STRONG
INTERACTION

Thomas Spence Smith

STRONG INTERACTION

The University of Chicago Press / Chicago and London

Thomas Spence Smith is associate professor of sociology at the University of Rochester.

The University of Chicago Press, Chicago 60637
The University of Chicago Press, Ltd., London
© 1992 by The University of Chicago
All rights reserved. Published 1992
Printed in the United States of America

01 00 99 98 97 96 95 94 93 92   5 4 3 2 1

ISBN (cloth): 0-226-76413-3

Library of Congress Cataloging-in-Publication Data

Smith, Thomas Spence.
    Strong interaction / Thomas Spence Smith.
        p.   cm.
    Includes bibliographical references and index.
    1. Social interaction.   2. Interpersonal attraction.   3. Social
structure.   I. Title.
    HM131.S574   1992
    302—dc20   92-16211
                                                          CIP

∞ The paper used in this publication meets the minimum requirements of the American
National Standard for Information Sciences—Permanence of Paper for Printed Library
Materials, ANSI Z39.48-1984.

CONTENTS

PREFACE

Three ingredients of social interaction tie together the arguments of this book—instability, transference, and the body. The first is an ever-present liability of social interaction, the second a psychological mechanism activating this liability, and the third the biological foundation from which this liability ultimately derives. I began to see these subjects as part of the same theoretical problem only when, starting in 1985, a developing interest in clinical issues caused me to suspect two things—first, that sociological models of social interaction ignored many of the strong forces psychotherapists faced on a daily basis; and second, that these forces actually were far more ubiquitous as ingredients of social interaction than even therapists commonly recognized. Transference in psychotherapy, as I eventually came to understand this complex and fascinating phenomenon, entails a rich family of somatic, affective, and ideational matters—feelings and emotions; illusions and wishes; cravings and wants; personal adjustments, defenses, and adaptations; conflict and growth; relationships and control; and many often obscure or latent biological, psychological, and social uses of interaction. Because prevailing theories of social interaction in sociology were insensitive to most of these phenomena, the difficulty I had appropriating them to my sense of social life established what I took to be a serious theoretical puzzle. The forces at work in transference had to be acknowledged in social theory, but how?

This book develops a theory of interaction and social life in which this question is tentatively answered. First and foremost this is a theory of these strong forces in social interaction—of *strong interaction,* as I shall describe it. It is a theory of how our cravings and passions, our loves and addictions, our fantasies and illusions, our appetites and wants, and our revulsions and fears are fed by our attachments and interactions. And it is a theory of how these forces, as they are introduced into interaction, work apart from intention or planfulness to create much of what a distant observer, looking down at our world from a far place, would perceive as the loose and disorderly structure of our social life.

The language we use to describe many of these strong forces—appetites, cravings, passions, wants, addictions—is a language of the senses. Interaction affects our feelings, feelings affect our interaction. Even as it is driven by hungers or wants or fears, interaction also works to control these states. Entering into interaction at every moment are the felt reminders of our condition as biological organisms—the feelings that signal an inescapable concomitance of the body in everything we do. The interesting thing about feelings, from a sociological point of view, is that they are deeply responsive to what happens outside the body, especially in the world composed of other people.

The presence of other people controls our senses, like an invisible vortex in the perceptual field. As readily as a blow to the knee produces a reflexive kick, the speech of another person turns the head. No less than a boisterous crowd entrains our full attention, a single person walking past lures the eyes. Such familiar effects arise, as we must begin to understand, because the proximity of other people portends a human richness in the near environment. It portends the potential onset of social interaction—a process whose origins in biological relatedness at the start of life evolves subsequently into nearly all of the complex patterns of human association studied by sociologists. In its seemingly reflexive aspects, interaction indicates ways human beings are dependent, for much of what sustains life and gives it coherence, on the biological, psychological, and social environments in which they are raised. The properties it develops among adults, as clinical practitioners have long understood, retain the qualities of these early caregiving environments—their emotional features especially. An intoxicant to some persons, interaction for others is a narcotic, a fantasy, a gamble, or a seduction. To these and other unconscious somatic, pharmocologic, and psychological functions of interaction, we seem by our human nature drawn—creatures of an innate readiness to search in social life for the care and responsiveness natural to our kind.

This embodied view of social interaction is rarely encountered in sociological writings, despite its obvious usefulness in making sense of behavior. The usual subjects of sociological theory are found across a change of scale, away from the felt experiences of real persons and toward matters having to do with the structure and process of groups and societies. Yet the truth remains that biological claims on social life begin with the human body—the corporeal foundation of personal and social life so unevadably real that theory can avoid considering it only at the risk of spinning groundless illusions. So disembodied are most contemporary views of what happens when two persons interact face-to-face that even plain somatic changes registered by attentive observers are ignored, and in their place appear analytically interesting but lifeless speculations about matters such as speech acts, utilities, choice points, or social roles. How we decide to acknowledge in sociological theory the part played by matters physiological, alongside these more familiar contemporary questions of utility and choice and role, is a matter of decisive intellectual importance, and has given direction to the project of this book. Though many of the issues raised by physiological claims on social life go beyond the scope of the argument developed here, this book nevertheless assembles physiological considerations into a theoretical perspective side-by-side with more traditional sociological subjects. In effect, it attempts to bring the body back into the theoretical work of sociology, first in a theory of social interaction sensitive to physiological and developmental considerations, and thereafter in a theory of complex interaction systems and social structure that expands to embrace social life more generally. Broad enough to accommodate the more traditional concerns of sociological work, this perspective aspires to reembody the subjects of sociological theory, putting life back into them.

Rethinking social interaction from a developmental angle leads along the interesting trail this argument follows. It is a trail that starts with considerations of infant-caregiver interaction and attachment, as conceptualized in relation to physiological homeostasis, moves toward models of strong interaction, and thereafter crosses a change of scale into the analysis of complex, n-person interaction systems and social structure. Traversing this change of scale—moving, in fact, across two such scale changes, from physiological considerations into dyadic arrangements, and then from dyads into complex, multiperson interaction systems and social structure—involves juxtaposing macrosociology in a theoretically tractable relation to microsociology, thereby establishing a micro-macro ladder by which to climb from one set of subjects to another. How this is accomplished I shall let the reader discover in the pages that follow. But the success of this argument, if it is successful, follows from returning the focus of social theory to the subject of social interaction it began to lose sight of thirty years ago.

A small but important shift in the way we are accustomed to conceptualizing social interaction radically alters some of its implications. Many of the theoretical tools for making this shift—the concepts, the empirical observations, the detailed research—are already at hand, subordinated, it turns out, to other theoretical agendas. What has been missing, as I hope to show, is a way of putting them all together—not so much replacing the old assumptions of theory, as showing how they have limited our understanding of important subjects. When we attend what actually occurs between persons who are face-to-face, interaction itself will reveal how we shall have to change our views.

Tracing the implications of these changed views, our subject will begin to surrender itself afresh into our grasp, and we shall find ourselves starting out along a road leading directly toward the reinterpretation of many other matters traditionally kept separate, as different subjects of sociological study, from interaction itself—matters including some of the central properties of large-scale social systems, complex organization, social change, and other subjects usually far removed from the study of interaction itself. Yet just how this reinterpretation can be done, as I must show in the pages that follow, will require us to alter our thinking about this seemingly most familiar of subjects.

The most important change involves recognizing just how unstable inter-action is—how easily it is unsettled, disequilibrated, and deflected from its course. When we recognize this, we are at the point of discovering a funda-mental problem with the main assumption by which the study of interaction has been driven for the past century. Interaction is never merely the integra-tive, ordering affair social theory in the main has assumed it to be, but a process of varying but often extraordinary sensitivity to even small and seem-ingly trivial disturbances introduced into it by partners or outsiders. Signals that would seem destined to fade into an interpersonal background, as so much insignificant white noise, are suddenly and inexplicably amplified by interaction out of all proportion to their initial magnitude. Trivial gestures thereby become preludes to encounters intensified by a mysterious respon-siveness that makes them suddenly affirming, exciting, inspiring, seductive, or acrimonious in the extreme. This potential is implicit in all interaction.

Strong interactions as they are conceived here are interactions controlled by feelings, particularly feelings we describe by using a vocabulary that is itself comprised of strong words: love, enthrallment, fear, excitement, pas-sion, desire, potency, craving, and so on. For this reason, this book could mistakenly be categorized as part of the growing sociological literature on emotions (Kemper 1978; Hochschild 1983; Scheff 1990). Although feelings and emotions are an important part of its subject, to categorize it thus wouldn't be quite accurate. It would be better to regard it as an effort at reconceptual-izing interaction itself, particularly at explaining how this complicated and in-teresting process, depending on its uses, serves either to control and regulate behavior or to undermine and destabilize it. Interaction is a foundational pro-cess in this sense—a place where matters social and cultural originate, where they are maintained, and where they are transformed. When it is used in one of these ways, it develops qualities—passion, interest, motivation, attach-ment, drive, energy, instability, sensitivity, inventiveness, speed, depth, and intensity—by which we recognize its strong forms. These excited, upbeat, enhanced qualities of interaction, not its stabilizing, integrating, or control-ling qualities, are the primary themes of this book. Bringing them into focus, and reclaiming this subject, will begin for us by our recognizing how the study of interaction has been controlled in the past by misleading assumptions about the nature of social order itself.

The way an eddy in a stream will put a spin on a drifting leaf, interaction can be understood to control the drift of social life. By turning persons in one direction or another, it sometimes draws them toward an intensifying social round and at others spins them further along on solitary journeys. Aggregate patterns appear in social life when these drifts and eddies are examined from afar, like the mix of clouds and storms visible in the sky. These evanescent patterns are created by the aggregation and disaggregation of persons in systems of interaction, entering and leaving as the forces in their lives permit. Many times such systems, despite being only emergent features of social life, can be recognized as peculiarly stable examples of social order, even though they remain wholly unlike those other forms of order we conventionally describe as social structure—complex organizations, kinship systems, public institutions, governments, and hierarchies of all sorts. They are specifically unlike the latter in that they are forms of organization or complexity that emerge in the aggregate only on the basis of forces at the level of individual persons that create instability. Typical systems of interaction are of this sort—forms of order that emerge on the basis of processes at the level of individual persons where individual behavior is both unstable and difficult to forecast—stochastic and hard to predict, rather than determinant and exact.

Once the concept of social structure is expanded to admit these emergent forms of structuration based on systems of interaction, rather than being restricted only to forms of organization based on constitutions and other normative means of regulating individual behavior, the theory of social systems will have taken another step further toward life as it really is. It is this step the present book also attempts to encourage—a step that depends ultimately on recognizing that older concepts of social order are plainly inadequate to describe the actual patterning and organization of the social world. This beginning I shall take in the pages to follow, where I hope to persuade the reader of how a simple argument about attachment and self, and especially about interaction as an unstable process, can be pushed across a surprisingly diverse terrain of subjects.

Because I foresee yet other ways these ideas can be put to use, I have become impatient to get on with the job. This book, as a result, will no doubt impress many readers, as it impresses me, as incomplete. This will especially be the case for readers who are experts in fields about which I have presumed to write. Where my patience and tolerance for revision have worn thin, or where I have plainly proved to be too ignorant to write about matters I have nevertheless tackled, I have still pushed on, mainly because I have been in the pull of an argument. No person these days can be the master of all the knowledge it will require to develop the fuller social theory this book attempts to glimpse. The subjects included here range from brain chemistry to the study of large-scale historical change. Because they are all interrelated, sometimes even in obvious ways, connections plainly needed to be developed in theory among them. These thoughts ought to be read, therefore, as a set of provisional hypotheses rather than as a finished product.

Because this book makes use of certain concepts of commonly recognized clinical phenomena, I have sought to deepen and confirm my hold on these personal and interpersonal matters by participating on a limited basis in a training program in clinical psychology. I have come away from a year's limited exposure to clinical materials with a deepened appreciation for how extraordinarily subtle are the ways our pasts shape how we behave. While the experience confirms for me the limited uses I have made of psychiatric concepts, it has also raised my awareness of many other parts of the clinical picture neglected in the argument that follows. The interested reader will want to know that some of these issues will be examined in a sequel to this volume, where I shall generalize the logic developed in these pages so as to interpret cognitive activity more broadly. Nevertheless, this book may give a false sense of closure on many of the fronts where my argument in fact remains incomplete.

ACKNOWLEDGMENTS

Several friends and colleagues have read parts of this book, and to them I owe debts of gratitude. To Donald Levine especially, I wish to acknowledge special thanks. After reading two working papers I had written in 1988, he pushed me to undertake the present book. Neither he nor I foresaw the scope of the project that would unfold for me, but none of it would have been undertaken without his enthusiasm for the first ideas. He has subsequently been a patient and close reader of the whole manuscript, and has served both to correct my mistakes and to improve the manuscript's quality overall.

Charlie Solky will recognize in these pages many ideas that took shape during long conversations with him. I trust he will forgive me my transmuted Kohutianism. Without Charlie's guidance through the literature of object relations theory in psychoanalysis, and without his generous responsiveness, I should not have taken the liberties this book contains.

At Rochester I have found students and colleagues who have been an important stimulus to my writing. Especially important has been my collaborator Craig Barclay, whose perspective as a cognitive psychologist has stimulated my work and helped to educate my imagination. My student Lancelot Braunstein encouraged much of the effort that this book contains to formulate thoughts mathematically. Others in the local community who read and commented on these ideas include Janet Wolff, Steven Kunitz, Klaus Roghmann, Dean Harper, Richard Ryan, James Connell, Christopher Lasch, and Dale Dannefer.

Numerous friends and colleagues undertook detailed criticisms of parts of the manuscript, and several of their remarks led to important changes in the argument. Harvey Molotch took time away from his own research to read the whole manuscript critically and to offer numerous suggestions to improve it. Arthur Stinchcombe's criticism caused me to rewrite a substantial portion of the argument in chapter 7. Neil Smelser's detailed comments on the manuscript have helped isolate several ways to strengthen and expand the general theory in subsequent work. Thomas Fararo showed me where there were ambiguities in my treatment of dynamical systems. Michael Farrell's comments on my early working papers were helpful in setting the scope of the theory. Norbert Wiley's criticism has helped orient me toward the sequel to this book. Edward Laumann's comments on portions of the argument also pushed me to clarify its differences from Parsonian theory. Others whose comments or encouragement have figured in my revisions include Douglas Crase, Jan Hajda, Deirdre Boden, Guy Swanson, John Wilson, and Kenneth J. Wilson. To all of them, I am deeply grateful.

INTRODUCTION

Interaction as an Unstable Process

For the last hundred years a project implicit in the theoretical agenda of sociology has controlled the conceptualization of social interaction: namely, understanding how the larger social order itself is possible. "Society stated in mechanistic terms," asserted Park and Burgess in their *Introduction to the Science of Sociology* ([1921] 1969, 341), "reduces to social interaction." Some such notion of "society"—if not as an aggregate product of elementary processes of interaction, then at least as a system depending for integration and stability on the achievements of interaction—has continued to inform distinctively sociological thinking about this subject. For this reason, most of the analysis of interaction welcomed by sociologists has been implicitly or explicitly concerned with how interaction creates, fits into, "reproduces," functions within, or contributes to a larger, encompassing society or social system. Important in shaping reasoning about this issue has been the concept of society itself—a notion conventionally equated among sociologists with ideas of order, stability, structure, and organization. Apart from whether particular theorists have knowingly sought to advance the disciplinary agenda of explaining how interaction creates social order in this sense—creates, that is, the stable conditions it assumes define it—the thinking of persons with an interest in how society maintains and reproduces itself has generally entailed the assumption that what people do in interaction somehow has this effect—producing (or reproducing) order, coherence, stability, and integration.

Though producing coherence and order is surely one of the things people *are* up to in interaction, that isn't the end of the story. And to exclude the rest of the story is to eliminate from theoretical analysis most of what this book will attempt to bring into view in relation to the concept of "strong interaction"—passion, interest, excitement, motivation, attachment, fantasy, conflict, and other signals of disequilibrium, danger, change, disorder, stimulation, emotion, escalation, and instability. In themselves, of course, these are also subjects with a sociological pedigree. And in truth, among sociologists concerned with how society is possible, it has been less the fate of these subjects to be excluded from the sociological curriculum than to be segregated from the study of society itself—kept apart from the study of social order, as if what they defined was what social order wasn't.

The notion that social order is some sort of unitary condition precluding instability is a contestable assumption. It is contestable mainly because it pivots on a narrow conception—let us call it the dominant conception—of social organization or order. The dominant conception is that change, instability, and uncertainty are antipodal to order and organization. In this view, indeed, organized and disorganized are two ends of a continuum. The organized end is associated with structure, stasis, and stability, and the disorganized end with process, change, and instability. Social structure for sociologists has become a reified version of this classic concept—by definition, the stable grid or organization of society. Corresponding to nothing real, some such comforting concept of permanance, set off against the confusing flux of actual experience, has become a central myth of sociological theory and only rarely has been recognized for what it really is—more an idealization than an accurate mapping of matters social and interpersonal.

What the dominant conception of social order has seemed best adapted to describe is certain kinds of groups and institutions, especially formally arranged, purposive structures—and then only, as in organization charts or written constitutions, when they are considered on paper. No real group is ever the stolid edifice the concept of structure suggests. While it is true that important forms of social order are relatively static and unchanging in this sense—bureaucratic offices, for example—other forms of order aren't. Relatively free of imperfections, for example, markets are highly unstable systems, based not on fixed and unchanging organization but on shifting and emergent patterns of association. Other forms of organization in society are equally unstable, from temporary crowds and demographic patterns of flow within populations, to electoral systems, temporal patterns, spatial arrangements based on social differentiation, and even communities and cities.

The argument I propose to develop in this book will make this point central to understanding "society." As much as society is based on order in the dominant sense, it is also based on order in this different sense. This different conception of society—as a "system" organized as much on the basis of processes characterized by instability and flux as by stability and stasis—will have important implications for analyzing social life, interaction included. The purpose of this book is to show some of these implications, starting by developing a theory of interaction as an unstable process.

To begin drawing out some of these implications, consider simply a distinction between formal and emergent organization. Interaction itself typically provides us with examples of organization best understood as emergent—organization based not on formal structural arrangements but on emergent patterns. Indeed, as I shall analyze it in a later chapter, interaction is best understood as a *self-organizing* system—not as an idealized arrangement of "actors" performing "roles," nor as a system of forces necessarily characterized by equilibrium, but as an unstable system marked by endlessly fluctuating mixtures of order and disorder simultaneously produced by complex feedback processes. Interaction as a self-organizing system, as we shall eventually learn to characterize it, can best be described with concepts of fluctuation, openness, nonequilibrium, and evolution (cf. Jantsch 1980).

Interaction in the Dominant View

In contrast to this view of interaction as an unstable, evolving, emergent system, the dominant conception of order has shaped the study of social interaction in two main ways. The first is by orienting theories of interaction only toward explaining how stability, order, and structure arise from face-to-face communication. When theoretical interest in interaction has been governed by the assumption that the larger social order arises as an ongoing and stable structure from interaction, the conceptualization and study of interaction have been implicitly organized by questions of how interactants establish equivalent patterns of order on a smaller scale. And the second main way the classic conception of social order has affected the study of social interaction has been to exclude from theoretical attention the possibility that unstable patterns of interaction sometimes produce stable forms of order on a larger scale. The second bias we won't consider until later in this book. But consider the first here.

Traditions in the Study of Interaction

A good example is provided by the study of communication. When the study of communication is controlled by the order assumption, it gives rise to questions of the sort asked by social philosophers like George Herbert Mead or Alfred Schutz. A typical question controlled by this assumption is, How do social actors come to understand one another? By contrast, altogether different questions are asked when the study of communication is controlled by the need to explain unstable phenomena like mental illness or addictive behavior. Studying communication then leads to questions like those posed by some "family systems" theorists and by students of pathogenic communication. One such question might be, How do implicit paradoxes in communication produce schizophrenia? These two different kinds of questions lead toward startlingly different images of interaction. The former, based on explaining order, dominates sociological thinking. The latter, based on explaining instability and pathology, dominates clinical thinking.

Just how these differing questions have influenced concepts of interaction can be illustrated by selectively considering, first, dominant sociological traditions in this area and, second, some of the clinical traditions.

The Order Assumption: Symbolic Interactionism, Role Theory, Dramaturgy, and Phenomenology

MEAD AND SYMBOLIC INTERACTIONISM   There is no necessary reason why studying symbolic communication *ought* to entail the conclusion that interaction produces understanding, meaning, *Weltbildung, nomos,* or any other comforting and integrative effects. Yet these are mainly what symbolic interactionist and phenomenological studies consider sociologically problematic in interaction: descriptions and explanations of how persons come to understand one another and produce intersubjectivity. Studying symbolic communication doesn't preclude recognizing conflict, disagreement, dissensus, and disorder, but these are not outcomes regarded by such interpretive theorists as central to understanding either the individual or society.

Mead (1934, 170) put the matter this way:

> *It is the unity of the whole social process which is the unity of the individual, and social control over the individual lies in this common process* . . . It is the ability of the individual to put himself into other people's places that gives him his cues as to what he is to do under a specific situation . . . It makes him a part of the community, and he recognizes himself as a member of it just because he does take the attitude of those concerned, and does control his own conduct in terms of common attitudes. (Emphasis added)

The "unity of the social process" is a way of invoking the dominant assumption of order. "Taking the role of the other"—the process, in Mead's view (1934, 253ff.), at the very center of social communication—ultimately became in his hands a way of explaining how "social control" made its way into every member of society. But just as often, of course, it is the reverse in social communication that occurs; interaction produces not social control but social disorganization—misunderstanding, discomfort, estrangement, and conflict.

Sociologists working in Mead's shadow have nonetheless continued to elaborate lines of argument consistent with his assumptions. Though Blumer (1966, 1969), for example, was a strong advocate of the point of view that social organization is a dynamic and not a static matter, what this amounted to in his scheme was a loose concept of interaction as an "ongoing" process—a matter of endless definition and redefinition.

ROLE THEORY AND DRAMATURGY Others in the Meadian tradition have also emphasized active, spontaneous, and emergent features of interaction, as in Turner's (e.g., 1962) concept of "role-taking." But even such healthy revisionism ultimately subscribes to the bias of classic assumptions. The telltale sign is that conceptualization is based on the language of "roles" and "role theory." Where theorists revert to speaking of roles, the study of real interaction is being subordinated to the classic theoretical agenda: preexisting images of social organization—society as a system of roles—deflect attention from actual interpersonal behavior. However inventively individual "actors" perform such "roles," role theories construe them as puppets of a wider society.

A subsidiary tradition has formed itself around so-called dramaturgical analysis. Even attending the deceptions and ironies of "managing" interaction in creative ways, however, didn't prevent Goffman from taking interaction's "stability" to be what was sociologically most important to understand about it, as in his effort to study "role distance" (1961) or to isolate the rituals by which disturbed encounters get stabilized (1967). Goffman's work, indeed, by disclosing a moral order underlying interaction, moved from analysis based on matters of interpretation into analysis geared to showing the stabilizing effects of shared culture.

SCHUTZ AND PHENOMENOLOGY Most sociological models of interaction, like Goffman's, are hybrids, including concepts both of subjective interpretation and of normative order. The phenomenological conceptions of interaction inspired by the writing of Alfred Schutz (e.g., 1962), for example, make use of both normative and interpretive concepts. Schutz's first work, a methodological reflection on Max Weber's program for a *verstehende Soziologie*, led him to emphasize in his own conceptions of social life the importance of ideal types. More generally, it led him to highlight the process of "typification" in what he described as the "construction" of the social world. Since it was his conclusion that organized social life rested on such processes, Schutz made central to understanding social communication an analysis of how persons face-to-face come to understand one another. Social reality, in Schutz's view, hinged on mutality of expectations, reciprocal typifications, and other considerations of agreement, all of which constituted a stable framework for society—the "stock of knowledge at hand," the "sedimented situation," the "paramount reality of everyday life," and other concepts all arranged, in

Schutz's analysis, for making sense of ongoing, stable projects and situations of social action.

Inspired by Schutz's writing, Berger and Luckmann (1966) and others have also proposed analyses of social interaction framed in phenomenological terms, some resting even more explicitly on underlying normative concepts.

ETHNOMETHODOLOGY AND CONVERSATION ANALYSIS Deriving from Schutz's work, and likewise conceiving interaction to be a normatively regulated process, is the elaborate project of "ethnomethodology" undertaken by Harold Garfinkel (1967, 1974) and his students. Ethnomethodologists seek to uncover the everyday world Schutz's actor assumes—to show by experiments and in "conversation analysis" how everyday social order is created and maintained in interaction. Explicitly, therefore, ethnomethodology is directly geared to analyzing order in the dominant sense. But the idea that society might not be rule-driven is foreign to the body of assumptions by which ethnomethodological work proceeds.

The Liability to Instability: Systems Models
in Action Theory and Clinical Theory

The one place where there is every logical reason not to find such a controlling assumption is in analyses of interaction indebted to cybernetics and general systems theory. It is least required in such theoretical reasoning because "systems" views should conjure an image of interaction as a process where *destabilizing* forces produce effects *stabilizing* forces reverse—or, more accurately, where stability or equilibrium is a contingent outcome, dependent on whether there is a balance between these two opposing sets of forces. In systems models, the effects of processes serving to produce *positive feedback* (amplifying, reinforcing, explosive effects) are controlled by processes serving to produce *negative feedback* (damping, modulating, equilibrating effects).

Adopting the perspective of systems theory means being alerted by this controlling conceptual imagery to the liability to instability inherent in many systems. Indeed, one reason to employ systems theory is to make this liability explicit, or to draw attention to the feedback mechanisms by which it is reduced. Yet so powerful is the classic concept of order that it sometimes appears even here, where it isn't required.

ACTION THEORY Consider the most familiar example of how systems theory has been used by a sociologist to analyze interaction—namely, Talcott Parsons's conceptualization of interaction as a process controlled by actors' mutual expectations. Parsons was alone among sociologists when he first recognized in systems theory conceptual tools for adding new analytical rigor to the analysis of social order. Against the processes by which social life was regularly and endemically disorganized, as the logic of systems theory perforce directed his argument, were those by which it was regularly and contingently stabilized. "A stable system of interaction . . . ," as he formulated his views in 1961 (42), "orients its participants in terms of mutual expectations, which have the dual significance of expressing normative evaluations and stating contingent predictions of overt behavior." But while Parsons's theorizing was thus sensitive to how feedback processes in communication served to stabilize interaction, it was nevertheless still controlled by the order assumption, mainly through his conceptualization of what constituted a "social system."

This was because Parsons used systems theory principally to conceptualize social order itself. Though he was quite explicit in directing theoretical interest to how phenomena such as "conflicting role expectations," "strain," and "alienative need dispositions" might cause social change and "deviance," these were subjects that stood apart from his analysis of a *stable* social system. Stability had become the property of social systems that emerged as the main focus of his theoretical analysis, so much so that "stable social system" (like "stable system of interaction") became a stock phrase in his lexicon. Interaction itself was central to this analysis, serving as an analytical pivot able to draw into itself forces arising not only from the social world but from both personality and culture as well. But only by shifting attention away from real persons and toward an idealized conception of the social world as a system of roles, however, was Parsons's theory able to construe interaction as a stabilizing process. Not systems theory but this traditional, order-dominated conceptualization of social structure—society as a system of roles—controlled his argument. From it emerged an equally idealized view of interaction—two or more "actors" in social roles, each constrained by reciprocal "role expectations," engaged in "role interaction." Induced not from study of face-to-face behavior but from the logical requirements of a theoretical analysis, this was a way to understand how interaction fulfilled the terms of social order—how it became, in another appropriation of systems language, a "boundary-maintaining" process. In effect, Parsons's theory showed how interaction might be understood to *maintain* social systems. In the context of this theory, a system of action marked by instability was disqualified *by definition* from even being treated as a "social system."

This exclusion was made explicit in Parsons's first sustained effort to use systems theory in conceptualizing large-scale societies. In the introductory pages of *The Social System* (1951), he isolated for the "action frame of reference" only those systems stabilized by shared expectations. This was the pivotal notion in his concept of role, itself defined as a "mode of organization of behavior relative to complementary expectations." By this matter of definition, social systems (qua stable systems of roles) didn't emerge until shared expectations presided over interaction. "It is a fundamental property of action thus defined," he wrote (1951, 5), "that it does not consist only of ad hoc 'responses' to particular situational 'stimuli' but that the actor develops a *system* of 'expectations' relative to the various objects of the situation." [1]

As with the symbolic interactionist and phenomenological views, this is a partial conception. It dominates Parsons's theorizing despite his reliance on systems concepts—concepts that logically entailed, even as part of the conceptualization of stable interaction systems, implicitly postulating the destabilizing effects of positive feedback. Though Parsons's systems framework was sensitive to interaction's liability to instability (why else, after all, place so much emphasis on negative feedback mechanisms?), it nevertheless failed to recognize how the processes serving to produce instability in interaction, apart from accommodating what he called "deviant" need-dispositions, might nonetheless produce patterns of order in social systems more generally.

PSYCHIATRIC MODELS   Outside sociology, the fate of models of interaction based on systems theory and cybernetic concepts is instructive. This is especially so within certain areas of psychiatry. Psychiatric thinking in the 1950s underwent numerous conceptual shifts, most of them progressively moving theory and research away from the psychoanalytic foundations which Parsonian thinking was only then beginning to exploit in sociology. One of these shifts involved the widespread growth and elaboration of so-called object relations theory, based on the original work of Melanie Klein in the 1920s and 1930s as it came to be extended, deepened, and changed by British clinician-theorists such as D. W. Winnicott and W. R. D. Fairbairn. Object relations thinking was based on the significance ascribed theoretically to early infant-caregiver relations, and especially to early forms of relatedness that, by the 1950s and 1960s, in several theories, came to be reconceptualized in view of new models of feedback and homeostasis, particularly by theorists such as Margaret Mahler and Heinz Kohut.

Second, psychiatry in the 1950s, in the United States especially, also increasingly took up themes of Harry Stack Sullivan's pragmatic, interpersonal school of psychiatry by moving from therapeutic models based solely on intensive patient-psychiatrist interaction to models based on analyzing group communication and on treating relationships, particularly marriages. Though some of the movement toward family and group psychiatry can be traced back to the 1930s, where it claimed psychoanalytic foundations, most of what today is known as "family systems theory" (or structured family therapy, etc.) had origins in the late 1940s and early 1950s—roughly at the time Parsonian action theory, with its new connection to psychoanalysis, was moving into the phase Alexander (1982–83, vol. 3) calls its "middle period." Within orthodox psychoanalytic circles, this new movement's focus on groups was regarded as heretical, and for many years its primary proponents carried on their work without publicity. The leading figures in this early work were scattered across the United States—Gregory Bateson, Jay Haley, John Weakland, and Don Jackson in California, Murray Bowen in Kansas and later Washington, John Rosen in Pennsylvania, Nathan Ackermann in New York, Salvador Minuchin in Philadelphia, and others. When they eventually came into contact with one another, what emerged were new ways of treating schizophrenics as well as new therapies for persons with addictions or behavior disorders. All of the new therapies were based on a clear recognition of families as complex emotional *systems,* readily conceptualized in view of the new feedback concepts of general systems theory and cybernetics. This conceptualization aided clinicians in recognizing patterns of dysfunctional communication among family members. As the thinking of family therapists evolved, great significance came to be ascribed, on the one hand, to the part played in destabilizing some families by processes backed by positive feedback—described, for example, as "escalation" (Watzlawick, Bavelas, and Jackson 1967)—and, on the other hand, to the part played in overstabilizing other family systems by processes backed by negative feedback—sometimes described as "rigidity." Marriage therapy, for example, often involves isolating the positive feedback implicit in endemic conflict. By contrast, behavior disorders like alcoholism are often shown by such reasoning to be maintained in families by homeostatic mechanisms based on maladaptive negative feedback.

Some of the most innovative work in this tradition originated in California with part of the so-called Palo Alto Group, including as its theoretical stimulus the extraordinary insights of the anthropologist Gregory Bateson and his collaborators Jay Haley, John Weakland, and Don Jackson. Bateson, with tools from cybernetic reasoning that appeared after World War II, had reconceptualized arguments about schismogenesis, originally introduced in his monograph *Naven* (1936). Based on his enthusiasm for communications theory, he along with his newfound collaborators began to study so-called clinical entities like schizophrenia as phenomena produced by disturbed and paradoxical communication. From the first, this work was based on the concepts of complementary and symmetrical communication Bateson had isolated in *Naven*—concepts whose underlying logic could be reinterpreted with notions of feedback. When this work was joined to Jackson's useful conceptualization of "family homeostasis" (e.g., 1957), the "double-bind" theory of schizophrenia emerged (Bateson, Jackson, Haley, and Weakland 1956). The Palo Alto Group, after Bateson's departure, subsequently reconstituted itself around clinical problems dealing with behavior disorders (e.g., Watzlawick, Weakland, and Fisch 1974, etc.) and, more generally, moved parallel to the whole developing area of "family systems theory" (e.g., Minuchin 1974).

Here then are two theoretical traditions—object relations theory and family systems theory—sensitive to forces overstabilizing some systems and driving others into disequilibrium—both of them, perhaps unsurprisingly, located within contemporary psychiatry, where the clinical mission is to treat disturbed systems. Even though neither object relations theory nor family systems theory is itself wholly emancipated from biases following from the order assumption, each nevertheless indicates that powerful destabilizing forces need to be taken into account in explaining individual and group behavior.

OTHER SOCIOLOGICAL MODELS   Among sociologists more generally, of course, there has been no want of interest in instability or disorder per se. Subjects such as conflict, social disorganization, war, collective behavior, competition, love, ideological solidarity, personal and social change, movements, and revolution are no less a part of the sociological canon than is the study of social integration, social order, and social stability. The order assumption has not meant blindness to instability. Yet, as is well appreciated among sociologists, some theoretical systems seem more at home with such matters than others, in part because they are cued by their own assumptions to the part played in society by disintegrative processes and processes of conflict, competition, and change. This is clearly the case in macrosociological theory. With the exception of Simmel's writings, however, it is less so in the study and conceptualization of interpersonal processes—at least by sociologists (Simmel 1950, 1955; Coser 1956). Even when the conceptual tools for isolating disequilibrating processes in interaction are present in a theoretical area—as they are, for example, in game theory, social exchange theory, rational choice theory, balance and dissonance theory, conflict theory, and elsewhere—the emphasis still tends to be on explaining phenomena of integration, decision making, choice, contract, relationship, solidarity, and order rather than on disintegration, instability, and disorder.[2]

Attention to positive-feedback-based processes like arms races, contagion, and circular reaction aside, few reflections on interaction have been broad enough to conceptualize it as a mix of stabilizing and destabilizing forces. Fewer, if any, have regarded the liability to instability in interaction as what is really of interest about it.[3]

The Task: Reconceiving Interaction

Between models of interaction geared to explaining stability and models geared to explaining instability there should be no necessary choice. Both have something to say about what actually goes on between persons face-to-face. Yet neither by itself is a full model. I have drawn out this contrast not so much to set the exact terms for the theory that is to follow as to draw attention to how even the best sociological models of interaction have ignored an important part of the subject. Thus, symbolic interactionist, phenomenological, and other order-based theories have difficulty explaining how two "social actors," without a word passing between them, can be driven into such disequilibrium states as "romantic infatuation." To explain such phenomena—indeed, to explain every example where interaction develops speed, depth, intensity, passion, and other "strong" qualities—we need concepts for how positive feedback enters into and drives social behavior. Some of these, as we shall see, can be derived from considerations like those to which family systems theory or object relations theory can sensitize us; others we shall find elsewhere. Many of them are scattered about sociology even now, isolated from the study of interaction proper.

What I have tried to do in the following pages takes its lead from such general considerations as these. Above all, it involves conceptualizing interaction as a "system" whose properties fluctuate in ways suggested by describing it as strong or weak in some degree. My aim has been to examine this variation, to account for its causes, and to illustrate how it manifests itself across various social settings. This is different from the conventional way sociologists and social psychologists have studied strong interaction, at least its most familiar examples—those arising in romantic love, say, or between parents and infants. The usual approach to the subject is to jump over the problem of describing and understanding the interaction itself, and to focus instead on the social relationships where strong interactions typically appear. Thus, the way to learn what sociologists know about strong interaction is to find studies of emotional relationships—analyses of love or passionate attachments or marriages or whatever. Such studies are often interesting and important, but they are usually based uncritically on the assumption that familiar culturally shaped relationships in our society delimit the important underlying psychological and sociological variation in interaction. This is the scientific equivalent of deriving a sampling frame not from theoretical reasoning but from the talk of one's friends and colleagues.

Too often, in fact, what culture recommends to sociological attention are the relationshps for which it has a good word—never wild interaction in the buff, *l'interaction sauvage*. There is little doubt that important differences do separate friendships, say, from pairs of lovers, and both of these relationships from others to which our culture also gives names—acquaintances, colleagues, mates, pals, relations, family members, and so on. Simply because such relationships shape social life in their terms, culture makes it important to isolate them for study by social scientists. But the first clue that such nominally different categories might mislead theory and research is that they do not isolate distinct phenomena. Lovers can be friends, friends colleagues, and acquaintances kin. A better approach to these diverse phenomena is perhaps to look underneath their cultural garb, and to search for other properties by which to make sense of what we find.

One thing we always find is that real relationships are never exactly what culture leads us to expect, particularly when we look hard at how interaction itself varies from moment to moment and place to place. Real interaction, wherever we look, subsumes an astonishing flux of feelings, speech, mentation, and affect. Many of these matters ride into and out of awareness so quickly they vanish before we grasp them, even though they may have left traces on ourselves and on our partners. Real interaction is thus a complex and multilevel phenomenon, typically involving interdependent states of relatedness our coarse analytic categories often plainly miss. What model of reciprocity, for example, is sensitive to the warm flush of attraction that arises mysteriously into consciousness as two strangers eye one another with interest across a room? How does the usual tit-for-tat notion of social exchange explain the violent emotion triggered in a patient as she interacts with her psychotherapist? What plumbing of reciprocal expectations explains the exhilaration adolescents experience dancing with one another? How can a person derive from schemata of culture, or rules of the road, or interpretive guidelines, or role theory, the awe induced in many listeners by powerful speakers? These are matters about which models of interaction ought to talk, but about which they are too often mute.

One reason, suggested above, may be that theoretical reasoning about interaction gives too much emphasis to conscious, intentional, normatively shaped, order-creating, and symbolic behavior, and ignores many forms of social orientation whose roots are preverbal—sources, we might suspect, of positive feedback. There is good reason to suppose that such roots are in fact where many of the strong forces in social life originate. Research in several fields—neuroscience, ethology, developmental psychology, biochemistry, genetics, anthropology—has made it plausible to argue that there are many such influences on social interaction, influences whose sources are innate, products of our genetic incompleteness at birth, our dependence on culture and caregiving, and our endogenous physiological and neurochemical homeostasis as organisms. This is an argument I shall begin to explore in chapter 1, a hunch leading to a redescription of interaction in view of forces generally ignored in sociological theory. By no means is this a redescription of the sociobiology sort, nor is it naïvely reductionist. What it does suggest, however, is an ineluctable chain of interdependence between matters biological and matters sociocultural. Recognizing this doesn't mean that sociologists ought to jettison their agenda, but only that they ought to make room in it for biological influences over social life. Though giving physiology its due, we shall quickly need to return the subject of interaction to the control of social and cultural forces, with the result that the largest portion of this book will attend these biological matters only indirectly. On the road to more familiar subjects, however, we shall have been sensitized to the subject of interaction in a way I hope will prevent us from ever again thinking about it in quite the same disembodied way. This is because this redescription should ultimately provide a way to say something new about interaction *au fond,* particularly about where some of the strongest controls over it originate.

Organizing the Subject

There is a certain temerity in what I propose to do, since nearly all of it carries me far outside of the usual intellectual terrain of a sociologist. Ultimately, the deepest foundations important to incorporate into a theory of interaction will probably turn out to be biochemical—especially foundations enabling us to speak of the ways brain chemistry is interdependent with a person's social behavior. A few steps in the direction of recognizing this interdependence in theory are taken here. My starting point for these initial steps should be a familiar one—the analysis of infant-caregiver interaction and attachment. Attending infant-caregiver interaction is important in this respect, since it is the first "system" of interaction in every person's life and, significantly, because it is this system within which the infant as a physiological organism is first socially regulated. This is where the argument in this book begins—in the first "uses" or functions of social interaction, which turn out to be physiological.

Models of psychological growth and attachment sensitive to these formative physiological considerations supply the basic terms of the argument pursued in the first part of this book. Around them we shall build a theory of self as at base a generative structure, along with an analysis of how infant-caregiver attachment is driven by forces akin to those operating in addiction. Powering the book's theory of attachment, in fact, are some of the same forces isolated in theories of addictive behavior—explosive systems of feedback, as we shall see, backed by extreme states of anxiety, that drive persons without certain psychological strengths to rely on external sources to control their feelings. The logic of these processes, in turn, enables us to build various models of strong interaction. These are based on an argument, made explicit in a model of interaction as a coupled system, about how partners to interaction regulate one another's feelings.

When the terms of this model are extrapolated beyond two-person into larger interaction systems, the theoretical relevance of a new area of thinking opens up—namely, the study of so-called nonequilibrium (sometimes called chaotic) systems. Studying the appearance of turbulence in systems, particularly systems in which some form of stability emerges from instability prior to the onset of turbulent behavior, provides a useful analogue for conceptualizing complex dynamics in all systems of interaction, as I shall argue. Particularly as this framework draws attention to embedded processes of positive and negative feedback, these ideas can be applied to unravelling complex properties of interaction in numerous examples—collective behavior, systems of stratification and differentiation, fashion, event structures of numerous kinds, and, significantly, political systems and markets.

Much of the second part of this book will be taken up showing how complex sociological examples can be explained with the theory that emerges from these beginnings. Seen in the light of this theory, traditional subjects of sociological analysis like love and power appear in a wholly new light. So, too, however, does the whole subject of social structure. Markets and hierarchies, in this perspective, become concepts for talking about two forms of structuration in systems of interaction. Analyzing historical materials on social change, the book concludes by illustrating how the theory provides a bridge for uniting the central issues of Durkheimian and Weberian sociology.

Nonequilibrium Functionalism

The driving logic of this theoretical perspective, as the reader will discover, is feedback. Homeostasis is achieved through a mix of positive and negative feedback, and complex interaction systems and social organization are stabilized or destabilized by the forms and levels of feedback running through them. This is not a difficult idea in theory, but it becomes a truly complex matter to sort out in empirical social systems. One of the more intriguing arguments following from this perspective, in fact, is that everything personally and socially organized depends in the final analysis not on processes that generate order but on processes that generate disorder. Disorder in this perspective is a sort of fuel for social life, and it is eaten up by engines that produce order. Or, as I have finally gotten used to saying, order arises only on the basis of processes that scavenge disorder. The meaning of this statement I will allow to emerge in later chapters, but the general idea is probably important to mention ahead of time. The kind of theory this project produces might be called nonequilibrium functionalism—a theory of how social order arises adaptively on the basis of all of the inexorable entropic processes which by and large make the social world a loose, gas-guzzling, and inefficient place.

1
Generative Self

The Unity of the Senses

Important discoveries in the study of infant perception have occurred in the last twenty years, many with direct implications for sociological views of interaction and for conceptualizations of self. Two areas in particular where new discoveries have a significant bearing on sociological theory are the study of affect perception and communication, and the study of infant-caregiver interaction. Although numerous statements by leading contributors to the research in these areas (e.g., Trevarthan 1980; Stern 1985) have been available for some time, little influence has proceeded from this work into sociology, where its bearing is no less profound.

There are two lines where this might have been expected to occur most directly. First, infant-caregiver interaction has always been suspected of producing precedents active in subsequent behavior—for example, by setting up what Bowlby (1969) called "inner working models" that enter subsequently into interaction with noncaregivers. Second, the ways infants appear to form such models or schemata of caregiving involve forms of perception and cognition that require revisions in concepts of self, particularly in formulating how deep structures of self actively shape subsequent motivation and behavior. The aim of this chapter will be to advance an argument, founded on observations about affect and cognition, derived from these lines of research. The outline of the argument is as follows:

1. Affect plays an important early role organizing the infant-caregiver system in terms of responsiveness and mutual regulation.

2. Affect is deeply implicated with early learning, especially in the initial formation of deep structures of self.

3. The fundamental logic of internal structural growth in self develops initially within a framework of physiological homeostasis, initially organized around attachments infants form to their caregivers.

4. Early self-development can be summarized in view of how infants derive such regulation first from external structures like caregivers and thereafter from internal structures developed in infant-caregiver interaction.

5. These internal "caregiver substitutes"—we shall call them structures of self—are founded initially on an inborn capacity for abstract perception, and hence operate subsequently as "generative" structures.

There are several conceptual foundations for this framework.

AMODAL PERCEPTION It has long been recognized—at least since Heinz Werner's (1948) studies of "physiognomic" perception—that infants translate stimulations of all kinds into affects, and that affects accordingly serve as generalized media for communication in early social situations. More recently, the research of Moore and Meltzoff (1978), Meltzoff (1981), Field et al. (1982), Bower (1974), Stern and Gibbon (1978), Spelke (1982), Meltzoff and Borton (1979), and others supports a related and equally general claim: namely, that infants possess an inborn and predesigned capacity to transfer information across channels of perception. Thus, for example, infants appear to "know" the visual equivalent of something they have only touched—having accomplished an internal transfer of information between touch and sight, presumably through some higher-order template. Stern (1985) and others have called this "amodal perception" and have used this notion as one of the empirical foundations on which to build a new and startling image of infancy. In this new picture, as Stern himself is quick to tell us, infants are not the "autistic" entities described by Margaret Mahler (e.g., Mahler, Pine, and Bergman 1975); nor do they begin life in an undifferentiated state of merger, unity, or fusion with their caregivers, as assumed in nearly all classical developmental theories. Rather, it is argued, they must now be understood as engaged from the very first hours of life in aggressive and continuous acts of self-definition and affective/cognitive sorting.

EARLY LEARNING While affect and cognitive schematization are difficult to separate at early stages of development, a number of implications of this image of early perception are becoming clear. First, affect itself is deeply interwoven with other elements of perception in the schemata in which an infant's experiences are stored—schemata that emerge, as Stern (1985) has argued, through processes connected with the appearance and change of what Tulving (1972) calls "episodic memories." Actively categorizing and sorting its experiences, the infant is believed to establish clusters of invariant perceptions, amodally represented, "yoked" together (in Stern's expression) because they are concurrent. According to this important new analysis, the emergent

organization of an infant's "sense of self" might best be thought of as generalized and abstract—abstract in whatever "higher-order" ways the unity of
the senses might be imagined. This is an important reconceptualization, because it implies that the deep organization of self is *generative*. To regain
access to perception, to support mentation, these abstract structures must be
given content; the processes by which they acquire concrete content are the
generative processes of self. Tracing out the implications of this conception
and isolating some of these generative processes become profoundly important for understanding social interaction.

FRAMEWORKS OF SELF-KNOWLEDGE   Whatever emerges in the way of organization in the sensory and experiential field of an infant arises within some
"framework." The initial framework is the physical body—its agency, coherence, identity, and so on. Later, the body is superseded but not supplanted by
a framework of "relatedness" to other persons—initially caregivers, subsequently other need-regulating or "self-regulating" figures. As successive
frameworks of relatedness emerge, older frameworks survive alongside the
newer frameworks and remain active as parts of an infant's interactions. Thus,
even after a child learns to use language discursively, the preverbal parts of
its self—the part, for example, that arises before the infant has a sense of
itself as a coherent physical entity, later the "core self" (as Stern calls it), and
then a "subjective self"—continue to be integrated into its responsiveness to
others and to its environment.

This image of simultaneously active multiple "senses of the self," each
corresponding to a developmental phase of self-organization and a domain of
self-other relatedness, presents a challenge to theories of social interaction
more generally. Beneath symbolic communication and yet subtly fused with
it are signals and perceptions associated with these active structures of self.
What is new in this thought is not so much the layered image as the logic
underlying it. There is nothing startling, for example, in the notion that affect
profoundly shapes social interaction, or that it often arises from sources outside of awareness. The question is how we are to conceptualize the many ways
its shaping influences are manifested. Aside from cataloguing varieties of
affect and feelings—the "thrills, twinges, pangs, throbs, wrenches, itches,
prickings, chills, loads, glows, qualms, hankerings, curdlings, sinkings, tensions, gnawings, and shocks," in Gilbert Ryle's (1949, 84) playful list, along
with, say, Darwin's ([1872] 1965) categorical affects and Stern's "vitality affects"—what are we to say about how particular chills or prickings affect
particular interactions? Or how our partner's throbs and hankerings affect our
own glows and qualms—even if we should never become aware of them?

HOMEOSTASIS   The answer I wish to propose is based on an argument synthesized from several of the newer views of self. It succeeds only by deliberately

oversimplifying the question. What I will argue is that psychophysiological precedents in the early experience of the infant, as they are defined in conjunction with the activities of caregivers in regulating an infant's feeling states, are the foundations on which subsequent structural development in self occurs. If not all, at least some fraction of deep psychic structure arises in conjunction with the homeostatic function of the caregiver—the shaping, educating, regulating, and modulating of the infant's inner states, in the presence of environmental turbulences over which the infant itself has little control. These regulatory activities, in their original perceptual status, get functionally organized by the infant, in ways we shall see below, and are eventually stored by the infant through processes analogous to those that produce memory more generally—episodes of regulation, generalized and made prototypic. Such original regulating episodes then serve as precedents for the subsequent elaboration of inner and outer life, differentiating in directions made possible by the emergence of later developmental capacities. Even in the face of subsequent personal change, as I want eventually to argue in relation to sociological materials, all social interaction seems thereafter to be patterned as if by the invisible operation of these deep homeostatic regulators.

The specific *ways* this influence operates also appear to have strong precedents in infant-caregiver interaction. In chapter 2, I shall argue this point more vigorously, specifically by developing the notion that an infant's attachment to its caregiver is like an addictive attachment. If this is true, we should be able to isolate in infancy certain psychophysiological templates for attachment and separation. To facilitate initial conceptualization and discussion along these lines, and to make clear a number of consequences of this kind of argument that would otherwise remain obscure, I propose to rely in this chapter on a number of familiar images of homeostasis. In subsequent chapters, models of homeostasis will be superseded by more complex models of feedback, which weaken the assumption of equilibrium in human systems. The first section of this chapter thus reviews the general logic of homeostatic systems, and illustrates it with respect to the qualities of interaction present between small infants and their caregivers. The argument then turns to related theories in the psychology of the self. I am particularly concerned to show that the logical structure of a number of psychoanalytic views of infancy is also homeostatic—in particular, work in "object relations" theory and in "psychoanalytic self psychology." These views provide clinically derived impressions of the subjective world of the infant. In them we shall find forces that continue to have a part in later social situations. In particular, I will argue below, for reasons that will by then be obvious, that the deep logic of "selfobject transference," as Kohut (1971) develops this concept, rests on homeostatic selfregulation. Kohut's concept isolates an important class of generative processes, especially significant in analyzing interaction.

Added up, these considerations will provide a groundwork on which to build a new theory of interaction. They suggest hitherto unformulated dynamics in face-to-face interaction, point to latent feedback structures in dyads, and indicate numerous important "uses" of interaction to which existing theory does not seem sensitive. Most interesting among the specific subjects this perspective opens up with fresh insights are the strong forms of attachment and interaction we shall study in later chapters. And as we shall eventually see, the general dynamics isolated by studying the infant-caregiver dyad also reveal processes that spread beyond such simple systems into complex interaction systems as well.

The Wisdom of the Self

Positive and Negative Feedback

Homeostasis was first recognized in the studies of the great French physiologist Claude Bernard. In his now famous reference to the "constancy" of the *milieu intérieur,* Bernard denoted the diverse capacities animals have to monitor and regulate their internal environments within certain limited ranges of variability. Homeostasis more generally refers to this capacity of living systems for maintaining the steady-state internal conditions necessary to their survival. In its general formulation, this was an idea readily appropriated by early social scientists for whom organisms provided models of societies. But beyond such simple theorizing based on primitive organic analogies, the concept of homeostatic equilibria has also had a more sophisticated theoretical legacy—mainly through the work of Pareto in general theory, through Henderson's use of the concept of homeostasis as it was originally developed in Cannon's *The Wisdom of the Body,* and in the influence of Norbert Wiener's work on cybernetics.

The general logic of homeostasis depends on the principle of *feedback.* Feedback is at the heart of all self-correcting behavior. Systems such as missiles, for example, can be built to correct their own performance on the basis of sampled information about their operations, thereby eliminating deviations in their trajectories caused, say, by environmental perturbations or by internal malfunctions.[1] Living systems must do similar things. They accomplish self-regulation through monitoring themselves—regulating their internal environments in view of continuously sampled information that describes internal states and surrounding conditions.

Feedback is of two kinds—positive or negative. Thermostats in houses provide the usual example of negative feedback, while processes of contagion or diffusion illustrate positive feedback. Human beings make use of both kinds. In a familiar illustration given by Roger Eckert (1983), for example, a game like Pin the Tail on the Donkey takes advantage of this dependence on "information feedback" by depriving persons of monitoring capacities. By blindfolding a player, slight disturbances in neuromotor or sensory systems that would ordinarily be compensated for by *negative feedback* can result in lopsided and meandering efforts to stay upright, culminating with small children toppling over. With the blindfold off, however, a child will correct a stumble or a drift and make its way directly to the target. The visual system of the child in this case serves as a sensor, enabling its neuromotor system to produce corrections in movement opposite to perceived errors. The neuromotor system acts then as an *inverting amplifier* to correct for deviations from a *set point* (in this case, upright posture and forward movement).

The elements of positive feedback appear in figure 1.1. The diagram shows a source of turbulence (perturbation) acting on a controlled system. A sensor picks up the output of the system, sending it as a signal to an amplifier. In this case, the signal is amplified but its sign (positive or negative) is left unchanged, and we have positive feedback. That is, the amplified signal returned to the controlled system has the same effect on the controlled system as the original perturbation had. Examples of this highly unstable configuration are familiar to anyone who has ever heard the loud squeal of a public address system, when the output of loudspeakers gets picked up and reamplified by a microphone. An initial small perturbation, even background noise in a room, can result in very large outputs from the speakers. Usually there is something in such systems to limit their output—as in the inherent limits of an amplifier or of the speakers, or limits arising through saturation of the microphone signal (Eckert 1983). In human systems, as we shall see, limiting structures are important regulators of the effects of positive feedback. And where such regulators are absent, are weakened, or fail, we find familiar examples of excitement, powerful attachment, and strong interaction.

Positive feedback is important in producing regenerative, explosive, or (in chemical systems) autocatalytic effects. In social systems, positive feedback is behind rumor processes in collective behavior, arms races between nations, bandwagon effects in voting behavior, the developing popularity of a celebrity, and the rising phase of cyclic events such as bull markets on the stock

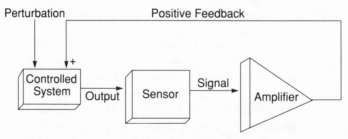

Fig. 1.1   Elements of positive feedback (after Eckert 1983)

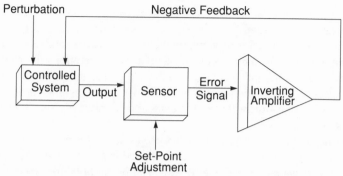

Fig. 1.2   Elements of negative feedback (after Eckert 1983)

exchange. (Coleman [1964, 1968] provides good examples of explosive and contagious processes in social systems.) All of these are unstable processes.

Negative feedback, by contrast, involves an inverting amplifier that changes the sign of signals entering it, producing output signals whose sign is opposite the input. Signal inversion in this sense is the basis for all negative feedback and is used to regulate parameters of many controlled systems. This is illustrated in figure 1.2. The feedback process depends on the sensor's sending an error signal to the amplifier, often scaled such that it is proportional to the difference between the state of the system as affected by the perturbation and the set point to which the system is supposed to be held. Before the input signal is sent back to the controlled system, it is amplified and inverted—that is, its sign is changed. Such negative feedback into the controlled system counteracts the original perturbation, enabling the system to stabilize in the vicinity of the set point.[2]

A classic example of negative feedback in social systems is provided by Malinowski's (1948) argument about the "functions" of magic—an argument suggested when he observed the Trobriand Islanders perform elaborate magical rituals before they would leave their protected lagoon to fish on the open seas. In our terms, ritual magic served as an inverting amplifier, changing anxieties over fishing on the open seas, if not from apprehension to confidence, at least from positive to negative. The "function" of ritual, then, was to calm and allay fears induced by risk and uncertainty (cf. Stinchcombe 1968).

As they are represented here, the diagrammed elements of feedback systems need not always be separated. Inversion can be accomplished at the sensor, for example. Where the elements are not separated, the principles of feedback nonetheless remain the same.

Homeostatic Structures and the Self

Homeostasis is central to the survival of all complex organisms, human no less than others. But above the purely physiological level at which its operations are well established, the ways homeostasis supports other levels of organization are perhaps less appreciated. Some of the most prominent instances of such regulation at supraorganic levels involve caregivers' attentions to their infants. To many theorists of infancy, observations of interactions between caregivers and their babies have suggested that it is this "social" matrix of early interaction where infants' own self-regulating capacities first emerge—in other words, that early interaction has precisely such homeostatic functions.

The newborn baby isn't equipped with the kinds of regulatory structures required to support its life. These are supplied initially in the caregiving activities of its parents. For this reason, newborns might be likened to the generalized system represented in figure 1.1: they lack the endogenous controls by which their internal environments might be regulated in the face of the perturbations entering their worlds.

Certainly infants behave at times like positive feedback systems, their excitement and level of stimulation seemingly damped only by limits on the capacity of the organism to make itself the vehicle of various disturbances. The "primary task" of parents during this period thus becomes what Sander (1962, 1964) calls "physiological regulation" and Greenspan (1981) describes as homeostasis. Parents accordingly spend most of their time during the first two months of an infant's life "regulating and stabilizing sleep-wake, day-night, and hunger-satiation cycles" (Stern 1985, 42).

Stern elaborates:

> When baby first comes home from the hospital, the new parents live from minute to minute, attempting to regulate the newborn. After a few days they may be able to see twenty minutes into the future. By the end of a few weeks, they have the luxury of a future that is predictable for stretches of time as long as an hour or two. And after four to six weeks, regular time clumps of three to four hours are possible. The tasks of eating, getting to sleep, and general homeostasis are generally accompanied by social behaviors by the parents: rocking, touching, soothing, talking, singing, and making noises and faces. These occur in response to infant behaviors that are also mainly social, such as crying, fretting, smiling, and gazing. A great deal of social interaction goes on in the service of physiological regulation. (43)

Repeatedly, the infant's sense of itself in relation to an environment is defined through such regulation of its needs and feeling states. This is important in understanding how the infant eventually develops the capacity to regulate itself. Tulving's (1972) concept of "episodic memory" is put to use by Stern to suggest how such moments of regulatory interaction with caregivers begin to thread though and organize self-knowledge. The infant apparently categorizes and sorts its experiences on the basis of their variant and invariant properties. It does this first by grasping these matters as they are enmeshed with the regulation of its needs and wants—such need "states" serving as invariant and recurrent templates of experience. Viewed in relation to the infant's homeostasis during this period, social interactions early in life are thus categorized in conjunction with their regulatory functions.

The infant's subjectively emerging sense of itself is imaginable in this light—as a field of sensations, certainly, against which particular clusters of feeling, connected with the regulation of inner states, begin to stand out like familiar beacons. Such subjectively invariant clusters of feeling begin then to serve as an incipient organizational framework for self-knowledge. Bundled together with them thereafter appear other concurrently invariant perceptions, mainly those of the infant's "self-regulating other" (Stern's phrase for the caregiver), along with amodally represented traces of changeover among interior feeling states—from a state, say, that is quiet, to another that is explosively stimulating, and then back again into a condition of quiescence and satisfaction (if such expressions mean anything in the world of the infant).

The turning points between these states, as they are represented in memory, are associated with the presence of the self-regulating other, whose actions are "yoked" into the emerging memory. On the one hand, for example, there is the sort of mother whose patting and stroking of her overstimulated infant serves to quiet it. Then there is the mother who plays "walking fingers" or "I'm going to get you!" or "peekaboo!" with the infant as she changes its diaper or seeks to fix its attention. The first mother, most of the time, is the same person as the second, yet the two experiences are wholly different. The first damps and inverts the signals exploding through the organism, the second introduces a perturbation she then amplifies positively. One calms, the other excites.

These are only two kinds of self-regulating others, each serving in the dual capacity of sensor and amplifier. They are external structures, doing for the infant what the infant is as yet unable to do for itself.

What is being regulated by the self-regulating other?

The argument advanced by Stern recognizes certain active competencies on the part of the infant itself, and also makes use of a concept of global or coenesthetic experience (Spitz 1959; Werner 1948). "The problem with [other concepts]," he writes, "is that infants do not see the world in [their] terms . . ."

> Infant experience is more unified and global. Infants do not attend
> to what domain their experience is occurring in. They take sen-

sations, perceptions, actions, cognitions, internal states of motivation, and states of consciousness and experience them directly
in terms of intensities, shapes, temporal patterns, vitality affects,
categorical affects, and hedonic tones. These are the basic elements of early subjective experience. Cognitions, actions, and
perceptions, as such, do not exist. All experiences become recast
as patterned constellations of all the infant's basic subjective elements combined. (1985, 67)

What, then, about this subjective world *is* being regulated? It is not the
yokings and invariant constellations, nor the emergent organization by which
the whole is experienced. The supposition supplied by the argument resting
on homeostasis is that such constellations themselves emerge first around
regulatory interactions and eventually are consolidated as structures of self,
which replace the external caregivers as sources of homeostatic control. This
follows directly from the observation that regulatory interactions constitute
the largest fraction of all caregiver interventions in the infant's world, at least
for the first two months of life, and it is supported by the related observation
that infants appear in these first few weeks gradually to acquire the early
homeostatic capacities parents want them to have. From these and other regulatory interactions, additional constellations thereafter emerge to control yet
further felt properties of early global experience—properties other than excitation or calming. It is these felt qualities of global experience that such structures eventually regulate.

Some of what comes to be regulated by caregivers also plainly amounts to
what they want to regulate, and thus merely reflects their own parental projec-
tions of subjectivity into their infants—the pains they imagine, the hungers
they feel, the wants they sense, the pleasures they crave, the security and
attachment they need, the presence and attention they demand, the anxiety
they want to still. Most probably, too, it reflects some interaction between the
affects infants express and each parent's own deep affective core. The notion
that parents eventually implant set points and regulators into the infant's experience, however, gives a considerable role in shaping subjectivity to powerful social and cultural forces of which they are the agents.

Homeostasis and the Bipolar Self

Several intriguing hypotheses about this early global subjectivity have arisen
from the clinical work of psychoanalysts, particularly object relations theorists who reject the drive-structure model of orthodox Freudian theory. Many
analysts now work with a concept of early subjectivity in which they have
made room for states and qualities arising from the infant's social interactions
with caregivers—a notion similar to current arguments appearing in devel-

opmentalists' theories of infancy. But rather than resting formulations of the infant's early psychological growth on developmentalists' concepts of learning, these clinical arguments usually employ variants on the classic idea of introjection.

Psychoanalytic Self Psychology

Consider the work of the late Heinz Kohut, the founder of "psychoanalytic self psychology." Along with the work of other so-called object relations theorists, Kohut's theories have been described as so radically different from Freudian theory as to constitute a fundamental paradigm shift. This is because Kohut, following in the footsteps of many other revisionist thinkers, moves the responsibility for psychological growth away from biological drive systems toward the external world—mainly toward the world of other persons, but also the world spreading beyond persons to other sociocultural "objects." The way Kohut conceived how others control psychological growth and development, as we shall see, makes his views uniquely relevant to reformulating sociological notions of interaction.

Kohut argued that an infant's self arises in connection with the way caregivers meet or respond to two fundamental narcissistic needs. The first of these needs is for admiration and recognition, especially of the infant's emerging capacities. When an infant's caregivers give it admiration and recognition, they are engaging in what Kohut and other object relations theorists call *mirroring*—that is, they are empathically attending the child by returning to it (in our language, amplifying back into it) a signal it itself emits.[3] Mirroring responsiveness from parents results in the appearance of what Kohut suggestively describes as the *archaic grandiose self*. This first structure of the self arises from what the infant grasps of itself in such mirroring responsiveness to its "healthy *exhibitionism*"—behavior in which the infant is demanding attention, in effect that caregivers merge with it. A smile might be just such an exhibition. Seen from the perspective of our analysis of homeostasis, the caregiver's response to this "merger demand" establishes a pattern of positive feedback. The smiling infant whose parent smiles back has its own smile reinforced. If the parent accompanies the mirrored smile with some other enlivening upbeat signal, like a laugh or a wiggle or another gesture of excitement, the mirroring response is being positively amplified as it is returned. With repeated cycles of such mirroring, the infant can find itself quickly filled with excitement—along with the initial sense, perhaps, of being able to bring about such enlivening responsiveness on its own. Because of the positive feedback involved in this process, and perhaps because of the infant's illusion of being able to produce this enlivened subjectivity by itself, this is a pattern of parental responsiveness resulting in an explosive accumulation of consequences inside the infant, an explosion, significantly, to which the infant knows no limit. Some such feedback loop, along with the caregivers' merger, is presumably behind what Kohut describes as the infant's *omnipotence*, a term commonly used by object relations theorists to denote both this idea of accumulating, limitless global capacity and, significantly, the related idea of magical control over "objects" (cf., e.g., Winnicott 1965, 1971).[4]

It is in the presence of this felt omnipotence that the infant's second narcissistic need makes its debut. Full of admiration and capacity, the infant now feels the need to "transfer" some of the inflated and perfect sense of itself to other "selfobjects" in its environment, as a way, presumably, of stabilizing and securing this newfound sense of itself. Specifically, Kohut argues that the infant transfers some of its self-perfection and omnipotence to an *idealized selfobject*—"an admired omnipotent (transitional) selfobject" (Kohut 1971, 25). Associated with this idealized structure, and balancing the exhibitionism of the archaic grandiose self, moreover, is the new pattern of behavior Kohut calls *voyeurism*. An exhibitionistic child is calling for mirroring. In effect, it is demanding, "Look at me! I am perfect, and you admire me!" The voyeuristic child is making the reverse *merger demand*. It says, "You are perfect, and I want to merge with you!" If this external *idealized selfobject* is introjected, the infant develops a second internal structure of self Kohut calls the *idealized parental imago*.

Kohut's theory develops from an elaboration of this *bipolar* conception of the so-called nuclear self. Fundamentally, this is an equilibrium conception, based on the emergence of opposite homeostatic amplifying capacities in the mirroring and idealized poles. The "selfobjects" in this system of thought eventually become introjects—the "mirrored" introject arising typically, in Kohut's analysis of traditional family arrangements, from interactions of the infant with its mother, and the "idealized" introject arising from interactions with the father (though, of course, this pattern reflects only a traditional family configuration). Think, perhaps, of the mother who excites the infant ("I'm going to get you!"), and the mother who calms it ("There, there. Mommy's here"). Merged with the mother being used as a mirroring selfobject, the infant's purchase on itself is through the empathic responses of this mirroring other ("I am perfect and you admire me," in Kohut's own formulation). "Toned-down versions" of the self arise from fusions with idealized selfobjects ("You are perfect and I am part of you").

The way a child's self develops thereafter will reflect special patterns in given biographical histories of responsiveness and interaction. In theory, however, the self can develop structurally along either or both of the two lines, one arising from the consolidation of strengths around the mirrored pole of the nuclear self and the other from the consolidation of strengths around the idealized pole—one from a tendency on the part of the infant to demand attention from others who mirror and admire it, the other through mergers with selfobjects the child can idealize. The optimal pattern of such structural growth balances idealized and mirrored strengths. But the fact that structural growth can emphasize one line to the exclusion of the other also helps to clarify another issue: mirroring does not only excite, and idealizing does not only calm. A mirroring selfobject *can* in theory and in reality amplify a negative exhibitionistic signal, as when a sad, crying child confronts a caregiver whose own sadness serves only to deepen the child's own subjective state. Likewise, idealized selfobjects can raise *or* lower, excite or calm, an infant's subjective state—the level of its boredom, say. An idealized parent, confronting a voyeuristic merger demand by a child who is obviously feeling listless and without direction, can excite the child by leading it with enthusiasm toward some enlivening activities.

In line with Kohut's shift of theoretical emphasis away from drives and toward the external world, his theory argues that all "structural" growth in psychological organization occurs in connection with a phenomenon he called "optimal frustration," an idea closely resembling Winnicott's (1960) discussion of the "good-enough mother." "Optimal frustration" involves the nontraumatic disappointment of the infant's narcissistic needs by an otherwise empathic caregiver and is a pattern encouraging the infant to take over functions previously managed for it by its caregivers. Slowly and incrementally, in a process of internalizing fragments of the caregiving experience— "transmuting internalization" is Kohut's name for it—the infant is encouraged by its caregivers to build up self-structures enabling it to regulate itself and grow apart from them. What this means is that introjected fragments of the caregiving experience—microinternalizations—get organized functionally by the infant around the two original poles of the self. Each fragment is added to one or the other pole in response to "optimal" failure of the relevant external selfobjects (the caregivers) to accommodate demands made on them for merger. In theory, therefore, the infant merges with these external selfobjects only to find itself unaccommodated in some portion of its neediness, and thereby is pushed to undertake such transmuting internalization of the selfobjects as would result in discovering within itself the strengths or responsiveness it previously located outside.

Viewed in light of arguments about homeostasis, Kohut can be understood as deriving from clinical impressions a set of concepts that describe a self-regulating system. The self emerges through the development of functional capacities that support self-regulation, as based on introjected and transmuted "selfobjects"—the caregivers who perform regulatory functions for the infant early in its life. These replace the "narcissistic homeostasis" Kohut imagines is present in the mother's innate physiological responsiveness to the infant before and shortly after birth. Subsequently, the infant-caregiver dyad,

as he imagines it, supports only an approximation of such narcissistic homeostasis—the imagined "perfection" of this regulatory interaction prior to birth
inevitably destined to being lost. The way this happens is in the failure of the
caregiver to sustain the perfect "in-tune" qualities of responsiveness present
earlier on a purely physiological level. Indeed, the best kind of parent is one
who "optimally frustrates" the infant's "expectations" of perfect empathic
responsiveness. (At one point, Kohut likens this "expectation" on the part of
the infant to the unconscious "expectation" of oxygen in the environment—an expectation of which we become conscious only when disappointed by its absence [Kohut 1977, 85].) Viewed in terms of homeostasis,
mirroring selfobjects can thus be understood as the equivalent of the kind of
amplifiers involved in positive feedback systems, and idealized selfobjects as
inverting amplifiers. Introjected, they work together in the healthy person to
affirm and strengthen the self in its ambitions and capacities (mirroring), and
to give it purpose, control, and direction by permitting merger with powerful
images of effectiveness and leadership (idealizing).

Driven by deep physiological forces and structured by a homeostatic logic
derived from the infant-caregiver system, Kohut's theory of the self and early
attachment thus has numerous implications for the analysis of self and interaction more generally. As reconceptualized here in terms of feedback processes, his theory isolates mechanisms behind the appearance of strong forces
in interaction. These appear in relation to his concepts of "disintegration anxiety" and "selfobject transference."

SIMPLE MODELS OF FEEDBACK   Interpreted in the light of systems concepts, Kohut's model of the self begins to look like Malinowski's model of
magical practices, though it is more complex. Both posit processes that give
rise to the emergence of functional structures for the control of fear and uncertainty or for regulating excitation. One way to represent the functional or
homeostatic aspects of such processes involves using linear directed graphs,
following the example provided by Stinchcombe (1968), based on Huggins
and Entwistle (1968).

In the case of Malinowski's argument, Stinchcombe (1968, 82–83, 89)
presents the linear graph shown in figure 1.3—where H represents the homeostatic variable, S the structure selected by the homeostatic variable to
maintain the system, and T the source of tension entering the system. The
variables are assumed to be linearly related and to influence one another according to the operators r, c, and k. More concretely, Malinowski talked
about uncertainty (T) caused by the prospect of fishing on the open seas,
influencing the level of anxiety (H; the homeostatic variable), calmed thereafter by the performance of magical practices (S). The way this is written, the
practice of magic has an effect on anxiety proportional to c. This same effect

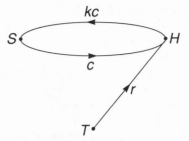

Fig. 1.3   Linear graph representing the causal structure of a functional explanation (after Stinch-combe 1968, 89)

subsequently reappears in the strength with which the homeostatic variable "selects" magic as a regulator—an effect then multiplied by a measure k of the "effectiveness" of H in selecting S. Two linear equations represent Malinowski's argument: $H = rT + cS$, and $S = ckH$.

KOHUTIAN FUNCTIONALISM   The same kind of directed graphs are useful in studying Kohut's notions about the self, though the rules for manipulating them must be relaxed in order to reflect subtleties in the Kohutian system of reasoning. First, a central variable in Kohut's system is responsiveness—especially the level and availability of empathic responsiveness on the part of a caregiver to an infant. It is mainly variability of empathic responsiveness from caregiver to caregiver, family to family, or environment to environment, that accounts, in his way of thinking, for differences in self-development. Thus, where external perturbation in Malinowski's argument amounts to "uncertainty," the equivalent term in Kohut's model refers not only to matters that normally produce anxiety but also to sources of responsiveness—mirroring and idealizing responsiveness. As such, T can be a variable that excites the self with surpluses of strength or depresses it by deprivations, or it can be any perturbation that arouses what he calls "disintegration anxiety."

Disintegration anxiety appears in relation to experiences threatening the "cohesiveness" of the self—any experiences, that is, which lead to "anticipations" of the breakup or fragmentation of the self. All this is "relative," of course, to the level of cohesiveness of the person in question. In the case of a person with "structural deficits" (i.e., a person whose self never grew structurally through transmuting internalizations that consolidated mirroring and idealizing introjects into a bipolar configuration), small perturbations can give rise to disintegration anxieties that would not appear in a stronger, more cohesive personality. The same level of perturbation, therefore, will not lead to disintegration anxieties in everyone.

An analyst can distinguish disintegration anxieties by attending certain signals—typically the spread and diffusion of fears. The particular fears signalling disintegration anxiety "have a hypochondriacal and phobic cast" (Kohut 1977, 105). The fragmenting self, for example, is endlessly fretful and worried, brooding over one or another potential catastrophe—moles become carcinomas, paint blisters on houses become signs of ruinous termite infestations, fluctuations in stock prices become signs of an inevitable depression, and so forth. These verbalized fears "give circumscribed content to a deeper unnameable dread experienced when a person feels that his self is becoming enfeebled or is disintegrating" (1977, 105).

Far from being observed only among persons exhibiting psychological disorders, disintegration anxieties are not at all unusual. Even the strongest personality can be enfeebled by circumstances that deprive it of empathic responsiveness over a period of time, or that overwhelm it with an excessive degree of excitation or fear. This is not the case when we speak of lesser quantities of such anxiety. For homeostatic reasons, in fact, all of us depend on maintaining moderate levels of anxiety. Moderate levels, indeed, are functionally necessary to sustain continuing "selection" of the structures of the self—that is, to sustain the "selection pressure" behind structures that under normal conditions work to maintain self-esteem and support self-regulation.

Using only the theory Kohut provides, it is not easy to see why this is the case. Kohut doesn't make explicit the homeostatic logic I have lifted from his theory. But to develop fully some of his theory's value for sociological analysis, this more explicit formulation is useful. It may also assist in understanding why his system seems to assist the clinician in dealing with certain common disorders of the self and also why certain of his central concepts describe processes that work as he argues. This is especially true in relation to his concept of selfobject transference.

Selfobject Transferences

SENSITIVE DEPENDENCE AND THE FOREGROUND   Selfobject transference in Kohut's thinking is a process in which current partners in social interaction are used as selfobjects—whether those current partners are analysts onto whom remobilized infantile narcissistic needs are being displaced, or current partners outside analysis who are distorted in terms of earlier unsuccessful object relationships. Particularly where earlier selfobject relationships failed in one way or another to produce transmuting internalization, a person's current interaction becomes vulnerable to being used functionally for the purpose of self-repair or self-consolidation. Kohut associated the appearance of these "transference phenomena" with injuries to the self, or with failures of the self to develop cohesively—in particular, with weaknesses of mirrored or idealized strength. Where these weaknesses showed up, as he recognized through his clinical work, was in the chronic tendency a person displayed in interaction to use, or to attempt to use, another person as a selfobject—that is, as a caregiver, or, in the language of systems theory, as an external regulator. Deficits of internal psychological strength manifested themselves in a person's chronic efforts to reconfigure current social interaction into the sort of caregiving scenario where, in Kohut's language, "structure building" might occur—where, in other words, deficits might be remedied, weaknesses eliminated, and a self consolidated.

When this is happening—when a person is attempting to use another in this structure-building way—the process becomes obvious. Its signals are those of the infant—*exhibitionism,* the merger demand of the person without mirrored strengths; or *voyeurism,* the merger demand of the person without idealized strengths; or some combination of the two. As we shall begin to see in subsequent chapters, there is another way to recognize such persons as well—namely, by their chronic readiness to be controlled by persons and events in the *foreground* of experience. I shall refer to this as *sensitive dependence,* meaning to indicate by this concept how vulnerable and unstable persons with psychological deficits are, considered as systems, to picking up and amplifying fluctuations produced in their near environments by the behavior of others or by immediate events. In effect, small proximate fluctuations get amplified out of proportion to their size, as they are transmitted from the selfobject milieu to the person in question. Petty interpersonal rebukes strike the person in question as devastating assaults on self-esteem; smiles as triggers for romantic idealization; repudiations by significant others as precipitators of suicide.

It is this responsiveness to the foreground of interpersonal life to which Kohutian thinking especially is alert—to the small signals of attention and disattention, to wants and likes of others, to the leads provided by significant others, to opportunities for exhibitionistic displays or voyeuristic merger, to subtle empathic failures—and that makes it uniquely useful, compared to other versions of psychoanalytic theory, for the purpose of elaborating a more general theory of social interaction. This is not to say that other kinds of psychoanalytic theory are not also useful—and, in fact, I have made use below of the work of several other psychoanalytic theorists. Nor is it to suggest that Kohut's theory exhaustively isolates and explains all variation pertinent to clinical work, or that the concepts of other psychoanalytic clinicians are not also relevant to the description of social interaction. But what we are presented with by Kohut is a framework already close to being in a form suitable not only for discussing in functional terms clinical phenomena but also, especially when reconceptualized in view of systems theory, for making headway in understanding everyday social interaction. Moreover, as I shall argue in a later chapter, Kohut's theory of the bipolar self can also be shown to depend on a more general logic of how *any* system produces "coherence," and thus helps to isolate processes at a personal and interpersonal level we may expect to rediscover in other systems.

THE LOGIC OF EMPTY ANTICIPATIONS   Transference occurs in the presence of disintegration anxiety. Pronounced levels of such anxiety arise from deficits of self-structure, and these deficits produce selfobject transferences. The reason disintegration anxiety produces selfobject transference is fundamentally homeostatic, but it is not easy to derive this consequence from Kohut's thinking without some outside help. This is because the argument requires us to understand how disintegration anxiety is inherent in the kind of memory by which introjects remain part of subjectivity. The circuitry here is complex.

Beyond suggesting that introjects are constructed incrementally and in fragments, Kohut isn't helpful on the question of their status in subjectivity. What is necessary to make sense of his idea is a concept of preconceptual memory—a concept available in the notion of "amodal perception" and useful allied ideas of self-schemata encountered in the literature of cognitive and developmental psychology. As reconceptualized with the help of these notions, introjects appear not as those homuncular entities some theories have parading around inside the head—choruses of snapshot relatives and significant others, carping about this and that—but as abstract and highly generalized templates for recollection, templates based on the invariant concurrence during early infancy of certain felt qualities of experience, a concurrence grasped in connection with regulatory interactions involving caregivers. These schemata include visual, tactile, olfactory, auditory, and other traces—all somehow stored, yoked together, through some higher-order code or suprasensory system. This is an image so much at odds with the assumptions of much traditional thinking that its implications begin to spill much beyond theories of the self. It is an image developed in numerous places—the cognitive side of it certainly in theories of deep cognitive structure; the mix of feeling and thought in the important essays on communication Alfred Schutz (e.g., [1951] 1971) wrote in the 1950s; and something like this mix in Daniel Stern's (1985) concept of the RIG ("representation of generalized interaction").

Transference and Instantiation

If introjects are actually functionally operating clusters of amodally represented perceptions—fragments of the caregiving experience, abstractly represented—then as regulatory templates having some homeostatic capacity they must actually occupy a status in subjectivity rather like Schutz suggests is the case for music. Music exists as a memory only in the abstract way a composition exists—as a translation of the tonal sequences of which it is composed into another form, as, say, into a series of notes and directions arranged on staves, or, say, into the abstract status it occupied through amodal perception. But actual music as heard and performed is then something quite different; indeed, it is a sensory experience *realized* through re-creation. A player performing a piece of music for the first time may be said to "realize" the music through re-creating it, just as a dramatic actor may be said to "realize" a dramatic role in a particular performance of a play. The realization of the music is shaped and affected, according to Schutz, by the player's foreknowledge of the kind of music of which the piece he or she plays is an example—thus, he or she sight-reads a sonata, say, with the knowledge that it resembles other nineteenth-century piano music of this particular form. To realize a piece, then, is not simply to repeat it, or to imitate a memory of it, but to create it anew, and to hear it only then—and to shape one's re-creation by the assumptions and expectations presiding over the type of which it is an instance. "The player's general knowledge of its typicality," as Schutz ([1951] 1971, 168) says of a musical piece being sight-read for the first time, "becomes the scheme of reference for his interpretation of its particularity. This scheme of reference determines, in a general way, the player's anticipations of what he may or may not find in the composition before him. Such anticipations are more or less empty; they may be filled and justified by the musical events he will experience when he starts to play the sonata or they may 'explode' and be annihilated."

If introjects have a status analogous to the types of which Schutz wrote, the way we should reason about self-development and related phenomena is dictated in part by the resulting process of "fitting" types to instances—*typification,* in Schutz's language.[5] Extrapolate beyond his musical example, and interesting consequences begin to appear. Insofar as lived experience is shaped by our memories, controlled by anticipations, and ordered through expectations, the suggestion is that some fraction of this process of self-realization involves *finding the equivalents in present interaction of deep templates of relatedness,* templates whose roots are in relationships to significant others. Moreover, *the generalized status of these deep templates requires us to instantiate them in order to have access to them;* otherwise, they simply are "forgotten." As structures of self thus constantly threatened by the prospect of their own decay and loss to mentation, *introjects are accompanied by an ever-present disintegration anxiety that is a constant feature of a person's apprehensions of his or her own fate*—an anxiety that waxes and wanes but is part of a person's necessary struggle to sustain self-regulating capacities, and part of the inherent dynamics by which a person gains access to self—concretely and in particular instances.

The import of this conceptualization of the self's deep structure begins to become apparent only as we start to think what it means to be continuously vigilant in some half-conscious way for the external equivalents of internal forms. This is what is implied—a selfhood alert always for the opportunities presented by experience to grasp itself through some recapitulation of its past. We are not talking here about some sort of neurotic Byzantinism by which persons are the captives of their own history—slavishly duplicating canonical forms locked into their identity, "prisoners of childhood" (in Alice Miller's expression [1981]). The person in this view realizes "self" the way a painter realizes a conception—by bringing the conception into being on canvas. We may always be seeking ways to realize familiar forms—replaying the same music, the same dramas, the same relationships, and so forth—but not to duplicate them without deviation from the precedents supplied by the past. A person's social life in this view does in fact amount to an ever-active drama unfolding according to a logic implanted in it by the deep-seated needs all of us have for empathic responsiveness and self-regulation. Every social setting has the potential to become the dramatic scene in which we discover partners who are "responsive" to the particular configuration of needs we bring into the social world.

For now, however, consider the immediate place of this idea in Kohut's homeostatic notions of the bipolar self. What these thoughts suggest initially is that "selfobject transference" for Kohut involves first creating and then instantiating introjects. Other persons are "used" as selfobjects when disintegration anxiety motivates one of Kohut's "merger demands"; this "functional" use of another person as an selfobject is a selfobject transference. The aim of selfobject transference is to recapitulate a caregiving relationship—to reconfigure the person in relation to external selfobjects in such a way as potentially to engage in what Kohut calls "structure building." We use selfobjects to strengthen self in either mirroring or idealizing areas. Moreover, the amount of anxiety necessary to motivate such selfobject transference need not be great. Transference indeed begins to look like an everyday process through which a person reestablishes self in concrete and particular instances—or, as we might now want to say, "realizes" self. Clearly, there are extreme forms of this phenomenon—those, in fact, Kohut mainly wrote about, where selfobject transferences are motivated by deep deficits, as when a person never developed nuclear structures of self to begin with. In such cases, a person's transferences are signals of his or her inability to function apart from external selfobjects—and hence of needs to build psychic structures, able to serve functional needs of self, where presently such structures don't exist. But what this reconceptualization also suggests is that the same process, manifesting itself in less extreme forms of selfobject attachment, is a normal route by which people grow and undertake self-realization.

Kohut's system requires this postulate, as indeed do most notions of personality based on concepts of introjection. Selfobject transference fits

generalized models of earlier experiences to concrete instances of present experience, attempting thereby both to reinstantiate deep introjects and to define
the present in view of the past.[6] Part of this involves reconfiguring present life
in terms of earlier object relationships, and in the process again finding regulation in view of external others.

Directly, then, this makes transference the interpersonal equivalent of the
intrapsychic process by which the self "selects" an internal structure to serve
its needs for regulation. Sandler and his collaborators (e.g., Sandler and Rosenblatt 1962; Sandler and Sandler 1978) would have such "selection" operating continually—operating, that is, as a more or less implicit sensitivity to
whether others are "responsive" to our needs. Since the precedent for transference is the original transfer to an idealized selfobject of some of the omnipotence of the archaic grandiose self, Kohut's reasoning implies that
transferences inevitably occur when persons are unable to regulate themselves, particularly to regulate the level of their own mirrored strength or self-
esteem. This allows us to think of selfobject transferences as strong forces
that come into play in our social interactions when the self is thrown out of
equilibrium—that is, out of a region in which it can maintain itself apart from
others, and where it thus must turn to others for the regulatory strengths it
lacks. Transferences shift the locus of regulation from endogenous to exogenous structures—from introjects to external selfobjects. Weakened, introjects
continue to provide general functional templates of relatedness a person subsequently attempts to reconfigure in interaction.

The Causal Structure of the Bipolar Self

Consider, then, the translation of these thoughts about Kohut's notions of
homeostasis into the directed graph in figure 1.4. T represents sources of
perturbation or tension—in this case, variations in circumstances that yield
disintegration anxiety (e.g., unprecedented danger such as combat; or a significant life transition, such as movement from one occupational role to another; or a narcissistic injury, such as repudiation by a significant other, etc.).

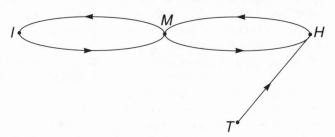

Fig. 1.4   The causal loop structure of the bipolar self

The homeostatic variable *H* registers the resulting disintegration anxiety itself.⁷ Depending on whether the level of anxiety affects the ability of the person to function cohesively (as it would at high and low extremes), selection pressure will build up behind one or the other merger demand and/or behind one or the other pole of self.⁸ These two structures are functional alternatives for dealing with the anxiety in question.

In the situation of the infant we have already reviewed, for example, empathic failures (but only "optimal" empathic failures) on the part of the caregiver—that is, moderate values of *T* and *H*—result in first "selecting" the "archaic grandiose self" and establishing the mirroring pole, *M*, as a focus for subsequently clustering mirrored introjects. The global subjective experience of mirroring alone Kohut suggestively labels "archaic omnipotence"—in our terms, the felt product of undamped positive feedback. As the infant finds itself increasingly excited through this process, it "transfers" some of this mirrored "perfection" to an external idealized selfobject, which then functions in the capacity of a negative feedback device. Introjected, the idealized selfobject becomes a structure, *I*, supporting self-regulation apart from the external object. Under normal functioning (e.g., when *T* is insignificant) and with the self otherwise exhibiting structural cohesiveness (i.e., when both *I* and *M* have been adequately strengthened through selfobject transferences and transmuting internalizations), the circuitry from *M* to *I* and back again is sufficient to regulate and stabilize the self in the homeostatic style Kohut had in mind. Such a state is referred to as a condition of "equilibrium."

The equations implied by the graphic representation of this argument are not immediately obvious because we have now begun to talk of comparisons and set points. Still, figure 1.4 itself facilitates investigating the consequences of homeostatic dynamics. As Kohut himself points out, structural development can proceed psychologically along either or both of the "selfobject lines," that is, through transmuting internalizations on the basis of repeated optimal mergers with idealized selfobjects or mirroring selfobjects. Using the graph, the consequences of structural deficits in either area can be visualized by examining how a person would be obliged to function in the absence of one or the other of the polar structures. The child raised by a cold and unempathic mother, for example, might exhibit weakness in the mirrored area. In the limit, weakness in this area means the mirrored pole vanishes completely. Such a child would be expected to exhibit chronic mirroring merger demands, manifested in one form of exhibitionism or another. Similarly, idealized weaknesses might result if an unempathic father regularly frustrated the merger demands of an anxious son. Idealized deficits in this sense would be expected to produce chronic voyeurism in one of its forms. In cases of fragmented personalities, where neither pole of self functions adequately, we would find ourselves observing a person seeking regulation entirely in view

of external selfobjects. These lines of functioning are suggested by the dynamics implied in figure 1.4. We shall ask in chapter 3 how social interaction
itself can be represented in these terms.

Generativity and Its Pathologies

Though Kohut does not argue as such, the deep structures of the "nuclear
self" are generative. Thinking of them this way aligns Kohut's clinical impressions with contemporary conceptions from developmental psychology of
early development. Revised in this light, what Kohut described as a nuclear
self is actually better understood as a foundation *for* self, that is, as a generative system formed from configurations of early cognitive schemata, organized initially on the basis of regulatory interactions with caregivers. In this
view, "self" becomes a complex emergent of these underlying schemata—a
more or less cohesive or stable system of information consisting, on the one
hand, of different forms of "self-knowledge" (Neisser 1988a) and, on the
other hand, of different "frameworks" of self-other relatedness (Stern 1985).
In reality, no such entity as "the" self exists, even though terminological convention probably requires us to continue using this locution. What actually exists (and only in varying states of instability) are the products of these various
deep generative schemata—different senses of self that emerge in mentation,
activity, and interaction as instantiations, realizations, and improvisations
(Barclay and Hodges 1988). This revisionist conception averts some of the
conceptual and philosophical difficulties inherent in reified notions of the
self.[9] This does not mean "self" isn't real, but it does require a nonessentialist
conception. Self in this view is shorthand for information—specifically, for
what a person "brings to mind" or "realizes" when he or she thinks reflex-
ively of himself or herself.

Our own admonitions to the contrary, let us follow terminological convention and speak of this structural configuration as self, avoiding the terminological awkwardness occasioned by the reconceptualization. What does it
mean, then, to speak of self as generative? Self is generative specifically in
the sense that these deep structures are abstract and generalized. To support
the person apart from caregivers or other external selfobjects, the schemata
on which self is founded require representatives. Thoughts and other illusions are such representatives and stand in some substitutive symbolic relationship to external selfobjects even as they represent introjects. Disintegration
anxiety in its extreme forms is what appears in persons unable to find self-
representations. These are persons whose self-representations are fragmenting, or who never developed generative structure to begin with. Disintegration
anxiety is also inherent (as argued above) in the generalized status of the
generative structure itself, and motivates ways of introducing into the person

the countervailing effects these structures otherwise would supply—effects then achieved through attachments, interactions, and selfobject transferences.

What I see as central to Kohut's logic, therefore, is the proposition that interaction is where people recapitulate the structure-building activities undertaken originally in relation to caregivers. Other matters also occur in interaction, but structure building is what interested him. This was because Kohut's own reasoning was concerned less with interaction itself than with the effects of interaction on the person—namely, the possibility that interaction might in fact result in strengthening people psychologically. This meant allowing them to function autonomously, without being driven by the strong fears and phobic forces signalling their anxiety. Deficits in self-structure interested him as a clinician. The same logic in the hands of a sociologist, however, begins to suggest interesting consequences interpersonally.

In the following chapters of this book, I examine such consequences. Eventually we shall make our way from the study of simple interaction systems, such as those we start to examine in chapter 2, to complex systems, such as those in formal organizations or in markets. Along the way, the concepts outlined in this first chapter will be refined and supplanted by others. But with these beginnings, we shall be able to build cumulatively across a diverse substantive terrain. Beginning in chapter 2, I shall suggest how these ideas can be related to neuropsychophysiological research on brain chemistry and to addictive behavior. From these beginnings, we shall then make our way quickly back into the study of personal behavior and social organization.

2

Strong Attachments

Prior to finding in its environment objects to which it can form "optimal" attachments—attachments from which self-regulating capacities can develop—the infant gears into experience in fragmented ways. The first relevance of objects appears in relation to their functional capacities: they excite, they calm, they relieve the pressures arising from needs. But without any coherent sense of all experience together, the infant's first attachments to objects have at most episodic and disconnected significances. Such experiences as the infant "knows," it knows only in the presence of the object itself. Experience is object-dependent. Only slowly and in certain "optimally responsive" environments does the infant learn how on its own to make objects appear, and hence to control experience itself. Attachments prior to the development of this competence are places where regulation and responsiveness are discovered—where life happens.

A basic quality of these locations is that they are powerful attractor states—strong attachments, as I shall call them. By characterizing these early attachments in this way I mean to suggest in particular that they constitute *addictive* forms of relatedness—connections to external objects the infant cannot do without. To recognize this, of course, is perhaps only to indicate that the infant's first attachments serve homeostatic functions for it, and thus constitute essential conditions to which it needs to return when it passes out of the caregiver's attention—that is, out of the region in which it is regulated. Putting the matter this way also suggests that "growing up" is psychologically akin to kicking a habit. Significantly, however, it is also to recognize the root of perhaps the single most important mechanism at work interpersonally in

every social interaction: the deeply implanted and wholly incorrigible tendency every human being displays to recapitulate just such addictive
attachments.

What makes attachments addictive? The fundamental force directing the
infant toward these "attractor" states is something like what Kohut had in
mind with his notion of "disintegration anxiety." The feelings connected with
being apart from the caregiver are feelings of disequilibration and fragmentation—deep fears of being in places where there is no responsiveness, where
one is utterly alone, and where there is danger of obliteration. By contrast,
attachments themselves are locations or structures the infant uses to manage
such fears and anxieties. Ignoring all the other things one might say about
how parents function when they are used in this capacity by their infants,
caregiving in this sense appears as a process deeply implicated with the infant's basic physiological and psychological homeostasis, as most developmentalists recognize. In some minimalist sense, it might be understood as
alternating between moments when the parent serves the infant as an addictive
opiate, calming and soothing its inner states, and as an exciting fetish, raising
the level of the signals passing though the organism.

So far as these thoughts take us, this remains too simple a model of early
attachment. What we need to do now is to suggest how the infant breaks
out of the pattern of external dependency. But if I am close to the mark
about the basic processes at work in this matter, it should be possible to
manipulate in interesting ways the ideas introduced so far—to show, for example, that we can get adults to behave like infants by depriving them of
whatever it is that supports their ability to regulate and stabilize their own
feelings. The infant in every adult, to overstate the case, is merely the adult
minus the internal capacity for regulating feelings. Or, to put this the other
way around, a full model of adult interaction should prove to have a degenerate case involving addictive attachment to objects—necessary and normal
in infants, but a sure sign of failed development or of a disorder of the self in
an adult.

Showing how this process works in infancy will also perhaps shed some
light on the addictively predisposed adult. Look again, then, at Kohut's basic
model of development. What is implied by my reconceptualization is that
phenomena like substance abuse, eating disorders, uncontrolled gambling,
promiscuity, fetishism, and related "behavior disorders" should all be understandable as variations on a common underlying attachment process—one
involving the addictive substitution of external objects, substances, or activities for regulatory structures of the self. The substitution may be understood
as "functional," in the sense that the objects or practices "selected" as substitutes for self-structures are meant to perform externally for the person in

the same functional capacity as might normal introjected "selfobjects," even though, for reasons to be shown below, they do not. In all cases covered by the theory discussed here, it is nonoptimal responsiveness on the part of caregivers that produces the disorder or disorders in question—sometimes all of them at once. Yet in all cases, the process out of which the behavior disorder arises must also be understood as the same process that in combination with optimal caregiving produces the healthy normal adult.

The Developmental Model from Self Psychology

Psychoanalytic self psychology rests on the observation that developmental progess, as measured by structural growth in the personality, occurs only in connection with a pattern of caregiving called "optimal." "Optimal frustration" of the infant, in particular, is meant to denote a nontraumatic, empathically guided process by which the parent's refusal to serve the infant's every demand encourages the infant gradually to take over functions on its own. By the process Kohut called "transmuting internalization," the infant slowly, incrementally introjects fragments of the caregiving experience, and subsequently clusters these fragments around what Kohut described as the "mirroring" pole of "the self." Roughly speaking, this first self-structure is the functional equivalent of what the infant can grasp of itself through the external caregiver or, in Kohut's language, the external "mirroring selfobject." This mirroring pole of the infant's nuclear self serves the general function of collecting what later becomes the equivalent of self-esteem—what, at this stage in the infant's life, Kohut deliberately calls "archaic grandiosity": the mirrored capacity and "omnipotence" that arises in connection with what appears to be undamped positive feedback.

All infants face the task of stabilizing such newly mirrored strength. To do this, Kohut argued, the infant "transfers" some of its omnipotence to a caregiving figure who performs for it as an "idealized selfobject." The idealized selfobject becomes a stabilizing force in the infant's world and serves as the basis for a second line of structural growth.[1] Mergers with this idealized selfobject, coupled with optimal frustrations of the infant on the part of the caregiver performing in this capacity, result in the appearance of an "idealized parental imago"—the second transmuted structure of the so-called bipolar self. The idealized parental imago operates either to soothe and calm the infant in the face of dangerous overstimulation or to govern and give it direction in the face of understimulation—or, put more generally, to stabilize or equilibrate feelings in the face of deficits or excesses of anxiety, excitement, and parental responsiveness.

Kohut crafted his unusual concepts precisely to suggest some of these dynam-

Functions

		Mirroring	Idealizing
Location	External	Mirroring Selfobject	Idealized Selfobject
	Internal	Archaic Grandiose Self	Idealized Parental Imago

Fig. 2.1 The self and its objects

ics of the self's development. They are reproduced by the cross-classification appearing in figure 2.1.

The mirroring selfobject (usually the maternal caregiver) serves as a witness to the infant's early behavior—to what, again suggestively, Kohut calls the infant's healthy *exhibitionism*. When mirrored back to the infant in conjunction with the pattern of responsiveness described as "optimal frustration," the mirroring selfobject is then introjected in fragments around the first pole of the self—what Kohut calls the "archaic grandiose self." Filled then with omnipotence in danger of being lost unless somehow stabilized, the infant transfers its sense of greatness and grandiosity to an "idealized selfobject." Again, following the pattern involving optimally frustrated merger with the external selfobject—a pattern Kohut labels *voyeurism,* as the infant merges with the idealized object—the infant then introjects the idealized selfobject as the "idealized parental imago." This process is diagrammed in figure 2.2.[2] Thus, to state the argument whole, we have the following steps: (1) optimal mirroring by the external selfobject, M, leads to transmuting internalization and the appearance of the archaic grandiose self, *M;* (2) the transfer of omnipotence to the idealized selfobject, I, then yields transmuted introjected strengths, this time organized around the idealized parental imago, *I;* and, in turn, (3) this intrapsychic structure subsequently serves the

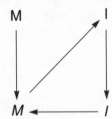

Fig. 2.2 The developmental pattern of the bipolar self

original mirrored pole of the self, *M,* in the same calming, enlivening, or directive capacity as the idealized selfobject.

The archaic grandiose self can thus be depicted as in figure 2.3, where *S* represents introjected mirrored fragments, *H* registers disintegration anxiety (the homeostatic variable), and *T* represents environmental tensions affecting equilibrium. This is the minimum structure of a functional system and is a representation we have already seen in connection with our discussion of homeostasis. Consider the diagram as written: without *I* to operate as an inverting amplifier, what we have in the archaic grandiose self standing alone is a positive feedback system. As *T* goes, so goes the system—explosively. Whether there is stability in this arrangement, then, is in the hands of an external selfobject, whose exciting or calming actions affect the organism equivalently.

It is thus important to understand how *T* in this logic can also serve to represent the presence of another actor. In the infant-caregiver interaction paradigm Kohut discusses,

$$T = \begin{cases} I, \text{ if case a,} \\ M, \text{ if case b,} \end{cases}$$

depending on whether (case a) the voyeuristic infant seeks merger with an idealized selfobject or (case b) the exhibitionistic infant presents itself for merger by a mirroring selfobject. That is, the infant's needs as a homeostatic system create uses for the objects in its perceptual field, as manifested in whether an object is looked at for mirroring or for idealizing. These alternatives manifest themselves as prepossessive distortions of external objects in view of either mirroring or idealizing needs. An object itself can then perform as required, or it can disappoint the infant's needs. Subsequently, such merger demands on external objects appear respectively as "mirroring selfobject transferences" or "idealizing selfobject transferences."

Selfobject transferences, as demands for self-selfobject merger in either of these modes, arise for several reasons. First, as chapter 1 reconceptualized this fundamental concept, a selfobject transference is a signal of structure building or an effort to instantiate an introject—a move to define an introject in con-

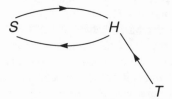

Fig. 2.3   Functional structure of the archaic grandiose self

crete perceptual terms. Instantiation arises because introjects, at least in their earliest fragmentary state, have a status within the infant akin to amodally represented perceptions and are probably organized similarly by means of episodic memory—episodes of attachment, represented via something like an amodal code, that are more or less "cohesively" organized (to use Kohut's word) within a representational system. One part of this system, following Kohut's reasoning, is centered around a pole of mirrored representations and another around a pole of idealized representations.[3]

On several grounds, it follows from this way of conceiving introjects that they are structures serving a person's needs to ward off anxiety as well as being sources of anxiety themselves—anxiety, that is, that persons will lose access to themselves unless they discover someone (or something) in whom they might, through instantiation or selfobject transference, recover themselves—gearing themselves into a concrete and particular world. Interaction and attachment, in this view, become processes through which a person gains access to "self." This is accomplished by searching in others for the equivalents of the mirroring responsiveness and idealized responsiveness grasped originally in strong attachments to caregivers. Such functional equivalences between persons (selfobjects) present in the here-and-now and persons (introjects) from the past—present partners conceived, say, as recapitulations of absent caregivers—operate in the way of metaphors to transfer qualities among distinct classes of objects. Reinstantiating strong attachments, in particular, results in transferring the concrete qualities of one class to another—in this case, the qualities of present perception across the barrier of time to an archaic structure (or to less archaic derivatives)—and giving to that structure renewed access to consciousness. At issue here is self-possession: the person's ability to find within himself or herself such structures as are required for self-regulation.

Without perceptual terms for giving content to one's introjects—one's representations of mirroring and idealized selfobjects—and hence for having access to oneself and for regulating one's feelings—the "self" is in danger of losing coherence, of becoming incohesive. The signal of this incohesiveness is the matter Kohut called disintegration anxiety. Disintegration anxiety operates as a homeostatic variable, as argued in chapter 1. In addition, because some degree of disintegration anxiety is registered by the person at all times, homeostatic support continues for *ongoing* "selection" of the basic nuclear structures used by the person in behalf of self-regulation. But the level of disintegration anxiety necessary to continue supporting these nuclear structures can be raised or lowered outside of functional limits—raised, for example, outside of the limits in which the person can remain self-regulating, or lowered beneath the point where structures will continue to be supported. This presumably happens when mirrored strength has been reduced below a

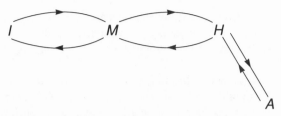

Fig. 2.4   The place of disintegration anxiety

critical threshold that supports ambition, self-esteem, or other mirror-related capacities, or when the person has been dangerously overexcited and fears "fragmentation" in the face of an inability to sustain self-control. Such deficits of mirrored or idealized strength arise from chronic nonoptimal responsiveness on the part of selfobjects in the person's environment. In the way concrete memories fade, introjects then weaken—or, perhaps more accurately, lose access to consciousness (or the capacity to support consciousness), and likewise their ability to serve the self functionally.

Figure 2.4 shows how we might think about the role of such anxiety in relation to the selection of new structures for self-regulation or for mirroring. Disintegration anxiety, registered in H in connection with the loss, say, of mirrored strength, promotes the selection of a structure A. As an "object," such a structure might be another person, a ritual practice, a substance, a belief—anything, in fact, the person might use to deal with the particular form of disintegration anxiety in question. When the problem is a deficit of mirrored strength, the self (i.e., the person as a system of self-knowledge) will search among objects for the kind of bolstering of self-esteem and mirrored strength it requires, and then attach itself functionally to such structures. When the problem is overstimulation, by contrast, the structure selected must be able to soothe and calm. More generally, the structure or object must serve the person in a functional capacity by supplementing strengths wherever they are weakened.

Addictive Attachment Processes

Attachment to an external object, then, arises in the face of disintegration anxiety and serves thereafter to strengthen psychic structures when optimal frustration by the object produces transmuting internalization. When the object in question is not optimally frustrating, however, there can be no introjection, and the person must then remain dependent on external objects for whatever functional regulation he or she requires. The general case of such external dependence subsumes the special case of addictive attachment. We may speak of an addictive attachment when the person lacks internal structures to manage disintegration anxiety, and turns to external structures for

regulation. Such addictive attachments typically lead away from strengthening the internal object world and may indeed result both in weakening such
structure as is in place and in commensurately increasing disintegration
anxiety.

The case of the infant attached to its caregiver is a limiting case of addictive
attachment—limiting in the sense that it occurs in the absence of structure to
begin with. The infant is dependent on the external caregiver to ward off such
anxieties as it may experience, and turns needfully in the direction of the
caregiver to find regulation for itself. What makes the case of the infant different from the addictive processes we can observe among adults is the likely
onset of optimal frustration, hence of piecemeal introjection of self-regulating
capacities. These capacities support independence from the addicting object
and hence change the quality of the attachment from addiction to something
else. This is not the case when we speak of addictive attachment more
generally.

A general way to represent this process appears in figure 2.5. Here we let
$S_{(t)}$ be the self (i.e., the person) at time t, $D_{(t)}$ be disintegration anxiety at time
t, $A_{(t)}$ be a substance (attachment, practice, etc.) selected at time t, and $Q_{(t)}$
be the total effects of A at t. We have fixed t to represent a process that exhibits
cycles. When the representation is expanded to show specific cycles, something of what is implied by this logic might be illustrated by the diagram in
figure 2.6.

Figure 2.6 shows two cycles in an attachment process—one that could in
theory be of longer duration. Useful in suggesting how to conceive the inter-
relationship of variables fundamental to understanding addictive-like attachments—attachments to structures (substances, practices, persons, imaginary
entities, etc.) by which certain "functions" are performed for the actor—the
diagram follows from those already presented and, as we shall see below, can
be understood as an extrapolation from the homeostatic model already
developed.

In this representation, I simplify certain arguments already derived in order
to develop a basic point. Again, let us imagine that S represents the "self" of
the actor in question—a system containing basic nuclear structures, as reconceptualized in terms of homeostatic regulators. The nature of these structures
(and of self as a more or less "cohesive" system) is such that they are characterized by a varying quantity of "disintegration anxiety," represented as d.
This quantity is also affected by whether the person in question has developed
what Kohut calls a "cohesive" self—that is, a self effectively organized by
its own internal regulators and understood by the actor in question as giving
rise to a coherent identity, stable relations to other social actors, self-esteem,
ambition, direction, and self-control.

A basic implication of this pattern of reasoning is that deficits of self-

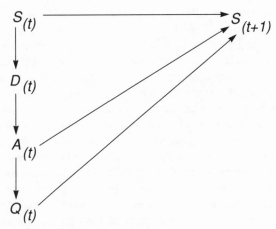

Fig. 2.5   Cyclic structure of addictive attachments

structure leave the social actor dependent for regulation on persons or things in the external environment. In addition, the environment itself can also undermine the adequacy of existing regulatory capacities—notably when it exhibits such instability as to produce events outside of the range of experience familiar to the actor.

Let us consider a common example. Imagine that figure 2.6 presents the process of attachment to external objects we might observe in a person who had achieved adequate developmental strengths. Suppose, however, an environmental turbulence appears in the life of this person, raising the level of disintegration anxiety he or she must cope with. By the terms of the homeostatic logic presented earlier, d_1 will then give rise to the "selection" of some structure a_1 whose function will be to deal with the anxiety.[4] Suppose the anxiety in question is met by the person through the choice of an activity he

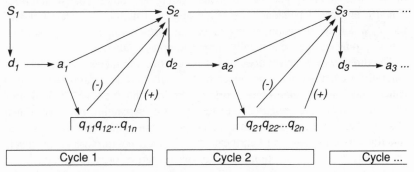

Fig. 2.6   Two-cycle diagram of an addictive attachment process

or she finds soothing or calming. Translated from self psychology into bio-chemistry, this notion of soothing (as well as the related idea of exciting) denotes underlying changes in organic functioning controlled or affected by environmental, social, and psychological behavior. Whatever the person chooses for "stress management," he or she ultimately will be attempting to regulate biochemical activity in the brain. This may not be consciously rec-ognized. But the choice of an activity like physical exercise, say, to diminish feelings of stress is one route from among many alternatives for changing the body's own chemical activity. In effect, it amounts to doing for ourselves what caregivers were called upon to do for us when we were infants: to introduce such practices (objects, perceptions, beliefs, etc.) into our experience as are known to have soothing and calming effects. Since physical exercise has calming effects, stressed persons often find themselves selecting exercise to manage their feelings. The biochemical reasons this choice can eventually become addictive might be roughly indicated as in figure 2.6, where a_1 can be seen to produce physiological effects q_{11}, which operate in the short run to diminish d but in the long run to augment it (q_{1n}). This establishes a relatively weak condition for describing something as addicting: the argument is that a is an addictive practice (object, etc.) if $Pr\{a_{i+1} \mid q_{11} \ldots q_{1n}\} \geq Pr\{a_i\}$. This is true because addictive attachments do not result in permanent decreases in disintegration anxiety and because the underlying biochemical effects of ad-dicting substances or practices can result in their abuse and in physiological dependence. How does this work?

Excursis on Neurotransmitters

Exercise triggers effects on neurotransmission in the brain not unlike the effects an infant can produce by sucking its thumb. Both are substitutes for the calming effects of sucking at the breast, and point to similar biochemical principles underlying mood changes.[5] If we can understand the biochemistry of exercise, we are on the way to understanding how other sedative activities can also produce dependence. Ingesting opiates, listening to certain kinds of music, watching television, eating a meal, or participating in a religious ritual can all produce effects chemically similar to opiate addiction.

The direct way exercise does this is by causing the release in the brain of naturally occurring opiates produced by the body to reduce pain—substances called endorphins. Endorphins work by diminishing the number of neuro-transmitter molecules released into the synapses separating neurons. When this number has been diminished below a certain critical level, such vital functions as breathing and heartbeat stop. In fact, neurotransmission levels are closely related to functional activity on the part of organic structures (up to an upper bound). In this way neurotransmission appears to perform for the organism as disintegration anxiety does for a person's sense of self. The two work in the same way in respect to stimulating functional activity of, on the one hand, organic structures and, on the other, the structures of "self." What an infant feels as anxiety may be nothing more than the direct and indirect effects of neuurotransmitter levels, as these, in turn, are registered in organic functioning and perceived, for example, as changes in pulse, heart rate, blood pressure, body temperature, and so forth. Such indicators of bodily functioning are themselves dependent on internal biochemical changes in the organism as it is affected by salient events. Even so, the person in question also registers d in his or her own perception, and it is d he or she wants to control—chemically, ritually, physically, and so forth. Disintegration anxiety, in this way of thinking, has an existence apart from reflecting organic activity and can indeed be one of the important causes of changes in body chemistry—a role also apart from being a covariate of environmental changes or turbulence.[6]

When d dips below the critical threshold required to maintain nuclear structures, the actor in question ceases to be capable of self-regulating activity. Likewise, when neurotransmission is weak, there is no support for physiological structures serving basic organic functions for the organism. Contrariwise, when d passes above an upper threshold of anxiety, the level of functioning demanded of the self's nuclear structures begins to exceed their capacities, and we observe dysfunctions of another sort. Stress might thus be thought of as one equivalent of what the infant recognizes as dangerous overexcitation. The infant manages its stress by turning to objects with the capacity to alter neurotransmission—objects, like caregivers, whose intervention in the infant's world produces the desired effects on its brain chemistry.

When adults do the same thing on a regular basis, external objects eventually get substituted for internal regulators. This can cause dependence on an object no less desperate than the infant's on caregivers. Indeed, as we shall see in later chapters, the object may be another caregiver, or caregiver substitute. In the case of an addicting practice or substance, the reason for the dependence is usually understandable in view of changes caused in brain chemistry by the habituation of the organism to the appearance of new compounds in the blood. The direct and indirect effects on biochemistry of the selected structures or practices a_i get compounded with those set in motion by the brain's own mechanisms for maintaining neurotransmitters at a fairly constant level. Since the chemistry in connection with different practices and substances differs, it makes no sense to try to summarize what is known of these complex processes here. It is enough to recognize, however, that it is the brain's own efforts to return neurotransmission to a normal level after an externally introduced variation in this level that probably result in dependence, tolerance, and addiction. "Dependence means that after repeated exposure to an event that decreases neuronal activity in the brain," as Milkman and Sunderwirth (1987, 33) summarize this argument in respect to opiates, "a person leans on that experience in order to feel adjusted or normal."

A typical consequence in the case of exercise is that in succeeding cycles of an actor's "attachment," he or she will gradually increase the level of commitment to the activities in question. A commitment that began as forty-five minutes every other day becomes, in this escalating pattern, two hours once a day: hence the addicted runner or weightlifter. Needless to say, this is only one of the mechanisms by which exercise can become a powerful attachment: another arises in connection with the so-called abstinence syndrome—the wish to avoid the dysphoric withdrawal that typically follows the elimination of exercise's calming effects. Addiction in such cases is sustained by anxiety over the imagined withdrawal, as in Lindesmith's theory of drug addiction.

THE CASE OF ALCOHOL   Easier to understand in these terms are addictive attachments involving the consumption of drugs or alcohol. Most people drink to make themselves feel better. They want to relax, or they want to be buoyed temporarily by alcohol above a bout of depression or low self-esteem. But the person who has a drink to feel better typically benefits only in the short run, as $Q_{(t)}$ reduces disintegration anxiety only at first. The initial drink at a cocktail party reduces the tension experienced by a person in social circumstances. Alcohol has this effect in the short run because it tends initially to depress inhibitory synapses, allowing excitatory synapses to predominate neurochemically. Our drinker will then temporarily feel exhilaration rather than depression. After this short-run effect, however, the lagged neurotransmitter effect is to depress excitatory neuronal pathways as well, and thus to serve as a depressant.

In the case of the person with chronic low self-esteem, repeated use of alcohol can lead to dependence and addiction. Subsequent cycles of selecting a_i as a regulator of anxiety will therefore require an amount of alcohol increased in proportion to the intervening increases in tolerance and depression.[7] Slowly, a physiological dependence will be built up, as alcohol consumption becomes something the person in question cannot do without—larger and larger quantities being involved on each cycle of the process.

THE CASE OF COCAINE   While some drugs produce genuine physiological dependence, others can be abused apparently without resulting in the same effect. Drugs of "abuse" like cocaine, it turns out, activate synapses of the brain's "reward system." It was the brain reward system that was isolated by James Olds and his collaborators in the early 1950s (e.g., Olds and Milner 1954; Olds 1958) and that subsequently spurred research in the field of neuropsychopharmacology. What Olds showed was that rats would push a lever to obtain stimulation from an electrode implanted in certain sectors of their brains. Since Olds's pioneering work, it has been demonstrated that direct intracerebral drug injections of the brain will produce the same effect. For a single dose of cocaine at 0.5 mg/kg, rats will push a lever 12,000 times (Yanagita 1973). Cocaine is so self-rewarding, in fact, animals self-stimulate to the exclusion of eating or drinking. Indeed, in the presence of unlimited supplies of cocaine, they will self-stimulate to death (Brown 1989).

As with their use of alcohol, people use cocaine to change the way they feel. Their objective is to experience the euphoria described as a high. At low doses, this includes feelings of well-being, confidence, creativity, self-esteem, and gregariousness. At high doses, however, cocaine produces an intense euphoria likened to orgasm. The memory of these intense experiences has been said to "persecute" the cocaine abuser and to drive them to ingest further quantities of the drug. More to the point, perhaps, is the pernicious neurochemistry involved. Cocaine mainly affects neurons that use one of the monoamines—norepinephrine (NE), dopamine (DA), or serotonin (5-HT)—as a neurotransmitter. Deborah Barnes (1988, 415) puts it succinctly: "A person takes cocaine; if it is smoked, the drug reaches the brain within 15 seconds. The person feels high, euphoric. The euphoria . . . occurs because cocaine blocks the sites on nerve cell terminals where dopamine is recycled back into the cell. This means that more dopamine than usual is available to stimulate other neurons in the reward pathway, an effect that is pleasurable and reinforcing."

In addition to causing pleasure by interfering with dopamine's "reuptake," cocaine in high doses also simultaneously creates anxiety. Crack cocaine abusers describe this as an effect so dysphoric that it drives them to consume more and more of the drug. Gawin and Ellinwood (1988) have argued that this anxiety signals a "supersensitizing" of the reuptake sites—a neuroadaptation that damps the brain reward system. In effect, their hypothesis suggests that cocaine's effects are so instantaneous that withdrawal symptoms occur almost at the same moment euphoria is induced. At high doses, that is, cocaine not only prevents dopamine reuptake and stimulates the reward system, producing euphoria, but also, at the same time, causes a supersensitizing of the reuptake sites that damps the reward system, producing a typical signal of withdrawal, anxiety. What it ultimately creates is a positive feedback system: withdrawal anxiety drives further cocaine abuse in order to produce euphoria whose aim is to override the anxiety. Such explosive dynamics are precisely what is behind the reckless, self-destructive behavior of the cocaine "addict" who pursues drugs at the expense of everything else, and who will ingest cocaine to the point of experiencing terrifying hallucinations, schizophrenia-like psychosis, and suicidal ideation.[8]

The Gawin-Ellinwood hypothesis is interesting in light of the self psychol-

ogy perspective, as well. While disintegration anxiety may be related to neurotransmission levels and to the maintenance of self-structures, as already
argued, this may occur because it arises in the presence of disintegrating attachments—"withdrawal" from attachments that had been used functionally
to serve some need. The anxiety the cocaine addict experiences as a byproduct
of neuroadaptation may be the key to a more generalized phenomenon: habituation to a structure (substance, object, practice, person, etc.) used to regulate feelings itself produces "anxiety" that motivates the continuing selection
of the structure. Some part of the anhedonic state Kohut described as disintegration anxiety is thus probably a withdrawal symptom. And like the
cocaine addict's anxiety, it motivates selections aimed at damping and overriding itself.[9]

Reduction of Alternatives

To describe addictive attachments in terms of their neurochemical consequences establishes a fundamental part of the addictive process—how such
attachments have their origins in efforts to regulate the way we feel. This style
of argument in no way diminishes the social and psychological side of this
process, since our attachments to others turn out to be the matrix in which
much of our physiological regulation emerges. Tryptophan in mother's milk,
for example, passes through the blood-brain barrier to become serotonin, and
eventually leads to decreases in excitatory neurotransmission. In this most
basic way we learn to associate ingesting warm food with the soothing presence of our caregivers—through the invariant effect (the release of endorphins) such a pairing has. Attachments to others, in this most fundamental
sense, are means first and foremost of controlling our feelings. Only for a few
persons, of course, are they a route consciously chosen for regulating the
release of neurotransmitters. Most of us get along quite adequately without
knowing about tryptophan or serotonin, though none of us long survive without knowing how to induce their effects. Similarly, we learn from other frequent pairings the ways to excite ourselves.

To analyze addictive processes this way suggests that they result from the
same cause on each cycle, but that each cycle involves increases (1) in the level
of the cause d and (2) diminished capacities to strengthen or regulate the self
in other ways. An addictive structure eliminates its competition—that is,
other "selections" the self has made or might make to deal with d in different
ways—at the same time it reduces the strength of even existing internal structures and controls.

Figure 2.7 substitutes for S_i the model of the functional structure of the
bipolar self, and thus makes explicit how the feedback involved in addictive
cycles is substituted for self-regulation. The small t appearing on the line

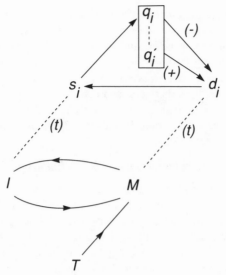

Fig. 2.7   Generalized model of an addictive process

connecting S_i to I or M in figure 2.7 is meant to denote the possibility of transmuting internalization as a consequence of the selection. This is necessary, of course, because the canonical form of this process—infant-caregiver interaction—involves not attachment to things or practices but to persons, and such attachments can produce transmuting internalization. (As we shall see in later chapters, the strongest of our social relationships involve such addictive attachments.)

One reason the addictive process lengthens into further cycles, in fact, is that it interferes with the "responsiveness" of the actor in question, causing him or her to become less and less able to sustain attachments to other, potentially optimally frustrating "objects" in relation to whom he or she might have developed new inner strengths. Such actors thus find themselves slowly made dependent on the addictive object alone.

An important characteristic of the addictive process, then, is that it undermines even existing self-regulating capacities. When we think of an addict, for example, we bring to mind a person who, say, can't have only one drink or who, more generally speaking, is immoderate in all consumption. The addict will drink until passing out, or eat to the point of illness and obesity, or use drugs until the loss of consciousness. The person who is addicted to painting or writing will likewise work until unable to work any longer. What this suggests, in view of the homeostatic notions we have been using, is that such personalities operate with serious deficits in the area of the idealized parental imago. Idealized deficits mean there is no inverting amplifier at work to control the level of excitation of the person in relation to mergers. In such cases, the person becomes like the positive feedback system I said was characteristic of the infant or the cocaine addict. The only regulators on the level of the signals passing through the person are those that are inherent in the addictive substance itself or that arise from physiological constraints of the organism. The infant's addictive attachment to its caregiver at least benefits from the caregiver's empathic efforts to regulate the infant's feelings. But there are no such empathic controls built into drugs or alcohol.

Exhibitionism and Risky Behavior

Closely related to addictive attachments of the sort discussed so far are those involving not diminution of anxiety but excitation and stimulation. The child deprived of mirroring responsiveness from a caregiver will find itself with disintegration anxiety manifested as something like a fear of "losing the self." Chronic weaknesses of identity, such as those typical of adolescence, for example, are often associated with the search for risks and thrills and by the short-run hedonism found among lower-class gang members (Short and Strodbeck 1965). Equivalent functional selections are observable in the consumption practices of criminal segments of the population (cf. especially Katz 1988), and in the shfting commodity fetishism noteworthy among *nouveaux riches* persons without settled preferences, a pattern increasingly apparent as well in the tastes of the audience to mass advertising.[10]

Self psychology would regard such "activity structures" in view of their capacity to introduce excitations into the undermirrored self weakened by one or another circumstance. Slightly different is fetishism, a common phenomenon involving the use of objects without which a person is unable to become excited, a pattern of self-controlled excitation by which the person attempts to amplify the low level of the signals that pass through the self in the absence of empathic responsiveness from a genuine partner. Instances of fetishism, needless to say, along with powerful addictions, indicate deficits of psychological strength and are signals of psychological fragmentation. Fetishism, in particular, often involves autoeroticism and related uses of the body of the person in question—indications of the unavailability of such strengths as are necessary to conceive the person cohesively, a condition resulting in the fragmented grasp of self as an aggregation of parts, members, organs, components, and acts. By suggesting that mirrored strengths are what is missing from the empty person who becomes dependent on consumption behavior or fetishism to substitute for self-esteem, I mean to denote such strengths as would result in "selecting" the structures of the self, including the optimal level of "disintegration anxiety" that is necessary, functionally speaking, to motivate the continuing functional maintenance of self-structures. In this

Table 2.1   Effects of Nonoptimal Patterns of Attachment

Structural Area		
Mirroring	Idealized	Consequence
Overprotective (surplus)	Absent structuration	Voyeurism
Deficit	Absent structuration	Exhibitionism

way of conceptualizing these matters, in addition, opiating addictions and excitatory exhibitionism also appear only in conjunction with an absence of strength in the area of the idealized parental imago, though each initially develops from the specific pattern of nonoptimal mirroring indicated in table 2.1. (By locating voyeurism in this table as an effect of overresponsive caregiving, I do not mean to suggest that it does not operate subsequently as an idealized merger demand, but only that it *first* arises, as Kohut himself argues, from the "need" to "transfer" qualities of the archaic grandiose self to idealized selfobjects.) Predispositions to seek calming attachments are established where there is chronic disintegration anxiety produced by maternal overprotectiveness, whereas excitatory predispositions arise where disintegration anxiety itself passes beneath a threshold critical to self-regulation, a matter portending the "loss of self" and associated with deficits of mirroring.

Figure 2.8 summarizes this argument: an infant's normal, healthy exhibitionism can lead in several directions, depending on the qualities introduced into its experience by the caregiver who performs as its mirroring selfobject. If the caregiver's mirroring responsiveness is optimally frustrating, then in theory the infant will be supported in ways that enable it to engage in transmuting internalizations—structurations of self in the mirroring area that are the foundation of its self-esteem. Such internalized mirrored strengths then diminish the amount of exhibitionism in the infant's behavior. But where nonoptimal mirroring has been the infant's fate, we can expect to observe further exhibitionism or a turn toward voyeurism. The exhibitionism is aimed at win-

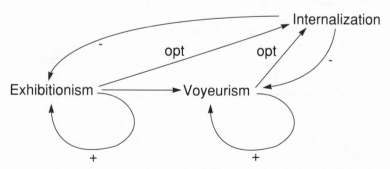

Fig. 2.8   Structuration and attachment effects of optimal and nonoptimal caregiving

ning attention from an inattentive, unempathic caregiver and is a renewed call
for the caregiver to merge with the infant. Voyeurism, by contrast, signals a
shift of the infant's functional orientations toward idealization. Normally this
shift is produced by caregiving that leaves the infant overstimulated: the infant
turns toward an idealized selfobject to stabilize its "omnipotence." It seeks
to merge with a selfobject it can use to calm itself. Sometimes this merger
demand is met by optimal responses that enable transmuting internalization
of strengths around the second pole of the self, and the infant benefits by
structurations that begin to make it self-regulating. Often, however, these demands are ignored or met nonoptimally, and we again can observe the consequences of a caregiving matrix in which the infant develops yet further
predispositions to addictive attachments of a different kind.

Strong Beliefs and the False Self

Stranger Anxiety

Calming and excitatory attachments, as this argument suggests, arise from
regulatory dysfunctions (surplus or deficit mirrorings, to use Kohut's terms)
that occur in conjunction with the absence of an inverting amplifier (the idealized parental imago, in Kohut's language). The problem thus conceptualized
raises into view the connection between disintegration anxiety in Kohut's
logic and the matter of so-called stranger anxiety discussed in the attachment
literature. This connection, in turn, opens the question of so-called transitional objects.

"Stranger anxiety" denotes the observed behavior of an infant in the presence of an unfamiliar experience (Bowlby 1969; Ainsworth 1973). The typical behavior of the infant at such times is an exhibition of distress—from
moderate amounts, where the mother is present, to massive exhibitions of
paniclike distress, when the mother is absent. Of interest here is how the
presence or absence of the mother—in fact her closeness and empathic availability to the infant—affects the amount of distress the infant experiences.

> The occurrence of fear of strangers . . . varies greatly according
> to conditions . . . [B]oth occurrence and intensity depend in large
> measure on how far distant the stranger is, whether he approaches
> the infant and what else he does; they probably depend also on
> whether the infant is in secure surroundings and on whether he is
> ill or well, fatigued or fresh. Yet another variable . . . is whether
> an infant is on his mother's knee or away from her. From the age
> of eight months onwards this makes a big difference, an infant
> sitting four feet from his mother showing much more fear than
> when sitting on her knee; this finding is no doubt related to the

fact that from eight months onwards an infant begins to use his
mother as a secure base from which to explore. (Bowlby 1969,
326)

Another way to make sense of such observed behavior is to see it as one
more way the infant's early experiences with its caregiver serve the function
of "tuning" the baby—much as we have spoken of the homeostatic tuning of
the organism in the first two months of life: the implanting of the parents'
sleep-wake cycles, and so forth. In this case, however, what is being tuned is
the fight-flight mechanism—the complex series of changes in the endocrine
system by which the organism, having registered and interpreted cues from
its surroundings as indications of danger, prepares the organism for activity
of one kind or another—flight, say, or aggression. The presence of a stranger
induces in the infant a kind of anxiety analogous in its function to disintegration anxiety. It predisposes the infant to turn toward structures for managing
the risks associated with strangers—namely, toward such external regulators
as are available and increase its level of security. When fear increases, the
infant turns toward the caregiver with the distinct need for merger. Idealized,
the caregiver is being used to mitigate and calm fear. Moderate levels of
stranger anxiety are forerunners of the search for idealized selfobjects and
thus are an important condition of the development of self-regulating capacities.
    The matter of tuning the body's chemistry in connection with such experi-
ence is a far from simple matter, however. The problem is to make the scanning apparatus "optimally" sensitive. Too much sensitivity or too little is
dysfunctional. Overly sensitive scanning means that any evidence of unfamiliarity in perception serves as a signal of danger, and causes hormonal changes
that keep the body constantly alert. Diminishing the sensitivity of the alerting
system is therefore an important accomplishment of optimal caregiving. It
encourages the system to admit into perception increasing levels of unfamiliar experience without ovewhelming the organism with fear responses. Gradually it encourages the development of strengths supporting the person in
dealing with more and more heterogeneous conditions. This is what the toddler is doing, for example, during those familiar experiments when it moves
away from its mother only immediately to return, subsequently repeating the
cycle—experimenting, so to speak, with apartness, separation, differentiation, and the unfamiliarity that are a condition of its psychological growth.
Only the mother who allows herself to be used as a "secure base" will encourage this pattern of exploratory strengthening of the infant's self.
    If overly sensitive tuning presents one dysfunction, undersensitivity pres-
ents another. Some infants in fact seem altogether untuned to dangers and
appear prepared to admit any new stimulation. The child of an unempathic
mother—a product of flawed mirroring and of neglect—will exhibit its

chronic mirrored deficits through patterns of behavior geared to raise its level of excitement. The coarse warning systems of these children behave so as not to register dangers that would alert others. In fact, such children are typically attracted to events their peers would fear.

Transitional Objects

Between such dysfunctions of stranger anxiety (oversensitivity versus undersensitivity to fears in the environment) and the pathologies of object relations that are predisposed by defective mirroring (the child inclined to calming or excitatory attachments), the connection, then, becomes clear. Calming attachments are predisposed by overly protective mothering—the same kind of mothering that infuses the child with the mother's own anxieties and paranoia—overtuning it, as it were, to the mother's own fears. Similarly, the unreliable, unempathic mother who ignores her infant's healthy exhibitionism creates a child desperately in need of responsiveness—a child untuned to dangers and predisposed by its inwardly troubled, flat and unresponsive mother to search for responsiveness in risk-taking, thrill-seeking, exciting activities. Excitement pumps up the empty self and restores to it the sense of being alive.

In the literature of contemporary psychoanalysis, this connection becomes even more interesting when reasoning about introjection. Some of the most famous work in this area centers around the observations made by D. W. Winnicott on the functions of so-called transitional objects. These are the blankets and teddy bears children use to comfort themselves as they rehearse separation from their caregivers.[11]

From Winnicott's perspective, the developmental problem for the child is to use such transitional objects to support introjection of the caregiver. This the infant is able to do because the transitional object "reminds" it of the caregiver. Implied by this capacity is the early operation of memory and cognition, in forms not unlike those I have discussed already in chapter 1. That is, the transitional object plays a role in the emergence of these active mental capacities. How this happens requires us to look in more detail at Winnicott's model of development.

It was Winnicott's thesis that objects become "real" when they are "incompletely adapted" to the infant's needs—an argument meant to subsume the mother as "object" along with everything else. Typically, the mother herself begins in a relationship of near perfect adaptation to her infant, and this blissful maternal synchronism to its needs creates in the infant a very special illusion about its environment. The illusion is that the environment is under its omnipotent control. The way this happens is suggested by the left panel of

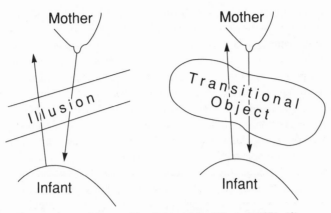

Fig. 2.9   The appearance of the transitional object (after Winnicott 1971, 12)

figure 2.9. The mother's role is actually to support this illusion. She does this by presenting the breast time and time again just at the moment when the infant needs it. This allows the infant to imagine the breast as its own creation; when it wants it, it creates it.

Both out of love and out of need, what emerges from this repeated experience of "creating" the breast is the infant's own subjectivity. Specifically, the subjective phenomenon initially created is the breast—or the illusion of the breast. This is by no means a ready achievement. The mother must support the infant's omnipotence by knowing when to place the actual breast "just *there* where the infant is ready to create, and at the right moment" (Winnicott 1971, 11, emphasis added).

When the illusion is in place, the work of "good-enough" mothering must begin. This is the piecemeal, incremental failure of the mother to stand so fully adapted to the infant—an empathically guided but limited frustration of its demands on her. The infant copes with such limited maternal failure through additional mental activity and cognitive capacity: it learns there is a time limit to frustration, and that there is ongoing "process" in experience; and it begins mental activity. Specifically, it begins to use autoerotic satisfactions as substitutes for the satisfactions the caregiver supplied, and it engages in "remembering, reliving, fantasying, and dreaming"—the "integrating of past, present, and future" (10). Mental activities such as these depend on vehicles of thought, and it is these vehicles of thought good-enough mothering shapes.

From Winnicott's perspective, regulating and shaping thought at this point in the child's developing mental life amounts to supplying an environment where "thinking" might occur in view of an *outside* reality. That is, once the initial illusions are in place, the job of caregiving becomes *disillusionment*. When Winnicott says "incomplete adaptation" begins to make objects "real," he is thus also indicating how good-enough caregiving strengthens the infant's trust in its environment. Trust that the environment is reliable encourages the infant to surrender its objects into the world. To become real in this sense means to be placed under the control of forces outside of the infant's omnipotence. This only happens when good-enough mothering has permitted the child to experiment with relinquishing its illusions, gradually learning that its feelings can still be regulated and its needs met even when it no longer magically controls the objects that served it in the past.

Allowing close adaptation to continue too long, however, results in pathologies of adaptation. The most obvious pathological pattern is where objects continue to seem perfect, and hence to be kept under magical control. Such objects, Winnicott says, become "no better than . . . hallucination[s]." The child not weaned of its illusions in this sense will be predisposed to manage life magically. It will fill its world with hallucinated and fantasied substitutes for their real counterparts. Such substitutes will perform for it like the caregiver who supported its omnipotence—the caregiver who eventually went away.

This reasoning helped Winnicott understand the many observations he had made as a pediatrician of so-called transitional objects. Blankets and teddy bears were external objects the observed infant used to remind itself of qualities located originally in magically controlled internal objects—objects corresponding to its primary caregiver. In Winnicott's observations of this phenomenon, the transitional object was always created with the tacit collusion of the parent, who never challenged the object's status in the child's world: it was permitted to be an object created by the child at the same time it was an object externally supplied to it. That is, the transitional object was simultaneously internal and external—both under the control of the infant's omnipotence and under the control of reality. Developmentally, Winnicott says, the infant is learning to replace apperception by perception—to experiment with surrendering the object to the control of reality. As it does this, it diminishes the part played by magic in its understanding of how objects behave, and it correspondingly increases the part played by forces not under its control.

We shall return to Winnicott's important ideas in later chapters. Right now, however, the important point to recognize is that Winnicott's discussion of the transitional object helps to deepen our conceptual hold on what Kohut would call idealized strengths. When in the realm of transitional objects, we are actually in the presence of the process by which the child brings about some adjustment of internal to external objects, and hence are observing the implanting within the infant's mental life of fixed mental constructs—constructs that, anchored externally, are not wholly illusory, and as such can operate to stabilize experience, apart from the forces of magical thought. Moreover, to say that transitional objects support a subjectivity on the way to becoming realistic and unmagical is to discern in them the functions of inverting amplifiers. Most culture operates in a like fashion. It appears as something, external to the child, with which to replace the activities of the caregiver—control systems, based in shared constructs of reality, supporting the regulation of experience.

The False Self

Deficits in the area of the idealized parental imago might very well be imagined in relation to Winnicott's analysis of transitional objects. In fact, Winnicott himself makes the point that the destiny of the transitional object is sometimes to serve the adult in later life as a fetish. That is, it operates as a positive amplifier of excitation, when paired with mirrored deficits. This would be the case where failures of good-enough mothering fall into the pattern of the mother who is unreliable and undependable—not available to accommodate the infant's own merger demands when they are pressing. The child of such a mother would never find itself in the sort of reliable environment where it might be disillusioned of strong magical controls over its experience. To such a child the environment would not seem trustworthy enough to permit the surrender of important inner objects. To surrender them would be to bring unmanageable fears and disorientation into experience.

One defensive reaction is for the infant to learn quite early in its life to hide what Winnicott calls its "true self." Rather than suffer another hurt from the inattentive mother, the infant's "true self" hides behind a "false self" that operates in a fashion compulsively attuned to the caregiver's needs instead of its own. In this flattering, obsequious style, the false self becomes a structure that serves the caregiver (later, the other) in a way the caregiver might have served the infant—fulfilling its every expectation. Perfect adaptation to the other is the defensive inverse of the caregiver's own remoteness to its needs. Connected to the growth of this false self is a nervous, other-directed addiction to audiences in general, where the false self looks to find admiration and control. Persons hiding behind such façades exhibit chronic stage fright—signals of disintegration anxiety—and seek to calm themselves by ritualized adherence to forms. The tastes and opinions of others then become forms by which such a self gears into its world.

Indirectly, the false self calms the anxious true self by diminishing the worry of the parent, who is thereby seduced by flattery and its equivalents into attending it. This evolves into a style made familiar by observations on many worried children—children who have themselves become caregivers, desperately worried about disturbing the sick or troubled parent.

Belief Saturation

The other flawed caregiving pattern in the area of the idealized parental imago involves deficits in what Winnicott called the "capacity to be alone." The mother so troubled by her own fears and worried about her child's love that she is unable to permit the child to "be alone" seriously impairs the child's development. Again, the pattern of good-enough mothering is absent, and the child is not motivated to replace illusion by reality. In this case, the child finds itself so overwhelmed by its mother's own anxieties that it retains magical control over its objects in order to secure to itself the protection and security it can't believe are present in reality. The pathological line of development following from such chronic anxiety is the elaboration of illusional substitutes—strong beliefs, as I shall call them, in all forms. In its extreme manifestations, this is the precedent in childhood for the sort of personality who is predisposed later to escape from real experience in hallucinatory and fantasy worlds—who becomes addicted to hallucinatory drugs, for instance, or who develops into the kind of belief-saturated personality who maintains obvious magical elements in thought: the prophet, the writer of great fantasies, the visionary artist.

Addiction to beliefs is no less pathological in its effects than addiction to alcohol, since it produces equivalent unresponsiveness. The belief-saturated personality stands apart from reality. Otherworldliness, sometimes religious, sometimes ideological, lends zeal and passion to such personalities. But it does so at the expense of their realistic adaptation to a wider life—particularly to life in all its quotidian disorderliness. In place of scattered reality appears a comprehensively elaborated scheme of beliefs to which the person is passionately, addictively attached.

The Spectrum of Addictive Attachments

The results of the argument developed in this chapter are summarized in table 2.2 in the form of a classification of patterns of addictive predisposition. By referring to the behavioral consequences of nonoptimal caregiving as "predispositions," I mean to suggest only that there should be a tendency in persons whose caregiving has been nonoptimal to compensate for resulting structural deficits of psychological strength by forming strong attachments in the patterns suggested. To regard all of these attachment patterns as addictive is perhaps to overshoot the terrain so far covered by solid evidence. But it has been my argument that they are addictive only in the weak sense developed

Table 2.2 Summary of Patterns of Addictive Predisposition

Structural Area	Consequence
Nonoptimal mirroring	
Overresponsive	Voyeurism, addiction
Underresponsive	Exhibitionism, fetishism
Nonoptimal idealization	
Overresponsive	Fantasy, "strong" beliefs
Underresponsive	False self

above—they supply regulation for the self in a way that does not support "apartness" from its objects, that is, $Pr\{a_{i+1} \mid q_{1l} \ldots q_{1n}\} \geq Pr\{a_i\}$, in the sense developed earlier.

Recall that, in the absence of optimal frustration, the canonical form of addictive attachment is the attachment of the infant to its caregiver. All other patterns of addictive attachment are manifestations of how the fragmented, incohesive self discovers substitutes for its caregivers in places, objects, substances, practices, or patterns that yield the excitation or soothing it requires as a homeostatic system, without also yielding transmuted introjects.

The successive steps developed in this argument are diagrammed in figure 2.10, which is an extension of the earlier model appearing in figure 2.8. Here, however, various feedback circuits connect exhibitionism and voyeurism, as primary behavioral modes of the infant, to various consequences, as these arise from either optimal or nonoptimal caregiving. Optimal caregiving

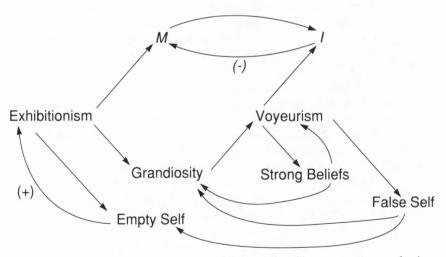

Fig. 2.10 Summary of structural effects and addictive predispositions as consequences of optimal and nonoptimal caregiving

gives rise to internalization in each mode—first to M, then to I—and forms
the initial bipolar self. But nonoptimal caregiving, in either the overresponsive or underresponsive styles, produces the various addictive predispositions
I have discussed above. Here, following Kohut, I speak of "grandiosity" and
related qualities of exhibitionism such as "omnipotence" when isolating the
effects of mirroring responsiveness. Likewise, deficient mirroring yields a
fragmented, "empty" self, disposed to look for stimulation. In addition, the
diagram makes explicit various feedback effects among these addictive predispositions, when they in turn are met by further nonoptimal responsiveness.
For example, archaic grandiosity can be reinforced by the appearance of the
false self. Arising from deficient caregiving, the false self typically involves
a form of exhibitionism in the area of idealizing merger demands. In addition,
the diagram shows how the false self can likewise be associated with feelings
of emptiness and fragmentation (the empty self) that in turn produce further
exhibitionism. Unresponsiveness in the mirroring area, which leads to an
empty, fragmented self, simply reinforces the tendency of the infant to manifest exhibitionism as a way of eliciting the attention it requires. Strong beliefs
and fantasy, by this same argument, feed back into voyeurism.

Conclusions

As figure 2.10 makes clear, the qualities of caregiving responsiveness elicited
by exhibitionism or voyeurism shape subsequent behavioral predispositions
shown by a person. In theory, moreover, all of the patterns discussed in this
chapter can arise within the same person. Not only *can* arise but *do* arise. I
have argued as if addictive predispositions were neat and separate, as if deep
divisions separated exhibitionist and voyeur and their derivative forms. This
seems to me true only for extreme cases. For one thing, the facts of addiction
tell us how easily one addictive practice substitutes for another—not with
perfect substitutability, but with an underlying functional logic. Strong beliefs
can wean an alcoholic from an addictive pattern, and running can calm an
ideologue's apocalypticism. Another look at the logic developed in this chapter, in addition, reminds us how deficits first arising in the mirrored area come
to underlie everything else we have discussed. Exhibitionism cycles into voyeurism and then back again; moreover, the derivative forms arising from nonoptimal responsiveness in each of these areas can also lead from one to the
other. Grandiosity and the empty self each can be subsidiary manifestations
of a false self; similarly, strong beliefs via the false self can cycle back into
exhibitionism. All these interconnections and cyclings are possible because
we are dealing here with mistuned, dependent personalities: persons so oriented to finding regulation for themselves externally in strong attachments
that the way the environment behaves toward them dramatically and instan-

taneously affects their own feelings. It is this mistuning, this excessive sensitivity to the *foreground* of immediate experience, that can transform the grandiose exhibitionist into the fantasy voyeur, or load the empty self with anxious conformity and dangerous overstimulation. One pattern blends into others, as responsiveness itself fluctuates across the nonoptimal spectrum.

Even in strong personalities, in fact, these patterns can be induced. With the right mix of environmental turbulence and social isolation, most people can be transformed into substance abusers, pathological conformists, or escapist dreamers. A boy from the country who goes to war and is repeatedly ordered out on dangerous patrols and finds himself in withering fields of fire may discover in drugs the only soothing adaptation to otherwise chronic and overwhelming anxiety. The adolescent undergoing transition from dependence to independence in our society, similarly, is typically moved from family-like circumstances into progressively unresponsive environments—from the warm, cosseting surroundings of grammar school into the vast, impersonal settings of high school. Many of the symptoms of adolescence arise in connection with addictive practices the teenager learns to substitute for the direction and nurturance such new and unresponsive environments put in short supply. Adolescence is the quintessential phase of sensitive dependence and strong attachment in American life—from traditional forms of attachment, as in romance and idealistic commitment, through sexual obsessions and desperate peer conformity, to drug experimentation, fashion consciousness, and exhibitionist group delinquency and rebellion. A few persons never undergo any of the strong forms of attachment in this list, but they are the exceptions. The typical adolescent in America is an addict to one thing or another, whether it is love or sports or drugs.

The study of these strong forms of attachment tells us something, therefore, about feelings everyone has had, most of us have learned to control, and a few of us chronically endure. Not just the feelings themselves—feelings of loneliness and worthlessness, paranoid fear and anxiety, hopelessness and plain craziness—but the "adaptations" we make to them—fantasies, illusions, poses, "attitudes," attachments—are more or less a part of everyone's life, or can be. These overriding states of neediness appear in such subtle and convoluted mixtures that our culture hardly has the terms to grasp exactly what we sense is going on inside of us—that sometimes we can only grasp by learning another language, say, or spending a month in Timbuktu, or visiting a great museum. Shadings then appear within our perception that we can render into consciousness, and perhaps understand. My point is not that otherwise imperceptible feelings ride into consciousness on strong attachments. Consciousness is always colored by feelings. But some of these affective signals create powerful states that dominate our behavior.

In all of us these dominating affective states arise, in some of us with less intensity than in others. The times when these states spread into groups of people tend to be of more interest to the sociologist than are isolated addictions, and they also tend to signal the appearance of dramatic social changes. Our task in this book will be to use the basic tools laid down in this chapter as a foundation for grasping theoretically and empirically some of these complex matters. In the next chapter, we shall see how these thoughts help in conceptualizing the appearance of these strong forces in social interaction.

CAVEAT My description of early infant-caregiver attachments as "locations," and my characterization of them as strong "attractor" states, is meant only to suggest a loose analogy between such states and those appearing as the outcomes of better understood dynamical systems, especially as such dynamical systems, under specified initial conditions, can be formally studied. Attractors in the latter sense—point attractors, cyclic attractors, chaotic attractors—denote various outcomes in dynamical systems and hence can embrace far more heterogeneous patterns of behavior than those narrowly implied by the notion of attachment. So far my discussion has isolated only intrapsychic conditions under which an attachment (or interaction) process unfolds, and these have to do with the consolidation of psychological strengths around the two poles of the so-called bipolar self—functional capacities allowing infants slowly to diminish the force behind their attachments. A specific strong attachment, in this sense, is only one way the general underlying attractor may manifest itself. Strong attachments, as well as the related qualities of addictive dependence arising in conjunction with such strong attachments, are therefore only particular instantiations of an underlying dynamical system. Only when the system in question is studied under conditions (or, alternatively put, when it is in a region of its parameter space) loosely described in terms of the psychological deficits (or the absence of intrapsychic strengths) of the persons comprising it would such strong attachments appear. As these psychological strengths build up, the conditions change under which the interaction process unfolds; and as these conditions change, these powerful attractor states will disappear. Loosely, therefore, this argument points the way not only toward more detailed analysis of how strong forces appear in interaction—as attachments as well as other instantiations of the attractor—but also toward the analysis of different regions of the parameter space where we find conditions not of strong attachment but of autonomy. But before we can make our way to the study of weak interaction, we must study strong interaction itself in more detail.

3

Dynamics of Strong Interaction

Interaction Revisited

Examining childhood socialization helps isolate interpersonal dynamics essential not just to infancy but to lifelong growth and development. In studying the addictive effects of attachment deficits, for example, an important proposition was formulated that can be generalized beyond infancy: from current partners in social interaction, no less than from original caregivers, certain broadly sketched patterns of "optimal" or "good-enough" responsiveness are necessary to promote and sustain psychological autonomy and growth. Not only the addictively predisposed person but every social actor has attachment needs—ubiquitous, exigent wants for strength and direction, causing in all of us a continuing search for responsiveness from others. How do these needs affect interaction itself? In this chapter we shall have another look at attachment processes, this time to analyze powerful states in interaction produced by our needs for responsiveness. The specific states I have in mind I shall designate as *strong interactions*, by which I mean interactions under the control of selfobject transferences.

To bring these matters into focus, we shall have to develop slightly different ways of attending interaction. The habit of sociological analysis is to think of interaction as dyadic, the unit of analysis as the "pair relationship." Here we shall start with two-person systems as well, but we shall want to preserve the option of generalizing our analysis to larger systems by focusing on "fields" of interaction. Beginning in chapter 4, our analysis will go beyond dyads to embrace complex *n*-person systems, and along the way the "field" concept will become more and more useful. This is because many of the same forces enclosed by dyads diffuse beyond them and enter into the dynamics of collective life on larger and larger scales. Anxiety, for example, knows no boundaries and is a force shaping large-scale collective interaction no less than the face-to-face variety. Bring to mind, then, a simple interaction field—a social space permeated by all the forces we have been thinking about up to this time, matters like needs, anxieties, merger demands, transitional objects, transferences, and so forth. Our angle on behavior has now subtly changed, for by focusing on field rather than person we conceive both the behavior of individual actors and of the system itself—plus, importantly, phenomena that emerge from interaction.

An interaction field obviously encloses individual acts by separate actors, but it also is alive with such emergent phenomena—states of feeling and acting that are interdependent states, that cannot occur in a one-person field, and that are themselves often transitional: temporary phases in the organization of a social system. Fluctuations of energy, tides of attraction and repulsion, phases of organization, disintegration, decay—all variously describe such fields, however strange this language may seem when applied to matters as ordinary as the familiar events that happen face-to-face. By speaking of strong interaction, for example, I refer to a phase of an interaction field, not a property of actors. It is a phase driven by the release of the strong forces identified so far as selfobject transferences. The appearance of transferences within an interaction field generally signals structure-building activity. Strong interaction thus sometimes indicates that a transition is underway into a new state of the system—but not always. It also can signal temporary fluctuations out of an established state—deviations that will be "corrected" as the system returns from this temporary phase back into its original state. Transferences are thus signs of these fluctuations and transitions, and strong interactions arise where these fluctuations or transitions are underway. In this sense they denote a phase into which an interaction field can move—at times temporarily, but occasionally heralding a transition into a new state.

After we have studied strong interaction as a dyadic matter in this chapter, we shall expand the discussion to phenomena on a larger scale. Strong interactions in some cases, as we shall see, are preludes to transitions—moments in the changing organization of a field from one state to another. This loose use of language from mathematics—states, phases, and transitions—will make familiar things at first seem strange and uncommon, but that is a price we shall pay to bring into focus matters that common sense about interaction often ignores. One reason for this shift of perspective is to suggest how feelings are controlled by the interaction field itself; another is eventually to argue that as we move from two-person to complex *n*-person systems, we actually observe patterns that remain constant across changes of scale. Interaction fields have important invariant properties, whether we are talking about 2-person or *n*-person systems. Just how this can be so, we shall not see until later chapters. First we must return to attachment and responsiveness.

Mutual Orientation

Two actors crossing into each other's perceptual fields are almost invariably interacting in some sense. They become, as Parsons and Shils (1951) used to say, "oriented" to one another. This does not require them to share a purpose, sign a contract, or even talk. But moving within reach of each other's perceptions changes the system of which they are a part. As soon as they are discernible to one another, they begin to generate a field of forces. This is no less plainly manifest in the subtle ways they immediately begin to control one another than is the effect caused on orbits when two objects pass one another in space. What had been two separate persons engaged in business of their own begins, *ceteris paribus,* to become something else—at first, a weak field of two, then, tentatively, something more coherent, organized and *sui generis.*

Attentiveness to one another is an incorrigible quality of social actors. Out of the corners of their eyes they monitor and scan the streets, even as they move through a crowd thinking about something else. Another person's movement will affect their speed and direction in the way a hidden shoal alters the direction of a wave—invisibly, beneath the level of their conscious perception, but inevitably. This mutual orientation—the capacity for "dissociated vigilance," as Goffman (1971) once described the way we scan the environment for the intentions of others—has been described as a "miracle of adaptation." Indeed, it seems so naturally a part of human behavior as to suggest there is something foundational about it—that it is one of those early adaptations of the active organism on which subsequent and higher-order skills stand. Or is it something even more interesting? Not merely an adaptation, but a ground form of social life itself—a tendency to return, at every chance, to a condition of attachment to others? Whatever it is—a mix, perhaps, of stranger anxiety in adult behavior and the predisposition to attachment—it remains profoundly there, a prime fact of our inherent social orientation. As a species, we exhibit this readiness to blend our lives with others, combining into larger systems that submerge the lone person into a field of others.

Optimizing Responsiveness

All of the ways this combinatorial predisposition affects social life are important to any theory of social organization, but one way is especially important. It is the tendency to "optimize" responsiveness, which means adjusting the level of responsiveness in a collectivity to the level of challenge in the environment and to related levels of merger demands on the part of members. Most combinations of persons show this tendency, even unrelated persons in a crowd. Turn your eyes toward any collectivity, even of strangers, and you will witness men and women moving toward one another as the chance arises or as they sense needs on the part of those within their fields of perception. It is a rare group indeed whose members never look one another in the eyes, or never are caught observing one another from afar, or do not gravitate into clusters as their orbits intersect. In these turnings and gravitations the forces of attachment have their say, and persons' needs for attention and responsiveness are being expressed. There is nothing particularly orderly about this, certainly nothing organized in patterns easy to see. It is part of the flux of attentiveness and indifference by which every group is characterized—no odder nor any less instinctive than the herding behavior of sheep, the parenting activities of a pride of lions, or, perhaps, the contagion of affects in a warren of prairie dogs.

In this minimal sense only, a dyad is a crowd of two. Affects communicate themselves between two people in about the same way they communicate themselves in a warren or are transmitted among infants in a nursery. One screams, they all scream. One cries, they all cry. But in an adult dyad, something more can happen. The cry that is merely echoed by an infant will be picked up by an adult and transformed into something else—a response. This is the nature of responsiveness—it is an indication, if not of genuine understanding, at least of some like deposit of feeling within the hearer, and of the hearer's capacity to turn in the direction of that feeling and to transform it. Affects in this respect are basic elements of constrained attachment behavior we sometimes recognize simply as styles of behavior. Constrained into patterns by deficits in self, moreover, affects trigger responsiveness in those who perceive them—signalling attachment deficits and dispatching the message that the sender can be adjusted and transformed by needed attentions. An affect, or a style of behavior, says to its perceiver, "By this signal, I communicate how I feel. By this signal, I therefore present you with a key to controlling me. Attend my feelings, and I will be strengthened and made responsive to you." In this most elementary of ways, we come under one another's influence. Before we have even spoken to one another, we are controlling each other's feelings and entering into dependencies. So nearly automatic are these patterns of responsiveness that at times we mystify even ourselves by the odd couplings in which we find ourselves. They happen to us—accidents of our openheartedness. Whether this means there is some "norm of responsiveness" is another matter—one of culture and morality that overlays this fact of biological and psychological relationship to others. What it does mean, without doubt, is that social interaction is structured by responsiveness in ways ignored in sociological theory. Before we can isolate strong interaction as a phase of interaction in general, we must thus develop some models of the dynamics of interactive responsiveness itself.

Coupled and Uncoupled Systems

The development of the capacity to see or imagine oneself into another's subjectivity is conceptualized by some developmentalists and "object relations" theorists as the marker of a stage in the growth of the person. We shall investigate this capacity more carefully in later chapters, since it is one of the important foundations of all social interaction. Here it is enough to focus on related dynamics: the way the "state" of each partner in interaction affects the "state" of the other. Infant-caregiver interaction can then be understood as a degenerate case of a more encompassing dynamic model of interaction. Such a model in fact follows from the discussion of addictive processes, and allows us to speak of interaction partners using each other as "objects" serving to regulate one another's feelings. Such mutual regulation is the first "function" of all social interaction.

The appearance of another person within an actor's perceptual field has a powerful precedent: the original appearance during infancy of a caregiver. One of the significant clinical discoveries of psychoanalysis is the observation that this precedent is wholly incorrigible. From it arises a powerful predisposition to grasp every new partner to interaction as the reincarnation of an original caregiver. Recapitulating patterns of infant-caregiver interaction in this way is not usually conscious, but appears apperceptively in the controlling activity within current perception of our introjects. At some level, all new partners are apperceptively grasped in this way. Half-consciously, for instance, we project into them qualities we wish to discover there, hoping, say, to find the mirroring responsiveness we got originally from a parent or the idealized strengths we lack in ourselves. Stated more forcefully, what this means is that *external others tend to displace the functions of introjects.* Just as we initially depended on finding in "selfobjects" the precedents for introjected self-regulation, so we continue to use others to reinstantiate these self-regulating capacities. This precedent of finding regulation in external selfobjects, then, tends to supplant and override the capacity to produce it in ourselves. This is such a deeply, perhaps biologically, implanted predisposition that it often happens apart from our conscious mental activity, and partners to interaction simply find one another relating at some level of awareness in ways that mutually control their respective feelings. Not every interaction follows this trajectory very far, but every interaction has at least the potential to initiate it.

This observation is fundamental to the way psychoanalysis has taught us to understand our grasp of others. It should thus never be lost to sight in attempts to understand social interaction more generally. All interaction has the potential to develop along lines in which partners eventually arrive at the point of being dependent on one another in the fashion of an infant's dependence on its caregiver. Only an adult's introjected strengths, along with the direction we have access to in systems of external cultural control, damp this addictive process. Where such introjected strengths have been weakened or have not fully developed, as during adolescence or other significant life transitions, actors attach themselves to one another in ways we must recognize as involving addictive dependence.

This is a claim I suspect would be uncontroversial among clinicians, and it follows as a derivation from the reasoning set out above. What is new here is the conceptualization. Given that our introjected strengths are chronically in danger of being lost, what this reasoning further suggests is that a permanent search is underway in all social interaction for the patterns of responsiveness from partners in which these strengths might be renewed. Responsiveness, that is, is motivated by disintegration anxiety that occurs when self-regulation runs down, and is structured by the inherent biological template of dependency out of which, under optimal conditions, these capacities emerge. Something of the same sort has been conceptualized by Joseph Sandler and his collaborators (1962, 1978) as a search for "role responsiveness."

Energic Regulation in Social Interaction

This most basic pattern of mutual interdependence—partners serving one another as regulators of their respective inner states—seems to resemble characteristic linkages within many physical and organic systems. Studying such systems has often been a way social scientists have sought to make explicit analogous patterns of dynamic interdependence postulated in social life. A close analogue to interaction conceived as mutual regulation, in fact, involves the coupling of thermodynamic systems, particularly where the state of one system is set to determine the state of the other.

In classic psychoanalytic theory there are other precedents for thinking about the energic side of life, and they derive mainly from older, drive-structure models of the mind developed in Freud's writings. Yet a close examination of assumptions and processes at work in so-called object relations models of personality harken back to some of the same notions, albeit conceived less purely in hydraulic and biological imagery. Kohut's formulation of the "mirroring" process, for example, can be understood as an "object relations" version of interpersonal matters founded initially on energic dynamics.[1] So, too, are Winnicott's concepts of mirroring. Basically, what is being regulated in interaction conceived along these lines is the level of energy and excitation of the infant—either by virtue of the infant's own capacities for exciting or controlling its feelings, or by virtue of its use of external objects. Initially, it is the coupling of the infant to the mother that introduces homeostatic set points into the infant. Later, the "adaptation" of each partner in interaction to the states of the other—a matter no more mysterious than a mother's adaptation to her infant—serves within limits to alter this endogenous homeostasis. Imagine this process in view of what happens between two empathic adults: as each has feelings the other registers, each can then function homeostatically within the context of their interaction, that is, each can serve to regulate those perceived feelings so as to maintain "cohesiveness" and diminish disintegration anxiety. In a way, this is like saying one acts on the other the way a thermostat acts on the temperature of a room: it compares the temperature of the room to a set point and then adjusts the temperature accordingly. Take this metaphor seriously, and you arrive at a way of representing analogous interpersonal dynamics formally.

Two-Person Interaction

Consider again the causal loop structure of the bipolar self, as it was represented in chapter 1. We can extrapolate from that representation by imagining the coupling of two such "bipolar" systems. The resulting image has direct implications for studying mutual regulation in social interaction—implications paralleling those we have considered so far.

Dynamics are implied, in fact, like those depicted by diagrams of coupled thermodynamic systems, where the state of each system establishes conditions for the other. Figure 3.1 shows what such a coupling might look like in a directed graph. As before, I_i (for $i = 1, 2$) represents the pole of the self where idealized strengths accumulate, M_i represents the pole where mirrored strengths cluster, and H_i is a homeostatic variable registering disintegration anxiety. The two actors' selves are shown as affecting each other through their respective homeostatic registers.

This is not infant-caregiver interaction, but interaction between two adults. Here the self of each adult partner contains its own "negative feedback de-

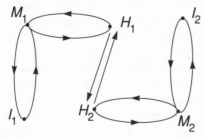

Fig. 3.1   Coupled bipolar selves

vice" in the idealized parental imago, I_i. Think of I for a moment as being like a heating-and-cooling apparatus, a combination furnace and air conditioner. As part of the same system, think of H as a thermostat and M as a structure where heat accumulates—a radiator, perhaps. Say we are speaking then of two rooms, each with its own separate heating-and-cooling system. Interaction then is *like* the process by which these two rooms have an effect on one another, especially if we move the rooms closer together or further apart or if we vary their temperatures. If they are adjacent to one another, the temperature of each will affect how much the furnace of the other will have to work, depending on the transfer of heat from one room to the other and the setting of the thermostat in each room. The furnace (or air conditioner) of each will have to work until the difference between the thermostat's setting and the actual temperature reading in the room falls within some preset range. Such is thermodynamic coupling.

If self-development is founded as I have argued on the emergence of homeostatic capacities, a model of this kind of coupling might be useful to us. In theory, such coupling to parents is required for the infant to develop self-regulating strengths (qualities clustered around the I pole of the self) and qualities like self-esteem and ambition (strengths clustered around the M pole). The infant needs a furnace, radiators, and a thermostat of its own, and it builds these structures when its caregiving is optimal.[2] Initially without them, the infant is externally dependent on its parents'.

Self-regulation does not develop in children without the appearance and strengthening of I, the idealized parental imago. This "inverting amplifier" Kohut saw as necessary to stabilize the infant's world. Yet as we have also seen, the qualities and inner strengths supported by a parental imago are subject to several operations that modify the imago's activities: first, the operation of decay, or the fading of the imago's strength that results from failures to instantiate it; second, disintegration anxiety that is a product of such decay; and, third, as a product of disintegration anxiety, the continuing search for selfobjects to recapitulate the imago's strengths in functionally equivalent experiences. Countering entropic processes, especially, is the tendency in interaction for external others to be apperceptively construed as objects in which to rediscover functional strengths the self requires. This in fact typically happens in more than a routine degree when a partner appears to be at all "responsive" to an actor's subjective states—attuned, that is, to his or her feelings. Interaction then follows a trajectory in which each actor's perceptions of the other are distorted by virtue of these functional usages—a matter involving, as we have conceptualized these phenomena, either (or both) idealizing transferences or mirroring transferences. Either or both of these transferences typically occur when the self has been weakened for one reason or another—or, in the cases that most interested Kohut, never developed cohe-

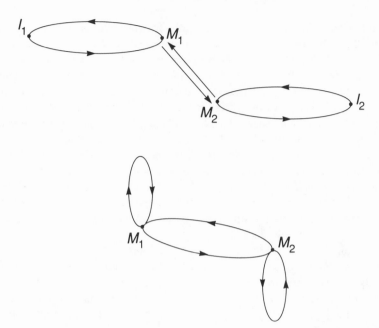

Fig. 3.2   Reduced forms of two-person interaction

sively to begin with. Failures that damage self-esteem or that impair the ability of the person to regulate self-esteem are typical forerunners of such transferences. They signal the tendency of the weakened self to seek sources of regulation for itself in an external environment. These are the forces that produce strong interactions: responsiveness potentiating responsiveness, transference meeting transference.

Allow the M_i in figure 3.2 to absorb the activities of H_i, so that the two actors configured there now connect, so to speak, at their respective "mirroring poles." The upper panel of figure 3.2 shows the corresponding graph. Now allow M_i to absorb the I_i, representing in this case the tendency of the actor to recapitulate idealized self-regulation by using the current partner as an idealized selfobject. This figure is represented in the lower panel of figure 3.2.

These simplifications suggest several ways implied by Kohut's reasoning to specify dynamics of two-person interaction. The bottom panel in figure 3.2 presents the interesting and typical case of mutual idealizing transference. (In the diagram, this is indicated by the absence of I as an operative endogenous structure of the self. Even though in the case of mutual idealization I does not appear in the self of the partner either, each is using the other as if the other might be taken as an idealized selfobject.) Here each partner seeks to merge with the other, there to discover strengths in which the self might regulate itself and find direction. When each partner uses the other in this way as an idealized selfobject, the other is being called upon to serve as a "negative feedback device" for the self. By contrast, mirroring transferences involve similar dynamics, only reversed: each partner's exhibitionism is then an invitation for the merger of the other, and establishes the other in the role of a mirroring or positive feedback device. (A graph of mirroring transference would accordingly show *I*, but not *M*, as a functioning self-structure.) The classic illustration of an idealizing transference involves the worship by a child of its caregiver. Beyond childhood, examples appear wherever one person worships another, as in romance or hero worship. The classic mirroring transference involves a child's demands for attention and praise from its primary caregiver. Exhibitionism has these mirroring demands implicit in it and appears in similar ways throughout life.

Coupling two persons as in this version of interaction, we find ourselves examining a dynamic system where each partner's feelings serve as conditions for the action of the other. One productive way this process can be further studied involves representing it mathematically in terms that sharpen the analogy to interdependent physical systems. Consider the following pair of differential equations:

$$(3.1) \qquad \frac{dM_1}{dt} = b_1 M_1 + b_2(M_2 - M_1)$$

$$(3.2) \qquad \frac{dM_2}{dt} = a_1 M_2 + a_2(M_1 - M_2)$$

Each includes the general form $dX/dt = b(D - X)$, typically used in control system theory to represent negative feedback. In the general form, X is usually a time-dependent variable like temperature, regulated by a thermostat set at D. This same argument, then, appears in equations 3.1 and 3.2, where D is replaced by the M_i corresponding to the partner. That is, the state of each partner serves as a regulating value for the other. The coefficients b_2 in 3.1 and a_2 in 3.2 are then measures of how much dM_i/dt is responsive to the "thermostatic" value of the coupled partner—a quantity proportional to the difference between the values of their respective M_i. The other terms in each equation define the self-amplifying or positive feedback properties of the system.

Models employing negative feedback concepts such as these are commonly used in the social sciences. These same equations were studied by Fararo (1972), for example, in relation to his concept of "status equilibration." Fararo's work is especially instructive because of the extensive mathematical analysis he undertakes. He is able to show, for example, that this system does not have a stable equilibrium. This is an important result. Starting at different points, the behavior of actors governed by these equations would show no inherent tendency to gravitate toward the same final position, nor would there be any inherent tendency on their part to gravitate toward an equilibrium if they start outside of one. Mathematically, if such an equilibrium existed, Fararo shows that actors would have to exhibit values corresponding to it at the beginning of their encounter in order to stay in its vicinity; otherwise, the system shows no tendency on the part of either to move in that direction. In self-psychological terms, of course, this consequence is appealing, since it is consistent with the observation that *any* interaction wholly dependent on giving itself direction through external regulation alone is unstable. Interaction is such an *unstable system*—or, better said, interaction fields are easily subject to being destabilized, depending on their uses.

A related aspect of this liability to instability appears initially in the attachment of infant to caregiver, and is part of what prompts the infant to develop internal strengths—introjects to replace unreliable or frustrating selfobjects. In theory, such unstable interaction can occur whenever actors exhibit deficits of idealized strength and confront one another in a mutually idealizing way. Psychologically speaking, each seeks voyeuristically to merge with the other. For example, such a circumstance can produce the meandering instability we readily observe in the behavior of romantically involved couples—a volatile connection, often out of the control of the participants, that is infused with paranoia and illusion. Again, this would be considered here as a *phase* of their interaction. Romance and love, moreover, also denote strong relationships and thus require for their understanding more than an analysis that stops, as we do here, only with the field of forces operating between partners to interaction. We shall give such relationships more detailed analysis in later chapters. Here let us concentrate on the forces of attraction and repulsion operating between two actors.

Numerous possible combinations of mirrored and idealized weakness or strength jump to mind when one thinks this way about fields of interaction. Nominal and classificatory habits of analyzing interaction are not generally subtle enough to discern these evanescent and fleeting possibilities, or the quickness with which these qualities emerge, combine, and succeed one another in endless modulation and fluctuation. In terms of pure energics, however, psychotherapists have known for a long time that it is possible to recognize these forces by observing their patients closely and listening carefully to what they have to say—often not so much to the content of what they say, as to the *way* they say it. One of the pivotal concepts in their clinical tradition, in fact, is the concept of transference, as we have already studied it in modified form in earlier chapters. It is the concept of transference that points to what might remedy the defects of stability we have just studied.

Dynamic models of interaction, such as the model based on coupling thermodynamic systems, require some concept of how stabilizing strengths enter into face-to-face encounters. Social interaction that moves beyond the level of an addictive attachment, for example, requires that partners possess endogenous structures capable of stabilizing them apart from their external attachments. As this logic would have it, weakened or absent introjected strengths produce transferences—illusory apperceptive distortions of the other as an object able to serve the self responsively in whatever way it requires for regulating feelings. But when these illusory transferential distortions themselves are weakened through what I have been calling optimal responsiveness—the pattern that allows the illusion to be surrendered and replaced by a "transitional object" on the way to becoming an introject—then and only then do stabilizing endogenous strengths of the self appear.

The model examined above configures actors who lack these stabilizing endogenous strengths, and thus must be revised with such mechanisms in mind. This time it must include a mechanism for linking precisely such stabilizing endogenous structures of the self to the process in which "external others" are used as something like regulators. Here Kohut's concept of the "idealized selfobject" has a role. This was Kohut's way of talking about a fixed external point by which the self stabilizes itself. Introjected as the idealized parental imago, this then becomes the structure that supports interactions that move beyond addictive attachments. Fararo introduces the equivalent "equilibrator" into his "controllable Galtung actor" with the notion of ascribed statuses—statuses, that is, that are not time-dependent. We assume here that the idealized parental imago is likewise time-invariant, at least within "perfectly adapted" (or near–perfectly adapted) phases of interaction, that is, when each actor is not disappointing the other, but instead is acting in the style of Winnicott's "perfectly adapted" mother, and the trajectory of their interaction accordingly is toward increasing identification with one another.[3]

The idealized pole of the self, then, serves homeostatically as an inverting amplifier or negative feedback device. This is the equivalent of the interaction field represented in the top panel of figure 3.2. If we transpose Fararo's argument about how ascribed statuses serve in similar capacities (as part of a process of status equilibration he was interested in) into our own argument, a more stable model of the interaction process emerges. Let us suppose I_i is fixed, operating on each M_i as a feedback device. Then for each of the two actors in our system, we can posit a mechanism that works as follows:

$$(3.3) \qquad \frac{dM_1}{dt} = b_3(I_1 - M_1)$$

$$(3.4) \qquad \frac{dM_2}{dt} = a_3(I_2 - M_2)$$

The coefficients b_3 and a_3 are measures of the responsiveness of each actor to invariant forces arising from within themselves—strengths clustered around the pole of the idealized introject. The suggestion is that the relative strengths of the idealized introject and the mirroring introject are compared, and that one of two consequences holds: for $M > I$, an effect inversely proportional to the difference damps the value of M; but for $I > M$, there is no sign inversion and the effect is simply in direct proportion to their difference.

The equations for the interaction represented in figure 3.2 then become a combination of the principles of feedback presented in equations 3.1–3.4.

$$(3.5) \qquad \frac{dM_1}{dt} = (b_1 - b_2 - b_3)M_1 + b_2M_2 + b_3I_1$$

$$(3.6) \qquad \frac{dM_2}{dt} = (a_1 - a_2 - a_3)M_2 + a_2M_1 + a_3I_2$$

Here actors can serve one another as external "self-regulating others," functioning in a homeostatic capacity, even as the whole system of their interaction continues to be stabilized with respect to their own internalized strengths.

The complexity of this process should not be exaggerated. Simple and quite common dynamics of interaction appear as a consequence of thinking in these terms, as well as fairly complex and subtle processes that require us to conceive of interaction as a matter occurring simultaneously on several levels. What is not suggested is that this process is wholly conceptual—that actors "think" about what they are doing, employing the full verbal armory of their language and all the cognitive capacity at their disposal. The process occurs both conceptually and by means of communications that are preconceptual and nondiscursive—by our readiness, so to speak, to recapitulate patterns of interaction deriving, in many instances, from the first weeks of our lives. The simplest regulatory dynamics, for example, appear to recapitulate just such early patterns of responsiveness. Overexcitement gives its signals to our partners, just as does disintegration anxiety and its related symptoms—fearfulness, perhaps, or shyness, or jumpiness. These are expressions of the way experience *feels* to actors and are compounded into behavior, communicated as affects. Among the things such signals tell us is that our partners may not be in a condition to respond fully and adequately to us—perhaps that they fall short of the conditions under which reason or its cognitive and moral relatives might serve to direct them, or perhaps merely that they find themselves incapable of attending us empathically. They may be too excited, too depressed and empty, too exhibitionistic, too utterly passive, too full of worries and paranoia, to engage life with us in an active, cognitively directed style, or in the pattern of a responsive and attentive companion.

What in fact we recognize as the "temperaments" and "styles" of our partners—characteristics variously labeled, say, as their optimism, or confidence; their explosiveness and lack of control; their toughness; their gracefulness and elegance; their ostentation and pompousness; their obsequiousness and timidity; their intuitiveness and sympathy; and so on—all are signals of their attachment needs. At some level of our own awareness, we depend on such cues to trigger the qualities imparted in our own responsiveness to them. It is difficult to open one's heart to a brittle, cold, and angry partner, and we recognize these qualities in how they attend or fail to attend our tentative displays of feeling. Sometimes this "reading" of our partners occurs outside of conscious awareness. It gets compounded into our verbal responses to them, as in theirs to us. At other times we simply "know" that a shy fellow needs to be mirrored, and that it would be cruel to demand of him that he become demonstrative. We likewise "know" that the last ingredient required by conversation with an arrogant braggart is a challenge to his self-esteem. Both would result in responses infused with disintegration anxieties—possibly also with "disintegration products" like aggression. We seem to move automatically to comfort a lost child, or to offer an elderly person help with directions, or to modulate the self-amplifying aggressiveness of a sociopath who happens in our path. The signals of failed regulation, or of chronic needs, or of a low spot in the day all make their way to us in how people act, and we respond to these signals by putting forth, when we can, acts of our own, themselves infused with homeostatic responsiveness. Just how we act—reinforcing a signal, transforming it, inverting it, damping it—depends on complexities we have not yet begun to analyze adequately. But one thing is clear: we act as the regulators of our partners no less than they act as ours.

Reciprocal Responsiveness and Strong Interaction

What amplifies this double-sided process beyond the moderate levels of intensity familiar in most interaction is the way these powerful transferential forces affect the level of partners' responsiveness to one another. Sandler's idea that we continuously and half-consciously "test" all of our partners for their potential responsiveness to us makes just this point. Implicitly, interaction is always a medium for discovering whether others seem at all suitable candidates for fulfilling the terms of our "wished-for" interactions. When, at some level of awareness, there is the slightest suggestion people with whom we are interacting are "role-responsive"—that is, are ready to make the effort to conform to our wishes or, in Sandler's more technical analysis, possibly to recapitulate interactively an infant-caregiver relationship of which we once were part—our own reciprocal responsiveness is triggered off. Partners' needs and wishes, then, potentiate their respective responsiveness and dramatically alter the qualities introduced into the space they share. This moves interaction into a new and different phase. Let us try to make this notion explicit.

The Strong Phase of the Interaction Field

Imagine that when we observed interaction we thought of it as a field described by the presence of certain fluctuating forces of attraction among the parties to it. In proportion as these forces were amplified on the part of one or all parties, we might characterize their interaction as strong. Making none of the usual distinctions sociologists and others commonly make among types of relationships—primary versus secondary, say, or marriage versus business—we would be led to calculate fluctuations in the force of such attraction across the range of observable values before us, and then perhaps to compare these values to numbers obtained from some other interaction field. What we would learn is not what our usual nominal classifications of the world into types of relationships would tell us, but something else: not just that relationships supposedly intimate according to normative expectations are typically marked by strong interactions and others not, but that all fields of interaction occasionally exhibit fluctuations in the forces of attraction and separation operating within them. Lovers no less than business partners occasionally display weak and separable fields of interaction, and business partners no less than lovers occasionally sense in one another the powerful resonances of trusted family relationships.

What accounts for these evanescent attractions is the appearance of the forces of selfobject transference. Men and women use one another, under conditions very rarely understood to themselves, as vehicles by which to serve their narcissistic needs—provisionally believing, if only momentarily, that the other person in their presence exhibits that special responsiveness to their personal wishes they hope at all times to discover in others. We know, of course, that many conditions affect the acknowledgment and deepening of these forces—norms proscribing them, fears that revealing such attractions make one vulnerable to the other's emotional manipulation or to their ridicule, the accumulation of "realistic" knowledge of the other undermining their capability to serve us in any illusory capacity, the plain repudiation of our transferences by the others in question, and so forth. Many such controls on transference are external—matters of the cultural specification of our relationships or interactions ahead of time. To such structural, cultural, and macrosociological matters we shall return in later chapters. More to the immediate point, however, are the ways the transference process itself exhibits self-regulating properties of its own. These are implied by an elaboration of Kohut's logic.

The Force of Attraction

Such narcissistic needs as Kohut isolated in his clinical investigations persist throughout life. They are, for example, the common forage of clinical interactions. Their satisfaction in diverse contexts renews our self-confidence and restores our direction in life. Rooted initially in the prime structures of self, they are decreasingly served in adequate ways by our original introjects, which are at best primitive concepts requiring repeated reembodiment through defining contacts with others who are thereby made "significant." The reasons for this have been discussed already in the theory of the introjects. Here, however, let us merely postulate that an introject has something of the status of a "memory," and as such behaves according to laws that describe memories—most notably, like a memory, being subject to the various sorts of attenuation we call forgetting, as well as to the specific mental transformations (repression, etc.) that stand among the many discoveries of psychoanalysis. We might say, in somewhat simpler logical terms, that the strength of an introject *decays,* and make the assumption that this loss of strength occurs as a function of the time elapsed since the introject last was reinstantiated or reestablished by something like one of Kohut's transmuting internalizations. Such transmutations of external objects—possessing them in the terms of the decaying introjects—both recharge and alter the introjects, in complex ways any theory of the introjects also needs to develop more explicitly. Most of these difficult problems must remain outside of the scope of our considerations here. But when the decisiveness of a strong leader, for example, calms and gives direction to his or her followers, we might well discern the recapitulation of a relational mode whose traces lead back to the idealized parental imago. Or when the respect shown a student by a professor affirms and strengthens the student's capacity to participate in a discussion, we also might find ourselves observing how mirroring responsiveness draws out archaic grandiosity from the most unlikely of candidates. How these processes affect interaction more generally can be discussed in straightforward terms, following the same logic so far developed.

One way to sharpen this reasoning is to attempt to represent it formally; another is to bring it together with our earlier analysis of coupled systems. The directions this should take are suggested by making explicit the interrelationships among the several steps in the logic developed to this point: (1) transferences appear with a force proportional to our narcissistic needs for mirroring and idealizing; (2) the "optimal" frustration of these transferences by a partner being used as a selfobject results in transmuting internalization; (3) by establishing and then strengthening introjects in this way, we undermine or diminish the operation of transference; (4) such introjects decay in the way memories lapse, again releasing narcissistic forces in the form of renewed transferences. This last development amounts to the searching attempt to rediscover in others the empathic responsiveness of our original caregivers, in both their idealizing and mirroring capacities.

These steps also translate into a familiar mathematical form, when we recognize that the "force of attraction" appears in ways described by a modified gravity rule. Let us define a variable F_{ij} to correspond to this attractive force and view it as time-dependent, $F_{ij}(t)$. (The domain of the variable is defined as time, the range as the force of attraction.) The process we have been discussing above is defined with respect to the transferential "role responsiveness" of persons i and j, $R_i(t)$ and $R_j(t)$ and the strength of their respective introjects, $Z_i(t)$ and $Z_j(t)$. The logic of the argument, then, allows us to discuss a function with the following properties:

1. if $R(t) > Z(t)$, then $F(t) > 1$;
2. if $Z(t) > R(t)$, then $F(t) < 1$;
3. $I(t) \neq 0$ for any value of t;
4. $F_{ij}(t) = y$, where y is a nonnegative integer; and
5. $\lim_{t \to \infty} F(t) = 0$.

Forgetting, for a moment, the filters on the transference process put in place by culture and social structure—the macrosociological circumstances of interaction—the canonical example of the function described by the properties listed above is a quotient formed as follows:

$$(3.7) \qquad F_{ij}(t) = \kappa \left[\frac{R_i(t)R_j(t)}{Z_i(t)Z_j(t)} \right].$$

Here we represent a time-dependent process and assume for purposes of discussion that we are able reliably to measure all of the theoretical variables and that they have been well studied and shown to exhibit no discontinuities—all assumptions made here only to examine what this representation of our reasoning tells us. If nothing else, this is a way of sharpening logic we may decide later on to discard. Defined more carefully below, the numerator in this expression includes the forces of transference (the R values), the denominator the introjects (the Z terms) as affected by decay, and κ is a constant of proportionality. As this function describes the theoretical argument of this section, then, we here isolate a "force of attraction" between actors i and j, directly proportional to the product of their respective "role responsiveness" to one another, and inversely proportional to the product of their respective introjected strengths. Actors will be drawn to attach themselves to one another by responsiveness to their needs, the more so when these needs are pressing—when actors are addictively predisposed; when there are high levels of challenge or unfamiliarity in the environment; when their capacities to act autonomously have been weakened in other ways by isolation, changes in the environment, biographical transitions, traumatic events, or sociocultural disjunctions that reduce personal or social integration and cause anomie, malaise, disorientation, or alienation. Any of these circumstances decrease personal or self-control, raise disintegration anxiety, and initiate external searches for attachment and responsiveness.

Mutual responsiveness, then, triggers strong interactions, and these can be studied in the behavior of $F(t)$. As we should now also understand, underlying this behavior is the operation of positive feedback, the phenomenon of unlimited amplification produced in interaction by each partner's use of the other as an idealized selfobject. As suggested in figure 3.2 (lower panel) or by the model in equations 3.1 and 3.2, this happens only when interaction can be represented by interconnected loops that carry idealization but not mirroring—when, specifically, the appearance of a partner displaces I, the pole of the self that serves normally to produce negative feedback in behavior. Without I, we have a coupled system without controls, and positive feedback results. It is only by virtue of such positive feedback that an interaction system can behave explosively in the manner suggested by dramatic increases in the level of $F(t)$. As we shall see in later chapters, positive feedback in some form is always present when a system moves far out of equilibrium—indeed, positive feedback is what carries a system into important phases we shall want in chapter 4 to study as far-from-equilibrium conditions. Such far-from-equilibrium conditions are highly unstable, volatile, and seemingly chaotic. But they are also fundamental, because no important personal or social change occurs without them. Developmentally speaking, for example, a form of this kind of far-from-equilibrium phase appears in infant-caregiver interaction fields and is a prelude to developmental changes marked by crucial phase transitions—sudden, critical shifts in the organization of "self" as a system, signified by the emergence of new and higher levels of complexity in perception, ideation, and behavior. This has profound and interesting implications for making sense of organization and complexity in social life generally. Before we can turn to this subject, however, we must continue to focus on the dyad itself, fleshing out the instability appearing interpersonally when $F(t)$ suddenly explodes.

Romance: An Illustration

For the purpose of studying the behavior of $F(t)$ under the control of positive feedback, consider the special case of an interaction field formed by two persons romantically attracted to each other. The "force of attraction" model argues that narcissistic needs, as represented here by the transferential "role responsiveness" of person i and person j, R_i and R_j, respectively, are at their most intense level where i's and j's respective introjects, Z_i and Z_j, are weakest (but where $Z \neq 0$). One indication of the inception of romance is indeed that our actors can become infatuated with one another even prior to meeting.

Consider, then, two adolescents who have "fallen in love" before actually meeting. Romantically predisposed actors of this sort, we would now say, are addictively predisposed. They typically give all the signals of mutual idealization, especially in perceptions of each other that outsiders would be blind to—powerful evidence of the operation of their selfobject transferences. Ignoring the subscripts in equation 3.7 for simplicity, what this model suggests is that the value of $F(t)$, when $t < 0$ (i.e., before the pair actually meet), increases with the weakness of our actors' introjects alone. This is so because the value of R, for both of them, is undefined in this range (i.e., neither can estimate the R value of the other prior to their interaction—though, as we assume for arithmetic convenience, $R \neq 0$). When they do meet and can confirm the other's wished-for responsiveness to their needs, however, the value of $F(t)$ increases dramatically over a subsequent interval of t. In this interval the product of their respective transferences saturates their field of interaction with mutually amplifying responsiveness—the positive feedback that kicks their interaction into a far-from-equilibrium phase.

On top of this, another influence on the behavior of $F(t)$ also appears after interaction has commenced. It is the tendency to "optimize" responsiveness and to engage in structure building or self-strengthening. Face-to-face, each partner inevitably learns the other is *not* the exact equivalent of his or her transferential preconceptions. Competing forces are at work here—the desire to demonstrate to the other that each is what the other wants (that one has a high R value), and the desire to "discover" in the other some of the values by which each has already prepossessed him or her (to strengthen one's Z values). Disappointment by the other's failure perfectly to embody one's wishes, according to my version of Kohut's thinking, will result in strengthening introjects when such disappointment is "optimal." That is, we begin to augment and change our Z values in this interaction by discovering the other is a dependable and trustworthy environment for our needs, that is, has compensating high levels of responsiveness or R levels, but is not "perfectly adapted" to our wishes. (A dependable and trustworthy environment is thereby defined as an "optimally responsive" one, the same thing as an "optimally frustrating" one.) Nonoptimal frustrations, by the same logic, do not augment trustworthiness and accordingly do not result in transmuting internalizations that strengthen our Z values. The influence of decay appears in relation to our needs for such empathic responsiveness. We can ignore decay as a force except insofar as nonoptimal frustrations in our interactions inhibit transmuting internalization, a matter causing the existing introjects gradually to weaken further because of lack of reinforcement or reinstantiation. The model as written includes a term for our own empathic responsiveness to others, and assumes the size of this term is proportional to our own needs for responsiveness from them.

The behavior of romantically involved persons is further described by this reasoning in ways that speak to the same forces in interaction more generally. When we study $F(t)$ over a sustained interval in which at first optimal frustrations have strengthed introjects but subsequently their strength has begun again to decay, we can imagine any number of monotonic or oscillatory trajectories describing the level of attractive forces in the interaction field. Romantic love, as one such instance, is typically marked by damped oscillations of fusion and differentiation—of identification followed by introjection and differentiation. This happens as the transferential forces distorting early perception of the other gradually routinize, and relationships are established on realistic grounds. (See chapter 5 for a more extensive analysis of romantic love along these lines.) This matter of routinization is especially important, because it describes how relationships rid themselves of the same *ausserall-täglich* qualities Weber knew made charisma incompatible with everyday life. The illusions by which transferentially strengthened relationships are marked in their early phases are replaced by reality in the course of each partner's optimal disappointments with the other. The powerful forces at work to preserve illusion inside romantic relationships, on the other hand, continue to strengthen dyadic withdrawal. Partners do not want to be reminded they are living in a world of fantasy. But disappointment is inevitable, and when it is also gradual and optimal, each associated moment of introjection pulls in its wake a phase of differentiation from the other—differentiation away from the control of the other's illusional expectations. Thus, reality replaces illusion in the logic of this model through the operation of disappointment— the slow disappointment that allows introjects to be strengthened even as it likewise encourages escape from the controlling force of a partner's own transferences.

This is described here by the steplike strengthening of introjects, in a sequence punctuated intermittently by optimal disappointments in the other, each leading to microinternalizations. Since introjects are simultaneously attenuated by the onset of decay, however, we observe a process that strengthens and then weakens, strengthens and then weakens the introjects. Combined, the forces of decay and introjection produce pulses of diminishing and

then enlarging responsiveness, appearing, as I shall illustrate in the appendix
to this chapter, in a trajectory of damped oscillations in $F(t)$.

Further Illustrations

Generalized though this discussion has been, it has widespread relevance for
analyzing both the mutual regulation arising within fields of interaction and
the powerful, far-from-equilibrium states occurring occasionally in conjunction
with transference and positive feedback. Interactions are interactions—not
relationships or roles or any other more or less permanent and norm-specified
interpersonal phenomena. A strong interaction can arise within the context of
a weak relationship, or within a purportedly "affectively neutral" occupational setting, or during a transaction in a commercial establishment—anywhere, in fact, where two persons come into one another's perceptual fields
and emit the signals of their responsiveness to one another, and even more so,
indeed, when they become attuned to each other in the fully "adapted" style
of the caregiver. There are numerous examples that serve to illustrate how
general the applications of these models are. I will first give some easy examples, based on two-person fields, that should serve to flesh out the terms
of the models again. Then I will suggest how to use these models to analyze
culturally induced states of strong interaction like those associated with important life-course transitions.

Many examples of what would commonly be considered strong interactions
fall short of the conditions where their partners actually strengthen each other
through their contacts. In the illustrations used above, interaction is assumed
to occur over a period prolonged enough for partners to establish trust in one
another, a condition encouraging their mutual disillusionment and hence supporting introjection—the self-strengthening operation that would allow them
to begin to stand apart from one another. But this is not the fate of most strong
interactions. Were we to enumerate them by categories based on how much
progress their partners make in disillusionment, most strong interactions
would fall short of the highest ranking—short, that is, of the disillusionment
stage. Thus, many fields of interaction don't produce introjection and are deliberately used by actors only for the positive feedback they generate. Some
of these are the scenes of addictive disorders—taverns, brothels, hunts, stadiums, and so forth. Other strong interactions arise in fields encouraging the
release of strong forces—fields suffused by anxieties, or structured by responsiveness triggers—but which lack other conditions that would enable
partners to prolong their contact. Yet others involve nonoptimal responsiveness, or turbulence, or asymmetrical responsiveness, or some other condition
that either results in the termination of interaction or permits only chronic

addictive-like episodes of attachment. Consider some examples based on whether partners have established trust in one another or in their environment.

Strong Interactions without Trust

Environments without trust are like those where infants discover high levels of stranger anxiety. Though distrust will not promote introjection, it can promote identification when it is associated with helplessness, fear, and dependency. Examples of such interactions, drawn from the literature on the defense mechanism Anna Freud (1936) called "identification with the aggressor," are familiar to sociological readers. Bettelheim's (1943) discussion of the relations between guards and inmates in concentration camps, for example, isolates "extreme conditions" in which this phenomenon can be expected. Weakened to the point of helplessness, inmates can be moved by small signs of favor to conform to the wishes of their guards. A strong interaction here may be the signal of an emergent false self—the behavior of a person so emptied of strengths by nonoptimal properties in the environment yet so full of fears that he or she obsessively conforms to what are perceived to be the wants of the tormentors. Again, sensitive dependence in such conditions works through positive feedback to magnify small signals of the guards' responsiveness into powerful identifications.

Another illustration draws on descriptions of crime. Robberies, for example, are strong interactions usually controlled by exceptional levels of apprehension on the part of both robbers and victims, and thus are common illustrations of how fears can affect both sides of an interaction. One of the motivations to undertake robbery, in fact, is not utilitarian gain but excitement—the thrill of confronting victims, controlling them with a weapon or threat, and then escaping. Such encounters can become part of a "way of life" and for some robbers operate the way addictions affect other persons— compensating deficits of strength in self with excitatory stimulation and temporary feelings of potency. There is no end to the testimony by robbers of the importance they attach to criminal acts as ways to relieve the emptiness and boredom of their lives (e.g., Allen 1977). Such attractions to crime are part of what Jack Katz (1988) calls the "moral and sensual pleasures of crime." From the victim's side, high levels of fear produce conformity to the robber's demands—or, more accurately, to the illusion or "front" presented by the robber. (The victim not controlled by such "front" often turns out to behave "inappropriately" within the context of a robbery and typically is its physical victim—the person who, by operating outside of the robber's omnipotence, causes the robber to use force to effect control of the interaction.)

Nonoptimal environments or deficits in self each support equally illusional strong interactions of other kinds. For example, conditions associated with the so-called empty self support various excitatory strong interactions, like sexual interactions with prostitutes or between persons unknown or barely known to one another. Impersonal sex in this sense can be fully controlled by various illusions, in which the "real" partner means little—in which, in fact, realistic knowledge of the other operates to damp sexual excitement. Such explicitly temporary interactions involve powerful transferential forces, terminated as soon as reality succeeds in damping the excitatory illusion about the other. Successful prostitutes acknowledge this by their readiness to conform to whatever fantasies their clients wish and to support fetishistic demands on their services.

Another interesting class of strong interactions involves sacred or supernatural selfobjects. In such interactions, illusional idealized selfobjects are formulated through an interactive process, typically involving priests or charismatic figures as intermediaries. Solitary prayer, on the other hand, as well as events subsumed by the more general class of "communion with Deity" (e.g., Söderblum 1911), typically involve personal disciplines by which the illusion of powerful idealized selfobjects can be induced. Again, these interaction fields become transferential by virtue of the readiness of participants to convert signals of responsiveness into positive feedback, potentiating their own responsiveness. Such signals may be supplied by a priest, a shaman, or other intermediaries, or they may themselves be imagined.

Strong Interactions with Trust

INTIMACY AND PASSION: ADDING DEPTH TO STRENGTH   Most everyday social interaction occurs within a preestablished framework of expectations, and thus ultimately is based on certain shared assumptions about reality. Some of these trusted interactions are characterized by high levels of $F(t)$, but the majority of them are weak and impersonal. Weak, for example, are routine encounters with clerks in commercial establishments and nonthreatening interactions with most mere strangers, with many casual acquaintances, with the majority of fellow employees in complex organizations, and with public authorities and bureaucratic officials acting in a formal capacity. Such familiar and common interactions are weak because they are generally based on limiting assumptions, usually public, that give specificity to typical encounters. Most interactions are limited and specific in this sense. These contrast sharply with other trusted interactions, also with low levels of $F(t)$, that may nevertheless become deep and important but typically lack what commonly would be called passion—a name for many of the qualities associated with transferences in the forms discussed so far. Interactions with friends, with colleagues at work or professional meetings, with comembers of voluntary associations, or with fellow nationals in foreign lands (among many other examples) are often deep and important, and sometimes we would describe them as diffuse and strong. Even so, such interactions are not usually suffused by the powerful mutual potentiation that arises from symmetrical idealizing or mirroring responsiveness. Clearly, therefore, transferential forces in the forms made familiar to us by the analysis undertaken to this point aren't the only ways to strengthen interaction.

Displaced from our analysis of interaction by this chapter's concern with the force of attraction, in fact, has been intimacy. Thus, the model developed so far ignores depth, an omission that prevents it from coming to terms with matters as important as friendship or love. Another way to strengthen interaction, plainly, is to allow it to become *deep*. Adding depth to an interaction field, in fact, is the recipe for establishing a relationship—a matter we can conceptualize as another of the potential *emergents* of an interaction field. Depth can develop in conjunction with idealizing or mirroring responsiveness, but it can also develop on its own. A relationship is based on what cointeractants jointly identify with and introject through time, and this only sometimes includes one another directly. In this sense, interactions with shared history—"growing old together," was Alfred Schutz's formula—are relationships. Temporally extended as an interaction field, a relationship deepens interaction through the shared memories occasioned by joint experiences, and can thus survive the interruption of face-to-face contact.

Intimacy is sometimes the way we describe a relationship in which this kind of joint introjection has emerged—in which, as we say, a relationship has deepened. This sense of shared knowledge and shared experience needs to be distinguished analytically from passion, despite common confusions of the two. Intimacy is a state of an interaction field produced in the course of establishing shared knowledge, often knowledge particular to partners—secrets, for example. This can certainly happen in an interaction field marked by powerful transferences—indeed, it is part of what is implied by the notion of introjection, which can occur in strong interaction fields where we find optimal responsiveness. Shared introjects establish a foundation of intimacy. But the process of sharing knowledge, or of reconstructing, during interaction, the shared memories out of which intimacy built itself in the past, can itself generate feelings of strong attachment—if not passionate attachment, certainly strong interaction. It does not have to begin with powerful idealizing or mirroring transferences. What generally is denoted as intellectual communion, for example, often involves such deepening interaction—interaction that is slowly strengthened by intimacy, even though most of the time it misses the passion of idealization. Communion in this sense is driven either by excitement over ideas or by the attractive forces generated within creative dialogue. Friendships are personalized versions of these same patterns of intimacy.[4]

The key to intimacy is a different kind of responsiveness—this kind based on partners recognizing in one another a shared world. Kohut spoke of such phenomena as examples of "twinship" (or alter-ego) transferences: discovering, in the abiding presence of another person, a responsive "selfobject milieu" that confirms in oneself one's essential aliveness and membership in a community. This can be signalled by something as subtle as the warm flush of feeling that mysteriously arises in us for no evident reason other than the presence of another person around us. Such sensations are like the comfort an infant apparently finds from the mere sounds of others' activities in its vicinity—continuing proof of the cradling embrace of a supportive world. Something like this also arises in us when we discover others share with us the same meanings and perceptions—when we thus know each other to be part of the same reality. Such evidence is itself a kind of responsiveness— proof that we are both sentient and alive in the same time and place.[5]

Consider a related phenomenon. No matter how often it happens, for example, the scientist who discovers the confirmation in reality of one of his or her thoughts is generally pleasurably surprised, the way a child is made happy to discover in pure mentation a way of anticipating and hence controlling experience. It can be pleasurable to release one's illusions into the external environment, if that world is benign and receptive in some degree. When that environment is another person, receptivity to one's thoughts can operate on interaction in the manner of positive feedback, charging and driving a few tentative speculations and offers of opinion into an explosion of constructivist activity. This is another kind of attachment process, this time based on coinstantiating a world. More to the immediate point, by isolating this special way of adding strength to interaction—the strength that comes from knitting together two worlds and from affirming alikeness of experience and existence with others—we can make our own model of strong interaction more comprehensive.

DEPTH PLUS PASSION   Consider, at first, a deliberately simplified way to introduce "depth" into our thinking about interaction—a simplification we can abandon in later chapters. By dichotomizing intimacy and passion into two levels each, we can generate a fourfold cross classification of fields of interaction. The results appear in figure 3.3, which lists four matters perennially among the subjects of sociological analysis of relationships. This is not to claim that this scheme is an adequate way to define these heterogeneous topics, but it does suggest some of the matters we might look for in each. Each will be separated out as a subject for detailed analysis in later chapters.

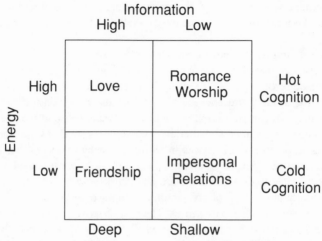

Fig. 3.3   Examples of relationships emerging from interaction fields based on trust

Implicitly we distinguish between "hot" and "cold" interactions, following Zajonc's useful distinction in psychology between "hot" and "cold" cognitions (Zajonc 1980; cf. Lazarus 1980). This distinction depends on the relative mix of *energy* (hot) and *information* (cold) in thought and is thus a way analytically of separating the two variables, information and energy, embedded in the familiar Parsonian concept of a cybernetic hierarchy of control (e.g., Parsons 1966). Worship and romance, in this scheme, appear as hot interaction fields, friendship as a cold interaction field. The affects we connect to each are based, characteristically, on transformations occurring in either energy or information—romance with energy transformations, friendship with information transformations. By contrast, love mixes transformations of high levels of information and energy. In addition, we can speak of worship and romance as relatively shallow interactions (as we have seen, each is based solely on transferential distortions and projection), but of love and friendship as deep interaction fields (based on sharing personalized information and a history of *Weltbildung*).

A more realistic conception along these lines is suggested by figure 3.4. Implied by the notion of intersecting "fields" based on the dimensions we have isolated is the idea that what most persons call friendship, say, actually corresponds to some region in a two-dimensional space established by the mix of energy and information—a region that overlaps with what others call love. Similarly, acquaintanceship in one person's mind is friendship is another's, and so on. Only a partial cultural equivalence holds among persons in such usages, and there are wide cross-cultural differences (see Brain 1976). Figure 3.4 suggests only that there are certain regions in this space where we can roughly locate the different mix of qualities persons associate with different kinds of relationships.

Figure 3.4 also introduces a notion to which we shall return in later chapters—namely, the argument that intimacy depends on whatever replaces the "information loss" or entropy we associate with weakening introjects. Following conventional usage in the theory of entropy, we shall refer to this as negative entropy or negentropy, since we do not want to lose sight of the fact that "structure building" in Kohut's sense arises in connection with information in many forms—any forms, in fact, that carry relatedness. We shall make more use of information theory starting in chapter 4.

Thus, not only can we multiply examples of two-person interaction fields based on the logic of this chapter, we can also refine the same tools with the addition of some simple distinctions. Still further examples are made available by shifting attention to collective fields of interaction, and in particular to culturally formulated selfobjects and their place in interaction. Though we won't discuss culture more fully until later chapters, it will be helpful to have a preliminary example of how cultural templates work in interaction, and how they can be conceptualized in view of the same models of interaction we have presented above.

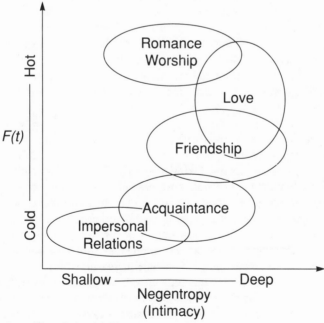

Fig. 3.4   Intersecting relational fields

Liminality: Strong Interaction in Collective Events

Status Transitions

Status transitions are prime candidates for discovering the forces of trans-ference in collective interaction, and models of infant-caregiver interaction address these matters directly. All shifts in self and identity after childhood arise through social learning, whose properties are generally understood in the same terms as those used to explain childhood socialization. The model of the one is thought to be the model of the other. Consider Van Gennep's ([1908] 1960) classic discussion of *rites de passage,* which for a long time provided a standard depiction of this process. Three phases, argued Van Gennep, are apparent in all status "transitions"—separation, margin,[6] and aggre-gation. The rites of transition from childhood to adulthood are the classic example. Their first phase separates and differentiates the candidate for adult-hood from an earlier status. In the case of male initiation ceremonies, the candidate suddenly is no longer a child—or, at least, is on the way to becom-ing an adult. This is symbolized by segregating him from contact with others, and by abrupt changes in the nature of permitted contacts with women, par-ticularly mothers. Separation as a phase is then succeeded by a mix of ordeals (scarifications, mutilations, hunts, vigils, etc.) and degradation rituals (in Garfinkel's [1956] sense) aimed at reducing the candidate to a condition of helpless dependency. This is where a so-called liminal phase in the experience begins. Here a candidate's own characteristics are obscured or obliterated (cf. Goffman 1961), and additional ordeals further reduce and disorient him. The now helpless candidate is ritually incorporated into a new status, in character-istic ways. Symbols of death and rebirth mark this final transition, as candi-dates are led from darkness into light and commence a celebration of their new status.

Such deliberately orchestrated phases in *rites de passage* have been studied in preliterate societies by anthropologists for nearly a century, but they are implicit in status transitions of all kinds—from obvious parallels like boot camp to less obvious ones like taking a new job, becoming a mental patient, or entering a new school. Consider how these phases might be conceptualized in view of the model of strong interaction. The first two phases are geared entirely to undermining self-regulation and lowering self-esteem. They rely on so-called disorienting or "unlearning" devices—practices like blindfold-ing, the use of darkness, isolation, and ambiguous stimuli. Candidates begin doubting their own perceptions and become increasingly dependent on ritual officials, elders, or adults. By this time as well, degradation rituals have sys-tematically reduced a candidate's self-esteem. At the end of the second phase, thus, the usual initiation rites have drastically weakened both mirrored and idealized strengths in those undergoing initiation. By this point, as well, liminality has induced immense structure hunger. Profound needs for responsiveness appear in the candidates, who have become very impressionable and suggestible. All interaction under these conditions is distorted by powerful transferences. But the conditions are not yet presented for structure building. At the beginning of these rites, the roles of adult figures in the rituals are structured along nonoptimal lines, a practice intended to increase candidates' dependency. Ritual leaders alternately frighten and ignore their candidates. This has the effect of inducing strong, addictive-like needs, along with powerful illusions about the environment as a place filled with magical forces and danger. When the liminal period has come to an end, all this changes. Then the nonoptimal posture of elders is abandoned for another marked by the accommodation of candidates' merger demands—in particular, the accommodation of their idealizations.

Now how does this differ, say, from romance considered above, and where does positive feedback enter to drive the ritual interaction field into a far-from-equilibrium phase? The way these interaction fields are set up, the examples of romance and initiation in fact look very much alike: mutual idealization appears in initiation as well as in romance, and the liminality spotted by Van Gennep and others in initiation ceremonies is very much like qualities associated with romantic infatuations (see Tennov 1979). Here mutuality and positive feedback arise from what happens to the candidates in the course of their initiation, particularly in the view of ritual leaders, observers, and adults. The stripping and freeing of candidates of their previous identities means that they literally begin to appear to elders as infants do to their parents—as blank, helpless vehicles in which parents can discern the fulfillment of their own wishes for perfection, strength, and value. Transference then meets transference, with candidates eventually inspiring leaders to engage in idealization as well. So, in effect, we find infants idealizing parents, coupled to parents idealizing infants, with results such as we have already seen in romance—another system of positive feedback, as represented in equations 3.1 and 3.2.

Except for one big difference: the mutual idealization at work in initiations is structured by powerful cultural templates. All such classic initiation ceremonial involves interposing between the reduced and helpless candidate, on the one hand, and the omnipotent elder, on the other, the symbolic terms by which their idealizations can be shaped. Initiations are full of cassowary feathers, lotus blossoms, bear claws, and magical dancing ancestors. Their actors wear costumes, enact stories, and chant incantations. They also dance themselves into excited states, use intoxicants, drugs, sleeplessness, and other practices that all serve to drive everyone into extreme conditions of exhaustion and excitation. Everything about these ceremonies, in fact, predisposes the search for idealized selfobjects—objects in which again to stabilize and calm the world and to get one's bearings. This magical, numinous, preternatural world of invisible spirits and abiding ancestors, just the other side of the line dividing everyday life from the precincts of the sacred, thereafter supplies the terms by which the feel of everyday experience can be given form, stabilized, and regulated.

Periodicity and Ritual Cycles

The peculiar statuslessness, timelessness, and amnesiac qualities of liminality have been given detailed attention by Victor Turner, who "infer[s] that, for individuals and groups, social life is a type of dialectical process that involves successive experience of high and low, communitas and structure, homogeneity and differentiation, equality and inequality" (1969, 97). Turner is here allowing rhythmic swings in social life, between the liminal condition he calls *communitas* and the nonliminal state of everyday life, to accommodate the structuralist dialectic of binary oppositions (Lévi-Strauss 1963; Leach 1970; cf. Rossi 1982). Still, his point is that social life no less than personal life is structured by various periodicities, generally marked in premodern societies by rituals of one kind or another. The transition from one profane period of time to another is where we find these ritual efforts to recreate *communitas*. Here, he says (1969, 97), "opposites [like high and low, *communitas* and structure] . . . constitute one another and are mutually indispensable." Here, as well, is where we find ceremonial structures driving interaction into phases of positive feedback and where, deliberately, there is an equivalent experience of the cycle of separation and fusion we just saw in puberty rites.

Analytically speaking, these cycles of separation followed by fusion are the equivalent of the oscillatory movement we have studied in interaction—the repeated movement of partners together and then apart. Separation is the equivalent of differentiation, which corresponds in the ritual cycle to the nonliminality or subliminality of profane everyday life; and fusion or *communitas* is liminal. This liminal phase functions religiously to tighten and reestablish the connections between the sacred and profane, between culture and the everyday world, and is generally a sacred time. The way this works, as we can see, is equivalent to generating strong interaction out of positive feedback, which produces powerful feelings stabilized in culturally supplied idealized selfobjects.[7] Liminality is amnesiac in precisely the sense that strong interaction is transferential: introjects are displaced, and cultural selfobjects are then used functionally for purposes of strengthening self-control and elevating self-esteem.

More generally speaking, this recreation of *communitas* has its equivalents in all periodic efforts to instigate the retrieval of "community" and *Gemein-*

schaft. Various equivalent quasi-periodicities appear in the ritual life of most communities, even in such mundane ways as the calendrical conventions by which weeks are organized in cycles of days and holidays fall on certain days of the year. Most of these practices and conventions have origins in religious calendars and thus are explicit survivals of communally directed efforts to institute positive feedback, often through disinhibiting and recreational practices, and to generate feelings and energies subsequently stabilized in cultural selfobjects.

Conclusions

Apart from what we are led to expect of our partners by virtue of the cultural and normative controls on interaction, any field of interaction can be described in terms of the forces of transference and responsiveness. Extrapolating from the kind of analysis undertaken so far, we should expect to discern in other fields of interaction a similar latent structure—one of fluctuations of diminishing and enlarging responsiveness. In a more general sense, we should also expect to find partners to interaction "testing" one another, in Sandler's sense, in the implicit effort to restore to their lives the environment of empathic responsiveness imaginatively and nostalgically echoing into the present from their respective childhoods.

The specific forms of transference involved in such responsiveness, moreover, will typically give rise to consequences of a general nature we may also specify. First, the appearance of transference in any positive form will have significant effects on the exchange ratio operating in interaction—most notably by increasing the degree to which partners thereafter are prepared to conform to one other's needs, that is, transference raises the costs partners are willing to bear. This development in turn will also raise the value each discovers in the other by investing them with particularistic significance, a matter making it impossible to regard the other as a person for whom substitutes are available. Partners are seen thereafter as uniquely and irreplaceably responsive to each other's needs. I suspect it is only the operation of transference that produces such particularism—seeing in others vehicles enabling the recapitulation of earlier significant relationships. The way idealizing, mirroring, and so-called twinning transferences are each served by the interaction field we shall have to consider in more detail.

Behind particularism in this sense, of course, stand the specific patterns of strong attachment we analyzed in chapter 2. What makes strong interactions different from strong attachments is that they occur in the presence of some preexisting self-structure, and it is such endogenous strengths that enable partners to regulate themselves while separate from one another. Nevertheless, the trajectory of an interaction infused by transferences—a strong interaction—is toward the circumstance where each partner is again singularly attached to the other. The partners' respective introjected strengths determine whether their responsiveness will potentiate to the point of mutual dependence and strong attachment, but each in theory can come exclusively to rely on the other for some part of the regulation each requires. The more exclusive this dependence is, the more desperate it is as well. What diminishes this addictive quality is adding depth to an interaction field, which happens with optimal responsiveness. It is this dimension of depth that opens the subject of relationships.

Before we turn in later chapters to analyze difficult but important examples of such relationships—love, on the one hand, and charisma, on the other—we must make several instructive diversions. By a sleight of hand, we have just shifted analysis from two-person to n-person systems. Implied by the ease with which this was accomplished is that the dynamics we isolated in dyads cross a change of scale into larger systems of interaction. In the next chapter, I want to explore this phenomenon even further and to develop conceptual tools for grasping how this occurs.

Appendix

Damped Oscillations in $F(t)$

The damped oscillation in $F(t)$ I have described on theoretical grounds can be understood mathematically as a combination of two functions—one describing the decay of the introjects and the other a periodic function in the level of $R_{i(j)}$.

We can observe how these functions combine by examining the damped motions of a spring—in fact, we can do this by translating the gravity model itself into an equation for representing just such damped motion.

Consider, for simplicity, the apparent pulses in $F(t)$ when we allow $C = 1/k$, $T(t) = R_i(t)R_j(t)$, and $P(t) = Z_i(t)Z_j(t)$. Reexpressed in these new terms, we then have

$$F(t) = C\left[\frac{T(t)}{P(t)} \right] = Ce^{-at} \cos t,$$

where $T(t) = \cos t$, and $P(t) = e^t$.[8]

Recall the first pair of equations (3.1 and 3.2) developed earlier to describe coupled interaction. The general solutions to those equations define, with respect to time, changes in the strength of the mirroring introjects of our paired actors. Those general solutions are

(A.1) $M_1(t) = (b_1 - b_2) \int^t M_1(s)\, ds + b_2 \int^t M_2(s)\, ds$

and

$$(A.2) \qquad M_2(t) = (a_1 - a_2) \int^t M_2(s) \, ds + a_2 \int^t M_1(s) \, ds.$$

Consider now the maps Ψ and Φ:

Ψ: $M_2 \to M_1$ such that $\Psi(m_2) = m_1$, $m_2 \in M_2$, and $m_1 \in M_1$;

Φ: $M_1 \to M_2$ such that $\Phi(m_1) = m_2$, $m_1 \in M_1$, and $m_2 \in M_2$.

Suppose these maps are independent in the sense that Ψ: $M_2 \to M_1$ is defined regardless of the action Φ: $M_1 \to M_2$ (and vice versa). Figure A.1 makes clear that as $M_2 \to M_1$, M_2 diminishes while M_1 increases under the action of Ψ. Since these maps are independent, the actions of Ψ and Φ can be seen to relate M_1 and M_2 in inverse proportion. This is the same relation as we have seen in equation 3.7, where the R's and the Z's are inversely related in the gravity model.

Following the reexpression of the gravity model above, let us consider the partial case where Ψ acts alone on the function $F(t)$. In this case, $F(t) = \exp(-\kappa t)\cos(\omega t)$, where $M_2 = \exp(-\kappa t)$ and $M_1 = \cos(\omega t)$. (Conversely, Φ acting alone on $F(t)$ would show the same pattern, inverted). We can then reformulate the general solutions for M_1 and M_2.

$$(A.3) \quad M_1(t) = \cos(\kappa t) \quad = (b_1 - b_2) \int^t \cos(s) \, ds + b_2 \int^t \exp(s) \, ds$$

$$= (b_1 - b_2)\sin(t) - b_2 \exp(-t) + c_1$$

$$(A.4) \quad M_2(t) = \exp(-\kappa t) = (a_1 - a_2)\exp(-t) + a_2 \sin(t) \, c_2$$

These reformulations of the original general solutions simply describe the specific behavior of the functions M_1 and M_2 relative to one another, under the action of Ψ.

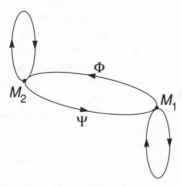

Fig. A.1   Maps Φ and Ψ in a directed interaction graph

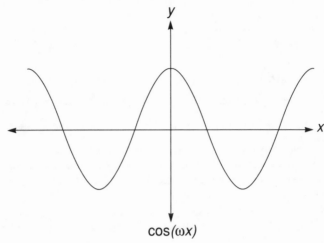

cos(ωx)

Fig. A.2   Graph for the function M_1

The graphs for the functions M_1 and M_2 are shown in figures A.2 and A.3. Finally, the combined graph of these functions is represented by figure A.4. Here then is the damped oscillation by which our theory described the behavior of $F(t)$, the force of attraction operating in the interaction of mutually responsive partners. Of course, this is how the damping looks from the point of view of one mapping. It should be clear by symmetry, however, that the other mapping produces the same consequence.

This exercise in analysis guides us toward several interesting and general conclusions: first, it is entirely reasonable to build a bridge between the model of interaction suggested in chapter 3 by equations 3.1–3.6 and these later notions founded on the concept of a "force of attraction"; and second, it becomes clear that the dynamics we have examined in the behavior of $F(t)$ can be read back into the earlier system. That is, studying $F(t)$ reveals how variation in the introjected strengths of interaction partners should show up in cyclic patterns of attraction and separation between them, whether they are business partners who have discovered a mutual responsiveness in one another or the romantically involved couple we examined earlier.

This conclusion probably deserves an even more forcible statement, since what this analysis suggests is that every field of interaction is marked by the same cyclic patterns—with the possibility of strong and potentiating mutual responsiveness enlarging $F(t)$ over an initial interval, after which it is subsequently damped through the operation of introjection, and so on. Of course, the absolute levels of responsiveness are not going to be equivalent when we compare, say, romantic interaction with an over-the-counter commercial transaction. But the same forces are subtly present, whether we are observing

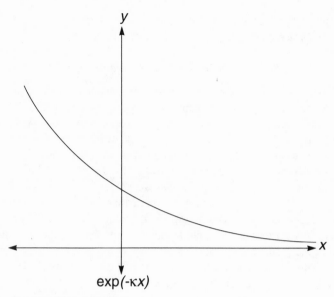

$$\exp(-\kappa x)$$

Fig. A.3   Graph for the function M_2

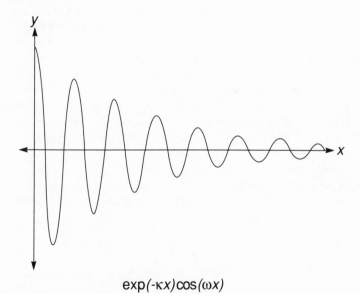

$$\exp(-\kappa x)\cos(\omega x)$$

Fig. A.4   Graph of combined functions M_1 and M_2

lovers, co-workers in a bank wiring room, speakers and their audiences, priests and parishioners, or clerks and their customers.

Two-Person Interaction as a Double Helix

With the bridging work we have just done, it also becomes possible to generalize our representation of both models of interaction by considering the separate variation of M_1 and M_2—or, equivalently, as in figure A.5, the $Z(t)$ and $R(t)$. Again, we shall impose the condition of independence on the maps Ψ and Φ. However, we shall now be concerned with what this independence says about the independence of M_1 and M_2. By definition, we have $\Psi^{-1} = \Phi$ and similarly $\Phi^{-1} = \Psi$. This implies that $\Psi^{-1}: M_2 \rightarrow M_1$ and $\Psi: M_2 \rightarrow M_1$. And finally, we have the composition of maps $\Psi\Psi^{-1}: M_2 \rightarrow M_2$. So in fact the independence of Φ and Ψ implies the independence of their respective domains. This permits us to conclude that we may consider the separate components of our model as separate "spaces" in the graphic representation. This simply means adding the implied behavior of the idealizing introject to the damped oscillation graph shown in figure A.4.

The damped oscillation in figure A.4 was graphed in two dimensions. Clearly, a more explicit representation of the forces at work in producing this behavior can be modeled in R^3. Let us revert to the symbolism in equation 3.7 and assign two of the axes (the so-called z-y plane) the values of R and Z, allowing the remaining axis (sometimes called the x-axis) to be a measure of time, t. The behavior of these variables with respect to one another and time then is maintained in R^3. Imagine that we were pushing a rotating rod through this R^3 space, allowing its endpoints to describe a double helix. What we would then be mapping in the tracelines of these endpoints would be the relative positions of the partners in our observed dyad.[9] Over a small part of the domain, we should then observe something like the graphed representation in figure A.5.

The double helix is a by-product of the dyadic formulation we have employed throughout the analysis. In an *n*-person system, of course, the equivalent representation would be an impossible snarl of interweaving

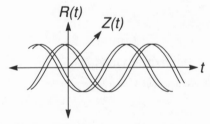

Fig. A.5   The helical trajectory of dyadic interaction

lines—assuming (quite unrealistically) no limit on the number of simultaneously responsive partners or possible objects of one's own responsiveness. Over a more extended range of two-person interaction, in addition, we should see the double helix contract in a pattern corresponding to the damped oscillation observed above. Nonetheless, here we see two functions describing one way our two interactants might be imagined as moving together and apart. Note that raising the value of Z diminishes the value of R for both of our actors, and that they are shown here slightly unsynchronized. Yet the forces at work between the two of them enlarge and then diminish their mutual responsiveness.

Instabilities, Attractors, and Sensitive Dependence

Explicitly I have been arguing in chapters 2 and 3 that systems of interaction under certain conditions enclose patterns of this kind—strong attachments and strong interactions, marked by cyclic movements together and then apart. These patterns arise when persons are *initially* liable, by virtue of their psychological deficits, to being controlled by such attractors. When they are liable to forming strong attachments, using substances, engaging in practices, or making object choices that begin to take on addictive qualities, they are giving the signals of weakened introjected strengths and of their inability to regulate their own behavior. The effect of this kind of deficit is to change the parameter conditions for the unfolding of any interaction process of which they become a part, in effect moving the interaction process into a region of the parameter space where the attractor operates. Since there are other conditions of interaction processes we have not so far considered, we shall not be able to discuss this process with greater qualitative precision until this analysis deepens in several ways.

Several important concepts are in danger of being conflated in this analysis and overlap with what I have called the "liability to instability" of interaction—that is, the incorrigible tendency of partners to interaction to come under each other's control. While I postulate that this tendency is incorrigible and universal, it is not inevitable or necessary. It is instead a liability—a potential development in an interaction process, depending on whether partners are mutually responsive, in the specific sense of being "role responsive" as this idea is developed in Sandler's writings. When responsive partner meets responsive partner, we have one of the conditions present for the interaction process to come under the control of the selfobject transferences—and, hence, for the interaction process to exhibit the positive feedback effects of this liability: because each partner's introjected strengths are then displaced and each subsequently comes under the other's control, the result is that their interaction can potentially give rise to a pattern of reciprocal amplification.

We would then have a system controlled by positive feedback, as analyzed above. This explosive possibility is a potential source of instability present in all interaction. By no means is such instability a universal feature of interaction, but one that arises in interaction only under the specified conditions.

In danger of being conflated with this analysis of such a liability in interaction is the notion that some interaction systems exhibit what is called sensitive dependence. Sensitive dependence arises in some dynamical systems under certain initial parameter conditions, and amounts to the property that small fluctuations introduced into such systems, under these initial conditions, can produce very large effects. An example is the "butterfly effect," where the minor perturbation in the atmosphere caused when a hypothetical butterfly fluttering its wings in China eventually produces a great storm over the United States. This would be an example of how a small fluctuation under initial conditions of sensitive dependence could lead to very large effects, as the perturbation got amplified out of proportion to its size in being transmitted to adjacent regions (Gleick 1987). I have so far suggested that sensitive dependence is a property of some interaction processes—specifically, those unfolding under parameter conditions where the psychological strengths of partners to interaction have been displaced, have been weakened, or never developed to begin with. This amounts to the claim that sensitive dependence in interaction is a special case of instability, especially as instability was conceptualized above. But I also want to suggest that this condition can arise in interaction when yet other parameters, not yet introduced into this analysis, also change. These other conditions of interaction are properties of sociocultural settings and will not be discussed until chapter 7.

4

Complex Interaction Systems and Dissipative Structures

Interaction as a Self-organizing System

Interaction is typically self-organizing. By this I mean that "structure" is imparted to it by the play of forces at work within interaction fields—structure in the sense of complexity, order, and interdependence. The specific forces at work generating structure in this sense include those we have been studying so far—the strong forces of selfobject transference and wishfulness, illusion, and belief. Such forces arise from chronic or intermittent attachment needs, and specifically from the weakening of our introjected strengths and of our capacities for self-regulation. When absent or lost strengths first lead partners to regulate one another's feelings, interaction begins to exhibit elementary structure. Later—in the case of the infant, at the moment coinciding with the achievement of verbal subjectivity—interaction moves beyond this elementary level of interdependence to yet higher levels of organization.

Since this is by now a familiar theme in this book, the argument of this chapter will move into the new terrain opened specifically by the study of interaction as a self-organizing system. Again, I shall be arguing by way of an analogy: interaction is self-organizing in the way biological, chemical, and physical systems sometimes are—by virtue, in this case specifically, of the appearance within them of stable "dissipative structures," patterns of order that arise spontaneously in fields characterized by information loss, or entropy. How this occurs we shall have to spell out in more detail below. But since this is a complex argument, let me anticipate it by first suggesting a simple connection between theories of entropy and theories of understanding. One connection has been pointed out before, though in slightly different

ways, by Mihaly Csikszentmihalyi and his collaborators (1984). Understanding in this view has a *negentropic* function: it imparts information to fields
where information is being lost. Explicitly, thus, we shall be equating information and structure, as in classic information theory. So general is the scope
of such thinking as a framework for considering energic matters that all of the
energic speculations about interaction we have so far undertaken might be
imagined as applications of the theory of entropy, culturally and socially
applied.

At first glance, such overgeneral claims seem to make "understanding" a
simpler matter than of course it really is. We cannot equate understanding
with matters like attraction and repulsion. Yet neither can we ignore the ways
the two are connected. Eventually, just such connections between energic and
cultural matters must become a concern for any social theory, and such connection is what our interest in interaction obliges us to address in this chapter.
First and foremost, the way people understand one another depends on the
kinds of culture they rely on to communicate. This matter of culture's diversity, in fact, lends complexity to the analogy we shall be following. Consider
how this occurs.

At each of the several levels of communication or relatedness, the qualities
of culture change. One way this can be seen is in the *amount* of information
communication conveys; and though this amount might be judged in some
objective sense to increase as we move, say, from communication based on
affect to communication based on language, information itself must still come
to be *shared* in order to make a difference in understanding. To convince one
another they share a meaning, social actors sometimes employ all the levels
of communication available to them. One argument this chapter will begin to
develop is that successive levels of organization arise in interaction through
the self-organizing requirements inherent in such communication—requirements depending on these different kinds of culture. But I am also going to
argue that "structure" in a more general sense first emerges in interaction the
way so-called dissipative structure arises in general—through driving systems
into far-from-equilibrium conditions where spontaneous patterns of order
emerge within them. This notion of emergent "dissipative structure," it turns
out, is a general concept for complex *n*-person interaction systems of all
kinds, and immediately provides us in this chapter with tools for dissecting
hitherto neglected aspects of many complex interaction systems.

The Organization of Interaction

Prominent among the implications we derive from developmentalists' and
clinicians' research on infancy is the proposition that interaction is a strati-
fied affair. It occurs on several levels of relatedness, not all of which are

conscious. Alongside the conceptualization of self as a homeostatic system, I have relied heavily in thinking about early self-development on the work of Daniel Stern (1985). Return for a moment to Stern's model of self-development—a happy mix of developmental psychology's "observed infant" and the clinical picture of the infant used by psychoanalysts to reconstruct an infant's subjective world.

The Senses of the Self

Stern's developmental model is based on an idea of sequentially reorganized subjective states, only the last of which involves full participation of the developing child in relationships mediated by culture. As we shall see, his postulated stages bear a close resemblance to what we shall soon recognize as successive "dissipative structures."

Stern speaks of what he calls "senses of the self." In his words, these are "invariant pattern[s] of awareness that arise only on occasion of an infant's actions or mental processes" and that are "form[s] of organization" (1985, 7). Later senses of the self arise out of (without displacing) earlier senses, but seem to bring with them a wholly altered person. "[W]hat is different about the infant [when new senses of the self emerge] is not simply a new batch of behaviors and abilities," writes Stern (8), "[but] . . . an additional 'presence' and a different 'feel' that is more than the sum of [its] many newly acquired behaviors and capacities."

> For instance, there is no question that when, sometime between
> two and three months, an infant can smile responsively, gaze into
> the parent's eyes, and coo, a different social feel has been created.
> But it is not these behaviors alone, or even in combination, that
> achieve the transformation. It is the altered sense of the infant's
> subjective experience lying behind these behavioral changes that
> make us act differently and think about the infant differently. One
> could ask, which comes first, an organizational change within the
> infant or a new attribution on the part of the parent? Does the
> advent of new infant behaviors such as focal eye contact and smil-
> ing make the parent attribute a new persona to the infant whose
> subjective experience has not changed at all? In fact, any change
> in the infant may come about partly by virtue of the adult inter-
> preting the infant differently and acting accordingly. (The adult
> would be working within the infant's proximal zone of develop-
> ment, that is, an area appropriate to infant capacities not yet pres-
> ent but very soon to emerge.) Most probably, it works both ways.
> Organizational change from within the infant and its interpretation
> by the parents are mutually facilitative. The net result is that the

infant appears to have a new sense of who he or she is and who
you are, as well as a different sense of the kinds of interactions
that can now go on. (8–9)

When Stern comes to graph what he has in mind by the several "senses
of the self" that succeed one another and yet coexist in a child's interaction,
he presents the diagram appearing in figure 4.1. With age in months on the
x-axis, the "senses of the self" are shown on the *y*-axis as successive cumulative structures. In fact, Stern has represented his conception by utilizing a
kind of diagram central to exhibiting how sudden, disjunctive changes are
also known to appear in physical systems, in particular those governed by so-
called nonequilibrium dynamics. This kind of change, familiar to students of
phenomena described as "self-organization," is typically represented with the
use of a *bifurcation* diagram. Though this representation is perhaps used un-
wittingly in Stern's case, it accurately depicts what he has in mind as the
underlying developmental process—one involving sudden "leaps" infants appear to take across the frontiers separating successive "domains of relatedness." The line of primary bifurcation is established at the appearance of the
"domain of emergent relatedness," and secondary bifurcations thereafter establish domains of "core relatedness," "subjective relatedness," and "verbal
relatedness."

Without relying on explicit concepts of bifurcation, Stern nevertheless describes developmental shifts in a language powerfully suggestive of this
model of disjunctive change and reorganization. This is explicit, for ex-

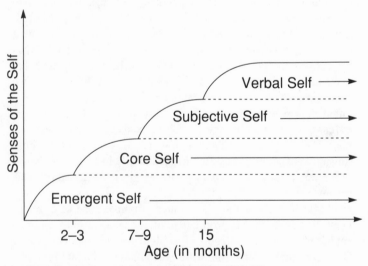

Fig. 4.1   Coexisting developmental domains (after Stern 1985, 32)

ample, in his repudiation of Freud's speculation that infants have inborn protective "stimulus barriers," and of Mahler's related idea that infants undergo a phase of "normal autism." "Infants," Stern argues, ". . . are predesigned to be aware of *self-organizing processes*" (1985, 10; emphasis added). In fact, the very first emergent structures of the infant's self arise out of the repeated activities of "yoking" together various abstractable qualities in perception and in consolidating smooth-functioning sensorimotor schemata—accomplishments depending on processes of amodal perception, physiognomic perception, and the perception of vitality affects—along with so-called constructivist activities like the identification of invariants. Detailed explication of these processes permits inferring the infant's self-organizing capacities, and Stern suggestively builds his case on the basis of developmental and clinical findings about matters such as contours of affect—arousal buildups and shifts in hedonic tone that result in characteristic vitality affects. All such processes involve perceived internal fluctuations—enlarging disequilibrium conditions from which arise new states of organization. The details of such "phase transitions" are not well known, though Stern describes their broad contours as "jumps" among domains of relatedness.

From our perspective, each successive "domain of relatedness" can be understood as corresponding to a higher level of *social* complexity, supported by increasingly information-rich "culture." In addition, each emerges from a prior relational field in which the parent has served as an amplifier of fluctuations in the infant's felt experience. In what Vygotsky (1978) called the infant's "proximal zone of development," for example, the amplifying role of the parent might be conceptualized along the line of Csikszentmihalyi's and Larson's (1984) notions of maintaining "flow," or, perhaps, in view of the use I have made of the Winnicott-Kohut notions of the "good-enough mother" and "optimal frustration." Optimal frustration would then be understood, as both Kohut and Winnicott seemed to understand it, as the force driving the nonequilibrium (but nontraumatic) states that motivate structural development in self.

Though Stern's "senses of the self" are inductively formulated on the basis of observations of infants and cannot themselves be "derived" from a theory of development, an equivalent notion of successive developmental stages *can* be understood as deriving from the theory of strong interaction—not the particular stages Stern isolates, but the interpersonal mechanisms for producing the kinds of developmental "leaps" he describes. Indeed, the mechanism for producing these leaps depends on the appearance of positive feedback in social interaction. It is only positive feedback in such systems that drives them away from equilibrium into conditions where they become vulnerable to change. So far, we have used one verison of how such strong positive feedback accumulates in interaction, derived from Kohut's theory of selfobject transferences—always a signal, in Kohut's theory, of the appearance of a process of "structure building." Can the theory of selfobject transference be understood in such general terms? Can we see it as one example of a larger class of positive feedback processes serving to drive systems into nonequilibrium states where they become vulnerable to change and reorganization?

Dissipative Structures in Social Interaction

When we postulate a "nuclear" self whose fundamental structures are decaying introjects that give rise to patterned force fields, the analogy to physical processes isn't exactly being concealed. At work here are images appropriated from the study of atomic and molecular events. But what we have learned so far with the use of such physical analogies—having started along this path by following Kohut, who was initially responsible for the concept of a "nuclear self"—is based on a kind of thinking since transcended in many parts of twentieth-century physics and mathematics.[1] Consider the work done since the 1960s on so-called nonequilibrium dynamics.

Ilya Prigogine's work on the thermodynamics of nonequilibrium systems, for which he won the Nobel Prize in 1977, postulates the existence of what he calls "dissipative structures." Such structures arise spontaneously when a system, perhaps like the interaction system we have been examining, moves into what Prigogine calls "far-from-equilibrium" conditions and, as a consequence, passes through a "bifurcation point" that results in a new and "higher" level of complexity or organization appearing within it. He speaks thus of "self-organizing" systems, of "order arising out of chaos," and of other phenomena not intended to sit well among adherents to more classic conceptions of the universe. In Alvin Toffler's words:

> Summed up and simplified, [the Prigoginian view holds] that while some parts of the universe may operate like machines, these are closed systems, and closed systems, at best, form only a small part of the physical universe. Most phenomena of interest to us are, in fact, open systems, exchanging matter or energy (and, one might add, information) with their environment. Surely biological and social systems are open, which means that the attempt to understand them in mechanistic terms is doomed to failure.
>
> This suggests . . . that most of reality, instead of being orderly, stable, and equilibrial, is seething and bubbling with change, disorder, and process.
>
> In Prigoginian terms, all systems contain subsystems, which are continually "fluctuating." At times, a single fluctuation or combination of them may become so powerful, as a result of positive feedback, that it shatters the preexisting organization. At this

revolutionary moment—the authors call it a "singular moment" or a "bifurcation point"—it is inherently impossible to determine in advance which direction change will take: whether the system will disintegrate into "chaos" or leap into a new, more differentiated, higher level of "order" or organization, which they call a "dissipative structure." (Such physical or chemical structures are termed dissipative because, compared with the simpler structures they replace, they require more energy to sustain them. (Prigogine and Stengers 1984, xv)

The Prigoginian view of reality is surprisingly like the dynamic picture of an interaction field we have been developing. Imagined as a complex space alive with energic pulses, fluctuations in interactants' anxieties, and momentary local equilibria, interaction appears as no less bubbling with disorder and process than Prigogine's physical universe.

Order through Fluctuations in Interaction

In particular, the notion of higher-order complexity evolving disjunctively from processes scavenging entropy is very close to the argument we have advanced to this point about the way decaying introjects and related phenomena of selfobject transference affect two-person interaction. Consider in slightly more detail what Prigogine has argued.

In the Prigoginian system, successive bifurcations arise only in nonequilibrium conditions. By contrast, in cases described by the second law of thermodynamics, systems are expected to evolve toward a state marked by thermodynamic equilibrium, which serves as an "attractor" for nonequilibrium states. When one considers, say, a system whose change can be characterized in terms of the variables $\{X_i\}$ on the horizontal axis of figure 4.2, the evolution of the system can be examined by studying rate equations of the form $dX_i/dt = F_i(\{X_i\})$. The equilibrium is where $\{X_i\} = 0$.[2] If this is an attractor state, perturbations in such systems, as represented by the movement of the system in figure 4.2 to point P, will disappear, absorbed, so to speak, by the equilibrium at point O (Prigogine 1980, 5–10).

THRESHOLDS OF STRUCTURATION   This behavior would not occur in systems "far-from-equilibrium," some of which were studied even as part of classic physics. The so-called Bénard instability in hydrodynamics is an example Prigogine uses in several of his writings and is conceptually close enough to the notion of coupled systems we dealt with in chapter 3 that we shall find it instructive. "Consider a horizontal layer of fluid between two infinite parallel planes in a constant gravitational field," he says (Prigogine 1978, 779).

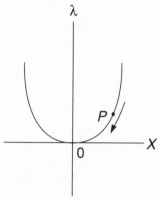

Fig. 4.2   Asymptotic stability in systems with thermodynamic equilibrium at point 0 (after Prigogine 1980, 7)

> Let us maintain the lower boundary at temperature T_1 and the higher boundary at temperature T_2 with $T_1 > T_2$. For a sufficiently large value of the "adverse" gradient $(T_1 - T_2)/(T_1 + T_2)$, the state of rest becomes unstable and convection starts. *The entropy production is then increased as the convection provides a new mechanism of heat transport. Moreover, the state of flow, which appears beyond the instability, is a state of organization as compared to the state of rest.* Indeed, a macroscopic number of molecules has to move in a coherent fashion over macroscopic times to realize the flow pattern. (Emphasis added)

Consider now a two-person interaction field with an equivalently large "adverse gradient" between the actors—between, that is, their respective mirrored or idealized strengths, as each actor *perceives* the relative strength of the other.[3] The theory of interaction developed to this point suggests that such large gradients arise when introjected strengths on the part of one or both partners decay below some critical threshold—or, in a measure connected to reasoning about "psychological entropy," when disintegration anxiety reaches a certain level. This sets up a critical value for the force of attraction, $F(t)$, as we studied it in chapter 3—a gravitational force related, in this discussion, to the convection rate. Consider this instability in relation to the gravity model developed in chapter 3.

Structural decay in self, as the analogy suggests, operates as the equivalent of a *constraint* on an interaction system—equivalent, under this analogy, to the perturbation that prevents the fluid system in the Bénard experiment from reaching an equilibrium (applying heat to the lower boundary, raising the value of T_1). As this constraint grows (that is, $T_1 - T_2 = \Delta T$ enlarges) in the

Bénard experiment, we remove the system further and further from equilibrium. At some critical value of ΔT, say, ΔT_c, we observe a discernible bulk movement of molecules—a movement that is not random, but that is structured in a familiar regime of thermal convection by the appearance of small so-called Bénard cells. Nonequilibrium, as Gregoire Nicolis (1988, 317) puts it, "enables the system to transform some of the energy communicated from the environment into an ordered behavior of new type, the so-called *dissipative structure*." When this happens, "we have literally witnessed the birth of complexity through self-organization." How does this work?

Thermal expansion of the fluid layer, under the constraint where $\Delta T \geq \Delta T_c$ (but short of the more extreme condition where convection is displaced by turbulence), introduces stratification into the fluid: in particular, the layer closest to the bottom plate becomes less dense than the layer near the top. It is this "density gradient" that produces convection; it does so by creating a condition (a less dense lower layer) *opposing* the force of gravity. Nicolis, one of Prigogine's collaborators (1988, 318), describes what happens this way:

> Consider a small volume of fluid near the lower plate, and imagine that this small volume element is weakly displaced upward by a perturbation. Being now in a colder, and hence denser region, it will experience an upward Archimedes force, which will tend to amplify the ascending movement further. If, on the other hand, a small droplet initially close to the upper plate is displaced downward, it will penetrate an environment of lower density, and the Archimedes force will tend to amplify the initial descent further. We see therefore that, in principle, the fluid can generate ascending and descending currents like those observed in the experiment.

The analogy to systems of interaction holds up even under this stricter appeal to the work of gravity. Weak introjected strengths constitute the constraint on a system of interaction that increases the value of $F(t)$. (Recall that $F(t)$ increases as the value of terms in its denominator, the Z values, decrease.) By the postulate of how responsiveness in interaction operates incorrigibly to displace such introjected strengths and to recapitulate the infant-caregiver system, interaction therefore appears as a system predisposed to transmit and amplify the fluctuations its partners introduce into it. Under this analogy, the respective strengths of the two actors should then fluctuate within a range established by the evolving "structure" in place between them. Subjectively, such fluctuations in the field then echo in internal changes in how each feels—attracted by the other, full of repudiation, confident, depressed, whatever.

The specific hypothetical "structure" in question here, analogous to the pattern of thermal convection in the Bénard instability, arises from reciprocal "responsiveness" and selfobject transference. It is not the same as selfobject transference, but arises from it. Transferences simply supply the mechanism that gives rise to "far-from-equilibrium" conditions in an interaction field. So far we have examined transferences in interaction in relation to the mutual adjustment of feelings, considered in chapter 3 in view of models of thermodynamic coupling. The present analogy alerts us to how the seemingly unstable process of regulating one another's feelings potentially can produce out of interaction new states of complexity.

This can happen in several ways. The Bénard instability illustrates one, and another is illustrated when the constraint on the system of interaction grows even stronger. The Bénard instability is a state of unstable organization that arises as a system is driven away from equilibrium; it introduces into a system qualities of order and coherence built on the nonequilibrium conditions maintained in the system by the constraint applied to it. If we imagine pushing this system even further from equilibrium, we can see a second phenomenon appear. Well beyond thermal convection—what Nicolis (1988) describes as the "first threshold of structuration"—we reach a point where the global organization of Bénard cells suddenly disappears, displaced by what then appears as "fuzzy," random behavior. This heralds the onset of the condition commonly described as turbulence, evidence of how the behavior of such systems can further evolve chaotically. What separates these regimes—the regime of thermodynamic equilibrium from the regime of thermal convection, and thermal convection from turbulence—are phase transitions that appear as points of bifurcation in the evolution of the system: sudden, disjunctive reorganizations of the behavior of the system.

What this analogy alerts us to, therefore, is how the seemingly unstable process of regulating one another's feelings can produce out of interaction something like a new "attractor state"—an unstable location reached after the interaction process passes a bifurcation point taking it to a higher level of complexity such as that illustrated by thermal convection. Such a bifurcation point is apparently traversed, for example, when an infant suddenly arrives developmentally at the position where it is capable of engaging in what Stern describes as communication based on "interaffectivity" with its caregiver. Such a point is reached, likewise, when two interactants, face-to-face, know each other to be "responsive" to one another's internal states and proceed to mirror and regulate one another. "Responsiveness" and "transference" thus provide a mechanism, analogous to convection, by which entropy production *increases*. This process accordingly accelerates the weakening of introjected strengths, and ultimately results in displacing self-regulation through the forming of "strong attachments" to new external selfobjects—rediscovering regulation externally, as we considered this phenomenon in earlier chapters. How introjects are modified by transferences we can now also understand differently: the process accelerates their decay by the mechanism it establishes on the basis of responsiveness, at the same time it substitutes for them new external regulatory structures (new "selfobjects" in Kohut's sense). If accompanied by optimal frustration, such external structures then encourage new introjection, with the result that existing introjects are again both strengthened and modified. Introjections thus are markers of *potential* bifurcations, events that support higher levels of complexity in the interaction. (This reconceptualizes what Kohut had in mind in his notion of "transmuting internalization.")

TRANSFERENCES AS NONEQUILIBRIUM FLUCTUATIONS   This process can also be understood by reconsidering the mutually potentiating effects of responsiveness in connection with $F(t)$. In this sense, transferences can be studied as *positive feedback processes between interaction partners*. Mutual mirroring, for example, amounts to the amplification of each partner's "states" in terms of such variables as self-esteem, ambition, and empowerment. Such amplifications drive an interaction away from equilibrium. Of course, so long as positive feedback does not produce large amplifications of each partner's feelings but is kept at a low level, each can serve as a stabilizing environment for the other, i.e., each can damp such fluctuations as perceptibly arise in the other during their interaction.[4] This is what typically occurs in what we might call "weak interactions." A condition of weak interaction is that transferences are not activated beyond some low level of intensity—as when, for example, partners don't exhibit the weakened internal structures that predispose responsiveness to begin with. Weak interactions, in addition, stay under the control of an inverting amplifier that introduces appropriate levels of negative feedback—the functional structure we have located in the idealized parental imago and its derivatives.

Consider the mild flirtation that arises between a customer in a department store and an attractive clerk. A certain kind of salesmanship in fact founds itself on just this sort of exchange: superficially arousing in the customer the sense that the clerk is responsive and attentive to them especially. For many persons the mild attractions that arise cumulatively in many such interactions constitute an important source of (false) mirroring, essential in some cases to balancing psychological deficits. Yet such transactions generally do not involve potentiating feedback of the sort that causes the partners to move toward establishing a new and different kind of relationship—a date, a one-nighter, a love affair, a courtship, a marriage. Flirtation is their limit—a mild affective background that is generally a factitious theatrical component of transactions everywhere, from pulpits to showrooms. Generally speaking, weak interactions like those involved in consumer behavior stop short of the point where partners use one another more than superficially as selfobjects.

When something passes between partners beyond the manifest content of such weak interactions, however, it appears in the perceptible attentiveness each gives the other. Sometimes a pattern of feedback will arise that does move their interaction into nonequilibrium conditions. It is then that the force of attraction has the potential to pass interaction through something like a bifurcation. Infatuated lovers constitute a positive feedback system in this sense, since the trajectory of their mutual idealizing explosively moves their interaction into far-from-equilibrium conditions. Double the idealizing transference in any dyad, and such patterns of positive feedback regularly appear. If idealization is mutually "accommodated" by each idealized partner, each quickly finds himself or herself absorbed by the other's world—lost, at times dangerously so, to the other's bewitching powers, submerged in the other's identity to the point where little stabilizing value remains in each considered separately. In fact, powerful patterns of illusional feedback like these can be damped only by the appearance of processes that interfere with transferences. But the transferences themselves, through the operation of positive feedback, produce Prigogine's far-from-equilibrium conditions. Whether these conditions find a new attractor state, in something like the Bénard instability, or constitute only unstable fluctuations in the interaction field depends on other matters.

Whatever supports the diminution of transferences in interaction—whatever, we might now say, undermines strong attachments—damps such positive feedback. The specific force that diminishes transference, as we have seen, is the force of "reality" in our actors' lives—the continuing adjustment of actors' illusions in the light of forces outside of their omnipotent control, motivated, as I have argued, by frustration and disappointment. "One becomes moral," Proust writes in *Within a Budding Grove* ([1919] 1981, 678), "as soon as one is disappointed." Introjections that strengthen an actor's own representational world and self-structure in this way—mental representations of external objects that are allowed (or that circumstances of trust permit) to stand under the control of reality—diminish transference.

REALITY AND AUTONOMY   All along in this conceptualization of how social actors adjust one another's feelings and internal states, we have been attending the work of several processes in combination. In general, such combinations simultaneously both weaken and strengthen each partner—or, as we can now understand such combinations, they mix entropy and negentropy. Indeed, transference in this light amounts to a narcissistically motivated apperceptive tendency on the part of a "structurally weakened" actor to generate in social interaction those amplifications of attractive (or repulsive) forces, based on positive feedback, that yield new psychological strengths. This depicts transference in a way close to the "feel" of the matter: a distortion of potential partners in view of "wished for" interactions (Sandler 1981). Transference, that is, arises out of entropy—out of the weakening or the decaying of introjects—and seeks "responsiveness"—the signals of similar decay in others. Responsiveness then initiates a reciprocal process based on scavenging entropy: collecting new strengths first through identification (surface mappings of the other's qualities onto oneself) and then through introjection (depth transmutations of the surface mappings). The companion process here is introjection: the securing to each person of such new information as will enable them to function at a higher level of complexity.

The "higher" level of complexity denoted by this claim has a reference initially to early developmental positions of the sort described by Stern, but thereafter to movement on the part of an actor toward a position outside of the powerful attractor states formed in strong attachments. Complexity accompanies the incremental development of autonomous capabilities, as we shall see in some detail below when I make more explicit a cybernetic formulation of entropy. In general, transferences undermine such capabilities by strengthening attachments to others: these persons become objects we depend on to regulate ourselves. Only optimal levels of disappointment in such attachments enable self-strengthening introjections that diminish the intensity of these relationships and enable partners to stand apart from one another. Self-strengthening yields the capacity for autonomy.

GAINS AND LOSSES OF INFORMATION   Implied by this further disentanglement of psychoanalytic concepts in terms of energics is another concept of how mixtures of entropy and negentropy can produce stable dissipative structures. Prigogine's "order out of chaos" does not arise automatically when entropy appears in the social field, but only when oxymoronic circumstances like "stable instability" arise. Stable instabilities can appear in interaction where there is a balance of entropic and negentropic forces—but this is only their simplest form.

Suppose, to continue in this simple vein, we characterize a system in terms of two parameters related to negentropy and entropy, α and β, measuring respectively the tendency of a system to gain information and the tendency of a system to lose information. When the ratio of gains to losses, α/β, approximates unity, the system is in a stable condition of organization. When $\alpha/\beta < 1$, the system is losing information; and when $\alpha/\beta > 1$, the system is gaining information. One minimal condition of the emergence of a dissipative structure is that this ratio begins to fluctuate around (in the sense of having reached a steady state around) a value in the vicinity of unity. This ratio α/β

says nothing about the quantity of information in a system, but only whether the system is capable of saving or accumulating information. Presumably, successively achieved dissipative structures in interaction involve raising a quantitative measure of information, and then stabilizing the quantity by instituting processes that balance gains and losses. But, of course, it is not only interaction that might be characterized by such ratios.

Implied by the notion that psychological strengths inevitably weaken, in fact, is the far-reaching consequence that personal and social organization are tied invariably to processes of dissipative structuration. This follows directly from the observation that any social or personal system might be characterized in terms of information losses or decay—a condition true of every system with "cultural" regulators—and, as such, is dependent for its stability on gains to balance its losses, or negentropy to balance its entropy. As we shall see in subsequent chapters, particular patterns of entropy and negentropy depend on the kind of cultural vehicles available to store information. But every stable social system, every stable personal system, can achieve its stability only by raising the level of $\alpha/\beta \geq 1$. Every stable structure, that is, must be characterized by mechanisms that scavenge entropy from its environment to supply it with a more or less constant level of complexity. Where such systems cannot maintain stable complexity, perhaps in primitive subsystems, we may in fact observe an information criterion of complexity serving as a principle of social differentiation.

Complex Interactions Systems

Bifurcation and Complexity

Following the analogy further shows that Prigogine's concept of the bifurcation point in the evolution of a system corresponds to matters like developmental shifts in personal growth, the consolidation of a "relationship" in an interaction field, or perhaps even to the evolution of successive "stages" of social organization—stages corresponding to different, higher levels of organization or interdependence. In fact, the notion of interdependence between systems might be defined with this notion in mind. Consider the graph in figure 4.3.

A, B, and C in figure 4.3 are successive bifurcations of a system, corresponding to the movement from the rest point λ_1 to the rest point λ_2 and beyond.[5] The system following the bifurcation at C *implies* the prior "historical" movement through branches A and B. That is, the only way the system *evolves* to C is through successive bifurcations at A and B. We might be talking here about the movement, say, from Stern's (1985) "core self" (A) to his "verbal self" (C), if such developmental movements implied, as the theory of bifurcations does, successive and higher levels of complexity and

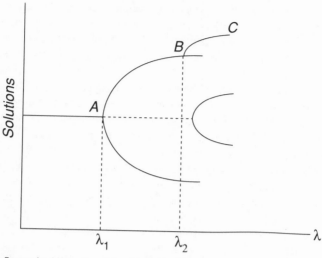

Fig. 4.3   Successive bifurcations (after Prigogine 1978, 781)

organization. (In general, as Stern makes clear, such developmental changes *do* imply fundamental qualitative shifts in the "senses of the self.") Or we might be talking about the evolution of a "social system" that arises initially, at *A,* out of the entropic forces in an interaction field between our two actors. Such a conception of a "social system" would recognize as a condition of the system's emergence a cybernetic notion of complexity. To develop the logic of this concept in relation to additional sociological examples, let us consider a range of illustrations—starting with cases where fluctuations do not produce bifurcations and moving subsequently to examples of how higher levels of complexity evolve out of entropic processes.

Amplification of Fluctuations in Collective Behavior

Many of the ideas about dissipative structures applied thus far to study two-person interaction might as readily be employed to conceptualize interaction processes in so-called collective behavior. Especially good examples of positive feedback systems are crowds. Occasionally, indeed, the state of crowd participants gets amplified into the equivalent of one of Prigogine's far-from-equilibrium conditions. Particularly when we focus on so-called hostile or expressive crowds—lynching mobs, say, or crowds that arise within holiday riots—we can see these dynamics clearly. What we bring into view in such cases are interindividual processes that chain together into a feedback system a population of persons who find themselves polarized about some focus. The excitability of crowds, their occasional destructiveness and uncontrollability, is the main reason they first attracted sociological interest. As Milgram and Toch (1968, 517) put it, "Historically, the most persistent question in the study of collective behavior has been: 'Why do the restraints that lead to conventional decent behavior in the average man break down when he is in the crowd?'"

Consider a simple model of how this might happen. Apart from the fact that crowds are not usually homogeneous aggregates, the issue of their excitability has a familiar explanation that can be found in the analysis of strong attachments. In particular, the reduction of inhibitions in the behavior of crowd participants resembles the reduction of inhibitions that occurs in addictive-like processes. Considerable evidence exists, for example, that "mammalian populations are controlled by physiological mechanisms that respond to population density, that extreme social disorganization may result from crowding, and that biochemical malfunction and even death [can] occur when animal densities rise above a critical point" (Milgram and Toch 1968, 518; cf. Calhoun 1962; Christian 1960; Parkes and Bruce 1961). Crowds appear to produce excitement partly on the basis of just such a physiological link. The most obvious examples of this appear when large numbers of persons are compressed by collective dynamics into a small space, resulting in "breakdowns of cooperation" like panics or in other forms of collective behavior. But many other aggregations of persons, apart from their spatial compression, also appear quite plainly to induce physiological effects among participants: they excite their members. In terms of neurotransmission, what is implied is that crowd phenomena act to stimulate naturally occurring chemical processes in the brain, very probably those associated with the underlying hormonal mechanism of fight-or-flight.[6]

As many students of collective dynamics have suggested, crowd processes themselves appear also to depend for some of their energy on the differential recruitment of persons psychologically predisposed to seek just such stimulation. This would result in raising the level of "responsiveness" among crowd members to the possibility of excitation. The wild-eyed, out-of-control appearance of excited crowd members who are experiencing the rush and "omnipotence" of immersion in an all-powerful acting crowd is familiar to any observer of riots. But interestingly, some of the same qualities are observable among so-called stress junkies and others who are attracted to risk-taking and fear-inducing situations. Hans Selye was the first to point out how such persons appear to self-induce a state of arousal by manipulating their own stress hormones. Basically, such individuals can become dependent on events or activities that stimulate their fight-flight mechanism—causing the brain to signal hormone-producing glands that prepare us for fight-or-flight. Similar alterations in consciousness can be induced with amphetamines, cocaine, or caffeine. "In terms of brain chemistry," write Milkman and Sunderwirth, "the symptomatic adventurer seeks the same mind-altering escape from depression, stress, or fear of nonbeing as the user of powerful stimulant drugs" (1987, 97). This is not an unusual or rare phenomenon, as many adolescent crowds would show (Smith 1968b).

Several hypotheses about the ostensible properties of crowds are immediately suggested. First, there may very well be a relationship between underlying psychological predispositions, akin to the sort of disintegration anxieties we have associated with the "loss of self" (anxieties arising from chronically unempathic, nonoptimal caregiving of the sort that produces deficits of self-esteem), and the "unrest" so much discussed as a property of the situations out of which crowd actions arise. Such psychological deficits are produced not only during infancy, but arise in relation to environmental deficiencies or are caused by the erosion of mirrored strengths connected with life-cycle transitions, by extreme social conditions like slavery, unemployment, poverty, disasters, illness, warfare, and so forth. Thus, we may imagine "unrest," "restlessness," and similar collective moods as feelings spreading by means of signals of the disintegration anxieties activated in such circumstances—signals picked up by one bystander and relayed to another and then another. McDougall (1920) speculated that such feelings were contagious and were spead by the "sympathetic induction of emotion." Signs of feelings like facial expressions, he observed, moved among members of a crowd like a cough. The mechanism of *circular reaction* discussed by Floyd Allport (1924) and Blumer ([1939] 1946) isolates the positive feedback in this process: person A stimulates person B, who in turn stimulates C, and so on until the process returns the stimulus to A, where it is reintensified. Another mechanism of transport here is *milling*, which involves the circulation of persons in the crowd such that a greater degree of uniformity of feeling and excitement emerges.

From these elementary processes arise certain macroscopic properties of crowds like the spatial "flow" we can observe among participants. The stratification of a crowd in terms of levels of interest and involvement has frequently been noted by students of crowd behavior and seems to appear as the result of the normal gravitation toward the center of activity (or toward leaders, or speakers, etc.) of those most involved, and of the movement toward the periphery of those least involved. Such circulating movement of crowd participants has the appearance of a dissipative structure: a ringlike flux arising out of the arrangement and rearrangement of participants in the space occupied by the crowd, based, so we might surmise, on the scavenging of entropy signalled in disintegration anxiety and on the circulation of information by crowd processes. Such a concept of "differential participation" fits well into the views of crowd dynamics proposed by Turner and Killian (1957) and Lang and Lang (1961). Moreover, the specific ways this occurs have been much discussed by theorists and observers of crowds since the writings of Ross (1908), McDougall (1908), LeBon (1903), Freud ([1921] 1953–74), and Park and Burgess ([1921] 1969). All point to underlying processes leading to the appearance (if not the reality) of the "mental unity" or *polarization* of crowds.

From the point of view of dissipative structure theory, these observed increases in the level of crowd excitation are understandable as positive feedback amplifications of the forces at work among participants, driving the crowd into far-from-equilibrium conditions. What specifically this means is that crowd members become far more volatile. First, they are submerged by a collective event wherein something akin to anonymity emerges, associated with the feeling of omnipotence or invincible power. Second, they are quick to adopt and transmit signals or information. And third, they are easily suggestible in the way of the hypnotic subject. What all of this sets up is the potential for a bifurcation—the traversing of a critical point in the history of the crowd when it suddenly gives rise to some new structure. The pattern of spatial flow and ring-like flux in crowd participation is an example of such temporary dissipative structure.

Event Structures and Anomie

Most crowds never make it so far. They simply assemble temporarily around a focus and then dissolve, leaving not a trace, failing certainly to spur new states of organization. They are simply events. Sociologically speaking, however, this is perhaps the most interesting property crowds have.

Crowds are so easy to generate; it is as if the conditions of collective behavior were constantly present in a population. Experimenters, for example, can readily cause unstable and shifting crowds to assemble. Their recipe is simple: On a busy sidewalk, place a confederate who is looking up into the sky at some nonexistent sight. Then count the number of pedestrians who stop next to the confederate and begin to stare up into the sky as well. The more confederates the experimenter uses, the larger the crowd the experiment can generate. The naturally occurring instances of this same phenomenon are too numerous to list. "Freely forming groups" of this sort were studied by John James (1953), who concluded they typically range in size from two to seven. Stochastic models of the underlying processes giving rise to the size distribution of these groups have been proposed by Coleman and James (1961) and by White (1962). But as instructive as these models are, what seems more interesting is the simple observation that crowds form so frequently and easily. Why is this? And what are its implications?

Strongly suggested by the link hypothesized above between crowd participation and neurotransmission are some obvious conclusions: perhaps the most interesting of these is that people respond to events like crowds as opportunities to change their feelings. No less than they use one another or drugs, they use collective behavior. Bring to mind the average population in any public place, and one has a sample disproportionately composed of persons in search of some kind of regulation. Shoppers, spectators, audiences, joggers, teams, people watchers, gangs, kids out of school, sunbathers, peer groups, discharged inmates from public institutions—all have an eye open in the direction of the wide world around them, looking for something to catch their attention or for possible threats. However intent they sometimes seem on getting from point A to point B, they are vigilant to the properties of their environments and can be stopped dead in their tracks by the least thing interesting: a loud noise, a yell, a horn, a bright light, motion anywhere. Disintegration anxieties, it would seem, are like other silent miseries and make one look for company.

Responsiveness especially is what crowd behavior often taps, though rarely exclusively. This claim oversimplifies the complex motives that bring some persons into crowds—patrons in a bar into a mob, townspeople into an audience for a lynching, teenagers into an expressive gathering—but to say all participants are predisposed to collective behavior by the want of responsiveness in their lives comes close to asserting the universality of this condition. Part of this claim amounts to arguing no more than that human beings have a universal readiness to find something about one another interesting, comforting, exhilarating, soothing, or transforming; also, part of what crowds promise, as in the case of what persons "wish for" in the company of others, is the prospect of relief—stimulation when one is feeling bored, solace or diversion when hurt, excitement when empty, soothing when frightened and anxious, justice when injured, or perhaps a mix of all of these at once. Crowds, that is to say, form out of the same motives that bring about our attachments as persons to all objects, human and other. We turn toward them, as toward caregivers in the first weeks of our lives, for responsiveness to our inner states. Some of us do this more than others, perhaps in proportion as we are chronically worried by the deficits of responsiveness that were part of our childhood environments. We use such events after the simple, half-conscious fashion of our first attachments. They catch our eye, hold our attention, and arouse or comfort us. They excite, they calm; they lead, they soothe.

With this in mind, a more general claim can be argued: the larger society is itself characterized by something we might describe as a *structure of events*—meaning by such a notion the collection of disconnected episodes to which individuals turn for precisely the same things they sometimes stop to discover in freely forming groups.[7] When one adds up all the evangelism, all the circuses and sideshows and entertainments, all the buffets and sales and contests, all the games and campaigns and street parties, all the holiday celebrations and parades and performances, all the secretaries' days, birthdays, wakes, fiestas, jamborees, banquets, dances, and garage sales—there is no end to the list of collective phenomena that in some degree are built up out of the processes crowds reveal in purer form. Feeding these structurally intersti-tial phenomena are disintegration anxieties. Running through the social order, in the behavior of its individual members, one observes this in the everpresent readiness of persons to turn in the direction of the qualities such events prof-fer—not all at the same time, certainly, nor even in any stable pattern of attachment. But for the person who is feeling fearful and alone, solace can be found in a tent ringing with music and the oratory of salvation and love. Likewise, the person bored and understimulated by his or her job can look forward to a night's gambling or engage regularly in fantasies of winning lotteries and luxuriating in limitless consumption. In such lives, going shop-ping is a substitute for attention, a salve for disappointment; watching TV an opiate.

The whole structure of this flow of persons into and out of such events, modulating their feelings in ways routine interpersonal life does not make sufficiently available to them, amplifies life into states where it is livable but stands short of supporting organization. Yet the claim might be made, were the totality of such movement visible to the social scientist, that it constitutes something of a dissipative arrangement: a complex system that scavenges en-tropy from the disorganized and understimulated, or worried, phobic, and frightened lives of individual members, and introduces such positive feedback into the feelings of individual persons as to capture their emotions in some more encompassing form, in the end modulating the way they feel. Without all the tent religion, the casinos, the barrooms, stadiums, and shopping malls, to say nothing of freely forming groups, modern societies might more readily succumb, not to the sort of malaise and *Unbehagen* Freud saw in their destiny, but to the forms of social pathology studied by Durkheim. The social correlate of disintegration anxiety is not the cake of custom or the book of laws; it is *anomie*—the failure of the social world to supply individual life with regula-tion. (See Hilbert's useful reconsideration of anomie, 1986, as well as Donald Levine's [1985] provocative analysis of the ambiguities in this concept; and below, chap. 7.) And out of anomie, so this analysis strongly suggests, arises another source of social pressure to engage in interaction and to be caught up in the marketplace.

Structures of Social Differentiation

A primitive foundation of social structure more generally is the ever-present process of social differentiation that arises ubiquitously in all social interac-tion. Out of repeated acts of personal and social differentiation on the part of individual actors arise alignments and separations within the social field that organize it vertically and horizontally. Differentiation in this sense is a source of information "gains" to social structure, continuously enlivening the field of social action with acts at once marking off both its local organization and its wider diversity. It matters little theoretically speaking whether these individual acts of differentiation or identification are shaped by a preexisting structural matrix into which actors attempt to fit themselves, or arise from the needs of individuals in amorphous social environments to locate and anchor themselves. The consequence is the same: out of the cumulation of such identification and differentiation, dissipative structures arise that either affirm existing social divisions or trace the outlines of emergent social patterns.

Sociological research documents such structure on a regular basis. Both in traditional studies of "social distance" and in more contemporary sociometric depictions of social networks, we find cross-sectional snapshots of these structures as they can be synthesized from the analysis of individual acts of evaluation, differentiation, and choice. The best of such studies (e.g., by Edward Laumann and his collaborators [Laumann 1966, 1973, etc.]) combine both distance and sociometric techniques and produce multidimensional "smallest-space" images of social structure. These images rest on one version or another of an underlying "distance matrix" constructed from responses to sample surveys. Social distance so measured arises out of pervasive acts of individual judgment stimulated in these surveys—acts on the part of each respondent of likening and differencing from others and from collectivities, aligning themselves with some individuals and social formations, separating from others. Research of this kind at times unintentionally resembles the use of projective techniques—its questions about social distance appearing to be the equivalent of presenting a respondent with an ambiguous stimulus and calling for an interpretation. But when we analyze the underlying processes these stimuli tap, we get something of a cross between social stratification and the ubiquitous dissipative processes that arise continuously out of disintegration anxiety: acts of distancing the person from some categories with which they are not identified, and gravitating toward others with which they are identified. On the one hand, such judgment is an objective location of the person in social space, while on the other it is a subjective alignment of the person in ways enabling them to deal with anxieties, the way, say, prejudices and related opinions serve functionally to define "self" by the repudiation of outgroups or "deviants." This sort of process is active, I have hypothesized, in proportion to individual actors' requirements for concretely instantiating introjects so as to have access to themselves, and it is one of the foundations on which identity everywhere rests, individual and collective. Smelling out witches in this sense is the functional complement of worshipping deities. Everything sociologists study as deference and demeanor, in fact, keys into this ubiquitous activity of social classification and evaluation, and provides all social actors with information that strengthens their hold on the structure of the social world.

The Fashion System

Not just one but numerous dissipative structures appear in connection with such differentiation, and the sociological tradition of studying them is indebted to the classic work of Georg Simmel for identifying so many of their dynamics (e.g., Simmel 1950). The most famous of Simmel's models of these processes of identification and differentiation appears in his analysis of fashion—an analysis his heirs have been able to elaborate successfully to describe fashion processes in far more complex stratification systems (see especially Blumer 1968, 1970).

As Simmel isolated its dynamics for nineteenth-century European societies, the fashion process was driven by dynamics of imitation—the imitation of elites by their social inferiors. Fashion originated among aristocrats. If a particular style became *de rigueur* among them, it was destined soon to be imitated by persons of lesser social standing. Always in such cases imitation was an explicit act of identifying with superiors so as to enhance social standing. Inevitably, of course, the imitated fashion would then be repudiated by aristocrats in favor of newer and more distinguishing styles. Extrapolated throughout the status hierarchy, this process resulted in the eventual circulation of fashions from the top to the bottom of society, as those at each level who found themselves imitated by their immediate inferiors moved to differentiate themselves by repudiating older fashions and adopting new ones. Simmel's analysis, then, leads us to recognize another example of dissipative structure, based this time on a dynamic process involving asymmetric or one-sided idealization.

Reconceptualized in terms of self psychology, the dynamics of this process circulate a fashion top-to-bottom through a status system, based at each level of the hierarchy on successive acts of identification, each motivated by subordinates' *idealizations* of their superiors, and each time followed by superiors' *repudiations* of these "merger demands." Cycle after cycle, the process continues without end. Each time elites adopt another fashion, imitation by nonelites prompts further status differentiation, as yet another distinguishing fashion is adopted. In this process the fashions themselves remain surface structures—never "introjected" because identification with them is itself always unaccompanied by the equivalent of optimal frustration (i.e., the merger demands implicit in identification are repeatedly repudiated).

However apparently chaotic all this seems on the surface, it is precisely this unstable and ephemeral circulation of the fashions themselves that describes the dissipative structure, which scavenges information from the status system and thereby is able to maintain something of a steady state. The total informational value of fashion derives from how it serves in this process as the equivalent of a boundary marker separating status groups: those with whom one shares a fashion are those with whom one wishes to be identified. So fashions are unlike many other kinds of culture that possess information apart from their relational significance. The way one dresses makes a statement only about one's location in the social order. Similarly, the fashions one repudiates are surrogates for the groups from which one distances oneself. Thus the fashion process, by the distinctions it makes, encodes social organization in dress and serves (as do other forms of culture) as a negentropic resource for locating and stabilizing oneself in a social world.[8] As in Simmel's acute sensitivity to such subtleties of social dynamics elsewhere, the fashion process appears as one of the ways the surface of life changes without altering the more fundamental structures beneath it.

Secrecy

Simmel's analysis of fashion illustrates plainly an important foundation of his sociology: his persistent concern with social differentiation. This was behind his interest in secrets, for example. The secret society, he argued, developed its distinctive traits "as mere *quantitative intensifications* of very general types of relationships" (Simmel 1950, 363; emphasis added). He had in mind general forms of social differentiation, amplified into the peculiarly intense solidarity secret societies illustrated. A simpler example employing the same dynamics is a friendship: a relationship two actors build by moving through stages of closeness marked by jumps in how much they reveal to one another of the "secret" parts of the self. Secrecy is an inherently relative concept, so this is not a perfectly clear conception. But what Simmel described was a relationship more or less impermeable to outward flows of information, a property making such social formations "closed." In part it is the *maintenance* of such closure—a process involving each actor in continuous revelation of personal secrets, a condition supporting mutual trust—that gives such systems the property that $\alpha/\beta \geq 1$. When friends no longer sustain secret sharing, this ratio diminishes and the boundaries of the relationship dissolve.

As Simmel developed the general logic of closure around the concept of secrecy, he repeatedly drew attention to phenomena we might describe in view of dissipative structure theory. "Secrecy," as he put it, "is its own sociological purpose" (1950, 355). Maintaining secrecy, for one thing, serves the critical sociological function of producing social differentiation, and it does so in several respects. First of all, *boundaries* can be made to appear around "societies" in which secrets are shared. In the simplest illustrations he used, those inside such societies "knew" something those outside couldn't know. This supported, in such a group, "the distinct and emphatic consciousness that [its members] form a society" (363). Sharing secrets is then an underlying condition of the consciousness that goes with being part of a society. This claim has no reference to the envy inspired by excluding outsiders from a "secret," but to the feeling of being able to communicate with insiders in ways outsiders do not have access to. (This theme reappears in George Steiner's [e.g., 1975] studies of language and translation. "Why," Steiner asks, "are there so many languages?" And his answer has to do with an untranslatable core every language preserves—a matter Steiner discusses in relation to the concept of secrecy—which creates community among those who speak each language, motivates the preservation of each, and thereby creates linguistic pluralism.)

From this starting point Simmel was elaborating a characteristic analysis of collective life's foundations. In his view, *group consciousness* maintains a complex balance between forces pulling in two seemingly incompatible directions: either to "individualization" or to "socialization." These two concepts refer to tendencies of the group member, on the one hand, to be separated from a "society" and, on the other, to be returned to it. A balance of the two is at issue in maintaining societies—examples like friendships certainly, but also other examples of organized social life. Apart from whatever content social life might have, societies are maintained when they serve as arenas of association where the unification of consciousness is possible—where there *is* some balance of individuation and socialization.

When Simmel's writing on such themes is viewed from a more contemporary angle, he appears to be arguing something iconoclastic indeed: as in the case of fashion, it is not so much the exact content or subject of consciousness but the very processes for sustaining common consciousness where we may find mainstays for social life. It is as if Simmel were saying to us that the contents of life are as so many fashions to the social order: they come and they go, but it is this evanescence that is the importance they have for social life. Contents are vehicles of social differentiation, the way school ties are signs of old boy networks. So long as they "carry" social differences, they gather commitment to themselves as the markers of solidarity. Implied by this perspective on "culture" (which is not Simmel's full view of the subject) are such "modern" notions as the proposition that cultural matters should lose adherents when they no longer carry social differences. (Do "paradigm shifts" [Kuhn 1970] occur in science when established scientific theories fail to carry emerging group differences within the scientific community, as between newer and older generations [Feuer 1974]? Are stylistic differentiations within the history of art, as between, say, impressionist and cubist painters, motivated in part by the failure of one style to carry their group differences?

Is the "exhaustion of a style"—what German aestheticians used to call *Stil-müde* or *Formermüdung*—a manifestation of these underlying processes of social differentiation [Kubler 1962]?) Such propositions might be seen to follow from a neo-Simmelian theory because Simmel himself so often argued about social life as if it were a dynamic entity, as alive with flux and instability as any dissipative structure studied by Prigogine. In fact, the apparent flux and instability of something like the fashion system, as with the dynamics of relationships like friendship, are what define its structure: all such matters are based on "quantitative intensifications" (amplifications of fluctuations) of general social processes (fundamental underlying matters of identification and differentiation). They arise as complex states of organization out of fields of entropy.

Conclusions

Extensions of the Analysis

Multiplying examples of dissipative structure is fairly easy.

GENERATING LEADERSHIP   All phenomena connected with the circulation of elites, or with successions of leadership, appear to arise in connection with fairly well studied patterns of fluctuation. When political elites are regularly replaced short of revolutionary structural change in a society, we are witnessing dissipative structure. Elections in democratic polities play a part in such structures analogous to selfobject transferences in relationships—they are mechanisms by which entropy production is increased and, as such, operate as principles of fluctuation. Elections amplify political beliefs on the basis of appeals by candidates to their followers: the aim of the best electoral rhetoric is always to set up a positive feedback system based on idealizing transferences (or negative idealizing transferences), and hence to drive systems into far-from-equilibrium conditions sufficient to move legitimacy from one candidate to another. In the macroscopic history of democratic systems, electoral cycles are thus ways of building order out of inherently entropic processes associated with long-term incumbency. Does it help to understand other patterns of elite circulation, say, revolutions or coups d'état, as "catastrophes" of the collective behavior sort? As bifurcations sometimes associated with the evolution of a system in a chaotic direction, sometimes with evolution in the direction of fundamental reorganization? In a later chapter, we will examine Max Weber's famous theory of charismatic leadership in this light.

THE INVISIBLE HAND   Market economies operate by competitive principles that in theory give advantages to participants who can organize the preferences of buyers. Order arises out of chaos in the aggregate behavior of the system—Adam Smith's "invisible hand"—where (so to speak) entropy is scavenged by suppliers of negentropy. The function of advertising, for example, is to amplify wants, the equivalent of fluctuations, so as to disorganize previous preference patterns and establish a "market share" for a new product. In less "rational" markets where "imperfect information" is not an "imperfection" but the sine qua non of the market form itself—as in the "bazaar economy" described so comprehensively by Clifford Geertz (Geertz, Geertz, and Rosen 1979)—the market, out of its inherent disorganization, generates structures based on the "reputations" of its participants: reputations for "honesty," treachery, and so forth. This converts such markets into status contests along lines familiar to students of noneconomic "contest systems," where "clientage" and other similar patterns of personal and semipersonal ties, based on trust and distrust, connect participants. (A more general analysis of markets as positive feedback systems appears in chapter 7.)

INSTITUTIONALIZED EXCHANGE The exchange of persons and objects among social groups is often organized normatively in societies. The circulation of women among kinship groups (Lévi-Strauss [1949] 1967; Mauss 1925), as analyzed by anthropologists in relation to the rule of exogamy, for example, can be understood as a practice functioning to avoid the indefinite segmentation that would follow from consanguineous marriage. Rules requiring exogamy, that is, are ways of constraining the flow of marriage partners among groups so as to guarantee the "dominance of the social over the biological" (Lévi-Strauss [1949] 1967, 479). "This is because the value of exchange is not simply that of the goods exchanged. Exchange—as consequently the rule of exogamy which expresses it—has in itself a social value. It provides a means of binding men together, and of superimposing on the natural links of kinship the henceforth artificial links . . . of alliance governed by rule" (480). Exchange relationships, as thus institutionally constrained, become supports for complexity and interdependence.

CONTEST SYSTEMS Alvin Gouldner's (1966) analysis of Athenian society in the age of Socrates discusses similar reputational dynamics, based on a contest system such as might be illustrated by (but was certainly not confined to) games. Whether one examined athletic contests and the society of the gymnasium, or studied the gossipy, competitive circle of friends who assembled around one or another brilliant figure of the time—Alcibiades and Socrates being only the most famous—the dynamics were essentially similar. Something close to a zero-sum logic presided over competitors; there could be only one winner. In a sense, the structure of rewards played the competitors, making status competition intensely personal. One "scored" in philosophic conversations as in athletic events, in drama as in discus, with the result that an intensely narcissistic culture evolved around these contests. It was left to the "winners" to define what was taken to be the standard of achievement for Greek life. In Gouldner's view, all Greek society might be seen as a complex ramification of the (dissipative) structure involved in such surface activity—competitors always preparing to take their turns, heroes always in the making. And thus the competitive process was one in which winners did not merely replace losers, but standards of life succeeded one another. The contests were negentropic—constantly redefining what it meant to succeed or to win.

The Growth of Complexity

All of these examples give content to an idea this chapter has attempted to elaborate, based on the groundwork of earlier chapters. It is the notion that social structure of all kinds, from personal relationships to complex organizations, arises out of dynamic processes scavenging the anxieties with which life is constantly and necessarily saturated. Disintegration anxiety in Kohut's sense signals entropy, and entropy is inherent ontologically in the "regulators" human beings depend on to support their lives apart from caregivers. I think we must posit something like an optimal level of anxiety in life, centered somewhere between disintegration anxieties of the extreme sorts discussed in chapter 2. Between understimulation and overstimulation, so to speak, is the pathway into which we are drawn by our own needs for coherence and integration.

Analyzing dyadic interaction in such terms reveals how dissipative structure is imparted to microsociological phenomena. But it has been my point in this chapter also to suggest some of the ways these same individual and interindividual processes give rise to macrostructures. A primitive index of what, pirating Smelser's (1963b) term but reversing his meaning, we might call structural conduciveness—the readiness of a system to accommodate those disequilibrium fluctuations on the basis of which supraindividual dissipative structures arise—is the ease with which persons aggregate into freely forming groups like crowds. But the measures of such conduciveness extend beyond crowd behavior to include all of the other structures also driven by disintegration anxiety.

Ever-present disintegration anxiety pulses into the social world in the signs social actors give off to one another of their needs for responsiveness. When circumstances are conducive to the amplification of these fluctuations, structures emerge in multiple, sometimes simultaneous ways: ranging, as we have seen, from the aggregation of personal and social differentiation into systems that carry stratification, like the fashion system; to the amplification of social distance that societies are witness to in campaigns against nonconformists and deviants, like witch-hunts and purges; to settled, institutionalized mechanisms of entropy production like elections, which move legitimacy among political contestants; to economic markets that aggregate consumer behavior by organizing preferences; to related contest systems where gaming constantly renews the definition of certain important social values like "success." All of these structures build complexity on the basis of entropy, and all alert us to how social organization thus arises out of instabilities inherent in personal and social life. Social organization, like social interaction, is self-organizing.

One peculiar advantage of this way of conceiving the appearance of macrostructure is that we can begin to see how the same processes at work in face-to-face interaction are also behind "structure building" on quite different scales of analysis. My aim in the next several chapters will be to make use of the basic theoretical tools discussed so far in this book to show how this matter of constancy of process across changes of scale is possible. Ultimately, the tools of strong interaction theory, along with the related concepts of embedded feedback appearing in analyses of nonequilibrium dynamics, should permit us to unravel not only dyadic processes but also those at work in complex organizations, markets, and other forms of large-scale social structure. To see how this is so, we shall begin by reexamining with these tools two fundamental subjects—the dynamics of love relationships, on the one hand, and of systems of power and domination, on the other. The next chapter accordingly addresses love and its transformations, and the two following chapters take up, first, personal power and charisma, and, second, systems of domination as they can be understood in relation to the analysis of markets and hierarchies.

5
Love and Its Disintegration

Two subjects above most others in sociology bring into focus the strong forces of transference and illusion—namely, love and charisma. In this and the next chapter, I propose to reconsider these subjects from the standpoint of the theory developed in earlier chapters. This means, at a minimum, seeking to explain love and charisma as examples of strong attachments and strong interactions. Beyond this, however, I shall also consider how the powerful feelings stirred up in love and charisma arise as far-from-equilibrium fluctuations in interaction, conditions that sometimes precede the emergence of new states of social and personal organization—concrete instances, that is, of bifurcations. Love and charisma, as Freud and Weber both knew well, are keys to understanding social change, and a model of such change is implicit in the study of nonequilibrium processes.

Love and Its Vicissitudes

Love is arguably the most powerful and important emotion experienced by human beings. Certainly nothing in social life has inspired more poetry and drama, and few things have been the subject of more philosophical discussion. This is probably so because the feelings associated with love are at once so complex, so wavering and volatile, and so profound. Whether love is discussed as friendship or brotherhood, devotion or romance, it takes hold of the imagination like few other subjects. Poets have worked this ancient subject like miners following a vein, endlessly seeking new ways to grasp and give form to the rich store of feelings that overflow ordinary discourse about it. And since it is a subject whose discussion exists only within a historical and cultural field, it is also one whose meanings have changed endlessly and necessarily.

What I want to present here is a new analysis, based, as before, on developmental considerations, again organized in view of reconceptualized psychoanalytic concepts, but further reconceptualized with the help of dissipative structure theory. The type case for this analysis will be romantic love, though the analysis itself rests on a generalized scheme enabling us to move to related subjects like fraternity or communion or charisma. Since the argument is complex, let me give it some initial shape in the form of a loose and preliminary definition of the subject itself: *Love, in this analysis, denotes the complex mix of feelings and ideation experienced by partners in relationships driven by dynamics that produce (or have produced in the past) strong attachment based on mutual idealization.* Note the special features of this definition. Love isn't a single, unitary, homogeneous state—it is a mixture of feelings and thoughts that arise out of interactions marked by strong attachments, attachments that, given the way interactions typically work, produce within us *changes* of state as well as recognizable feelings. Some of what we associate with love are these *changes of state*—unstable, fluttering, agitated, anxious fluctuations in our feelings and thoughts when we are in the presence of persons to whom we are becoming strongly attached. These complicated feelings—quickenings, crashing fears, paranoid horrors, sudden elations—are part of the whole *rush* of emotion a great love can induce. Typically, such powerful feelings displace anything in their way and can result in desperate attachments that utterly and totally unhinge a person's world. People thus fall "madly" in love. The mythology of romance celebrated in the West includes the stories of lovers for whom nothing is so important as the perpetuation of these passionate attachments. And for such prototypical pairs as Romeo and Juliet, even death is preferable to parting. Any useful theoretical models of love must explain features like these.

We have already taken a few steps toward constructing such a model. Chapter 3, for example, developed a brief sketch of romance to suggest what we mean by strong interaction. Now, however, we are ready to take the additional steps in our analysis made possible by the theoretical gains of the last chapter, uniting an analysis based on concepts from self psychology with the analytical apparatus appropriated from the theory of nonequilibrium dynamics and dissipative structures. Self psychology, as we already know, helps to isolate the features of love that arise from the appearance of transferences within the interaction field—the dramatic potentiation of actors' illusional distortions of one another in romantic ideation. Mutual idealization, in particular, is what accelerates the attachment process commonly observed in romantic couples. Idealization is also behind the damped oscillations of fusion and individuation examined in chapter 3. We shall consider this interesting property of romantic interaction again in this chapter. In addition, by following up chapter 4's reconceptualization of these matters as properties of far-from-equilibrium systems, we can begin to understand the importance within romance of *sensitive dependence*. In particular, adding dissipative structure theory to the strong interaction perspective brings directly into focus what would otherwise be features of romantic love neglected in alternative theories—namely, the flux of feelings this perspective helps us to recognize as *systematic instabilities,* seemingly chaotic properties of romantic interactions analogous in some sense to the appearance (and disappearance) of turbulence in a system. These amount to orderly features of love's volatility—the characteristic flux of emotion and feeling that is among romantic love's most defining features. The sensitive dependence concept allows us to understand these fluctuations as the effects of one partner's responsiveness to another's merger demands—effects, in particular, of how each partner accommodates the other's merger demands. And, finally, the same joint theoretical perspective also enables us to discuss how these turbulent relationships sometimes exhibit self-organizing characteristics like those we studied in chapter 4.

The model of love we shall study in detail thus appears as a synthesis of conditions and dynamics separately investigated in earlier chapters. Strong attachments arise in addictive dynamics, and strong interactions characterize interaction fields marked by these attachments. Let us consider the model of this process step-by-step. To make clear the special theoretical gains won by this conceptualization, it will be helpful for us to ask how the same matter might be understood in other theoretical frameworks. The one best suited to describing systematically some of the dynamics of the sort isolated here is social exchange theory. But, as we shall argue, exchange theory in its present versions has more success describing interpersonal dynamics marked by steady states and equilibrium than by powerful emotions. Nonequilibrium dynamics like those central to love raise different forces into theoretical view. Even so, as we shall see, we can deepen the exchange perspective by introducing into it appropriate psychological foundations, and with this new hybrid perspective better explain romantic interaction.

The Theoretical Analysis of Love

What most people seem to have in mind when analyzing love is the appearance and deepening of romantic attachments, not the related phenomena of attachment and commitment Swanson (1965) has discussed as forms of love, from love of God to friendship. Romantic love is the most compelling case sociologically because of its powerful shaping influence, especially while it is developing. The force of this attraction is sometimes unrelated to its reciprocation, as is evident in the case of infatuations on the part of partners who have never met. Each partner to a romance sees the other in ways third parties are blind to, the surest evidence, as in therapy relationships, that powerful transferences are at work.[1] Exchange theory and rational choice theory generally ignore this phenomenon, though it is not clear they are unable to extend themselves to accommodate it. The case of social exchange theory is instructive.

Market Price and Social Exchange

Analyzed merely as a case of social exchange, romance appears without the shaping work of selfobject transferences. Blau's "Excursis on Love" in *Exchange and Power in Social Life* (1964), by rejecting psychological analysis in any form, is obliged to address the central illusional features of romance only obliquely. Lovers' judgments of how valuable each is to the other get based, in such an analysis, on something like market price. "How valuable a woman is as a love object to a man," Blau argues, "depends . . . on her apparent popularity with other men. It is difficult to evaluate anything in the absence of clear standards for doing so, and individuals who find themselves in such an ambiguous situation tend to be strongly influenced by any indication of a social norm for making judgments" (79). As if to confirm this judgment, social research has long made it clear that such variables as popularity, sex ratios in dating markets, reputation, social class, and other matters sociological and demographic all enter into the calculus for determining a partner's value. Among Coleman's (1961) high school students, for example, these considerations invariably influenced whether a person was even considered as a partner; and, similarly, among Waller's dating couples (1937, 1938), they determined whether one partner could exploit the other by virtue of occupying the powerful position of "least interest." But if market price, or popularity, or reputation, were the only considerations determining the value we attached to our partners, then in theory all persons equally evaluated in such markets would serve in our eyes as marginal substitutes for one another. Obviously false consequences of this kind leave no room for the particularism and devotion of real love.

This is a blind spot common to most work in the tradition of social exchange theory: the failure successfully to conceptualize, in romantic dyads and elsewhere, the interpersonal dynamics producing particularism and devotion. Selfobject transferences, by contrast, make particularism inevitable. To say this, of course, is certainly not to suggest that love hasn't been amenable to some kind of analysis in terms of social exchange, but such analysis has generally been off the center of the target. Homans (1961) considered the subject only implicitly in his analysis of liking, but others in the exchange theory tradition have tackled it directly. The work of Harold Kelley and his collaborators, in particular, has always exhibited sensitivity to the complexity of love relationships, and has succeeded both theoretically and experimentally in exploring many of their dimensions, including the difficult matters of commitment and conflict (see Kelley and Thibaut 1978; Braiker and Kelley 1979; Kelley et al. 1983; Kelley 1979).

Much of the work centering on Thibaut's and Kelley's (1959) original and revised analyses of dyadic interdependence, however, remains narrowly focused on what Levinger (1979, 171) calls the "pair situation." To expand this focus, Levinger and Huesmann (1976) construct what they label an "incremental exchange" revision to this notion of situational interdependence, and define "deep relationships" in terms of partners' coming to share "a large number of outcomes in diverse pair situations." As relationships deepen, partners develop extended temporal frames of reference, become less insistent on immediate reciprocity, and are reinforced by increasingly "particularistic exchanges" (Foa and Foa 1974; Levinger and Huesmann 1976, 175). Arranging outcome matrices of the Kelley-Thibaut sort in sequences corresponding to situations of deeper involvement and greater depth, Levinger and Huesmann can trace how continuing exchanges result in "the partner's payoffs [being] increasingly weighted into one's own payoffs—an explicit acknowledgment . . . that deepening intimacy implies increasing mutual identification" (175).

Building a pair's history into the analysis of the dynamics of their exchange, as this kind of analysis does, broadens the ability of the model of exchange to subsume aspects of love that "situational exchange" notions must ignore—matters like the tendency of partners to discount current low "outcomes" in the light of the high cumulative payoff or "credit balance" their relationship supports. In addition, isolating such sequences or phases in close relationships forces an analysis of how developing interdependence between partners changes their exchange, but it also begs the question of why partners identify with each other to begin with. Blau's reliance on market evaluations doesn't help dispel this problem for exchange theory. Arguing, as he does, as if lovers were related to one another like the participants in an Asch experiment merely ignores the problem of introducing into exchange theory some understanding of the emotional underpinnings to motivation and personal attachment. And simply postulating, as Levinger and Huesmann do, that increasing interdependence "implies" partners' identifications with one another only gets around this problem in the backward manner of behavioral research—ignoring inner states of the actors being observed, deriving identification from intimacy, and inferring intimacy on the basis of increasingly interdependent exchanges.

Such logical and conceptual shortcomings in exchange-based analyses of close relationships were among the problems that encouraged Richard Emerson to urge that social exchange theory should develop a psychological footing. What Emerson had in mind was theory of precisely those interdependent exchange relations that economic theory, with its simplifying assumption of the perfectly competitive market, explicitly ignored (esp. Emerson 1976, 1962, 1972a, 1972b). Along with directing attention to "exchange networks" and "longitudinal exchange relations," Emerson's agenda for exchange theory urged upon his colleagues the evidence of diverse exchange rules from such imperfect markets as had been disclosed by comparative anthropological research and isolated analytically by Meeker (1971) and Cook (1975). Another direction for theory to develop, he argued, was suggested by considering each partner's "needs"—"a concept that," Emerson argued (1976, 349), "we should develop rather than derogate." The logic of diminishing marginal utility, or satiation-deprivation as it is called in behavioral psychology, merely conceals the underlying work of these fundamental personal forces. To attend them properly requires us, as Emerson demonstrated, to recognize "every rewarding stimulus as part of a feedback system, a cybernetic, self-regulating system" (1976, 346). At least one respect in which the fruitfulness of this theoretical admonition can be demonstrated, though not in the way Emerson expected, appears in attending the powerful needs operating in selfobject transferences—forces that openly shape the mutual expectations and evaluations of partners in close relationships.

Indeed, when we attend these subjective forces, the model of exchange becomes far more powerful. We can then isolate with it a number of peculiar features of love relationships that result from partners' serving as vehicles for each other's selfobject transferences. Something like the "transference value" of the other, or their "role responsiveness" in Sandler's sense, can readily be brought to the center of the analysis of exchange. When this is done, and when the analysis is further deepened psychologically by consideration of the bipolar structure of our wishes regarding significant others, we develop a more complex grasp of an inherently complex phenomenon.[2]

Spirals of Exchange and Cycles of Transference

How, then, does self-object transference as we have studied it affect romantic interaction examined as exchange? It does so by bringing into the analysis of social exchange the features typically regarded as love's defining qualities—matters of affect and illusion. This does not mean we no longer have in view an interpersonal process we can regard as an exchange. Any interaction can be viewed as an exchange, even if the partners to it don't think so. But it does alter the way we shall now make sense of how these partners evaluate one another—not by looking to *others'* judgments, nor to the market price each commands or to other such "cold" cognitions, but, plainly put, to their own feelings in the presence of one another. Most important among these initially are the worshipful feelings romantic partners inspire in one another.

Idealization has been at the center of efforts to analyze love at least since antiquity. In the *Symposium,* for example, Socrates argues that love is what leads us to the *ideal,* which constitutes our own special excellence—"our *potential* perfection," in the phrase of Norton and Kille (1971, 85). Indeed, by contrast to the usual social exchange analysis, none of the important observations on love in Western philosophy and literature after Plato—those, say, by Aristotle, Augustine, Dante, Shakespeare, Stendahl, Kierkegaard, Schopenhauer, Ortega y Gasset, Simmel, R. W. Emerson, Nietzsche, Nygren, Scheler, and de Rougemont—has failed to locate the part played in attraction to others by these deeply rooted ideals. In the conceptual framework of this book, we would paraphrase this by saying that love leads us toward others in whom we both instantiate and redefine ideals such as perfection—ideals, as self psychology has sought to make plain, of greatness and protection, warmth and beauty, leadership and inspiration, that are rooted in the nuclear structures of self.

Consider again the "responsiveness" Sandler and his collaborators postulate we are by nature constituted to seek in our social relationships, but consider it now in light of the exchange process in which partners are implicated. Let us postulate that every romance begins with each partner finding something valuable to admire in the other—strength, beauty, achievement, leadership, wisdom, talent, whatever. Each begins, that is, with idealizing transferences—the projection onto the other of wishes founded in the original transfer to an idealized selfobject of some of the infant's own archaic grandiosity and omnipotence. Partners to romance approach each other scanning their readiness to play roles required by their respective "wished-for" interactions. They come away elated by each other's responsiveness, generally believing they have witnessed significant "inner objects" bodied forth in the other's behavior. Initially, that is, a double-sided idealizing transference is in place, and the implications this has for analyzing their interaction as exchange begin to become clear.

By definition, idealization *raises* the value a partner is seen to bring into interaction. Even outside of romantic contexts, this most natural transferential process profoundly affects *initial* rates of exchange between partners relatively unknown to one another. It does this by increasing what they are willing to pay to maintain an interaction.[3] When *mutual* idealization is involved, the transference process compounds this exchange rule in a self-amplifying way. Positive feedback enters the calculus. In this situation, *each* person values the partner's contributions *more* than his or her own. This follows from the double-sidedness of the idealizing—each perceiving the other, compared to the self, as a person of greater worth and interest. If this were not the case, we would not be observing idealization. The idealization works such that each is reminded by the other of ways in which he or she could be better, ways, that is, with which the self wishes to be identified. A spiralling movement is imparted to their exchange as a result and is typically what is regarded by love's observers as among the most defining of its first features. Plato's *theia mania,* for example, signals the worried preoccupation with one another this escalating pattern of contribution can produce. It denotes effects that appear only from each partner discovering in the other the equivalent of a god—the pattern of worshipfulness and mutual obsession so much the subject of subsequent commentaries on love. Such "madness," as Ortega y Gasset (1957) analyzed it, also points to insecurity about partners that is typical of lovers' early worries concerning each other, insecurities that sometimes pass into paranoid fears.

Such early worries include the familiar fear that partners don't evaluate their exchange in the same way—that one partner has lost interest, perhaps, or no longer thinks what he or she receives from the relationship is worth what they contribute to it. Such worries establish a powerful force behind the escalation of exchange. Each partner in these circumstances seeks renewed proof of the other's sentiments. And, in turn, each also moves to contribute *more* to the relationship—enough to *raise* the value of his or her own contribution to what they perceive to be the level of the other's. Since the same perception is held on both sides, moreover, the exchange spirals, each party on every round raising the level of his or her contributions. The mechanism here seems to be one of attempted discrepancy reduction, where both partners wish in turn to minimize the difference between the value they assign their own contributions compared to the value they assign their partner's. This has something of the same wishful logic to it as stands behind the escalating bets made by a hopeful gambler—the conviction that one is in the game for all it is worth, and that the only strategy enabling ultimate success involves increasing bets on each round until one finally does win. (Obviously, too, what we are observing in such spiralling exchanges are the addictive side effects of dramatically strengthening attachments. More on this below.)

Part of the usual solution to overcoming perceived discrepancies between partners involves some of the same magical and superstitious thinking found around a gambling table—the compulsive imitation of the winning partner's behavior. So long as mutual idealization is operating, that is, each partner comes to act as if one of the ways to raise the value of his or her contributions to the level of the other's is to *become* the other. Out of idealization comes identification, motivated by the same half-conscious and magically induced merger with the other we can see in the infant who, we are told, wishes to become a part of the omnipotent parent. One's contribution becomes identically equal to the other's only when one *becomes* the other—a matter of magic by which partners strengthen or calm themselves in interpersonal dealings. Among romantically attached adolescents, the signals of this merger soon appear in the exchange of clothing and other possessions, along with the adoption of common habits of speech and demeanor.

Such identification, of course, has its limits—those imposed by society along with those deriving from the finiteness of time and resources. Evaluated psychologically, partners reach this point in their exchange only after appearing to undergo a kind of regression—usually signalled by baby talk and mutual infantilization. These signals appear at this point because spiralling exchange by then has reduced each partner to a condition of deep dependency vis-à-vis the other, a condition wherein each plays baby to the other's parent. Sometime during this regressed interaction, we can observe with great clarity how idealization appears to change into mirroring. "This being in love stuff is great," wrote Scott Fitzgerald in *The Crack-up* (1945), ". . . you get lots of compliments and begin to think you are a great guy." Eventually, that is, idealization has the positive effects on self-esteem that derive during infancy from mirroring responsiveness. By the feedback circuits relating idealized to mirrored strengths, worship gets converted into self-esteem.

When mutual dependency reaches this point, we are observing interaction where each partner's idealized strengths have been displaced by a partner serving externally as an idealized selfobject. Given that interaction is necessarily structured by turn taking, external dependency imparts a functional logic to the sequential organization of interaction. That is, interaction becomes functionally differentiated by turn taking into acting and observing—two roles corresponding functionally to exhibitionism and voyeurism. Analytically, this may sound more complex than it really is. What it means is that the observing partner is always "using" the acting other voyeuristically, while the acting partner is always using the observer exhibitionistically. Consider this step-by-step. Whoever acts is being presented, by the observing partner, with merger demands to behave in ways worthy of idealization. Accommodating such idealizing merger demands thus implicitly calls upon this acting partner to become exhibitionistic for the observing partner. Functionally understood, idealization and mirroring are therefore simultaneously present at the same moment of interaction. Moreover, at the moment when this exhibitionism appears in the active partner's responsiveness, *mirroring* merger demands become part of it. It is this unstable functional differentiation of romantic interaction that converts idealization into mirroring. In the flip-flop, active-passive logic of turn taking itself, each partner switches from exhibitionistic actor to voyeuristic observer, and from voyeuristic observer to exhibitionistic actor.

Interpersonal Differentiation

This mix of mirroring and idealization in romantic interaction produces interesting but convoluted patterns. All along in this double-sided process, each partner is in part motivated to shape himself or herself along lines suggested by the *idealizations* projected by the partner. The situation is analogous to that of infancy, in which, we are told, the infant learns that it maximizes the likelihood of securing love (and minimizes the chance of abandonment) by conforming to its parents' wishes. At stake here is not only the matter of becoming the other (identification), but of becoming what the other wants one to be (false self). At work in romance, if not in infancy, there is thus a double-sided effort to convince the partner that one is what the partner wants—the fulfillment of the other's wishes—and to convince oneself that the partner's wishes are within reach—that one is truly a great guy. The partner's idealizing helps to secure this image, even if it is held in place only within the context of the relationship. Yet this is by far not the end of the matter.

Complex issues are introduced into this pattern of interaction by the illusions at work between the partners. One first-order problem arises from disjunctions between reality and idealization—from the fact, for instance, that the partner with whom one *identifies* is not the equivalent of the *idealized* partner. Clearly, our sense of a partner is in part the product of our own prepossessive transformation of him or her in the light of our own wishes, and it is this distorted impression we wish initially to identify with and are motivated to defend. This, however, is not the reality we confront. A second, confounded issue is that we are being pulled in different directions: on the one hand, there is our identification with a partner we ourselves have idealized—that is to say, with a partner as a result of our own idealization of the partner—while at the same time, on the other hand, we have the partner's different idealizations of ourselves to body forth in our own behavior. Our partners may be flattered by identification, just as we are, but we automatically begin to disappoint them if we seem subsequently not what they wanted us to be but mere edited versions of themselves.

The conclusion that interpersonal matters can become this convoluted only begins to approximate the true convolution of real relationships, particularly those involving love. The tension introduced into relationships between identification with the other and role responsiveness, between reminding the other of himself or herself and seeming to the other that one is what the other

wished for, is precisely what yields yet another of the characteristic movements in the history of every personal tie. The movement is equivalent to
differentiation. It is an oscillation on the part of one or both partners away
from the *other* as a model for the self and toward an actor's *own* idealized
self-representation, as it has been affected by the other. This sounds like a
very subtle matter, but is really only a question of acting so as to keep the
other's interest. If this process operates as it does developmentally, differentiation in this sense is always supported by the equivalent of internalization as
well. Or, in Kohut's language, by a *transmuting* internalization of the
other—an accomplishment induced by the partner through an optimal mix of
frustration and responsiveness. Such differentiation, then, stimulates growth
in relationships, away from simple identification, toward mapping onto each
partner such values as enable each to maintain the other's interest, not mere
reproductions of the other, but new values or qualities that reestablish one's
uniqueness in the other's eyes.

   In a sense, this is a way to derive from notions of exchange what optimal
frustration is. One is optimally frustrating to a partner when one is driven to
keep their interest by *reducing* one's identification with them. The more they
see themselves in us as a result of our growing identification with them, the
less they are able to idealize us; so differentiation from them on our part is
partly aimed at recovering qualities in ourselves that will inspire them to idealize us again—qualities different from their own. The way this works psychologically, reducing one's identification with a partner is one equivalent of
retreating from the kind of relationship with them in which they are being
perfectly served by us, particularly where they are "using" us to derive mirrored strengths. So reducing identification produces reductions of adaptation,
and these are in effect reductions of mirroring. Indeed, viewed economically
this way, "perfect adaptation" to a partner (as in Winnicott's notion of a mother's "perfect adaptation" to her infant) is actually a condition of attachment
that eventually diminishes our value in a partner's eyes. Optimal frustration,
thus, becomes another way to talk about *diminishing marginal utility,* or about
the principle of satiation-deprivation as it is studied by psychologists—both
notions well understood in other theoretical frameworks. We can understand
it here as leading us to replace our idealizing of a partner by active merger
demands for responsiveness, a change implicit in the renewal of our own
exhibitionism. This says to a partner, "OK, enough of this idealizing of *your*
sterling qualities. That kind of flattery is beginning to bore you. So you idealize me for awhile, especially this *new* me I'm about to exhibit for your
admiration." In other words, differentiation appears both as a way of reestablishing the partner's interest in us by diminishing how much we identify with
them, and it goes hand-in-hand with establishing for them an idealized image
they must then maintain to keep *our* interest. Satiation cuts two ways.

An economic analysis in terms of joint utility would suggest, oddly enough, that optimal frustration *of a partner* appears side-by-side with keeping oneself on the highest indifference curve within reach of *their* budget line: one wants to stay an *idealized* selfobject for *them*. But one does not want to get so far beyond their reach—that is, so far outside the range of their capacity to identify with us—that they find our superiority a frustrating, nonoptimal challenge. In Csikszentmihalyi's and Larson's (1984) sense, we must allow them to remain part of the "flow" our differentiation establishes. We want to maintain a relationship to them that sustains jointly enjoyable experience, rather than separating so far from them as to constitute by our behavior an anxious challenge for them. This is an interesting consequence of conceptualizing romance in this way, since it suggests that what we mean by optimal levels of responsiveness in relationships is the equivalent of the mix of frustration and idealizing that supports a balance between differentiation and identification. By a balance of these two forces—the one force drawing partners together, the other pushing them apart—we mean whatever level enhances the "cohesiveness" of the relationship. This ultimately turns out to be a changing value—one that begins by keeping partners strongly attached, but that eventually diminishes their attachment by strengthening each partner individually.

Damped Cycles, Separations, and Introjection

Spiralling exchanges, therefore, lead to identifications, and such identifications, by diminishing the value of what one contributes to a relationship, induce differentiation in the direction of one's own or one's partner's ideals, reestablishing something in the self the other can value. This is a logic of oscillations, with cycles of identification following cycles of differentiation, ad infinitum. Such oscillation would maintain relationships at a high pitch of exchange, of course, were it not for the fact that differentiation and identification are typically damped in successive cycles of this process by the operation of introjection. We thus derive from our reasoning the argument involving *damped cycles* of interaction that we first saw in connection with the analysis of transferences in chapter 3.

When we separate from a partner to reestablish our differences, something of the other ends up transmuted into an object representation with a status of its own, apart from the other as an external object. Each cycle amends the inner representation of the other, augmenting its significance in our inner life, the product of repeated microinternalizations. This gives us a hold on the other apart from our public exchanges with him or her, and proportionately increases our capacity to function apart. There is an obvious analogy here to growing up, with both partners on successive cycles made less the infant to the other's parent. Something, too, of a slow routinization to the intense pitch of romantic fervor accompanies the damping of these cycles, as each partner's increasing hold (i.e., introjected possession) on the other diminishes the other's bewitching power.

Beyond Transference

To speak of love's routinization, of course, is to indicate how relationships move beyond early transferential cycles to accommodate something each partner accepts as reality. Analogously, Greenson (1971) speaks of the "real relationship" between the patient and psychiatrist to denote how analysis can rid the psychotherapeutic encounter of transferences and allow each party to perceive the other realistically. The fact that selfobject transferences inevitably make their way into personal encounters points to some of the same work partners must accomplish to develop their own ties on realistic grounds. Of necessity relationships must follow a course shaped by the need to correct transferential distortions. This is part of what the differentiation cycle accomplishes—the movement away from perfect adaptation to a partner's wishes or needs. Simultaneously, however, this same movement opens up a space between partners that is then available as the place where each can refind the direction and confidence imparted to life by illusion and understanding.

TOWARD REALITY When an analyst "differentiates" from a patient and asks the patient to attempt to explain his or her own actions, something of the same antitransferential disappointment, appearing as the force of reality, is also being called into play. The analyst disappoints the patient in the piecemeal way a mother presumably fails her infant or the lover his or her partner—each incrementally retreats from the other's illusional and magical hold on their shared interpersonal space. Differentiation from the shaping control of a lover's transferences aims at correcting distortions occasioned by conformity with them as well as at diminishing costs of sustaining them. Inevitably, for example, some of these costs appear in the form of lost benefits arising from forgone exchanges with others—opportunity costs. This is sometimes recognized when others excuse our failures on grounds of "love sickness" or some related explanation. Needless to say, there are several modes or patterns of corrective differentiation, as familiar to us already as are various modes of withdrawing assert to the controlling acts of authority—from rebellion in the face of what may finally seem an inescapable tyranny to the near routine reassertion of self-sovereignty one observes in so-called healthy adult relationships. The motivation to undertake such micropolitical assertions of autonomy and self-governance appears in the form of pressures to live one's own life after all, especially when, as in our analogous response to the failure of political authorities, partners fail our needs or disappoint our expectations. Pressures of work or from other personal ties exert a push back into a wider life.

TOWARD ILLUSION   Of perhaps equal importance to the way differentiation enables us to escape from an other's potential tyranny or from the other's delusional manipulations is how it opens up an area between self and other that can be filled with matters newly discovered or created. This is the fundamental accomplishment of our discovery during infancy that the other is part of some larger not-me. When the "good-enough" mother fails to adapt herself in perfect sympathy to her infant's needs, room is created for the infant to do for itself what it has hitherto had done for it. Encouraged by the mother's reliability, by trust in its environment, and by the mother's incremental frustration of its needs, the infant opens up a "potential space" between itself and the mother—a place where the infant, in relation to the mother, develops a primitive concept of its autonomy, where its capacities, waiting to be developed, are called forth by a mother who allows her own mysterious powers to stand apart from the infant's magical control, outside of the sphere of its omnipotence, and finally, perhaps, to be mirrored back into it, when its moments of faltering discovery and inept replication are saturated with her pleasure.

The fact is that there are such rewards to differentiation, just as there is a logic to merger and identification. Such rewards come to lovers as they do to infants, both by the discoveries relationships enable and by the rewards they elicit from partners. The discovery or rediscovery of a novel competence, the exploration of a side of oneself never before grasped or understood, the deliberate cultivation of capacities that infuse oneself with "value"—such are among the ways differentiation and individuation establish and reward the person. Insofar as each phase of differentiation is supported by the piecemeal introjection of the other, some aspect of the value one originally found in the other can now be found in oneself. Indeed, both self and other find something of interest in this transmuting achievement. The mother who responds with pleasure at her infant's exhibition of a new strength or capacity is finding in her infant the signs of its conformity to her wishes that it be perfect, and she rewards its self-assertion. The lover who recognizes a partner's differentiating refusal to continue their mutual idealizing is likewise initially driven to interpret such potentially estranging behavior as evidence of strengths that confirm his or her original idealization, even if such signs are in fact only preludes to abandonment. And on top of all this is the access provided by intimacy to further growth and further understanding.

Beyond their normality, a complex importance thus attaches to those moments when partners begin to seem strange or aloof to one another. These are occasions not necessarily for amplifying differences, but for tuning each to matters not before perceived. The other-as-stranger can be sustained as the subject of one's interest, the way a topic never before discussed can be kept as the subject of one's conversation: each is the horizon of some expanding understanding, some deepening hold on an external otherness. In the repeating phases of such ties, reality corrects illusions by substituting itself in self-strengthening ways. But it is in the potential space opened up by such disenchanting individuations that the good-enough mother or the idealized partner establish themselves in other modes as well—as constant and trusted foundations for the play of their infants and partners.

Interpersonal Addictions

Especially in the first phase of romance, extraordinary qualities of mentation and feeling become characteristic features of an emerging strong attachment. Each partner becomes something the other can't do without. Imaginary or real perturbations of this condition result in panic, as partners desperately cling to one another to ward off the paranoia even temporary absences induce. Indeed, there is something in these desperately strong attachments resembling the abstinence syndrome students of substance abuse have observed in heroin addicts: each partner's attachment to the other feeds on the fear of a traumatic withdrawal process.[4] Eventually partners have to develop such trust in one another that their temporary absences will not be construed as going cold turkey. When we hear a lover asking a partner for "space," by contrast, we are observing a countervailing need to relieve the suffocations of such strong attachment. Such feelings are relieved in differentiation. But before this can happen, partners must learn to trust one another. Building up this trust involves instituting a "potential space"—a place into which each can learn to relinquish illusions. This area of overlapping play is where we observe the phenomena of baby talk and infantilization already noted. It is also where the pair can play at being apart from one another—doing separate things while together, as a rehearsal for doing separate things while apart.

The fragility of this arena is evident in how readily small modulations of responsiveness on the part of either partner will affect the other's feelings. As we have seen, the disorienting result of their fusion is that each has come to serve as an exclusive external regulator for the other. Where on the part of most people this tendency to use others as external regulators reaches a point short of complete external dependence, interaction in romantic infatuation is carried much closer to this limit. Recall from chapter 3 what this means: we then have an unstable interaction system, one in which there is no inherent tendency for interaction to reach a rest point. Such a rest point can eventually be achieved, but only after the romantic process has permitted each partner to introject the other in some fragmentary degree. Only introjection enables internalized self-regulation. When introjection has clustered strengths again around the idealized parental imago, as Kohut's bipolar model of the self indicates, internal regulation begins to replace external dependency. But until that occurs, romance is an extremely volatile system, easily affected by any nonoptimal properties of responsiveness on the part of either partner.

Another way to put this is to observe that a correlate of this extreme attachment is the phenomenon of sensitive dependence. What in fact we have described in the development of a mutual interpersonal addiction is a volatile interaction system susceptible, by virtue of the positive feedback inherent in selfobject transferences, to being driven into far-from-equilibrium conditions. One way nonequilibrium dynamics can be recognized, in fact, is by the appearance of fast adaptations—resonance, responsiveness, heightened perception—on the part of each partner to external conditions presented by an other. In interaction systems not subject to selfobject transferences and hence not powered by positive feedback—systems, that is, closer to an equilibrium—the same external conditions ordinarily would not be perceived. But in romantic interaction, the signals of extreme mutual sensitivity are endless. In fact these signals arise out of an elusive internal flux of feelings that is frequently so strange as to baffle and frighten many inexperienced lovers, and stand beyond the conceptual grasp of most. Persons recognize such agitated internal states often without being able to give them exact names.

Optimal departures from perfect adaptation to one another, of course, are necessary to structure building in each partner, as I have repeatedly argued. I have even defined optimal frustration as that degree of departure from perfect adaptation able to diminish this extreme external dependence. But sensitive dependence exists when internal strengths have not developed to the point where an actor can stand apart from a partner. The numerous possible effects appearing then in each partner's feelings and mentation, particularly as the result of nonoptimal responsiveness, are what make up the agonies and the ecstasies of romantic infatuations. One way to come to terms with some of these unstable feelings is to recognize that they arise out of variations in responsiveness equivalent to those from which we derived the addictive patterns studied in chapter 2. Qualities like grandiosity and emptiness, or false self and fantasy, then, have their equivalents in the effects partners can have on one another during romance. Indeed, these *are* the effects partners have on each other—effects typically observed in lovers' endless obsessive efforts to secure their partner's attachment to themselves.

Since the appearance of these phenomena in romance follows the same logic as does their appearance in infancy and childhood, I would be repeating myself to go over it in great detail again here. But review briefly what I have claimed, this time in light of far-from-equilibrium dynamics. In this newer perspective, romance can be understood to produce sensitive dependence by instigating a process of increasing entropy production. It does this through mutual idealization, which creates the equivalent of an "adverse gradient" between two interaction partners—a gradient large enough to fuel instability. Potentiated by responsiveness, the transferences then work to enlarge this gradient and thereby to establish the mechanism, based on positive feedback, for increasing entropy production. This results in the near-complete displacement of internal by external controls; external dependency grows as entropy production increases. The flux of feelings and the onset of crazy thoughts during romance are manifestations of this circumstance—products of the loss of internal orientation, of the growth of helpless dependency, and of dedifferentiation and loss of structure.

The logic of this matter, as we have seen, makes the operation of these entropic processes contingent on the responsiveness of partners to one another. Since optimal frustration by a partner supplies responsiveness in a degree that supports introjection, this is a development that can reverse entropy production, or create negentropy. When negentropy begins to equal entropy, a new steady state may have been reached. Some of these "new" states of personal and social organization can be described as stable forms of complexity. One such form of stable complexity appears in relationships that "grow"—that is, where old adjustments of partners to one another are constantly being displaced by new achievements on the part of each that sustain idealization at the same time they strengthen self-regulation. Love, as a postromantic emergent, is one such form of stable complexity. But romance itself, by producing increases rather than decreases in attachment and transference, falls short of this condition of stable complexity. That is, it remains a matter of unstable, far-from-equilibrium fluctuations. Only when introjection passes some threshold of self-structuration that supports apartness does this process traverse something like a bifurcation. Though it is hard to specify what this means exactly, the equivalent of a phase transition seems to occur that reorganizes relatedness into more stable patterns. Wherever apartness and autonomy begin to characterize relatedness, we can speak of complexity in one form or another. Other forms of stable complexity will be examined in later chapters.

It is because romance arises in connection with entropy production that sensitive dependence is also so characteristic of how it *feels*. All of the small signals of a partner's responsiveness are magnified by strong attachment and can set up self-amplifying resonances that carry feelings and thoughts into extremes. As each partner is made more dependent on the other, desperation or elation is not unusual but typical. Indeed, as I suggested earlier, it is this state of strong attachment that makes understandable not only romantic volatility per se but enables us to describe certain of its characteristic forms as *systematic instabilities*. Each different pattern of addictive relatedness is one manifestation of such systematic instability—an unstable form of attachment corresponding to the kind of nonoptimal responsiveness a partner can introduce into interaction. Thus, depending on how one partner responds to another's merger demands, we will discover a romantically involved person affected in ways that can produce grandiosity, emptiness, false self, and fantasy. Grandiosity and its various forms—ebullience, optimism, over-confidence, ambition—arise from a partner's mirroring responses to exhibitionism; and emptiness and its forms—depression, listlessness, low self-esteem, timidity, shyness—from a partner's indifference to or repudiation of exhibitionistic merger demands. In the area of the idealized parental imago, the false self can appear in a person when their partner's own deficits are too overburdening to permit them to be responsive to anyone else's. And the pattern we called fantasy and strong beliefs will appear when the partner is too impinging—so preoccupied and worried, usually over the possible loss of love, that he or she cannot bear to separate or to be apart and is moved by anxiety to create illusory futures that fix and hold the qualities of responsiveness from their partners they most fear losing. All of these patterns are in some degree characteristic of lovers' feelings and thoughts about one another at one point or another in their attachment. It takes only a small indication of nonoptimal responsiveness in each of these directions by a partner to produce any of them, and they may appear alone or in combination. By recognizing these effects as instabilities, moreover, we draw attention to the essential mutability of each as an adaptation.

Though these are "normal" fluctuations in romance, they can become the basis for developments other than introjection and growth. Indeed, some of these patterns are what get exaggerated in relationships that fail. They then become signals of disintegration.

Disintegration and Aggression

Especially when we bring into greater resolution the forces at work in differentiation, we can see how to make sense of some of the dynamics of failed relationships. Failure, in the logic of transference, amounts to unresponsiveness—in the other's unwillingness or inability to mirror us or to accommodate our idealizations. A mother's failure to serve her infant's needs both frustrates and disappoints it, as Edith Jacobson (1946, 1964) once argued from a different psychoanalytic perspective. While frustration in Jacobson's view had to do with "drive demand," disappointment arose from the altered quality of the emergent mother-infant object relationship itself (cf. Greenberg and Mitchell 1983, 304–27). Jacobson argued that such disappointment led to a devaluation of the mother as object, for which the psychophysiological precedent was disgust with unpalatable food. "[Frustration, like a bad meal,] leads to the desire to expel, to get away from, to be separate from the noxious object," as Greenberg and Mitchell put it (1983, 308). Aggressive drive energies, as Jacobson argued, are released in this devaluing repudiation of the noxious object and give rise to "derivative sequences of attitudes toward the object."

Aggression as a Disintegration Product

Part of this logic appears in Kohut's suggestion that aggression is a "disintegration product." Normally a component of healthy assertiveness on the part of the child, nondestructive aggressiveness is mobilized to delimit the self from its environment "whenever optimal frustrations (i.e., nontraumatic delays of the empathic responses of the self-object) are experienced" (Kohut 1977, 121). Analogously, nondestructive aggressiveness is part of every partner's movement to delimit himself or herself in the environment of identification and fusion with the other. It is when the partner is no longer such an optimally frustrating environment that the equivalent of a child's destructive rage can result. The nonempathic lover arouses in his or her partner anxieties analogous to those the infant experiences in situations verging on the traumatic frustration of its needs. More than the fear of the loss of love is inherent in these anxieties. Since to the infant the parent is the world, losing the parent is the equivalent of losing contact with reality. Some of the paranoid horror the child fears from an inhuman environment appears in this disintegration anxiety—fear of exposure to "the coldness, the indifference of the nonhuman, the nonempathically responding world" (Kohut 1984, 18). It is a fear behind which, Kohut reasons, stands the horror of death itself, threatening to erase the slim purchase a child has on life in the warm connection it maintains with an empathic parent.

Love relationships are suffused by corresponding anxieties. Especially in their early phases it is these fears that motivate partners to cling ever more dependently to one another, willing to contribute whatever is necessary to secure their attachment. Such anxieties commonly appear in the need to know where the lover is, and promote desperate and paranoid demands for contact and communication. The quaking horror of a lover's disappearance is akin to the infant's fear that losing sight of an object, as in the *fort-da* game that so fascinated Freud (Ricoeur 1970), amounted to its obliteration. Disintegration anxieties are in each instance evidence of inadequate trust in the environment—a product initially of partners' mutual inexperience and of the weakness of introjected strengths, a function in turn of the correspondingly small number of cycles of mutual separation and individuation. In economic terms, these anxieties act like a multiplier on demands for empathic response from others—demands for giving more and more, and for proofs of commitment.

To many young lovers, the partner's absence is an intolerable cost, the reduction of which demands their return.

Asymmetrical Mirroring and Negative Transference

Meeting one another's empathic needs is at best an unstable achievement on the part of lovers, especially when their needs have been multiplied to the point of desperation and paranoia by anxieties of disintegration. Indeed, paranoia generates something of a cycle of necessary failure and disappointment. This is largely because such exaggerated needs interfere with responsiveness. Consider the simple case where one partner's paranoia becomes overwhelming —a pattern often merely doubled into a trajectory of disillusionment and estrangement that results in the termination of a relationship.

Anxious, demanding, and clinging actions on the part of one partner reflect a state of neediness that interferes with empathic sensitivity. Such overwhelming neediness may result in the other partner's own needs in this unempathic environment being left unmet, or being met in a half-hearted way that is frustrating and disappointing. One response to such impinging frustration, as we have seen, is for the deprived partner to defend against the evidence of unresponsiveness on the part of the other by elaborating strong beliefs and fantasies. The unresponsive other is then perceived as "worth" the trouble they create by their demands, or their insensitivity is thought to be counterbalanced by positive qualities. Or the deprived partner will elaborate a fantasy of future happiness and responsiveness that will be reached as soon as the troubled partner crosses some imaginary bridge. At the same time, the attachment on the part of the deprived partner may have developed strength simply by virtue of the positive feedback inherent in selfobject transference, enough that an abstinence syndrome also has grown into place—the fear that giving up this unresponsive, bad partner will produce even more pain and unhappiness than keeping him or her. These are all signals of the deprived partner's addictive attachment.

Yet another response to this asymmetrical situation is for the disappointed partner simply to diminish the level at which he or she is willing to sustain attachment. Such withdrawal is typically accompanied by the release of aggression in support of his or her subsequent individuation and by the progressive devaluation of the needy other. Nonoptimal frustration in this case both augments the disintegration fears of the first and motivates the separation and individuation of the second. The amplification of this estrangement in subsequent cycles is such that heightening disintegration anxiety produces ever more assertive demands for mirroring on the part of the anxious partner, deepening his or her selfish preoccupations and insensitivity, and is perceived in turn as yet additional evidence of disappointing unresponsiveness by the other. Eventually, with the disappointment all on one side, and the desperation on the other, this cyclic process can lead the disappointed partner to conclude that the only escape is in traumatic repudiation of the relationship, confirming the worst fears of loss on the part of his or her unempathic partner.

Aggression is a signal of this cyclically enlarging disintegration and is interpreted as such by both parties to the relationship. Like energy released in the decay of organic structures, aggression is a disintegration product—a force released by the failure of the relational template to accommodate the partners' needs. The failed object is repudiated like an unpalatable meal, if Jacobson's physiological precedent is right—expelled like a noxious taste, repudiated aggressively the way a disgusting object is expelled. Indeed, failed responsiveness on the part of the paranoid partner results in the transformation of his or her lover's idealizing transference into a *negative transference,* a phenomenon amounting in Jacobson's language to devaluation and in ours to deidealization. Such deidealizing, in the eyes of its recipient, amounts to diminishing contributions and decremental responsiveness, an outcome that slowly adds its costs to the equation by which other losses in the relationship are calculated. Slowly, as these costs accumulate on top of the pain and anxiety of disintegration, the other is finally seen as reciprocally unempathic and is likewise aggressively repudiated. What had been positive transference in his or her direction then also becomes negative, and the relationship is finished. All that remains are introjects, as they have been affected and transformed by their own disappointments—suffered now, in the immediate shadow of yet another defeat, as a palpable emptiness, as the place where once there had been an important other.

Feedback, Disequilibrium, and Negative Transference

When we study how mirrored and idealized strengths are related to one another in view of the feedback circuits outlined in chapter 2, it immediately becomes obvious that all nonoptimal patterns of responsiveness in the mirroring area ultimately lead to the pattern of disintegration I have just described or to one of its variants. Desperate, clinging behavior need not always be the signal of unjustified paranoia, but can indeed be induced in a person by an emotionally flat, unempathic partner. The empty self, in relation to such a partner, can drive itself into this deeper neediness by the positive feedback inherent in repudiation. As the result of an unempathic partner's repeated repudiations, such deepening neediness eventually becomes the condition that initiates the cycle of negative transference—the desperate, anxious, clinging behavior that is a prelude to disintegration. When unresponsiveness becomes symmetrical, the feedback involved in mutual negative transference will then quickly drive interaction back through the point of zero attachment and into yet another zone of disequilibrium dynamics—the zone of conflict and strong negative relatedness.[5]

Negative transferences, by a logic deriving from the analysis in chapter 2, can then serve to *raise* self-esteem. This happens in the first place by "changing the sign" of the repudiating selfobject, or, in the logic of homeostatic amplifiers, by inverting any signals he or she sends. This is what deidealization and negative idealization are all about. Disliking someone who dislikes you makes you feel better about yourself. After a time of living with emptiness and feelings of worthlessness that accompany the end of a relationship—particularly an other's indifference—negative transference allows an actor to transform such depleting attachments into supports for self-worth.

If Kohut's argument about anxiety is not off the mark, such endings affect us like the death of a loved one. When the death is not sudden and traumatic but occurs in a long process of disintegration for which we have been prepared by anticipatory mourning, then separation should be supported by numerous antecedents rehearsals that have substituted strengthened introjects for our external dependence on the living and present other. But if we have not been so prepared, the trauma can be devastating in its effects, and we must mourn the other's loss to avert chronic melancholia. Indeed, in the logic of self psychology, melancholia becomes understandable as another variation on the theme of narcissistic "injury"—that is, a manifestation of how "repudiations" can affect a person's feelings when paired with structural deficits, the weaknesses of psychological structure caused by nonoptimal caregiving first in relation to our parental partners, thereafter in relation to all the others who fail as substitutes for them in meeting our needs. Indeed, it is in part the insecure foundation bequeathed by failed early object relationships—insecure, undependable, untrustworthy attachments to our parents—that results in the greater readiness of some persons to find their adult love relationships disturbed by the sort of paranoid disintegration anxieties that lead to their failure as partners—desperate, clinging, needy, and selfish.

Transference in Exchange

Attachment Theory and Self Psychology

So many of love's vicissitudes are drawn within reach of this kind of analysis that the value of hybridizing these various theoretical perspectives—social exchange with self psychology and "object relations" theory in psychoanalysis, and both of these in turn with the analysis of nonequilibrium dynamics—might seem to have been established. New work in social psychology by Hazan and Shaver (1987; Shaver and Hazan 1987) also presents evidence consistent with the exchange-attachment perspective.

Hazan and Shaver (1987) argue that we should think of love as an attachment process, as conceived along the lines established in Bowlby's (1969) work. Romantic love, as they reason, looks strikingly like the bonds of attachment between infants and their caregivers. Indeed, they argue that something like Bowlby's "inner working models" of attachment form in the initial infant-caregiver bond and serve subsequently to influence adult relationships. Secure infant-caregiver relationships, for instance, have properties resembling secure love relationships—confidence, happiness, exploratory behavior, and so forth. Likewise, insecure love relationships resemble infant behavior troubled by problematic attachment. Interestingly, anxious-ambivalent lovers in Hazan's and Shaver's studies fall in love quickly and easily but evaluate as unreciprocated their wishes for merger with their partners—a pattern exactly parallel to the consequence derived above from argument about disintegration anxieties. Very probably, a condition of the neediness appearing in disintegration anxieties is the structural deficit diagnosed by Bowlby as problematic attachment. These are two ways of talking about the same thing.

Bowlby's "inner working models" are matters conceptualized in the tradition of psychoanalytic self psychology as introjects. What is at issue in evaluating the present argument in view of Bowlby's notions or the work of Hazan and Shaver is not so much self psychology versus attachment theory but the usefulness of hybridizing either of them with the social exchange tradition. My argument has been that new consequences can be derived from exchange theory as a result of adding to its perspective the wants and needs that derive from our early object relationships. Hazan's and Shaver's work supports the notion that such paradigms are operative, as would the work behind clinical observations reported countless times in the literature of modern psychiatry and psychoanalysis. Adding them as forces to be reckoned with in the exchange perspective—particularly the mutual evaluation of partners under the control of these inner images or "inner working models"—allows us to address additional dynamics of their attachment that seem to have been missed elsewhere—in particular, the cyclic trajectory of their relationships through time. Indeed, it is precisely the operation of these transferential forces that makes social exchange violate the assumptions of independence found in theories of economic behavior—forces that create the complex interdependence in relations of social exchange Emerson thought we might begin to treat more trenchantly with the help of some such concept of need.

What gives psychoanalytic self psychology the advantage over plain attachment theory with its inner working models is its unique specification of the self's bipolarity. It is this clinically based conceptualization of psychological organization from which we derive the sources within the personality of idealizing our partners. And it is this matter specifically that yields the dynamics of romance we have attended here. Attractive as it is, neither Bowlby's theory nor the extrapolation of it by Hazan and Shaver can produce predictions at odds with those derived from the hybrid of exchange and self psychology. The advantage of the self psychology model then arises, in turn, from its unique ability to predict certain observations—the spiral of identification and exchange, the cycles of fusion and differentiation, the addiction-like phenomena of abstinence syndromes and sensitive dependence, and so forth—that cannot be derived from these alternative theories.

The Attraction Paradigm Revisited

If we are to follow through to its further implications the logic we have derived from this conjunction of self psychology and social exchange theory, then we must also understand that the matter of love as analyzed here is the key to a far greater range of interpersonal dealings. The attraction we feel toward the "other-as-stranger" and the "other-as-self" represent alternating pulses of those two deep structures within the self—the idealized parental imago and the archaic grandiose self—that generate natural sequences of separation and merger. If we think of analyzing love as a step toward constructing a new paradigm of attraction, many other matters also begin to fall into place in relation to this analysis. Consider, for example, the vast and contradictory literature on attraction that has appeared in social psychology.

Not only does the logic of the present book produce implications not appearing in other theories, but it also serves to resolve contradictions and logically incompatible observations in the literature on attraction. Two of the most widely investigated propositions about interpersonal attraction, for example, simply restate contradictory axioms of folklore—"Birds of a feather flock together" asserts the importance of similarity; "Opposites attract" argues contrariwise that differences between partners, perhaps in the version of the complementarity hypothesis, somehow establish their interest in one another—the way, say, Socrates saw love grow from the capacity of others to help us discover excellence. When these hypotheses are regarded as contradictory, research produces a mixed picture. On the one hand, the similarity-attraction paradigm has produced remarkable support (as, e.g., the fifty studies mentioned in Byrne 1971). Similarity—whether it leads to attraction or is a product of frequent interaction that itself is based on attraction, generated on some other ground—almost always is reported to play a part in keeping partners together, particularly in the early stages of relationships. On the other hand, dissimilarity also enters into attraction under some conditions. When experimental subjects are told they are liked by persons dissimilar to themselves, for example, they prefer dissimilar over similar partners (Walster and Walster 1963). Likewise, the more confident a person is about interpersonal skills, the more likely he or she is to find dissimilar others attractive (Aron and Aron 1986, 46). When conditions like proximity that facilitate attraction are present, in addition, "best friends," such as those studied by Murstein (1972) in a woman's housing cooperative, differ significantly in physical attractiveness—a criterion otherwise important in choice of friends, especially where other supports for attraction are absent (Cash and Darlega 1978). Similarity, in other words, appears to be important where there are few conditions other than likeness facilitating relationships. Aron and Aron (1986) argue that in selecting mates people first judge whether a relationship is possible on grounds of either similarity, proximity, reciprocal liking, or shared norms, and then, having at least one basis in hand, prefer a partner different in one or more of the remaining ways—an argument, in other words, in which first likenesses and then differences have a part.

What the mix of psychoanalytic self psychology and social exchange brings to this debate is a similar double prediction. It follows from combining the logic of selfobject transference with the logic of diminishing marginal utility, as reviewed earlier. In optimal relationships (i.e., relationships in which partners optimally frustrate one another and hence grow), partners first identify with one another—motivated to produce similarity in their evaluations—and then differentiate from each other—motivated to produce differences. So in their perceptions of one another, partners who are attracted to one another at first perceive increasing similarity and then increasing difference. Whatever motivates their attraction initially, the operation of marginal utility as part of the transference process yields increasing similarity and then increasing difference, in cycles. Extrapolated to interpersonal dealings more generally, the same phenomenon appears. The *less* a person "has" of identification from others, the more that person is likely to *want* similar friends or partners. But then the more of such identifications persons accumulate, the less they want further identification from others—the more, that is, they will find "differences" attractive. This implies, say, that sociometric stars would be more likely to choose friends different from themselves than would so-called isolates. The reason identification reduces the value of similarity is diminishing marginal utility, but the reason similarity is valuable in the first place is scarcity. And the equivalent of scarcity in psychological terms is a structural weakness—a deficit of structuration, or a weakening of existing strengths (cf. chap. 7).

Weaker expectations follow from the postulate of the bipolar self, considered alone. For example, the evidence from studies relating attraction to self-esteem, or attraction to confidence in interpersonal skills, is helpful in developing a few of these arguments. Self psychology would look at this literature from the point of view of introjected strengths or structural growth and might argue that deficits in mirrored strength lead to attraction based on similarity rather than complementarity or difference—based, that is, on mirroring transferences—whereas either deficits in idealized strength or excesses of self-esteem (interpreted as exhibitionism) would support attraction based on differences, particularly, of course, valued differences—hence, based on idealizing transferences. Thus, with a simple logic that derives directly from the concept of a bipolar self, we can produce predictions about when attraction will be based on similarity and when on difference—a double prediction that helps to bring a degree of order to observations that might otherwise seem inconsistent or understandable only ex post facto.

By this reasoning, persons with low self-esteem and a background of mirrored deficits (underresponsive caregiving), for example, would be predicted to choose friends similar to themselves at rates greater than would persons with high self-esteem. When we turn to the idealized area, persons without self-control (idealized deficits) would be expected contrariwise to choose persons different from themselves, whom they might idealize. The reason for each of these expectations, as we should now be able to understand, is that such choices can be interpreted as behaviors shaped by disintegration anxiety. Thus, exhibitionistic persons with apparently very high self-esteem (though actually a form of archaic grandiosity) would be expected to choose dissimilar friends—persons whom they might use as idealized selfobjects to help regulate the anxiety behind their exhibitionism and grandiosity. The precedent in infancy for this choice is the infant's original transfer of grandiosity to an idealized selfobject. Choices along these lines, in other words, would be predicted because they could be explained as efforts at structure building. Derivations about attraction should be like derivations about strong attachments. Persons will find something to like or idealize in others depending on what their own deficits are. If they have no deficits, then (just as significantly) the strength of their choices should also diminish, along with the relevance in their interpersonal choices of others' similarities or differences.

The ways others can be used as selfobjects to strengthen the self or to make a person feel better about himself or herself probably should be understood to follow any of the various lines we have discussed in this and earlier chapters. A person, as we have seen, can be strongly related to another even in a negative attachment, since mutual negative transference can be converted into self-esteem. An attraction paradigm must deal with hatred and dislike no less than with liking and attraction. All of these so-called derivations amount to hypotheses based on Kohut's developmental logic. Numerous other implications can also be seen to follow from the same framework; persons with low levels of self-control (idealized deficits) would be predicted to find persons different from themselves attractive. But specific predictions such as these should always follow a *ceteris paribus* assumption, since a person's history can make the way his or her deficits manifest themselves difficult to discern. This is especially true when we are considering persons who display deficits in both structural areas. Simultaneous deficits do not produce implications as clearly derived as the first-order considerations just examined. But such hybrid patterns could readily be studied in biographical research. In such cases, attachment patterns based on compound deficits should be isolated as separate styles, and the underlying regularities in attraction associated with each style then catalogued and studied.

Creatures of Feeling

In point of fact, much of the literature of the West, and a good deal of the painting and music and sculpture, is about the greatly moving personal feelings and volatile relationships we have been dissecting in this chapter. One claim, not far removed from Langer's (1942, 1953), is that art itself stands as a memorialization of such feeling in the perception of the artist; another is that art constitutes a merger demand upon an audience for recapitulating relationships that were once home to the feelings in question—that is, for responsiveness in one form or another. What is the connection? The main reason art and love are so much connected in the culture of the West is that both are dominated by idealization. Artistic activity attempts to construct cohesion out of fragmentation, esteem out of emptiness, responsiveness out of indifference, order out of disorder. Romance attempts to do the same. As a constructive process on the part of the person, not all the feelings associated with love are necessarily pleasant; but the good feelings generally outnumber the bad. Love makes persons feel better about themselves. This is because the good feelings associated with love, as with art, are feelings of transformation from a worse to a better state—feelings of growth and betterment, of being completed and strengthened as a person, of being uplifted and energized, of being protected and cared for, and of being worshipped and admired.

Yet the tumultuous and romantic lives led by many painters and writers document in stark and convincing detail—in dairies, letters, confessions—a rich mixture of feelings and ideation, often in bizarre patterns, that we have already considered in relation to our study of addictive attachments. So dependent are certain styles of art on feelings of one kind or another, in fact, that it is at least plausible to entertain the hypothesis that such feelings are sought by artists as conditions of their work. The artist who is in love with love, or the poet who luxuriates in a chronic melancholia, or the painter for whom rebellion is a condition for establishing artistic validity or who idealizes and then loves his model, have become so archetypal within Western society since the Italian Renaissance as to have become character types themselves. Many artists of this type impress us as feeling junkies. They use their art as a means of controlling their feelings in one way or another, or as a vehicle for imagining environments of responsiveness attuned to their deficits. No less than many others are addicted to TV or alcohol, these great creative figures

return to their feelings to replenish and energize the imaginative visions powering their work. In forms of experience like the strong attachments we studied earlier—forms where feelings are shaped—they can intensify and
energize these creative states. It is toward such experiential forms, therefore,
that many artists often seem compulsively drawn.

Comparable claims can be made about romance (Peele 1975). Some persons are addicted to it, or to qualities of experience associated with it. Often
it is the romance itself they crave, not just the partner as selfobject. Relationships in which romance flourishes are themselves forms enabling partners to
feel better about themselves—its dynamics pump them up, raise their self-
esteem, and underwrite their self-worth. While these effects on feelings happen in all romantic attachments, only some become permanently addicting in
the sense developed earlier—namely, in failing to produce the transmuting
internalizations that strengthen self, and thereby in not proportionately less-
ening the strength of a person's attachments. For this reason we call them
strong attachments. Even so, there is an early phase in every romantic attachment when the dynamics of interaction produce what appears to be mutual
addiction. Partners cannot do without one another, they become so desperately dependent.

One consequence of this way of thinking appears in reasoning about how
multiple dependencies get combined. No less than addicting substances can
be combined in extraordinary patterns, so can interpersonal attachments. Joint
dependency on cocaine and heroin by an addict, despite the contradictory
neurochemical effects of these two substances, is no more bizarre than odd
combinations of subversive political activity and religious communalism we
find in the lives of some nineteenth-century utopians. Similarly, some forms
of strong attachment can be used to wean a person from other forms, just as
when one drug is used to diminish an addict's dependency on another. One
place this clearly appears is in the trade-off between love and politics. Lord
Acton's famous admonition—"Power tends to corrupt and absolute power
corrupts absolutely"—is another way of saying that power is addictive no less
than romance. Among some persons typically vulnerable to romantic attachments, like adolescents, certain forms of idealistic political activism are thus
alternatives to romantic love. Each form of attachment is based on idealized
deficits, and each runs on processes of positive feedback like idealizing transference that drive systems into nonequilibrium conditions.

Power in something like Acton's sense might thus be conceptualized as a
variable generated interpersonally by dynamics of interaction that drive social
systems into far-from-equilibrium states and produce extreme dependencies.
Some of the conditions and by-products of these dynamics are among the
important foundations for the organization of social life more generally—
particularly complex social life. Our analysis of romance, thus, points toward

an analysis of power. In the next chapter, I begin this analysis by reconsidering the phenomenon Max Weber called charisma, and in particular charismatic power. We shall be able to see in considering the nonequilibrium dynamics involving charismatic power a number of critical phenomena we weren't able to see clearly in studying romance and love. One of these is how such dynamics sometimes produce phase transitions marked by what earlier I called bifurcations—sudden changes in the organization of a system marked by the emergence of greater complexity.

6

Power and Charisma: The Release of the Romantic Impulse

Personal Leadership and Personal Power

Every romantic relationship is marked in some degree by its partners' attempts to control one another. The main reason for this is that each has become so deeply dependent on the other. Sometimes their mutual control can appropriately be described in terms of *power,* a concept by which sociologists generally denote the capacity one person has to produce effects in a second, apart from whatever the other person's wishes or interests are.[1] Sometimes these effects are predetermined by factors exogenous to the partners' relationship—for example, by the control each exercises over resources the other needs. As often, however, they arise on the basis of strengths or capacities each has that develop within their interaction itself—like the capacity to serve the other as a responsive selfobject. Understood in this small-scale way, power arises as a relational phenomenon—that is, as an emergent capacity of actors to produce effects in others, as described by their effective personal control over one another. Although we can see quite clearly how such control appears in fields sustaining romantic attachments, power is a far more general phenomenon. Indeed, it is an emergent property of *every* field of social interaction. Even when institutionalized in social organization as part of relationships of authority, power still fluctuates in interaction fields by virtue of forces of personal control emerging within them.

Because power in this emergent and personal sense sometimes is manifested in the effects it has on feelings, it too can be addicting. This is evident both in what Lord Acton described as power's corrupting effects on persons who exercise it, as well as in the deep dependency it sometimes generates in those who are manipulated by it. These dependency-generating and "corrupting" effects can readily be understood through an analysis of interaction fields controlled by selfobject transferences. The subject of power, thus, becomes another extension of the basic theoretical and conceptual tools developed so far in this book. To analyze power as emergent control in interaction, moreover, by no means limits the relevance of this concept to understanding only small-scale interaction. This becomes obvious when we remember that Max Weber's depiction and analysis of charismatic leadership is one of the foundations in sociological theory for the analysis of power more generally. Grasping and extending Weber's analysis of charisma within this newer framework, therefore, may provide a way for us to approach other sociological phenomena, beyond personal power and leadership, that he also had in view. In this chapter, we shall examine personal leadership and charisma. In the next, we shall consider structural phenomena in society that are based on the depersonalization of leadership and power.

Charisma Revisited

Every effort to conceptualize a purely *personal* element in power should stand indebted to Max Weber's theory of charisma. Most discussions of extraordinary personal leadership, for example, have been drawn quite naturally to the legacy left in his analysis (Willner and Willner 1965). This is because Weber came very close to isolating, as part of leader-follower relationships, the ways elementary social organization ultimately rests on foundations of personally exercised control. Implicitly, Weberian theory developed from the premise that social organization of every kind finds its origins historically in intense small-scale relationships between extraordinarily creative (or destructive) figures and their followers.

The widespread appeal of Weber's concept of charisma, of course, flies in the face of his own stringent efforts to define it in a limiting way—as a fleeting quality of great instability, appearing in response to "all *extra* ordinary needs, i.e., those which *transcend* the sphere of everyday economic activities" (Weber 1968a, 1111). Weber chose examples of charismatic figures— Saint Francis, Achilles, Cú Chulainn, Joseph Smith, Napoleon, Jesus, and others—intended to delineate historical and sociological conditions of charisma's appearance and to purge the concept of superfluous content. A certain narrowness in Weber's conceptualization resulted from this qualifying work and has been the subject both of commentary on the part of later generations of Weberian scholars (e.g., Alexander 1983) and of efforts to deepen and extend his thought to its full potential (esp. Shils 1965, 1975; Eisenstadt 1968). As this critical tradition has occasionally implied, therefore, a view of charisma acknowledging its ubiquity in social life would have been more in line with the real premises of Weber's thought and of his own wide-ranging historical and comparative research—work always informed by a sense of sociological phenomena as complex mixtures of forces.

One effort after another has been made in the sociological literature to transfix once and for all the shimmering and pure image of charisma Weber deployed so confidently in his many discussions of leadership, prophecy, magic, power, and authority. My aim here is not to produce yet another exegesis of Weber's mixed usages, but to follow a line of thought that promises to clarify some of the underlying conditions of charisma's appearance and spread. The methodological scaffolding of Weberian analysis—its use of ideal types to grasp multidimensional sociological realities—probably has tended to confuse the empirical issue of where we shall find charisma: as Weber claimed, nowhere but in its fleeting traces, like vapor trails in a cloud chamber, or, as others have argued (Shils 1975), wherever we are sensitive enough to discern it. Reanalysis of the inherent psychology of charismatic claims and attributions will help to clarify this matter, mainly by allowing us to understand charisma as part of a larger class of affective phenomena. In the first place, the extreme dependency of disciples or followers immediately suggests that there is a root for charismatic appeal in experiences somehow analogous to those of infancy. In particular, the propensity of followers to attribute charismatic qualities to a leader seems akin to the developmental readiness of an infant to "discover" greatness in a parental figure. If this likeness is taken seriously, the hypothesis suggests itself that charisma's appeal is rooted in what we have discussed in earlier chapters as the "idealizing selfobject transference." A focus on selfobject transferences, in addition, will enable us to take as problematic a leader's own acknowledgment of charisma in himself or herself, and will also direct us to look for the dynamics of this self-empowering acknowledgment in transferential arrangements sustained with followers.

Natural Supernaturalism

Examined in the longer course of the history of ideas, charisma is but one of the concepts by which nineteenth-century writers made their way toward a secularized idea of divinity. Weber himself appropriated the idea from the German church historian Rudolf Sohm, who had used the term, taken from the Greek translation of the New Testament (2 Corinthians), to describe the Roman church as a "charismatic organization" (Sohm 1892). In the hands of a believer like Sohm, charisma was understood to denote divine possession and inspiration (see Roth 1968). For Weber, however, the idea became a vehicle for conceptualizing empirically how sacredness entered the world, a matter understandable, he thought, from observations of the behavior of actual men. Weber's own use of the term thus begins in his *Religionssoziologie,* where he examines the activities of religious and near-religious figures— prophets, magicians, priests. It is only later, in a generalization of his thinking from religious to political subjects, that the more familiar concept of "pure" or "genuine" charisma appears as part of the argument he advances about authority and leadership.

As an example of typical nineteenth-century ideas, charisma should also be understood as a variant on one of the recurring themes in the Western concept of love—the theme of passionate and inspiring personal attachment and devotion. Profoundly romantic in nature, charismatic qualities were typically embodied in idealized portraits of heroic figures produced by nineteenth-century writers. Grafted onto the public personalities of men such as Byron, images of heroism were elevated into popular regard by the works of poet-prophets like Shelley or philosopher-seers like Fichte, Schelling, and Hegel. Romantic concepts of this force—Carlyle ([1836] 1908) called it "natural supernaturalism" (Abrams 1971)—are thus connected to Weber's analysis of charisma, making his thinking about leadership and religion akin to the larger but parallel effort of Dilthey (1962) and others to situate biographical facts in a framework amenable to systematic reflection, all the while appropriating for examination under a temporal light hitherto religious and philosophical subjects. Here was an idea, not the preserve of ecclesiastical scholarship, of inspired relationship—of dutiful connection to another person marked by the full force of religious devotion.

The mixture of religious and political themes in Weber's concept has created what Clifford Geertz (1977, 171) has described as a "difficult richness." While absorbing Weber's sympathy toward emotional forces modern society seemed to be purging from everyday life, it also signalled the potential inherent in all personal relationships for the abuse of power and the triumph of despotic forces. Such divergent and competing tendencies within charisma were the source of Weber's own ambivalence toward the notion. The positive side—the prophet, say, leading his or her flock toward freedom or salvation—celebrated great personalities who stood apart from the ordinary preoccupations of everyday life. The negative side—the demogogue demanding obedience—pointed to the abuse of power. Despite such inherently mixed qualities, the positive side had the upper hand in Weber's view of history.

In particular, Weber's fears about the obliteration of the individual by industrialism and rationalization turned his mind favorably toward the transcendent figure of the great man in history, and gave a certain passion to his defense of heroic ethics against the claims of democracy (see Brubaker 1984; Levine 1985; Schwentker 1987). Against the relentlessly impersonal forces of reason and modernity, charisma represented for Weber what Dow (1978) calls the "incarnate life-force." Ultimately, as many Weber scholars have seen, charisma was a force associated in his mind with emotionality and the release of feelings—a force capable of discovering and giving expression to deep energies of instinct and feeling, with the power literally "to revolutionize men from within."

Signalling an emotionality in danger of being lost from modern life, charisma thus resonated conceptually with the intense and persistent *Kulturpessimismus* of German intellectual life throughout the nineteenth century and beyond—its romantic preoccupations with the irreclaimable *Gemütlichkeit* of simpler times, its pervasive antimodernism, its ambivalence regarding the spread of functional relationships and the disappearance of community, its Nietzschean despair over apparent moral nihilism (Kalberg 1987, 1985). Objectivity in Weber's view required analyzing such emotional forces in the history of civilization as no more than events in nature itself, like the "caprice or carelessness of lightning, rain, or wind" (Dow 1978, 85). Loathsome or worshipful, they represented moments when people's worlds were turned by forces arising from what Weber sensed to be foundations of life itself. In this intuition, Weber came close to Freud's correspondingly pessimistic conclusions about the destiny of feelings in civilization.[2] This deep similarity between their systems of thought has its limits—it has been noted on several occasions (e.g., McIntosh 1969; Hummel 1975)—but nowhere is the convergence more relevant than in the context of making sense of charisma.

The Hidden Transference

As recent attention to Weber's concept has sought to reveal, the two sides to charismatic relationships—the ambitious leader with his or her claim, the dependent followers who acknowledge it—are alive with a hidden psychology Weber himself largely ignored (McIntosh 1969; Bord 1975). Charles Camic's (1980) work, in particular, moves the discussion again in the direction of psychoanalytic ideas, where numerous conceptual tools are available for refining and differentiating earlier discussions. The power of Camic's analysis comes from using a logic derived from the classic psychoanalytic drive-structure model.

Weber himself characterized the needs giving rise to attributions of charisma as *Ausseralltäglichkeit*, a condition implying, in view of his overriding preoccupation with the conditions of economic rationality and political stability, charisma's much discussed incompatibility with regular (economic, occupational) activities. Following suggestions from the ego psychology literature (e.g., Rapaport 1957), Camic argues that ego passivity with respect to various needs—id needs, superego needs, ego-ideal needs, or dependency needs—is a precondition for the attribution of extraordinary qualities to "objects" in a position to gratify those needs. He thus offers an analysis capable of differ-

entiating the types of specialness attributed to need-gratifying leaders—
respectively, uncanniness, excellence, sacredness, and omnipotence—based
on the types of needs in respect to which the ego is passive. Camic also
recognizes from psychoanalytic writing that the prototype for these attributions is the phenomenon of transference, generalized, following Freud's own
analysis in *Group Psychology and the Analysis of the Ego* (1921), beyond the
clinical setting.[3]

Charisma and Its Transformations

DOUBLE-SIDED TRANSFERENCES   But consider Camic's deductions about
the basis of charisma in unmet needs of the personality. If Camic is right in
his deductions, he is still only half-right—half-right, that is, in respect to the
double-sided transference structure inherent in relationships. Heeding the ad-
vice of object relations theorists (Sandler 1981; Kernberg 1975), what our
own analysis directs us to attend are the ways *mutual* transferences influence
the course of relationships, charismatic no less than others. To double the
transferential picture of a charismatic relationship is then to admit both the
leader and the led, the prophet and the disciple, the warlord and his band, or
the great king and his *trustis*. This demands a double-sided (or multisided)
analysis, for which the reasoning developed to this point has prepared us.

Like Camic, many others have analyzed charisma exclusively from the
point of view of the onlooker, emphasizing in its development the role of the
audience. Without doubt, charisma in Weber's sense is an inherently social
phenomena, undefinable outside a group context. This has been powerful
justification for analyzing charisma in relation to the needs of onlookers.
Something of a small industry has arisen, for example, bent on showing the
respects in which charisma thus amounts to a phenomenon of attribution
(among the most intelligent papers along these lines is Bord's analysis, 1975).
Weber himself, fully aware of how followers' circumstances affect their readiness to respond to charisma, nevertheless gave equal attention to the leader's
side in the charismatic arrangement. A charismatic leader, he reminds us, has
to *claim* his or her charisma.

The fact so often observed, and so much emphasized by Weber, is that
charisma as claimed is often *perceived* as a disembodied, cosmic or meta-
physical force, something by which persons become "possessed" and want
others to acknowledge in them. A magician must perform tricks, certainly, as
a warlord must plunder villages and come away with booty, or a prophet
deliver moral orations or exemplary actions (and perhaps, like Jesus, do a
little magic as well). But on top of these "proofs," leaders must also appear
to be full of conviction—as convinced of their own powers or message as
they expect others to be. Like the "ideologue" Nahirny (1962) discusses,

leaders might then think of themselves as the mere instrument of a transfiguring purpose. Between their beliefs and their audience, they would typically interpose themselves in a salvationary role, urging their audience to believe in the imminence of catastrophe or apocalypse, in the ineptitude, waywardness, or depravity of reigning authorities, or in the corruption and ineffectiveness of established practices and institutions. Or, if they are figures closer, say, to the example of the "beserk" warrior Weber frequently employed to illustrate what he meant by "genuine" or "pure" charisma—the *echt*-heroic figure, like Cú Chulainn, inflamed by the rage of battle—they would exhibit in their own behavior such inspiring or contagious states of excitement as would compel "unreflective imitation" on the part of their audience—the way, say, members of combat units are expected unreflectively to follow the trained heroism of junior officers, who are taught (Weber perhaps would say "charismatically educated") to orient their platoons, through their own example, in the direction of the greatest incoming enemy firepower. As Weber emphasized, such belief-possessed and heroic behavior initially serves to emphasize, in the eyes of its observers, some crisis or need and then to make a claim upon them for merger, a claim that subsequently becomes a matter of duty.

A purely skeptical outlook on charismatic behavior would suggest that it is undertaken with this claim in view: to develop and maintain the devotion of follows. Leaders in the prophetic mode, for instance, must persuade others the moment of truth is near (if they don't already believe it is) and must convince them the leader knows how to save them. It is the leader's ability "to accentuate the sense of being in a desperate predicament," in Robert Tucker's (1968) analysis, that encourages others to follow him or her. "You are my children," he tells them in one way or another, "follow me as you would your father."[4] But as observation of charismatic figures has revealed, there is in their own conviction about such claims a matter as much to be explained as in the devotion of their followers. To dismiss such figures as mere charlatans or con artists would be to dismiss as unreal the social and psychological dynamics that enable such illusional conviction to develop.

THE HUNGER FOR CHARISMA   What is charismatic in one person's eyes won't necessarily be charismatic in another's, of course. Their respective cultural settings and their various needs and competencies make charisma a relative matter to different onlookers. There are thus patterned reasons why only in some cultures an epileptic or hysteric is regarded as holy while in other cultures such persons are shunned or banished. (For example, as Liah Greenfield [1985, 132, n. 40] notes, in traditional Russian culture the word for "excitable insane" is *blajeny,* "blessed," a connection echoed in many other cultural settings.) Clearly, there are also conditions of deprivation or stress—

fasting, flagellation, ordeal, drugging—with which communities in the past have induced in neophytes (sometimes in the incumbents of specific "charismatic roles") "typical" experiences of extraordinary behavior—visions, most often, but also heroism, self-sacrifice, and so forth. Such practices "produce" a charismatic arrangement—an intrusion of charisma to feed the "charisma hunger" (in Erikson's [1958] phrase) of the audience. The same is true of national holidays, rituals, coronations (Shils and Young 1956), and other ceremonialized charismatic moments—periodic occasions for the revitalization of practices and values depleted of salience by routine life.

A number of the sociological and other conditions supportive of charismatic arrangements Weber himself catalogued, such as the removal of followers from regular economic activity, causing them to live on gifts or booty. Some of these conditions, as we can now recognize, clearly amount to disinhibiting practices centered on positive feedback mechanisms that enable the "systems" composed of leader and led to be driven into far-from-equilibrium conditions. Weber typically illustrated what he meant by "pure charisma," for example, with instances of excited states, like "ecstasy," that he knew might be induced "by drugs, tobacco or alcohol," or by "sexuality," or in connection with "ritual and dance" (see Weber 1968a, 401, 535; also chap. 3 above).

On top of these considerations of feedback in interaction are those conditions of charisma more to the center of the Weberian perspective—profound moments of world-historical disorder and change, when people looked beyond their own lives for solutions to questions of meaning or personal direction or for help in the face of catastrophic order-destroying events—plagues, battles, natural disasters—that have left them helpless and adrift. Such times make people vulnerable to the claims of powerful personalities, presumably, as Camic sees, by making the gratification of their own needs and requirements matters over which they seem to themselves to have no control. A leader at such moments is like an extension of the self, prepared to do for it what it cannot do for itself—gear it into the world, into a baffling and disordered reality, full of fearful omens and threatening prospects, all to be controlled, circumvented, dispersed, subdued, dispelled.

According to the Kohutian logic we have developed, what the leader actually does is to present herself as a vehicle for idealizing transferences. She must then be prepared to accept from a weakened audience a transfer to herself of some part of the "omnipotence" of their own "archaic grandiose selves"—actually, she must call it forth. The way she does this, psychologically speaking, is to offer her idealizing audience a degree of responsiveness that results in its *over*stimulation, a condition that must then be dealt with on their part through further idealizing transference. The transferential paradigm here is again the model of the infant and the overresponsive, nonoptimal parent. Both leader and audience must be predisposed in one way or another to seek the replication of this relational configuration. What makes for this predisposition? In the case of the audience, Kohut's logic would have it that the sociocultural "environment" (understood as the equivalent of an infant's primary caregiver) must somehow have failed or frustrated its dependent population, undermining its capacities or failing to mirror or call forth such strengths as might support self-reliant and autonomous behavior. This would predispose strong attachments of all kinds, including those on idealized self-objects.

Consider this argument about the cultural environment in more detail. A sociocultural environment so unadapted to the needs of a population is a condition that can be understood in several senses: it may be the product of a long-term historical drift of the conditions of life away from those for which a population's culture has prepared it, so that something like *anomie* predisposes its members to search for "solutions." Rumors of a messiah, for example, riddled the sectarian Jewish world in the century or so before the appearance of Jesus, as Roman rule and schismatic tensions undermined the capacity of traditional rabbinic values or practices—study of Torah, scriptural exegesis—to meet the needs of the illiterate Jewish majority (Neusner 1973, 1972; Smith 1973, 1978; Wilson 1954). In such circumstances, the sociocultural world itself must be understood as failing to support self-direction, its own "objects" having failed in relation to the needs of the population—as, for example, Neusner has argued rabbinic exegesis failed the mass of the Jewish population by finding in Scripture only esoteric and legalistic matters far removed from the popular wish for an ingathering of exiles and the coming of messianic times.

More visible perhaps are catastrophic events within a single lifetime—epidemics, incurable illnesses or injuries, natural disasters, economic ruin, criminal victimization—that can presumably so unhinge a person's world as to predispose a search for new cultural selfobjects (Kohut 1984, 194; Wolf 1980; Ornstein 1981). This is a matter on which the strength of traditional or other culture can act as a brake, even in the face of such catastrophe. What anthropologists (Fortes and Evans-Pritchard 1940) used to call "dispersed stateless societies"—by which they had in mind decentralized and fragmented tribal societies such as the Ibo of eastern Nigeria in the nineteenth century—were far more "receptive" to Western values, for example, than were traditionally hierarchical tribal societies such as the Zulu or the Yoruba or the even more centralized Islamic Fulani and Hausa (Ottenberg 1959; Green 1964; Jones 1941). In the traumatic and culturally disorganizing period of colonial intrusion—a period, in the Nigerian hinterland, as much disorganized by indigenous slaving as by contact with the British—Ibo "receptivity" to Western values thus proceeded at a pace far exceeding the assimilation of these values into Yoruba and Hausa culture. (LeVine's [1971] study of "achievement motivation" in Nigeria documents these tribal differentials among the major Nigerian groups.) The search for new cultural selfobjects, as these comparative considerations suggest, can thus be inhibited by the strength of traditional culture and social organization. Or, to put this another way, the degree of integration and "cohesion" (Kohut's word) of a "selfobject milieu," either personal or cultural, serves to diminish the force behind any transferential process—any process aimed at strengthening self or at structure building.

There are many examples of this in the history of the West, including most prominently those illustrating the absence of these inhibiting strengths of culture and social structure. The preoccupation of the nineteenth century with heroic figures and with questions of how life should be lived, for example, is said to have its roots in the way the French Revolution so dramatically served as a watershed for the "conceptual scheme" of feudalism (Ford 1963)—revealing how empty the surviving terms of the feudal image of society were as a model for a society already much transformed in the direction of bourgeois and industrial values. In such populations we may expect to find a readiness to transfer to new selfobjects some portion of the grandiosity and omnipotence attached in other times or by earlier generations to different selfobjects—from royal houses, say, to revolutionary prophets, from revolutionaries to heroic dictators, or from grand aristocrats to the heroes of popular imagination. Kohut's logic similarly leads us to expect hunger for charisma in environments marked by defective mirroring or repudiated heroes—defects, that is, in the capacity of existing sociocultural models to map adequately the true qualities or resources of a population or to call forth its undeveloped (or release its repressed) capacities. As Weber himself emphasized, the hunger for charisma appears because there is failure to meet the "needs" of a population facing extraordinary and unprecedented circumstances.

Cultural selfobjects thus have an important role in relation to understanding charisma, and help explain why charisma sometimes becomes the extraordinary force for social and cultural change Weber studied. An important difference between romantic love and charisma, for example, is brought into view by the part cultural selfobjects have in promoting charisma. Whereas romance, as we have analyzed it, appears typically among persons who exhibit deficits of personal strength, charisma as Weber attempted to study it is understandable not alone as a product of personal disintegration and weakness but as a social and cultural phenomenon. That is, it depends for its spread on mechanisms that tie together into a common system of interaction persons for whom cultural selfobjects have failed in some sense. All such interactively coupled persons then would be engaged in search behavior responsive to similar appeals—predisposed, in particular, to look for idealized responsiveness and, perhaps, for new cultural selfobjects. Also caught up in the same collective search, of course, might be persons who are undergoing personal fragmentation, apart from the failure of cultural selfobjects to serve them adequately. But charisma on the scale that became interesting to Weber was a function of matters like sociocultural disintegration or disjunction—these and any other circumstances that produced systemic responsiveness and attachment needs within a large population. Charisma, naturally enough, can arise in or be confined to small-scale settings, as well. But where it plays a role in large-scale social or cultural change, this capacity to affect large populations made it of interest to Weber. It then became a key to sociocultural change. This potential to spread and to affect large-scale systems becomes understandable in view of several kinds of analysis, including the perspective of dissipative structure theory.

Where Kohutian (and much other psychological) theory fails in dealing with matters like charisma's spread is in operating with primitive notions of the feedback mechanisms at work in such complex, large-scale systems. Since this is precisely the area where the analysis of nonequilibrium systems has deepened in the last decade or so, new understandings of complex feedback processes become tools to refine and expand Kohutian analysis. Complex feedback relationships, for example, are precisely what are at issue in understanding charisma's growth and spread, and these we can begin to understand only by grasping the connection between larger selfobject milieus and smaller interaction fields.

FEEDBACK PROCESSES IN SELFOBJECT MILIEUS   The questions raised by the integration or disintegration of sociocultural systems in the immediate environment of an actor, in particular, are two: first, whether the larger "selfobject milieus" of which such an actor is a member will operate so as to amplify or damp the fluctuations occurring in his or her own responsiveness to an idealized selfobject; and, second, whether these fluctuations will spread beyond the immediate region of their interaction. Both of these questions raise the issue of whether external selfobject milieus contain negative feedback structures, or whether the organization of such milieus is such as eventually to produce a damping effect in the immediate region of the milieu where a fluctuation arises. A small charismatic circle in Weimar Germany, for example, had more chance *not* to find its effects damped than a similar circle in Victorian England. Charismatic circles could arise in either place, but on the whole would encounter greater resistance to growth and spread in the latter.

These ideas about milieus become very abstract in theory and are hard to grasp apart from concrete examples. As a general rule, however, any surrounding structuration of milieu acts to damp fluctuations spreading outside of itself from charismatic activism and recruitment. For this reason, as Weber emphasized, such collectivities are often withdrawn from the world and seldom if ever thrive when members are obliged to conform to expectations or fulfill obligations arising from external commitments to structures like workplaces or families. Jonestown could *only* exist in isolation from civilization, corrupt as civilization was believed to be. Such segregation of charismatic collectivities from a larger culture and society effectively creates circumstances that support positive feedback, amplifying inherent dynamics of charismatic relationships into far-from-equilibrium conditions. Members' commitments and dependency thus deepen, as transferential forces work steadily, on the one hand, to increase the degree to which every member relies exclusively on the regulation supplied by an idealized external selfobject, the leader, and, on the other, to make the leader wholly dependent on the idealization supplied by followers to support his or her own fragile self-esteem and convictions.

In effect, the segregation of a charismatic circle from a surrounding society supports positive feedback within it the same way as would the *dis*integration of some larger selfobject milieu. By disintegration, in this sense, I refer to some separation of culture from person, such that culture no longer supplies negative feedback or serves as a vehicle (or set of vehicles) to stabilize omnipotence. In Kohutian theory, it must be remembered, cultural systems need to be viewed in the first place as the systems where infants find substitutes for their caregivers and for responsiveness—hence, *cultural* selfobjects. Cultural systems are surely *more* than that, but they nevertheless function as caregiver substitutes and selfobjects in some minimal developmental sense as well. So a cultural system that fails as a caregiver substitute undermines a person's ability to get along apart from strong attachments. Cultural disintegration, therefore, predisposes the search for responsiveness that can yield the potentiating feedback effects we have been examining in relation to romance and charisma.

What does cultural disintegration mean? In this analysis, it means the loss of stable cultural objects related to the self as selfobjects and as introjects. The Ibo whose native religion dissolves in the face of Western rationalism's challenges, thus, might be said to be witnessing cultural disintegration. The Puritan after the seventeenth century who finds his or her religion similarly unadapted to the conditions of life, as did Emerson in the nineteenth century, likewise could be described as signalling in his or her behavior effects of cultural disintegration. Emerson's Divinity School address, calling for an end to Christianity, is a strong signal of cultural disintegration in this sense— of the outmoding or failure of cultural selfobjects, predisposing the search for their replacements that, in Emerson's case, resulted in his own cultural celebrity.

Plainly, then, Kohutian theory, along with most social systems theory, works implicitly with a model of the acting person as one level of functioning to be taken into account in the analysis of self or system. This much is clear in such distinctions as those we have used between personal and cultural self-objects, or between external selfobjects and introjects. It is also implicit in the dynamic analysis of external "selfobject milieus" like the family or the small groups immediately surrounding an actor, and the more distant milieus formed by yet other small groups, by associations and organizations, communities, and so on. But even while these multiple levels are present in theory, they tend to be collapsed in practice by the focus of psychological explanation on individual self. So long as the focus of theoretical explanation is on self and not milieu, this kind of theory will help to isolate the immediate psychological and interpersonal aspects of charisma, but will not address the issues of amplification or damping.

Of course, a connection between these problems at different levels is at work. The psychologically relevant property of selfobject milieus is whether they support integrated or cohesive functioning, which means that they contain structures and selfobjects enabling self-regulation and supporting self-esteem (and related functions). If they do not have these structures, we would then characterize them in some degree as fragmented and incohesive. This fragmentation clearly has consequences for phenomena occuring on a scale larger than that of the single self or two-person interaction.

But before we turn to questions of charisma's role in social change, we need to explore further its dynamics in interaction.

Magic and Awe-inspiring Omnipotence

Consider these dynamics of interaction in a more focused illustration: the magician who discovers in his audience an unusual degree of credulousness. As Miyahara (1983, 370) suggests, it is magical charisma "that comes closest to being [Weber's] generic conception."

The readiness on the part of an audience to "believe" in magical powers arises, in psychological terms, from the "need for an awe-inspiring idealized parental imago," as Kohut (1971, 302) argues. This might come about from any number of structure-depriving experiences in childhood—the absence of parents, for example, a condition not at all uncommon as a consequence, say, of catastrophic natural events or warfare—as well as from sociocultural disjunctions of the sort just discussed—the failure of cultural selfobjects. In such circumstances, children fail to develop the psychic structures that transform and stabilize the "archaic grandiose self," structures that gradually accommodate and then transmute strengths mirrored into the self from others and retrieved through mergers with yet other objects of which they can be a part. Subsequent transfers of omnipotence to idealized selfobjects are manifestations of the hunger for powerful figures, an appetite that arises out of the inability of the child to stabilize its own sense of self-worth or to give direction to its life. The charismatic magician plays on these needs and impulses and hungers, and indeed works to reinforce the regression that carries the audience back to the credulous position of childhood's hopes and fears about the universe. The magician presents an illusion, and presents it to convince an audience of the ability to manipulate forces beyond their perception.

Numinousness saturates this illusion the magician creates, the way it presence is felt by the credulous in cathedrals or at the edge of great canyons or staring into the deep night sky. Tremendous mystery, creeping flesh, the sense of something unperceived, incomprehensible, overwhelming, imminent—we respond, as in Otto's (1925) exposition of the idea of the holy, with fascination, attracted and repelled simultaneously, attracted by the availability of a vehicle immense enough to serve our archaic grandiosity's needs, repelled by the fear, perhaps, that immersion in such an object would lead irrevocably into disintegration and incoherence, a step beyond the point from which we might recover control of ourselves.[5] Yet it is precisely this pneuma, this breath of the *Ganz Andere,* that is so extraordinarily exhilarating to the person psychologically predisposed to be "responsive" to charisma.

Whether the magician's tricks or the audience's needs initially establish the charismatic situation is beside the point. There is a certain symmetry of needs on the two sides of this arrangement. In some situations it may very well be merger demands made by needy members of an audience that activate a performer's charismatic posture. What clinical material makes perfectly clear is that an audience to a show of magic is not usually passive. The demands made upon caregiver surrogates for accommodating omnipotence induce the caregiver's need to conform as much as possible to the infant's wishes—not to disappoint them, if possible. Fear of losing such an imagined audience, an audience all the time craving yet additional mystification, for example, is said to have motivated Harry Houdini to push himself time and time again to perform ever more dangerous illusions. Couple the demanding observer to the caregiver who is desperately afraid of losing the audience and you have a potent charismogenic situation. What this mix produces in the behavior of the prophet, the magician, or the warlord we have seen—risk-taking exhibitionism supported by conviction and grandiosity, and connected within the area of the idealized parental imago to predispositions to fantasy, illusion, and strong belief. But when we look for this mix in the larger context of the charismatic group, we now have behavior of several parties to fit into the pattern—the audience or followers in a relationship of strong attachment to the leader, as well as the leader. The leader now demands and gets idealization, and we have a situation that amplifies her grandiosity and conviction to extraordinary heights. In return, she produces in her followers an ever more adventurous, stimulated, and exhilarated condition that substitutes for their deficits of mirrored strength. It fills them with excitation, which they continue to stabilize by repeated idealizing transferences. This circle of transference—the leader's exhibitionism and mirroring, the followers' voyeurism and idealization—is what constitutes the positive feedback in such extraordinary groups.

EXHIBITIONISM, FLIRTATION, PROVOCATIVENESS   No real encounter of a leader and an audience is ever quite so uncomplicated as even this discussion of magician and audience suggests. Nor is it ever the pure and undiluted product of a single sort of neediness confronting a single figure specialized in one pure kind of need gratification. Just as in all real relationships there is a mixture of transferences, so the leader-dependent case is no different. A powerful warrior might seem exemplary in the moral sense, a perfection of his type, or a prophet might perform miracles alongside sermonizing. Every real connection of leader and led, therefore, requires its own explication and analysis. Even so, each real case is no less historically specific for yet seeming an instance of the general model of charismatic relationships, and the general form of the relationship is clear. The leader is a vehicle for the idealizing transferences of an audience, the audience for the leader's mirroring transferences. Lasswell (1948, 62) pointed to this element when discussing the "dramatizing" character of certain political figures. "The term [dramatizing]," he wrote, "is not in general use but refers to several well-understood phenomena whose underlying feature is the demand for immediate affective response from others. The dramatizing character may resort to traces of exhibitionism, flirtatiousness, provocativeness, indignation." If she adds to her appeal with magic, what she seeks is the response from an audience that will keep in place what Kohut calls the "unaltered omniscience" of an archaic grandiose self, the idealizing response that supports her primitive grandiosity. Robespierre, says Hannah Arendt in *On Revolution* (1965), had exactly such a "theatrical" character, a disposition he shared with the other men who "enacted the Revolution" (cf. Trilling 1971, 69).

There is always present in the performance of such persons the implication that they will abandon their audience the moment it fails to adore them or to amplify their grandiosity. Vulnerability to slights is a sure signal of the sensitive dependence this personality carries into reading the smallest cues from those in its audience, moving its performance here and there, hovering to cover the greatest possible combination of needs, and always keeping individuals enthralled by whatever devices necessary. What structures this relationship from the standpoint of leaders is a failure to find within themselves a selfobject sufficiently strengthened in their own unmirrored history to shape realistic ambitions, firm the ego for self-initiated action, and support a realistic level of self-esteem. For all these reasons, the leader needs idealizing disciples or followers.

The dramatizing element in charisma has its analogue in one side of the "adaptation" (to use Winnicott's word) of the parent to an infant's developmental readiness. The parent tuned to respond to an infant's burbling and faulty exhibitions is something of an "environment" in which the infant can discover its as yet unperceived capacities—particularly when they are matters others want to amplify or shape. Often a parent's dramatizing response amounts to an appropriation and enlargement of the infant's own behavior, mirroring back to it on a larger scale what it has just done. Even when this mirroring amounts to no more than a playful echo of the infant's own sounds, the infant is learning to trust an environment attuned to itself. At the same time, amplification by the parent also enables the child to find in this trusted environment vehicles large enough to accommodate its own grandiosity.

SELF-ENCLOSING MYSTIFICATIONS Related to dramatizing and amplification is the parent's fascination with the infant's behavior. In this we can also find the root of another property of charismatic figures—the tendency to discover in themselves the magical, mysterious forces others also perceive.

A parent's sense of baby's "magic"—finding in the infant evidence of things enchanted and miraculous—is clearly one of those "projective identifications" with the baby akin to transference—and is also one source of a baby's "power" to inspire in its parents a superficial mapping onto themselves of its own baby talk and gestures, the mapping that amounts to mirroring. It is but a step further along in this chain of thought to realize how such parental mirroring is motivated by the wish to maintain baby's love, a wish that in some cases gets confused with the parent's own fears of abandonment. The parent who fears not having the unconditional love of the infant is signalling a deficiency of his or her own childhood. Such persons, scarred by evidence from their own lives that parental love is not unconditionally available—an ambivalent, distant, or distracted mother, say, or a mother unable to allow her child to be "alone"—give proof of the repetitive search for ever-new ways by which the sense of self-worth might be secured. The failure to find interesting and strengthening objects within oneself, coupled to the absence of structures to neutralize and diminish grandiose pretensions, produces a personality given to the kinds of dramatizing effects and spacious claims Lasswell had in mind.

Beyond mere dramatizing behavior, charismatic appeal also rests frequently in illusional constructions that are central to the defense against fears. The special case of the charismatic figure who announces his or her divinity, for example, reveals a selfhood marked by such delusional defenses—by the paranoid fear, for example, that relinquishing omnipotent control over objects will result in obliterating them. A delusional world is the only place such figures can find security. The apocalyptic preoccupations appearing in their claims are symbolic of desperate fears of their world's obliteration—fears of inner emptiness and of abandonment, defended against by self-deceiving convictions in a magically controlled alternative. Persons and objects in such magical worlds do not have an existence apart from the delusional powers of the leader. Particularly in the lives of prophets and saints, we often see the symptomatic correlates of these convictions—an unstable selfhood half the time depressed by its own empty sense of worthlessness, the rest of the time artificially inflated and energized by self-deceiving beliefs that tap into archaic grandiosity. Recall Saint Anselm's ontological proof for the existence of God: "And so, Lord, do thou, who dost give understanding to faith, give me, so far as thou knowest it to be profitable, to understand that thou are that which we believe. And, indeed, we believe that thou art a being *than which nothing greater can be conceived*" (Anselm 1910, chap. 2; emphasis added; reprinted in Mandelbaum, Gramlich, and Anderson 1957, 532). Here is grandiosity stabilized in an illusion of incomprehensible immensity—something like the mystery that suggests itself to a person looking into the deep night sky.

A troubled parent's desperate conviction in the paramount reality of such illusions infringes upon the "space" in which an infant might develop apart. Pulled into such delusional places, made to participate in the parent's fears and to attend the parent's needs, the baby is arrested developmentally by being overwhelmed and saturated by the parent's own needful claims and demands. Considered as the "environment" of a child's growth, such needful parents establish in their offspring a chronically worried outlook that reflects an experience of the world as undependable—a place that cannot be relied on to meet their needs. There are in such children simultaneous predispositions to engage the world in the search for objects who are at once calming and yet who also appeal to magical and omnipotent forces.

This symmetry of needy parent and child, two sides confronting in one another self-strengthening illusions, approximates more closely the ideal type of prophetic rather than exemplary charisma.[6] Pairings of messianic figures and their followers, in particular, illustrate a double transferential pattern receptive to illusional control, as conjunctions of archaic transference needs yield the fusion of subjectively controlled perception central to Weber's notion of pure charisma. Delusional relationships such as these arise where interaction is left unmodulated by introjected selfobjects. It is the absence of modulating self-structure on the part of all parties to genuinely charismatic interactions—profound deficits in the cohesiveness of their respective selves—that results in the delusional predispositions I have described. The effects of such profound personal deficits are amplified by the failure of cultural selfobjects, and establish the conditions for charisma's spread.

Indeed, much of the rest of the logic of charismatic circles follows from an elaboration of these basic notions. What is important to bear in mind, however, is that no real instances of charismatic leadership fulfill the terms of the ideal type. Most conjunctions of such transferential expectations are probably far more quickly disappointed by the forces of reality than those rare instances of successful magical prophecy and heroic self-sacrifice Weber had in mind.

Subsidence and Routinization

Magical Realism and the Surrender of Omnipotence

In the ideal-type formulation, Weber argued that charisma was always recognized *in statu nascendi*—thereby implying, of course, that even as it was instantiated by what were taken to be extraordinary manifestations, it was also dissolving continuously into the everyday (cf. Greenfield 1985). This ebb-and-flow version of charisma has been taken up Edward Shils (1975), who has argued that charisma must also be understood as merged into everyday life, although in diminished and subsided versions. From the developmental perspective of psychoanalytic self psychology, the same conclusion about charisma might be reached from the supposition that society itself is the beneficiary (or the victim) of the qualities of caregiving each of us derives from his or her infancy and learns early in life to impute to the social environment. This is a notion that requires elaboration.

Consider, to begin, the Winnicott-like assertion that elements of the adult social world—language, culture, group life—amount, developmentally speaking, to creative generalizations of earlier so-called transitional objects—substitutes, in some sense, for the initial caregivers. This is an argument we have repeatedly considered in earlier chapters. Like the toddler's blanket, transitional objects are part of an illusory security system that opens up between the dependent infant and its initial caregiver, just at the point where the infant is ready to make progress toward separation and individuation. Into this space the child can move objects it is as yet unprepared to relinquish omnipotent control over, allowing them a kind of halfway status in reality—objects then half under its magical control, half controlled by forces outside of its omnipotence.

One important early illusion such magical realism supports for the child is the notion that its caregiver is always present. Even when mother is in another room and the toddler must learn to play by itself, the child can still imagine mother is at hand. The disposition to sustain such a belief is no more than would be inferred by Kohut from the child's need to stabilize its own mirrored strength in idealized parental imagoes. Such imagined presences, in this sense, amount to instantiations of nascent structures of self—structures that, after more progress in the transmuting internalization of actual caregiving figures, subsequently support less magic and more realism in the time a child spends alone. Needless to say, among the comforting early illusions a child carries with it into the world is therefore some notion that it is accompanied by an omniscient observer—an idea that amounts to a projection of its own omnipotence first into parental objects, thereafter, perhaps, into gods and other distant protectors, with teachers, police, firefighters, priests, soldiers, and other authority figures or need-relieving public servants functioning in a like capacity along the way.

A further step in this logic makes us realize that we are all attached to society and culture the way infants are attached to their caregivers. Each structure of the adult's social world is a like environment for activity—a place where we are invited to be alone, yet where we can nonetheless derive strength by imagining the presence of comforting observers, persons or objects we imagine can support our capacity to be alone. The strength of our adult world likewise stands in direct relationship to the relinquishment of magical omnipotence as a force within it. The man who talks to himself as he works, or perhaps sings or whistles old melodies, is merely introducing into his solitude the calming presence of such imagined others. More accurately, perhaps, he is introducing such fragments of the idealized and omnipotent other as were introjected in some initial generalized status—the mix of soothing sounds, quieting pats, and cradling support of the mother, say, who moves to lull and pacify a dangerously overexcited infant. Listening to our own interior monologues, we likewise hear the empowering and soothing voices of men and women who have been caregivers and preceptors in the course of our own movement toward adulthood—parents, of course, but also others who have subsequently served in some substitutive capacity as idealized imagoes.

The worlds we inhabit, therefore, are full of imagined presences. What varies among such worlds are the qualities typically projected into these imagined others. The original matrix of responsiveness and caregiving provided by parents shapes such an imagined world and its inhabitants, along the lines argued so far. For many men and women, some of these imagined presences remain full of incomprehensible immensity, and clearly derive from deep imagoes of archaic care—or, more likely, from their absence. For others, the world as imagined is a largely muted and unmagical place, dominated by real persons with only ordinary strengths. Between these two extremes are the places most of us ordinarily inhabit. The variety of such places and imagined others, and the qualities we imagine them to have (or are persuaded by others they have), nonetheless speak plainly to the questions raised by persons who claim charisma and those who acknowledge it. More to the point, the same thoughts suggest some of the ways charisma makes its way into everyday life.

To see this in further detail, we must begin to understand the routinization of charisma as a process both analogous to and connected with the introjection of caregivers, particularly caregivers in whom the infant or child first stabilizes and thereafter is able to recover the omnipotence of its archaic grandiose self. In some senses, routinization is like disenchantment, when we surrender omnipotence, or at least retract our transference of it. To the extent the child eventually becomes self-regulating and autonomous in this respect, that is, is able to calm and soothe itself in the face of danger and is able to empower and direct itself apart from the presence of mirroring others, it exhibits a cohesive self able to support independent behavior—apart from parents, leaders, gods, and so forth. Deficits of self-structure not supporting such independence, however, yield the readiness to see charisma in persons or places where others see only a settled reality.

Second, we must also learn to see how idealized others are shaped in view of cultural selfobjects, as when the child learns to trust and rely on a teacher or police officer—or, more abstractly, to discover how its introjects and their functions might be instantiated by playing a musical instrument, reading books, or perhaps even writing stories or music. Such connections between deep introjects and culture—symbolic constructions of all sorts—establish a ready route by which charisma and its derivatives make their way routinely into everyday life. This is particularly so when we recognize how culture itself sometimes serves as a transitional object or "potential space"—a place whose magical realism enables us to play creatively with objects half controlled in our omnipotence, yet still in view of reality. Culture is the vehicle of imagination.

While our readiness to believe that life is saturated with magical forces arises from deficits in the area of the idealized parental imago, these deficits are in some sense always "relative." That is, selfobjects are adequate relative to the range of environmental variation to which we are accustomed. Few of us are fully self-regulating in the center of a combat zone, or when facing natural disasters like fires or great storms, or in the presence of menacing sociopaths. Such circumstances cause us to recognize a limit on the extent to which we can become self-regulating. This limit arises from the finite nature of our own experience, as well as from the inherent intransmutability of much of what we do experience—the limit, that is, that arises from our capacity to process and store information and that therefore leaves us in the presence of unknown, strange, or unperceived forces.

The best psychoanalytic predictor of charismatic predispositions, then, is this deficit of transmuted idealized strength. The developmental sources of this condition should now be familiar to us. Weakening of introjects, of course, can amount to absence of introjects and so lead to similar consequences. Weakening of structures in the area of idealized parental activity is typically the product either of environmental variations that carry the person outside of the range of familiar experiences—as in natural disasters or warfare—or of the traumatic failure of the environment to meet needs (where by "environment" I now mean any substitute for the original caregivers, substitutes like language or culture or personal relationships). Note again that this condition isolates not only personal but social and cultural variability— matters that affect everyone in an environment, interacting with the transmuted strengths or weaknesses of each. Variability of the environment outside its accustomed range typically elicits a need for stabilizing leadership and should be associated with the wish to recover an environment whose properties might be regulated by omnipotent control. Traumatic frustration of needs for safety or mirroring, in addition, similarly induce the wishful search for these need-relieving circumstances.

Bringing Up the Charismatic Family

Viewed from this perspective, charisma is incompatible with everyday life only in the obvious way infancy's untransmuted omnipotence is incompatible with adulthood. Each situates life in a world where autonomy and independent action are unimaginable, and where life is dominated by forces in whose palpable presence we are reduced to observers and credulous disciples, waiting to be excited or palliated, empowered or soothed. Yet in each case the former is the foundation on which the latter builds. Weber had something similar in mind.

All social structure and culture, in this view, are understandable in part as substitutes and elaborations of the matrix of growth and responsiveness the infant comes to know in the family. Something of the same assumption is implicit in Weber's image of society, except we must substitute "charismatic circle" for "family" in order to bring the assumption to the surface of his analysis. Weber himself sought to teach us that charisma can be embodied in traditions or laws or funeral practices, in kinship lineages or bureaucratic offices or belief systems. The notion that, once routinized, it is always implicit in social order, buried in the origins of cultural patterns (as remembered, say, in the celebration of their beginnings), becomes only another way of putting more simply the thought that the originating matrix of social and cultural forms is the charismatic "family."

To Weber's own discussion of the routinization of charisma, then, psychoanalytic self psychology adds the proposition that charisma's course into everyday life should follow a path produced by disappointments—the same sorts of optimal disappointments that stimulate children toward development apart from their caregivers. In instances of charisma presumed to be close to his ideal type, the subsidence of followers' readiness to attribute charismatic specialness to leaders should appear in proportion to the failure of their leaders to serve as effective transference vehicles. The constant demand for "proofs" of charisma lead inevitably to disappointments, and the cumulation of such disappointments gradually allows followers to recognize the limits of their leader's extraordinariness, even to the point, in some cases, of appropriating it. Indeed, the leader's failures can function as do the incremental disappointments of a mother or father to mirror every fantasy or craving of their child or to embody the omnipotence of the child's archaic grandiose self. Slowly, in a drift away from the position of absolute dependency, the followers, replicating the path out of their own infancy, build up psychic structures enabling them to function effectively and with direction on their own.[7]

In theory, the leader's own disappointments with his or her followers may be equally important in motivating this process. Followers' failures to conform to the wishes of a charismatic figure, or to serve their leader's needs, may result in the leader's refusal to serve as a vehicle for their merger demands, in turn producing disappointment on the subordinates' side of the ledger. Only the pattern of mutual disappointment we could describe as "optimal" presumably would be able to produce a slow antitransferential withdrawal of each side into a more adult "developmental" posture.

The Direction of Routinization

Much of Weber's political sociology can be seen as an answer to the question of how charisma's routinization shapes the subsequent evaluation of power, leadership, or authority—or, to put this into the psychoanalytic framework, how the originating charismatic context bequeaths structures that both constrain the subsequent exercise of authority or leadership and call forth in them the reinstantiation of an original (or transmuted) introject. Weber of course pointed to the ways charisma embodied itself, or was transmitted, beyond the original circle of disciples or followers—and how such embodiments or forms of domination constrained the incumbents of authoritative roles to behave in ways consistent with their charismatic origins, however much submerged, attenuated, or reinterpreted.

When charisma was routinized in an anti-authoritarian direction, opportunities in the form of plebiscites or elections were normatively instituted for the periodic reevaluation of the exercise of authority. This meant that the audience got a chance occasionally to judge whether a leader was doing what the audience expected—whether, in our terms, he or she was an adequate vehicle for idealizing transferences. When charisma was institutionalized in an authoritarian direction, the evaluation was the other way around: it was the superior who was now entitled to evaluate the adequacy of subordinates—whether, in our terms, they were idealizing the leader's own greatness and claims, or, somewhat more plainly, whether they were doing what the leader expected them to do. More precisely, the superior in such an arrangement *authorizes* subordinates' actions, that is, judges them to be consistent or inconsistent with some values, ends, or premises of action that are instantiations of a transmuted parental introject, whatever executive status the introject now has. Legitimacy flowed upward from the constituents in the former set of arrangements, downward from the superior or leader in the latter set. In both cases, however, the process involved Sandlerian role responsiveness: idealization looked for a vehicle in *legitimation,* mirroring for a vehicle in *authorization.* Behind authorization and legitimation, therefore, are the very processes of selfobject transference by which, all along, we have studied how persons control *feelings*—how, in this context, they gain confidence and security (authorization), on the one hand, and stabilize omnipotence and excitation (idealization), on the other.

Weber's notion of routinization, of course, was also informed by realistic struggles within the charismatic "family" for political and economic power and by the administrative exigencies of expanding charismatic dominion. Needless to say, these also have some analogy to important ideas in classic psychoanalytic thought—mainly to Oedipal dynamics. (See the way Hummel [1975] makes his way to some of these matters from Freud's so-called totem theory.) The "succession of leadership" issue serves as a pivot in the Weberian model, separating what we might call a charismatic from a postcharismatic phase.

Of more interest here than this further theoretical likeness to psychoanalytic ideas, however, is the attitude toward charisma Weber apparently carried into the rest of his theoretical logic. His sense of "genuine" charisma's disruptiveness and anti-institutional qualities, and of its instability and evanescence, points the way toward the critique of charisma that is simultaneously at the root of his ambivalence toward rationality and modern society. While it is clear he viewed charisma as a manifestation of what Thomas Dow (1978) calls the "basic life-force," regarding it as somehow behind or submerged in routine social order, he nonetheless held firmly to the proposition that in its "pure" manifestations charisma was disruptive, unstable, and anti-institutional.

Schematically, charisma's routinization followed upon the succession of leadership occasioned by a leader's death or disappearance. Charisma's subsequently diminished status in relation to routine life had much to do with the way it was thought to be embodied by those charged with perpetuating the charismatic legacy. Thus, when Weber talked about matters like "kinship charisma" or "office charisma," he was arguing that charisma perpetuated itself in transmuted and (sometimes) depersonalized forms, embodied in such ways as might be observed in traditional kingships or, less obviously, in bureaucratic rules. In all cases, however, the motivation to routinize charisma arose from the necessity of stabilizing and making predictable a pattern of domination, inherently unstable so long as it rested purely on the charisma of a single person.

The chemistry by which Weber saw instability and impermanence as the by-products of charisma was central to the logic on which his analysis of all other ideal types of order was built. Every other form of social life beyond the charismatic circle was founded on ways not of retrieving charisma but of preventing its return, or, perhaps more accurately, of filtering it out. Despite his bow in the direction of the *Veralltäglichung des Charismas,* both rationality and traditionality, in their ideal-type formulations, suggested patterns of social order that depended upon such filtration; they were incompatible with the radically dependent, subjectively fused, unstable and incalculable forms of personal charisma. This does not mean that Weber, in his analysis of empirical cases of what he considered traditional or rational forms, was oblivious to the appearance within them of personal and charismatic elements. Traditional order in particular was mediated through personal ties and particularistic loyalties. He was also attuned to reappearances of the charismatic in rationalized everyday life. Indeed, the family logic is nowhere so useful as in making sense of this peculiar status.

The critical variable here is reliability. The ultimately personal dependencies involved in pure charisma are one source of subsequent attitudes toward all leadership and authority. The analogy is to the "reliable" caregiver—the mother who can be counted on to meet her infant's needs, without allowing them to be frustrated or to pass over into traumatic disappointment. Weber's analysis can be construed to imply something similar about systems of domination—namely, that the political "environment" of social life, like such caregiving "environments" of childhood, is "successful" when, to use a variation of one of Kohut's expressions, it is "optimally responsive." In charisma's capacity to call forth the attitude of reverence and respect toward the incumbents of creative or authoritative roles, it might be understood as the deep force that infuses with similar feelings all beliefs in legitimacy. It not only affects an incumbent's political responsiveness, but it also establishes certain expectations on the part of constituents about institutionalized qualities of domination. Such would be implied, for example, by the logic we have derived from self psychology, and comes close to what Edward Shils has argued as well.

Authority, that is, calls forth idealizing selfobject transferences, though not always without disappointment. Disappointments follow when incumbents of authoritative roles possess qualities of unresponsiveness that isolate them and make them unavailable to their constituents' needs for merger. They might be austere or distant, absorbed in personal gratifications, unempathic, morally obtuse, corrupt, abusive, or despotic. Any examples of the exercise of authority with these qualities would disappoint wishful transferences in short order. In such cases, incumbents would be repudiated by their constituents the way an infant repudiates a noxious object. But authority itself, or the institutions of authority, produce in constituents patterned "expectations" whose roots reach back into their respective infancies. Such expectations derive from our first caregivers' activities in regulating and meeting our needs. Structures of authority, to put this more generally, are analogous to idealized selfobjects, culturally constituted. Methods of solving the succession-of-leadership problem—elections, say, or coronations—are then normative occasions to instantiate selfobjects beyond the sphere of kinship. Insofar as a political regime is legitimate, attitudes toward it are infused by its citizens' memories of responsive parents calming their fears, saving them from dangerous circumstances, and accepting their demands for merger. Such roots are hidden deep in the very notion of authority itself—*auctor, auctoritatem,* creator, god.

Power, Charisma, and Sociocultural Change

Particularism and Power

By this reasoning, *personal* power is always an emergent phenomenon within fields of interaction—every field of interaction. Charisma was Weber's way of isolating the pure, powerful manifestations of this unstable, emergent control as it arose historically in interaction systems where all participants were similarly predisposed by personal and cultural weaknesses to search for idealized responsiveness and direction. Personal power more generally, though, arises as the actual or potential effect one person has on another when each uses the other as selfobject. I have argued that these effects sometimes appear quite outside of conscious control, as when two romantically predisposed adolescents become dependent on one another. Their efforts to secure each other's attachment are sometimes manipulative in precisely the sense often associated with power relationships, yet manipulativeness is not the defining feature of such mutual dependency. Rather, it is the capacity of the one person to produce effects in the other—a capacity enabled by the inability of the other to avoid experiencing those effects. In this case especially, such effects appear when a person serving as an idealized selfobject acts so as to control the feelings of another. But is emergent power in other sorts of interaction different?

A powerful and charismatic person in this sense is always distinguished by an ability to elicit responses of an idealizing nature from those in his or her audience. They create the illusion, as Emerson reportedly was able to do during his public addresses, of speaking to each person in an audience intimately and alone and of thus standing in a special relationship to every one of them. Such a person seems magnetic, and others find themselves drawn to that person, hopeful of attaching themselves intimately to someone so obviously superior and inspiring. Responsiveness on the part of such figures converts the hopefulness of their admirers into devotion. But as we ought by now to suspect, the illusion of intimacy they are able to create is not the special gift of such political figures or leaders alone; it is one of the potential magical emergents of every field of social interaction. What makes us think of the emergence of such personal control as power—as, by the terms of the hidden metaphor, some disembodied and transient force passing through fields of interaction—is that it appears sometimes to "happen" apart from our own wants. We "find" ourselves, as we say, in another person's power.

Such transient feelings of dependency, and of being drawn to persons we perceive to be great, we can now recognize as products of idealizing selfobject transferences on our own part—potentiated, perhaps, by their responsiveness to us. As such, an immediate consequence of this reasoning is that emergent power's roots in feelings ultimately make it particularistic. Used by others functionally as idealized selfobjects, responsive leaders serve to recapitulate relationships to caregiver figures whose omnipotent qualities we "rediscover" in them. When we engage leaders this way, we tend to distort them in our perception by just such particularizing, transferential wishes—seeing them somehow as *our* leaders, and hence as persons just as irreplaceable to us as our parents, our children, or our spouses. This particularism is not generally appreciated about power, especially when concepts of power are employed in political analysis.

Consideration of large-scale power phenomena, of course, draws attention to geopolitical and material factors in power relationships—matters that can create dependencies of other sorts—rather than to evanescent and subjective fluctuations of feelings on the part of powerful figures and those dependent on them. Yet the exercise of power in any field of interaction, as by a person empowered by great wealth or influence or force, is not unrelated to the exercise of power in personal interaction. In some degree, it will ultimately elicit the same idealizing transference. Thus, for example, interactions between concentration camp guards and their prisoners—relationships marked by the most dramatic asymmetries in actual and potential power and resources—elicited idealizing selfobject transferences, despite the opposite interests at work in such relationships (Bettelheim 1943). Interactions among the representatives of different nation-states—soldiers on the battlefield, diplomats at the conference table—similarly involve idealization of the other as a powerful, responsive selfobject. Indeed, the crafty diplomat uses responsiveness as a means of manipulating her adversary. On the battlefield, mere copresence of enemy soldiers (in the sense of their mutual perceptual availability to one another) eventually diminishes feelings of personal dislike and increase feelings of sympathy—manifestations in feelings, perhaps, of Kohut's twinship transference, mingled with idealization. A soldier can continue to hate the enemy in general, but the particular soldier visible across no-man's-land is another person just like himself—and, if that other soldier *appears* better armed, clothed, supplied, and trained, then perhaps he *is* in some ways superior (Leed 1979). Idealization in such circumstances can find its purchase in mere difference.

Ultimately, therefore, an argument like this one that ties the logic of idealizing transference together with the workings of power must draw attention, especially where power makes itself *felt,* to the inherent particularism in power relationships. This becomes important for understanding stable power *systems*—institutionalized arrangements of power in the social world. If my reasoning is near the truth, then the dynamics of such systems will always be visibly affected by the infusion of transferential forces as part of the political process. As argued in chapter 4, for example, election campaigns in democratic political systems provide examples of how legitimacy gets moved among parties, policies, and candidates for office, based especially on candidates' abilities to call forth idealizing selfobject transferences from the electorate. Such campaigns are institutionalized processes for moving legitimacy, and hence for stabilizing elite circulation. Where other principles for the succession of leadership or elite circulation are operating in a power system, we can observe quite different dynamics.

Bifurcations

DISSIPATIVE STRUCTURE IN CHARISMATIC CIRCLES   Successions of leadership have the potential of producing bifurcations. This is because elections and other practices of elite circulation serve as entropy-producing processes that can drive systems, on the basis of transference-backed positive feedback, into far-from-equilibrium conditions. In general, when systems like those studied by chemists and physicists enter such conditions, their behavior becomes less predictable, and it is necessary to describe them in terms of stochastic rather than deterministic models. The linear equations that describe what happens near equilibrium give way to stochastic versions of nonlinear differential equations of the kind studied in chapter 3.

Models of social change often acknowledge exactly such complex dynamics when they attempt to describe and then generalize about the disorderly, seemingly chaotic events that typically precede and are part of important social transformations. What this suggests, of course, is that *all* such theories implicitly recognize how important sociocultural change ultimately depends on embedded processes that produce, amplify, and spread destabilizing positive feedback. My own argument has emphasized how developmental models of psychological growth, for example, can be reconceptualized in view of dissipative structure theory. In this newer perspective, fundamental psychological shifts appear developmentally as bifurcations—basic reorganizations of the "system" in which far-from-equilibrium conditions have emerged. The same logic can be applied to interaction systems and larger social systems, since the logic of bifurcation is potentially applicable to the behavior of all systems subject to feedback processes. Thus, I have described charismatic circles as far-from-equilibrium systems in precisely this sense. Such circles are based, so to speak, on entropy production and on the scavenging of entropy, along the lines suggested by combining idealizing and mirroring transferences in the patterns I have isolated. In addition to what I have already said about them, therefore, charismatic circles often partake of other characteristics of dissipative structures as well—characteristics we have seen elsewhere but that do not generally appear in relation to analyzing charisma. For example, charismatic circles themselves are far more unstable demographically than is typically implied in analyses of leader-follower relationships.

THE MAGIC FRIEND: AN EXAMPLE   An example of a "self-appointed" charismatic figure whose group illustrates this point is one I happened to observe a few years ago in upstate New York. The leader was an energetic young man who lived in a cabin high up on a mountain overlooking one of the Finger Lakes. Surrounded by various full- and part-time dependents, including two close companions, he lived a delusional life that was incompatible with regular employment, though he occasionally tried his hand at it. More to his style was the self-sufficient communal life of his household, in which he benefited from the support and charity of his friends. The house he shared was a center for musical and craft activities and was regularly visited by other persons who styled themselves self-sufficient in one way or another. I will not describe the full dynamics of this circle here, since they generally approximate those discussed earlier. But a number of revealing observations can be made about this circle, based on the organizational demography to which its cabin setting regularly was home.

On cold winter days the view from the front windows of this handmade house was straight down for five miles through a gentle sloping cut in the evergreen forest to the frozen lake a thousand feet below. An icy wind blasted from the lake through this cut and screamed against the front of the little cabin on bad winter days, and created drifts in the snow and swirling witches of vapor that danced along the pathways. The cabin's location was so far from the nearest city's glare that at night cloudless skies seemed to the eye to grow ever deeper, and the evidence of natural forces all about dwarfed its human inhabitants. It was the right setting for a delusional figure to convince himself of strange and momentous happenings. As the self-designated head of this household, its young leader was always enthralling his followers with stories of one kind or another. Frequently at night a great fire would be built in the "family room" fireplace, and guests and the group's members would sit around singing or listening to stories. Sometimes following a meal and in keeping with the *Gemütlichkeit* induced by communal work and a fine local wine, the group engaged in joint recollections of shared experiences, which served to objectify their intimacy in memories. But once in a while, when the wind and snow locked the little cabin into its own magical vault, members seemed more disposed than usual to accommodate the strange and outlandish delusions to which its leader seemed susceptible. The temptation to offer himself then as selfobject to the waiting group was too great to be resisted, and the leader invariably would use such occasions to present claims of one kind or another about himself. It went without saying that his personal extraordinariness would be the usual exhibitionistic theme of his stories. This theme appeared artlessly as part of what he was saying, as if it were only natural for others to want an explanation for why he was special. Something inside himself did not question others' natural interest in him—and, indeed, others often demanded that he tell them stories about himself, or just tell them stories.

One of these was the foundation for a strange delusion, the "truth" of which his close friends would corroborate in detail. It was the story of a spaceship that had more than once landed farther up the mountain behind their cabin, and that on one occasion had abducted two of them for a night and a day. The burn marks on the hillside where the ship had most recently set down were still visible to the doubting observer. The details of this wonderful story sometimes seemed to alter, but they invariably led toward another delusion about how the leader communicated regularly with a "spirit guide" he called Salpervius. On nights when he was feeling expansive, and when his audience seemed receptive and credulous, these two stories would be elaborated and combined. A further claim was then made. The leader had learned from Salpervius, he said, the strange story of his own birth. Details aside, it was that he had been born on another planet and was accordingly gifted in many ways that seemed incomprehensible to earthlings. The first evidence of this, surely, was his ability to perceive Salpervius, but the proof moved beyond Salpervius to embrace other mysterious talents he also possessed, such as his ability to read minds. In proof of this, he would then proceed to do just that. Sometimes, in addition, he would perform tricks of magic, and otherwise seek to enthrall and persuade his waiting, sometimes astonished, and uneasy audience.

Over time, many of these stories of unalloyed omnipotence accumulated—so many, in fact, that a large fraction of his otherwise quite gullible followers eventually began to doubt him. On any given day at the cabin, there was always some undercurrent in the air about the leader's lunacy or his lies and tricks. Some of this discontent served as part of the usual climate of opinion that in fact seemed forever to motivate this quixotic figure to deepen his claims and their defense. Always, it seemed, there was some challenge to his ascendancy. The most loyal of his companions, closest to the leader, seemed impervious to suggestions that he was delusional or plain crazy, or even that he was just a liar of some considerable talent as a storyteller. They did not worship him in every respect, but they were unable to tolerate protracted criticisms of him. They had evolved their own convoluted defenses of his behavior, and sometimes seemed so irrationally attached to him that observers suspected he must somehow have been blackmailing them to preserve such loyalty, particularly in the face of what occasionally appeared to outsiders as delusional tyranny and manipulativeness on his part. He was, for example, financially irresponsible and was constantly creating bills for the household the others would be obliged to pay. For many followers, of course, the leader's unbelievable delusions by themselves were enough to undermine loyalty to the household, and they would sooner or later drift away. The result was that a large fraction of his group's dynamics might better be described as group demographics—that is, as the coming and going of a transient audience.

The workings of the outer circle in particular were marked by the continuing recruitment of these temporary hangers-on and disciples. Demographically, this amounted to instability in the membership, but recruitment and loss always seemed to balance each other. The group's size fluctuated within a narrow range: attrition roughly approximated recruitment, with the small core of close disciples strongly attached to the leader at the very center of the group remaining more or less stable. My own impression of some of the shifty, impermanent "followers" was that, gullible as they were, they bore a considerable resemblance to the kind of persons attracted to shows of magic. None of them seemed genuinely gifted or talented like, say, the disciples of a great leader-prophet like Gandhi, or of a great intellectual figure like Emerson, or of a charismatic general like MacArthur. They were typically disorganized, fragmented persons desperately in need of strong leadership to salvage something of their own lives, and were always on the lookout for stimulation of one kind or another to override their feelings of personal emptiness. Only ghost stories really substituted among them for what they were told about Salpervius, and for stories of Salpervius the most dependent of them had insatiable appetites.

The way the shifting movement of persons in an active crowd can be described by models of convection, this unstable charismatic collectivity might also be characterized as a system of convection. Newcomers moved first toward the group's center but then invariably drifted out toward its periphery. In this sense, the leader's "charisma" and the related selfobject transferences of his listeners and followers created demographic currents, as his circle acquired something of the form it had by the intermittent but unpredictable ability he possessed first to enthrall but ultimately to disappoint his recruits.

Fusing itself into charisma's much discussed instability is therefore the special dissipative structure that arises out of processes like these—basic demographic gravitation occasioned by fast rates of recruitment and attrition of membership. These processes both produce and scavenge entropy. A similar scavenging arrangement, motivated by anxiety over the discontent of his followers, was also behind the leader's own compulsive exhibitionism and his claims and proofs. In other systems of power and status, like those, say, of small urban gangs, similar dynamics sometimes produce equivalent dissipative structure.

VIOLENCE, GROUP COHESIVENESS, AND PARANOIA A related example of unstable, quasi-charismatic principles for the succession of leadership can be found in James Short's and Fred Strodbeck's *Group Process and Gang Delinquency* (1965), which describes how violent encounters between inner-city gangs, or between these gangs and the police, provided occasions for "status threats." Younger and lower-status members of such gangs apparently used violent displays during such encounters to draw attention to themselves, and potentially to win status, "respect," and possible leadership roles.

In general, violent circumstances destabilize entrenched status orders and bring charismatically gifted figures to the forefront, both in such gangs and in national warfare. But in gangs, violence precipitates rearrangements of persons in terms of status by drawing those most talented as fighters (or related charismatic skills) toward the center and top of group life. Violent exhibitionism in gang fights, as a special case of this, elicits idealizing selfobject transferences among observers. Again, the associated structural destabilization of gangs constitutes a dissipative arrangement based on membership circulation, supported by idealizing transferences and mirroring responsiveness. Occasions calling forth charisma therefore regularly get cycled into the life of such groups as ways of destabilizing and opening their status systems. Group conflict and gang delinquency are in part motivated, therefore, by the exhibitionistic needs of newcomers and lower-status members—the same needs for attention, that is, we have elsewhere seen at work causing persons with narcissistic injuries and mirrored deficits to engage in other delinquent patterns. Here exhibitionism feeds status dynamics and creates a dissipative structure by scavenging the disintegration anxieties typical of adolesence.

Marxist-Leninist theory about revolutionary solidarity and the consolidation of revolutionary regimes rests implicitly on a similar anxiety-generating, entropy-producing principle. In this familiar argument, solidarity can be encouraged by campaigns against inner enemies or by warfare against external enemies. Stabilizing a revolutionary regime, in this way of thinking, depends on fomenting constant anxiety, principally over external threats to society and over internal enemies. This principle also has well-studied equivalents in experimentally created group dynamics (see, e.g., the studies on "group cohesiveness" in Cartwright and Zander 1960). Such patterns of "stable instability" depend on increasing levels of entropy production above those observable in more stable social forms, and thus are good examples of dissipative structure.

Systems theorists and psychotherapists have discovered similar patterns in clinical data, particularly in families. The best known of these patterns arises where families manage to maintain stability as systems only on the basis of sustaining instability in the behavior of members—in effect, building up a pattern of "stable instability." Examples of how families create patterns of communication endlessly amplifying the particular symptoms of their members—for example, as alcoholics or as schizophrenics—are persuasive illustrations of these dynamics (e.g., Watzlawick, Bavelas, and Jackson 1967).

Some of the most difficult psychiatric conditions to treat successfully also appear to be sustained in part by entrenched dissipative dynamics in systems of interaction, maintained by patients. Particularly interesting are dissipative structures manifested in temporal patterns, arising from underlying "self-organizing" dynamics of a type I have discussed but not isolated as examples before. Borderline personality disorder, for example, is marked by patients' exhibiting regular, quasi-periodic oscillations toward and away from unstable attachments (see Melges and Swartz 1989; cf. Kernberg 1975).

Micro-Macro Dynamics

CONSTANCY OF PROCESS ACROSS CHANGES OF SCALE   Another important conclusion suggested by these examples of far-from-equilibrium states is that there is a certain constancy of their properties across changes of scale. It is certainly not fortuitous that the same models used in sociological analysis often have precedents in models of psychological processes. Just as a model that fits psychological development also is useful to describe systems of interaction, so the same model can be seen to have applications to even larger-scale social phenomena. An interesting and suggestive illustration of this point involves Weber's model of charisma, which has the same logical structure as Freud's analysis of the just so story of the primal family (Freud [1921] 1953–74, [1930] 1953–74). Both Weber's and Freud's "stories" center on the dynamics involved in successions of leadership; indeed, each makes the displacement or replacement of leadership a condition for the appearance of subordinates' autonomy and for the emergence of culture in general. While this certainly proves nothing about the way things are in real life, it is a remarkable convergence in social theory. Freud's thinking clearly had something to do with his view of (and anxieties about) the politics of nineteenth-century central European society, since his model of the mind eventually had an aristocracy (superego) dominating but nevertheless being pushed around by an active middle class (ego), both of which had a hand in maintaining barriers of repressive control over a dangerous lower class (id). The sociology of knowledge aside, the main point about this convergence still holds; models of processes at work in the person are sometimes found to be useful as models of processes in interaction and society. Moreover, as the Weber-Freud example illustrates, these processes, particularly those involving excitation, feedback, and growth, appear to many analysts to exhibit constancy across changes of scale.

Take this point seriously, and one arrives at startling arguments about social structure. Not, certainly, that it is understandable as having been produced by sudden, disjunctive leaps into stability out of conditions of disorganization and chaos—mysterious phase transitions following upon far-from-equilibrium fluctuations. But certainly that the appearance of many of its distinctive characteristics follows upon political reorganizations of society, as Weber's and Freud's models of change and development would have it; in addition, that these distinctive characteristics have to do with the specific properties of the information systems—the patterns of negentropy, to oversimplify the matter—on which the reorganization of simpler into more complex patterns rest; and, furthermore, that the transitions from one level of structural complexity to another, either forward or backward, always seem to be coupled with dynamics of far-from-equilibrium instability.

This seemingly abstract argument will be given more development in the next chapter, when we study some of the distinctive patterns of routine social organization. It will be seen there that I am really advancing another version of one of Weber's arguments, namely, that culture is one of the "environments" of social action and varies in ways supporting different levels of complexity in social organization. The historical appearance of "rational" social organization, for example, really depends on changes that create cultural (negentropic, informational) conditions able to "carry" complexity. But here it is enough to suggest that all such changes do involve developmental and organizational shifts, and that these shifts appear to be associated with bifurcations. That is, the underlying dynamics of "growth" socially involve producing far-from-equilibrium shifts toward bifurcation points, and these can potentially produce phaselike movements of social organization among different structural patterns.

Consider simple examples, again based on materials we have already reviewed. If this kind of thinking is useful, we should be able to observe something like phase shifts when the underlying cybernetic conditions of social life are changed—that is, when the conditions associated with the production of negentropy and the creation of entropy are dramatically altered, with the result that the ratio (α / β) diminishes dramatically. Consider some small-scale illustrations. What happens when we raise the level of conflict in a group? Take a fight in a barroom as an example. One reason barroom fights break out is that other means of social control aren't working. Apart from fighting to resolve their differences, that is, there are only other "information-poor" resources available to the contestants to control each other. Fights are common in barrooms, it is sometimes argued, because drinking alcohol is disinhibiting. What this means in the framework of this book is that strengths clustered around the idealized pole of the self have been situationally weakened by alcohol consumption, such that persons in these contexts use others as external selfobjects in a greater degree than normally they would. Any bartender can tell endless stories of how he or she gets used by patrons as an external selfobject. Barrooms are therefore marked by many forms of instability—by what amounts to normatively supported and externally managed sensitive dependence. Tavern owners employ various sources of stimulation like dance bands or fancy lighting to enhance this condition, as well as inverting amplifiers (like bouncers) to modulate instability within bounds. Excitement in such milieus spreads rapidly.

One instability often observed within crowded barroom settings, for instance, is the endless aggregation, disaggregation, and reaggregation of patrons into small circles of sociability. This process creates a swirling, turbulent flow of patrons that can easily isolate and conceal unstable pockets of interaction. Participants' moods in such pockets are occasionally destabilized into spirals of conflict that end with fights. Under some conditions, moreover, such fights can spread. One patron pushes another on a dance floor, the push is returned, ugly looks are exchanged, a third party is elbowed in the process, more glaring occurs, and before long a contagious process has taken hold of a section of the tavern. Suddenly the bouncer has his hands full. Typically this sort of process produces a rapidly disorganized flux. In the flash of an eye, the dance floor will pass from a merely excited state of interaction through an explosion of disorganized conflict into what appears to be random action and disaggregation. Only the intervention of strong stabilizing forces can return such systems to a condition of stable complexity—at first, usually only as an audience controlled by a public address system, thereafter sometimes into other more complex arrangements of order supported by different sources of negentropy. Many such events provide examples of "chance" happenings that set into motion a contagious process (i.e., one built on positive feedback) that abruptly carries a system near the point where a phase transition might occur. The movement here is from stable equilibrium on the part of patrons before they enter the tavern, into the excited and disinhibiting conditions of the tavern itself, thereafter into the progressively more far-from-equilibrium conditions appearing on the dance floor, and finally into the explosion of conflict that results in the system's disaggregating.

If such a scene of conflict and riot were to emerge in a prison yard as prisoners milled about, we might then observe a transition in the system that would include reassertion of control by the guards. This would be a more primitive pattern of stability and negentropy than had prevailed in the prison prior to the riot, since it would be based merely on control of force as a sanction, and it would therefore exhibit simpler complexity. (Force is a "low-information, high-energy" source of social control; see, e.g., Parsons 1966). But it nevertheless for a time would be a stable pattern.

By contrast, a stable electoral system involves stirring up emotions and feelings along some of the same lines of separation and disintegration in the social order. Ethnic solidarity, interest-group loyalty, and moral commitments are activated by these competitive processes, but they are generally contained by inverting amplifiers like rules and customs, and by the legitimacy of the system. All of these factors govern (mostly successfully) the kinds of conflict and competition that can emerge, with deviant episodes like Watergate then celebrated as evidence both of a system's great weaknesses and its evident resilience or of its fragility and failure. Groups whose members are always elbowing one another on dance floors are brought into the same interaction system by electoral processes, and their emotions are stirred up by the feedback inherent in the electoral appeals of candidates. Such processes depend on raising entropy production by inducing idealizing selfobject transferences, and then scavenging it in commitments and in transfers of affect to external selfobject milieus.

LEADERSHIP AS NEGENTROPY, CULTURE AS LEADERSHIP   The analytically useful point here is that candidates, like leaders more generally, are sources of negentropy. Sometimes they are themselves regulated by a "cultural selfobject milieu" that includes information and sources of negentropy of which they become representatives and relays. This is generally the case with elected "officials," who have legitimacy to act as leaders and regulators within the framework of a larger system of information and regulation. What varies about such frameworks is the degrees of freedom they leave to their incumbents. Senators have more degrees of freedom than members of the House of Representatives, for example, because their accountability is looser.[8] Where degrees of freedom increase, there are inducements to personal leadership, and leaders sometimes seem (like charismatic figures) to be promulgating their own negentropy. A leader appears in a system as a structure to supply stability and organization to it, including direction. In the chaotic disorganization of a prison riot, a guard is an institutional source of negentropy, and an emergent leader in the rioting crowd of prisoners is attempting to become one—a focus around which others can stabilize themselves, find direction, and diminish their anxieties. As we must learn to see, it is something about the negentropic properties of such leaders we have known all along that determines the course of change open to a system in a state of disequilibrium.

What I mean by this admittedly ambiguous assertion is something the full implications of which will have to await development until the next chapter. But there is nothing mysterious in the basic idea—namely, that leadership, whether spontaneous or institutionalized, and the properties of leadership, whether personal or impersonal, make all the difference in the way a system gets organized. Leaders are information nodes in systems. And the simple point here is that different informational-negentropic properties of leadership support different kinds of complexity in social systems. Just how this relationship between cultural variation and social complexity works—between negentropy and organization—we shall have to wait until later to spell out. Needless to say, however, something like this kind of argument is precisely what was behind what Weber and Freud both were arguing about social development. When we learn to recognize negentropy in leadership, we are only a step or two in logic away from seeing how culture is a leadership substitute the way it is a caregiver substitute. This is an argument we have seen in other forms in earlier chapters on psychological growth. Culture is what allows individual actors to stand apart from leaders, the way children eventually weaken their attachments to caregivers. The theory of this relationship involves a theory of weak interaction, as I shall develop it in chapter 7.

THE IDEA OF THE PHASE TRANSITION   As a model of change, the most difficult notion to grasp in this argument is the idea of the phase transition— the event capping off the far-from-equilibrium phase with a sudden bifurcation that results in the reorganization of the elements in a system. A physical analogue here is when gases become liquids, or molecules suddenly become magnetized. Whatever in the social world we decide to count as examples of equivalent phase transitions should exhibit comparable suddenness and comparable changes in structure and complexity. Is this the case?

Many efforts to conceptualize the abrupt events within active crowds, for example, satisfy some of these conditions, and I have exploited the "collective behavior" tradition in sociology to develop several of my illustrations. But by contrast to most examples from collective behavior, phase transitions sometimes result in *higher* levels of complexity emerging suddenly out of far-from-equilibrium instability. In all cases, as I shall argue in the next chapter, this denotes a form of stable organization whose complexity rests on aggregating individual autonomy into one or another pattern. The general dimensions of complexity in social organization—hierarchy, on the one hand, and markets, on the other—appear in this argument to have properties that are a function of the supports for autonomy. (More on this in the next chapter.) Moreover, all dynamics leading in a far-from-equilibrium direction are either toward disorganization and chaos or toward dependency and centralization, undermining autonomy. But all movement out of these disequilibrium states involves a phase transition equivalent to a succession of leadership. The sequel to the succession-of-leadership problem in the charismatic group involves members traversing the gap between dependency and autonomy— growing up, sociologically speaking, by becoming suddenly responsible for themselves and no longer dependent followers. Traversing this gap is a phase transition, in the sense developed by this theory. In point of fact, of course, it need not occur instantaneously, the way water vaporizes in a flash when it is heated to a certain far-from-equilibrium temperature. But in some comparable sociological time, an equivalent disjunctive transformation of the group must occur if its structure is to become more complex.

Needless to say, such disjunctive transformations need more detailed empirical and theoretical study. It may be that they occur not to whole systems simultaneously but only to regions of interaction within such systems, and that the effects of what occurs in one region then spread into adjacent regions according to principles akin to those that describe the spread of fluctuations through physical systems. In some charismatic arrangements mentioned by Weber, for instance, a group of close disciples around a great figure eventually gets transformed into something like a staff, in others into a status group. These transformations, theoretically speaking, are phase transitions of two different types, supported by different negentropic processes. A status group, for example, emerges as a dissipative structure based on the kinds of negentropy generated by subordinates' opposition to the centralizing and entropy-generating interests of the leader or of the leader's successors, eventually the monarch. Type cases for this pattern might be found in the competitive relationship between feudal aristocrats and their monarchs. This oversimplifies complex historical processes, but it makes the general point. The staff appears by the promotion of personal retainers into a patrimonial relationship to the leader, which does not involve opposition to the interests of the leader or monarch and hence eventually supports bureaucratic administration. These and other such developments are not instantaneous events, but nevertheless they presume a prior "history" of development within a system.

Bifurcations out of far-from-equilibrium states, then, involve phase transitions connected sociologically with the appearance of the supports that enable persons to stand apart from one another and to weaken their personal dependencies. This makes the organization and reorganization of power and depen-

dency relations the background of everyday social life's complexity, a point
made repeatedly by Weber in his studies of historical change.

The Disabuse of Power

Personal power as we have studied it here is what worried Weber, especially
the tendency of powerful persons to abuse their control of others. Power is
often addicting to those who exercise it because it makes them dependent for
self-esteem on the responsiveness of those they control. Power itself does not
require reciprocity; it exists apart from mutual relatedness. Thus its exercise
is independent of the forms of optimal association from which introjected
strengths can develop. A powerful person can come to be wholly dependent,
therefore, on the exercise of power itself in order to make himself or herself
feel adequate. Exercising power is exhilarating in numerous ways and is often
a substitute for psychologically more adequate mutual relationships. One is
made to feel better about oneself by manipulating others, whose idealizations
are converted into mirrored strength.

Disabusing oneself of such powerful leaders, or of a partner, opens the door
to important personal and social developments. In this chapter, we have seen
how studying the appearance and disappearance of personal power introduces
the whole complex subject of change and organization in the social world.
Moreover, with the tools now in our hands for making sense of the phenomena
of power, we are poised to extend our analysis toward a terrain even more
familiar to social scientists—the organization of large-scale, complex societies. Using the same tools in the next chapter, I want to show how we can
further exploit classic sociological ideas about power and culture to develop,
first, a theory of weak interaction and, second, a general framework for understanding social structure and large-scale historical change.

7

Markets and Hierarchies: Social Structure and Strong Interaction Systems

Conceiving the Impersonal Other

Settings for modern economic activity are notoriously inhospitable to the particularism isolated by the concept of selfobject transference. The tendency we all exhibit to reconfigure interaction partners as persons responsive to basic attachment needs just doesn't fit well, in the theory of economic life, into arrangements of rational activity. Norms instituted in business settings, thus, presumably have exchange partners establishing relationships on the basis of criteria other than their respective "role responsiveness." For reasons similar to legal rationalism's efforts to exclude favoritism from hiring and victims' relatives from juries, rationality in economic life, particularly as it is conceived in theory, assumes decision making from which such particularism has been excluded. Ridding its world of real men and women to reflect this assumption, economic theory achieves formal elegance by imagining business transactions in every instance negotiated with a kind of "impersonalized other"—a fictive actor the equivalent in theory of the "market." In Emerson's (1976; also Cook and Emerson 1978; Cook et al. 1983) analysis of these matters, positing such an "impersonal other" supports the critical assumption of independence among market actors—a matter nonetheless contradicted by "imperfections" of real interdependence encountered in actual social relations. Such economic fictions may never occur in nature, but their manipulation in the abstract provides a baseline for evaluating empirical phenomena.

Starting from psychological foundations where matters like selfobject transference are prominent, by contrast, we can derive a distinctively different argument about particularism. Contemporary self psychology, for example, would take the question of how we construe our partners in economic life as a far more complicated theoretical and empirical matter than is the case in economic theory. Understanding economic life from this point of view would not lead to contrasting real observations to those derived from a fictional construct, but to understanding how it is possible for men and women to act as if their partners *were* fictions—cold, impersonal, unempathic fictions, at that. This, after all, is perhaps the more remarkable phenomenon empirically, evaluated from the point of view of human life's emotional foundations. Not good economics, perhaps, but a way to locate a sound footing for culturally shaped perceptions, economic or other. In addition, self psychology would direct us to compare this conception of the affectively neutralized partner to conceptions of partners in different economic or social systems. Viewed in the larger framework of comparative economics or comparative culture, modern settings for economic life are special cases—of necessity understandable only in relation to complex cultural and social developments. Where these developments have not occurred, we find strikingly different patterns of conceiving economic partners—or, for that matter, any kind of partners (Brain 1976).

To frame an analysis of particularism in this way, of course, is again to be reminded of the life's work of Max Weber (1968a). The central questions in Weber's macrosociology derived from his efforts to understand how matters of culture and social life interacted with individual psychology to serve the rationalizing needs of modern capitalism. His analysis was undertaken in exactly the comparative economic and cultural framework we have been discussing—one where we might eventually pinpoint how particularism was gradually excluded from the ways men and women conceived their economic activities. I believe, in agreement with many others (e.g., Schluchter 1979, 1981), that we might still profit by following Weber's lead on these questions and attempt again to construct a bridge by which microsociological concerns with social interaction—particularly this problem of depersonalizing our partners—can admit the forces of culture and social organization Weber took to be the conditions of modern social life. The problem most central to constructing this bridge, as I see it, is understanding the way cultural and social developments damp and filter from interaction the powerful forces of self-object transference we have attended in earlier parts of this book.

In what follows, therefore, I want to extend this theoretical project into a terrain more familiar to macrosociologists and examine several cultural and social filters on transference. This requires us first to reanalyze what Weber described as foundations for the legitimation of political authority, since his typology of these foundations suggests ways we may refine the discussion of some of the pertinent variation embedded in rationalization. Through this reanalysis we shall isolate structural and cultural filters on the powerful forces of attraction and repulsion deriving from our attachment needs, as conceived in self psychology. In addition, this reanalysis will enable us to conceive in Weberian terms the markets-and-hierarchies logic made useful again in economic theory by Oliver Williamson's work (1975, 1981). In turn, this framework will provide a way to link Weberian macrosociology to Prigogine's analysis of far-from-equilibrium systems. We shall then have come full circle in this book—from our start in a theory of strong attachment, through our analysis of responsiveness, sensitive dependence, and strong interaction, all the way into the study of strong forces of dependence in romantic love and in dissipative structures like power systems and markets.

Systems of Domination

The Ambivalence about Particularism

Max Weber's theorizing, as we have seen, exhibited a common liberal ambivalence toward matters of affect and particularism—interfering, as these forces did, with the historical project of dismantling political tyranny and undermining patriarchalism. In his comparative sociology, therefore, Weber produced thoughts about modernity which both attracted him—the capacity of rationality to support political freedom—and repelled him—the denial of basic life forces by impersonal bureaucratic decision making. Despite this ambivalence, his "ideal types" depicting modern life purged particularism from it utterly and left behind a landscape not of personal relations but of constitutions and offices, impersonal rules impersonally applied (*sine ira et studio*). Looking at society through the curtain of official life, men and women seemed to Weber drained of blood and warmth, specters conjured by the forces of efficiency and rationality celebrated in his terse rendering of bureaucracy. As a matter of theoretical logic, the analysis of bureaucracy included a despairing conclusion: rationality operated best when it suppressed matters of affect and inhibited particularism. This was a conclusion about which Weber was clearly of two minds. The side of his mind Mitzman (1969) identifies with Weber's mother was uncomfortable with this image of a world drained of feelings—a world without responsiveness.

This ambivalence about affect is preserved in Weberian theory, and has become one of the ways sociological thought sometimes blinds itself unnecessarily to the powerful operation of feelings and affect in contexts where they are proscribed by such wintry images of rationality. Subsequent theorists working in the Weberian tradition have gotten around problems left behind in the ideal types in numerous ways, usually by recognizing a "multidimensionality" whereby affect and rationality become interdependent notions.[1] They have rediscovered community in cities, the force of personal ties in combat, primary groups in industry, and other such familiar matters. It remains an open question, however, how exactly to conceptualize these affective forces. Are we to regard them, say, as would economic theory—as forces to be suppressed and ignored in view of the operation of utility-maximizing rationality? As equilibrating forces in task settings, like the social-emotional figures in Bales's (1950, 1953) early versions of problem-solving groups? As simple information codes (Zajonc 1980) used by persons to interpret environments? One view is developed in Weber's own scheme of thinking: we are to regard matters of affect as but one of several foundations on which social life might build, and to which it occasionally returns to replenish itself in different ways.

Foundations of Legitimacy Reconceived

FOUNDATIONS AS ENVIRONMENTS OF ACTION   We can begin to grasp Weber's foundation argument more clearly by developing some of its underlying logic. This appears most clearly in his speciation of the social world into ideal types, each based on different ways of organizing political life. Rather than simply listing these types, as he does, consider how they might be arrayed in terms of underlying variables—in particular, how Weber's typology of foundations for the legitimation of authority, as discussed in his political sociology, might be reanalyzed in view of implicit underlying variables. These four foundations—affect, tradition, purposive rationality, and value rationality—can be ordered conceptually by constructing a scheme where each is viewed as an *environment* for social action, a scheme calling upon us, in turn, to understand each such foundational environment as the joint or compound product of several complex variables. These must be spelled out. By reconceptualizing Weber's four foundations in view of these underlying variables, we shall be in a theoretical position to say something more precise about filters on personal life—specifically, about sociocultural filters on affect. First consider the scheme itself, then the underlying variables.

Figure 7.1 presents the argument in summary form. What it argues is that two complex forms of variation—one called cybernetic level, the other neutralization—combine to produce the foundations for authority systems Weber isolated in his comparative studies. The overlap between this scheme and Weber's isn't perfect. In particular, I have supplanted his concept of *Wertrationalität* with a generalized category of "values," but there is enough of an overlap to serve my purposes here. Note, as well, that running through this analysis is an important, implicit logic having to do with market forces, on the one hand, and hierarchical forces, on the other. In particular, the cybernetic dimension is related to variation in social organization (simple versus complex organization), and the neutralization dimension to different features of market behavior (dependent versus autonomous action). The markets-and-

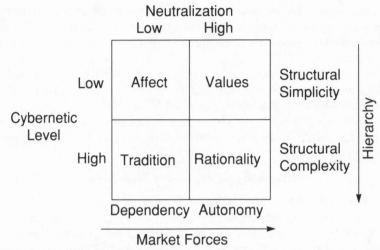

Fig. 7.1   A revised approach to the foundations of authority

hierarchies distinction will become an important theme in the argument, developed in subsequent sections of this chapter, about interaction systems. Here it helps to capture several of the themes in Weberian sociology.

This is principally so because throughout his life Weber had sought to find a way in sociological theory to comprehend the interdependence of historical conditions supporting individual freedom with those enabling rational economic life—all the while preserving a way for us also to talk systematically about premodern social arrangements. In the revisionist presentation of the component logic as it appears in figure 7.1, we can begin to see quite clearly how some of the forces Weber had in mind also might be understood as "filters" on personal life. Consider first the logic of this scheme and then how it can be illustrated with some of Weber's own examples.

THE COMPONENT LOGIC   One matter clearly at work in Weber's thought is a process I shall call neutralization. Rational market forces in his view demanded impersonal social relations—"neutralized" by having been made independent of transferentially complicated connections like kinship. As Weber saw it, for example, a hallmark of modern bureaucratic rationality was the appearance of impersonal rules and standards of conduct. Impersonality arose in connection with generalization of standards for evaluating performance apart from personal considerations like kinship or personal devotion—with abstraction in criteria of evaluation. Connected to impersonality in this sense were highly generalized "values" such as justice, salvation, and charity at the heart of the great world religions, as well as generalized standards like thrift, honesty, and efficiency, embodied in settings for modern work.

Values formulated apart from personal relations, to put this differently, become abstract and generalized. This happens when purely personal relations cease to be the sole or principal matrix of evaluation in the social world, and what people value can be formulated in increasingly generalized and neutral terms. An important example of neutralization appears historically when money becomes a medium of exchange.

Of equal importance in Weber's thought is another dimension—the capacity of certain cultural patterns to "carry" complex social organization. Weber thought of law, for example, as an environment of social action, and argued that rational law in particular was one of the conditions for the appearance of modern capitalism. Religion, similarly, he saw as another environment of economic activity, as in his familiar arguments about this-worldly asceticism. If we think of culture more generally as forming such environments of action, then in Weber's reasoning it was certain properties of these cultural environments—especially the properties he associated with traditionalization and rationalization—that appeared historically to be related to the development of "complexity" in social organization. Hierarchical forms in their traditional or modern instances would be examples of such "complexity."

But what is denoted by this concept of complexity? Such an idea readily translates, for example, into the terms of contemporary organizational theory. Suppose, as in prominent organization research (e.g., Blau and Schoenherr 1971), we allow complexity to be measured in an organizational sense by some variable that maps "administrative intensity" ("spans of control") and "levels of hierarchy." [2] By this definition, then, the more levels of hierarchy, and the greater the average span of control, the greater the average "complexity" of social organization.[3] Complexity in this sense is a matter supported (or, in our terms, "carried") by the cultural developments Weber associated with tradition and with rationality. The highest forms of complexity, in the case of rationality, were supported by cultural developments that included the appearance of systematic, written forms of culture such as rational law, accounting, and written record keeping. Less complex social arrangements, by contrast, rested on other cultural foundations.

Complexity is also related to the process Parsons (1966) called specification. Specification, as I use the concept here, means fitting culture normatively to social action, as by elaborating expectations, divining a truth, deriving a moral consequence, interpreting an oracle, discovering justice, reading a contract, or writing down a constitution. These modes of specification are typical responsibilities for authorities—bosses, rulers, judges, priests, leaders—and result in supplying the roles of subordinates—employees, subjects, juries, parishioners, followers—with direction. Where the activities of specification rest on culture with cybernetic properties we can abbreviate as "information richness," specification produces a sociocultural environment able to carry increased spans of control—and hence, complexity.[4] Specification does this by establishing cultural foundations for autonomous activity.

How complexity varies with specification can be documented by observing that superior-subordinate relationships loosen when there are increases in the autonomy of subordinates: specification then diminishes the need for supervision. Just how far along toward supporting subordinates' autonomy specification gets, of course, depends on the amount of information superiors possess about tasks and settings. Only in "information-rich" environments, that is, will the specification of cultural values or models establish norms and expectations by which persons in subordinate positions can regulate their own behavior.[5]

As defined in these terms, therefore, one can argue that the particular cybernetic properties of culture Weber thought supported "complexity" were a product of "information richness" and specification.

Weber's ideas on the subject of bureaucratic administration, as with his ideas about freedom, eventually led him to understand what we call "autonomy" as a concept that made sense only within a framework of legal or normative limitations. He spoke, for example, of independent "spheres" of responsibility connected with "offices." Such reasoning is approximately represented in figure 7.2, where the "autonomy" in roles or offices is viewed as a function of the specification, down through different levels in a hierarchy, of "information-rich" versus "information-poor" culture—the premises or models in terms of which a division of labor is organized.[6]

Organizational complexity from this perspective was a matter growing as much from concerting the limited or "bounded" autonomous capacities of offices—the separate "spheres" of official responsibility—as from coordinating their incumbents hierarchically.[7] This conceptualization is implicit in ar-

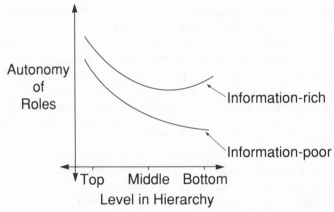

Fig. 7.2   Hierarchical distribution of role autonomy as a function of specification

guments that bureaucratic administration depends on clear divisions of labor, as specified, for example, in constitutions or codes. Codes specify exact terms of office, enable clear divisions of labor, and establish precise arrangements of authority—the hallmarks of rational administration.

Dramatic consequences of his reasoning, both about specification and autonomy, can then be presented as in figure 7.2: most important, spans of control by this reasoning can be larger in information-rich environments than in information-poor environments. Where subordinates already know what is expected of them, that is, fewer supervisors or superiors are required to coordinate or direct their activities. And subordinates can know what is expected of them only when their roles and offices have been specified.

This relationship becomes fully obvious only in comparative organizational research. It is especially clear, for example, when "spans of control" in organizations with fully specified, public cultures—like the administrative and support sectors of an army—are compared with "spans of control" in organizations without such specification—as in combat sectors of an army, where subordinates follow orders but don't have much autonomy. Since fewer officers are needed to supervise clerks than to lead men to face an enemy under fire, clerical offices easily outscore combat units on measures of spans of control (Smith and Ross 1984).

When this reasoning is placed within the developmental argument of earlier chapters, the derivation shown in figure 7.2 appears as a proposition reasserting the relationship of two different substitutes for caregivers—leadership and culture. In organizations and families, leadership is needed where cultural supports for autonomy are missing. The matter is more complex than this statement makes it seem, but this is the basic point. Organizations can develop complexity only when they are favored by environments (or create conditions) that allow supplanting leadership (supervision, caregiving, etc.) with some mix of external and internal culture—organization charts, constitutions, written rules, "offices," professional culture, internalizations, and so forth. The patterns of organization Weber considered make this obvious. But the general point applies to families as well as to bureaucracies.[8]

GENERATING WEBER'S EXAMPLES   Weber himself developed many examples of how different patterns of "organization" were associated with different cultural foundations for legitimate authority.

Charismatic groups, patrimonial households, rational sects, and bureaucracies came close to providing for him pure illustrations of his four foundations of authority, as he defined them. As we should be able to see, each example can be understood in terms of our reconceptualization of the variation underlying Weber's foundation argument. But to make this clear, let us first show how our scheme for generating Weber's foundations can also be used to gen-

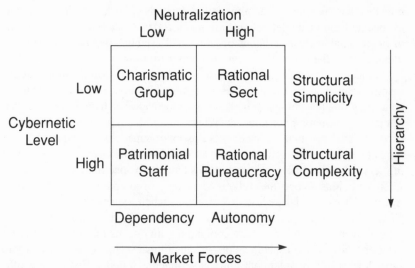

Fig. 7.3   Cross-classifying Weber's examples using the revised approach to the foundations of authority

erate his examples. Consider the examples as they have been arranged in figure 7.3.

When Weber talked of the disciples of a charismatic figure, as we saw in chapter 6, he used terms that made these followers seem the forerunners at times of an aristocracy, at others of a staff. In either case, the "organizational" arrangements of charisma in his view were not "neutralized" in our sense, and likewise would be regarded as structurally primitive or simple. Little organizational complexity arises around a warlord.

Structurally more complex, by contrast, were examples of traditional organization like the personalized household of a patriarch or the patrimonial staff of a king—again, arrangements still not neutralized, but now resting on richer cultural foundations. Illustrations of the richer cultural content of patrimonialism, for example, would include the appearance of named household officials (e.g., chamberlains) and other administrative appointees (e.g., sheriffs).

When we look at the example Weber discussed as the "rational sect," we find a collectivity he characterized as *Gesinnungsverein*—founded on the "voluntary association of individuals motivated by adherence to a set of common absolute values" (Weber 1968a, 41). What he had in mind here were the ascetic Protestant sects he had studied in conjunction with his argument about the historical origins of the ethics of bourgeois capitalism ([1904–5] 1958). Though subject to numerous empirical variations of which he was aware, these sects characteristically emphasized voluntarist individualism, sovereignty of the sacramental community, and strict moral discipline. Especially because such groups vigilantly concerned themselves with the purity of their sacramental communities, their members were obliged repeatedly to prove themselves persons worthy of inclusion. But because the qualities taken to exemplify worthiness and to qualify one for inclusion were not laid down by authority (in accordance with their individualist orientations toward Scripture), the emphasis was on proving oneself before God and gaining signs of salvation. Accordingly, the "pure" rational sect typically appeared as an example of simple organization—indeed, among groups like the Quakers, typically illustrated principled opposition to complexity, even as their ascetic disciplines were evidence of rationalization in respect to absolute values like salvation. General values such as salvation, in the absence of having their implications authoritatively and doctrinally specified as in a church, proved to be poor in information and thus able to support only primitive organizational arrangements; in addition, such absolute and abstract values worked to undermine personalism.[9]

Among Weber's examples, rational bureaucracy alone illustrates a pattern of organization benefiting both from neutralization and cybernetic richness. His famous essay on bureaucracy can be read as an explanation of why the organizational properties of this type—hierarchy, professional employment, clear divisions of labor, and so forth—not only are associated with efficient administration but also are supported by information-rich cultural environments and impersonal social relations.

Cultural Coefficients on Social Interaction

The immediate reason for undertaking this revisionist presentation of the component logic behind Weber's analysis of authority systems is that it enables us to see how some of the forces at work in his comparative sociology might also be understood as "filters" on personal life. When we try to imagine the "impersonal other" rational economic life requires, we need merely interpose between ourselves and the outer world the sort of filter Weber himself conceived—one that neutralizes the affect in social relations and sets those relations in an information-rich context of complex organization. On the one hand, this filter damps the operation of particularism in social relations, and on the other, it makes "offices" and not persons the building blocks of social structure. The neutralizing forces—money as a medium of exchange, norms of emotional neutrality in official relations, formally free labor, and other abstracting and generalizing cultural conditions—are those supporting rational market activity: calculability, substitutability, alienability, mobility, and divisibility of resources. The cybernetic and specifying forces—systematic record keeping, written constitutions, rational law and morality, explicit objectives, elaborate recruitment and socialization, professional training—create an information environment able to sustain hierarchical organization: a formal division of labor, separate spheres of responsibility, concerted autonomy, and efficient administrative ratios.

FILTERING THE INTERACTION FIELD How do these forces enter into social interaction? Imagine again the interaction field we have discussed throughout this book—a place entered naïvely by two social actors, sometimes burdened by the strong force of personal deficits, as each searches for responsiveness in the other. Now, however, let us define the setting of their interaction in the terms we have established above.

The filters on particularism Weber discussed, and the supports for complex organization he implicitly analyzed, stand now as a combination of variables we could write as a coefficient on the force of attraction $F(t)$ as it was formulated in chapter 3—a force that otherwise would be fully at work between our hypothetical actors, depending on their respective "role responsiveness" (the R values in equation 3.7) and introjected strengths (the Z values in equation 3.7). And depending on whether we are talking about low or high states of the filtering variables, we end up with a coefficient—let us call it λ, defined below—that damps or amplifies our gravity-like representation of $F(t)$.

Consider $F(t)$ first within the context of each ideal type. By filtering affect from relationships, neutralization (considered now as one component of the value λ takes on, the other being cybernetic richness) plays an important part undermining transference. It causes us to attend others not as potentially responsive and empathic vehicles for our needs—in the light, that is, of some personal and local significance—but in ways establishing their relevance apart from our relationship to them. This generalized way of establishing "relevances" (cf. Schutz and Luckmann 1973) is the beginning of what Parsons and Shils (1951) called universalism—the departicularized alternative within their scheme of pattern variables.

UNIVERSALISM AND PARTICULARISM IN DEVELOPMENTAL PERSPECTIVE
Such nonlocal contexts of information, knowledge, relevance, or culture allow or direct partners to construe each other in ways that are interpersonally distancing. For example, the facilities and media enabling profit-oriented market exchanges yield instrumental relevances to partners. Viewed in terms of psychological development, the capacity to construe partners in view of their instrumental relevance is often interpreted as one of the markers of developmental strength—the capacity to "use" an object or a partner generally being understood developmentally to be more "advanced" than simply attending a partner personally.[10] (This is a point made, for example, by Winnicott [1971, 89] on the basis of clinical observations.) In Winnicott's argument, this instrumentalizing capacity gets its start during infancy where caregivers allow infants to develop trust in their environments. When infants know their

caregivers are reliable, they are enabled to relinquish objects they otherwise would keep subjectively under their "omnipotent" control. Objects then begin to develop properties in "reality"—that is, apart from their statuses in subjectivity. Especially as coupled to information richness, therefore, neutralization goes hand-in-hand with disenchantment and the rationalization of the social world.

As a basis for reasoning about what culture needs to do to make complex instrumental structures possible, it helps to recall such reasoning about psychological growth. Neutralization cannot occur unless objects and partners are instituted into external realities where they have properties unamenable to modification or control through the operation of wishes, paranoia, or omnipotence. When we remember that "optimal frustration" is the occasion in the Winnicott-Kohut model for relinquishing control of the object and for introjection, we also locate psychological roots for establishing subjective representations of "objects" simultaneously having external statuses. More generally, we discern psychological analogues to the process of distancing a person from objects.

Rationality in social life, as in bureaucracies, is supported when such neutralism in social relations is coupled to cybernetic conditions able to carry complexity and bounded autonomy.

One of Weber's points about the pattern of social order he described as traditional was that it failed to support such neutralized relationships, particularly those between authorities and their subjects. In terms of our scheme for making sense of his types, particularism survives when cybernetic conditions add information but not neutralization to a social environment. In the logic behind figure 7.3, therefore, "information richness" alone produces conditions able to "carry" complex social arrangements, but such arrangements become complex only because they are able to extend and ramify the affective relationships present in simpler patterns of organization. Feudalism with its attendant process of subinfeudation illustrates how "organizational" complexity can grow out of such hierarchical ramification of essentially personal ties—with a lord's vassals, by developing vassals of their own, replicating arrangements of loyalty and service. Because of the emphasis placed by this structural logic on particularism (low neutralization), this is a concept of traditional social organization that makes traditional order dependent on sustaining a network or hierarchy of personal dependencies. Traditional order aggregates systems of personal ties—kinship groups, feudal alliances, village communities, and so forth.

Though this can be seen most clearly in the case of European feudalism, many of the "sacred" tribal kingships studied by anthropologists—the Zulu as described by Gluckman (1963) and Basoga society studied by Fallers ([1956] 1965, esp. 1966), for instance—also illustrate how "tradition" itself often becomes dependent on particular figures—particular kings, particular chiefs, particular elders. Even though a structure or arrangement of offices or roles is instituted through custom or traditional law as the framework for incumbents' conduct, royal offices in some degree become personalized and stand open to their incumbent's interpretation within broad limits.[11] Family metaphors likewise work in these and other societies as a concrete traditional language for hierarchy, shaping subordinates' "expectations" about leaders as persons with whom to recapitulate archaic (i.e., early caregiving) relationships.[12]

As we have already seen, Weber's main example of the pattern of social life founded on pure affect was the arrangement of a charismatic figure and his or her followers. Without neutralization or specified information, we end up, as argued for the case of charisma in chapter 6, with arrangements like those uniting a needy infant with a delusional caregiver. Cultural developments within charismatic groups that diminish followers' dependency on leaders establish foundations for transforming charismatic authority into other systems of domination—traditional or rational forms, as described by Weber. The routinization of charisma is the process by which these cultural foundations (particularly those supporting autonomy) supplant purely affectual relationships, and one or another pattern of everyday social order emerges.

Add the abstraction and impersonality in neutralism to conditions of low information, and the picture changes to one resembling the ideological collectivity described by Nahirny (1962) or the rational sect studied by Weber. Utopian groups, seen in this light, are able to generate responsiveness in needy followers in part because they serve as generalized templates for wishfulfillment. Brook Farm was filled with dreamers and philosophers.[13]

Ordered, Low-Energy Structures

Boundary Conditions

Weber's preoccupation with culture as an environment of social action derived from his lifelong interest in understanding how stable, modern forms of organization emerged historically. A straightforward way to translate his ideas into the language of dissipative structure theory comes from attending these cultural environments of organization. From the dissipative structure point of view, the environment of a system is where we locate boundary conditions. Weber's concern with rationalization—with information-rich, systematic, and specified culture—translates, in this perspective, into discovering the boundary conditions for a social system that make it *least* compatible with personal fluxes of the sort we have made the focus of our study in this book—namely, boundary conditions able to damp particularism and its roots, the selfobject transferences, as well as all of the instability associated socially with such feedback-based fluxes.

As we shall see later on, this argument also permits translating the hidden dimensions uncovered in our reanalysis of Weber's foundation typology—the dimensions of market forces and hierarchical forces—into the same general framework for studying dissipative structures and far-from-equilibrium instability. Market forces, as we shall see, are based on positive feedback processes, hierarchical forces on negative feedback processes. Culture is one such negative feedback condition or environment—a source of negentropy and stability in social life. Without such cultural sources of damping and inversion, positive feedback appears in interaction systems. Though details of this argument have appeared already and others will be worked out below, what this suggests should be anticipated here: the important implication is that the large-scale structure of social systems—what we shall begin here calling the macrostructure—evolves from a mix of market processes and hierarchical processes and can be described, just as the structure of "self" as a system can be described, as *bipolar*. Or, at this level of analysis, as having the property of *bistability*.

"Coherent" social systems, by this reasoning, can be treated conceptually as if their coherence were the product of *two* subordinate processes of structuration. What this means more specifically is that market processes operate macroscopically with the same functional role that mirroring processes have microscopically (i.e., in two-person interaction systems and in "self"), and likewise that hierarchical processes operate macroscopically with the functional significance held microscopically by idealization. The mix of these two kinds of processes affects the evolving macrostructure of social systems the way the mix of mirroring and idealization functions in relation to the development of "self." In theory, therefore, social systems may be described as more or less "structured" in each of these areas, and as having evolved with greater or lesser emphasis along a "developmental" line emphasizing market structuration or a "developmental" line emphasizing hierarchical structuration— though all will display both forms of structuration in some degree. Examples of social systems where hierarchical processes dominate macrostructure would be those with so-called command economies and other nonmarket arrangements of economic life, for example, totalitarian oligarchies like the Soviet Union prior to *perestroika* and *glasnost*. Examples of market-dominated social systems would be most so-called free enterprise or capitalist economies. In reality, coherent societies always contain some mix of both market and nonmarket structuration. Indeed, the peculiar mixtures of market and hierarchical forces account for significant qualitative differences among societies.

The microscopic-macroscopic distinction in use here is one of *scale*. Across the change of scale produced as we enlarge a system of interaction from a dyad to n-persons, we eventually introduce into social systems interpersonal matters described by concepts familiar from evolutionary, economic, demographic, and ecological theory—for example, scarcity, demand, competition, carrying capacity, mortality, conflict, accommodation, assimilation.[14] Viewed in terms of their contributions to positive or negative feedback within the systems encompassing them, these are equivalents to processes at work interpersonally in small-scale systems. Some, like competition under conditions of scarcity, introduce positive feedback into social systems, and hence are able to drive systems into far-from-equilibrium conditions. Others, like cooperation and contract, denote processes geared to producing negative feedback, and hence are capable of introducing stability. Social organization, just like personal self, is structured by the mix of these two simultaneous kinds of processes—those founded on positive feedback and those founded on negative feedback. Market processes, by being based on the positive feedback inherent in interaction systems, give rise to dissipative structures—high-energy forms of structuration based on scavenging entropy. Hierarchical processes by contrast are based on negative feedback and give rise to low-energy forms of structuration functioning to supply negentropy. The way the two kinds of processes mix suggests a concept of social structure far more dynamic, accidental, evolving, and process-based than those currently in use in social theory. We shall have to work out this logic by steps, beginning with what we have learned from Weber about the importance of culture as a boundary condition.

Culture as a Boundary Condition

As argued in earlier chapters, all culture establishes boundary conditions able in some degree to damp internal fluctuations in social or personal life. When we are speaking of individual actors as systems, culture functions as a caregiver substitute and thus serves to diminish phenomena like sensitive dependence and role responsiveness. When self is viewed homeostatically, culture is what works as a negative feedback device or inverting amplifier. Both sensitive dependence and role responsiveness, as we have seen, can give rise to far-from-equilibrium conditions in interaction, based on the positive feedback operating in attachment behavior and selfobject transferences.

Yet not all culture works equally well in damping these matters. The damping of such fluctuations occurs in proportion to culture's possession of properties like those Weber isolated in his studies of rationalization. Especially when cultural systems are public, systematic, and information-rich, they support autonomy and thus enable persons to function apart from strong attachments. That is, they enable persons to stabilize and regulate themselves apart from depending on external selfobjects—caregivers, other persons, and so forth.

This is ultimately a condition for the emergence, in any form, of stable complexity in social life, as I have argued. Only when separate actors have well-developed self-regulating capacities are they themselves in possession of the strengths to override the inexorable tendency that arises in face-to-face interaction of using external others as selfobjects—of recapitulating, that is, the infant-caregiver system, and the strong forms of positive feedback inherent in such interaction.

From a macroscopic viewpoint, therefore, the absence of cultural supports for autonomy predisposes strong interaction systems and strong attachments; indeed, such sociocultural "absence" is the boundary equivalent of "deficits" in self. In both conditions personal dependencies become common, and, as a result, a chronic condition of sensitive dependence emerges—or, to put this in Prigoginian terms, systems become liable to far-from-equilibrium fluctuations. Such unstable, personalistic systems are marked by high levels of entropy and give rise to high-energy structures—structures like romantic dyads, arrangements of "status despotism" (cf. Fallers 1966, 1973), or systems of power and dependency that scavenge high levels of entropy.[15] Ordered, low-energy structures like complex organizations depend on damping sensitive dependence and supporting personal autonomy.

Microscopic and Macroscopic Dynamics

An arrow drawn diagonally through figure 7.1, from affect through rationality, would describe a trajectory of social development away from circumstances where personal feelings were dominant forces in social organization toward circumstances where feelings, personality, and self had all but disappeared as relevant considerations. This means that in studying organized systems built principally on rational culture, a level of social life comes into view whose dynamics override those of smaller, less encompassing systems. From a macroscopic viewpoint, such dynamics typically presuppose a decentered sociological analysis, where the unit is not the person but a structural feature like role. These structural features are defined by their depersonalization and by effective cultural supports for autonomous persons acting universalistically.

By contrast, studying systems built principally on affect keeps in view dynamics able to override those associated with rationality, and sustains a person-centered perspective. Affective dynamics don't exclude rationality, nor does rationality eliminate affective dynamics. But as we move from affect toward rationality, we move from microscopic dynamics of self and interaction toward macroscopic dynamics of complex, large-scale systems. What Weber had isolated in his concepts of rational organization were thus conditions in which macroscopic processes overrode and damped fluxes arising from microscopic processes. The personal was overriden by the social.

Viewed realistically, all social systems can be understood as mixtures of competing processes pulling in these different directions—toward, on the one hand, the strong forces present interpersonally in two-person interaction, and the weak forces arising, on the other hand, from the ordered macroscopic systems in which interactions are more or less always embedded. An important property of macrostructures in this sense is that they exist apart from particular incumbents. With dynamics able to survive the loss or replacement of particular persons, they routinely override the dynamics of their incumbents—at least when incumbents are taken singly.[16] While this suprapersonal dominance can be celebrated in ways that naïvely ignore the workings of affect, the complex processes embedded in many macroscopic systems tend to operate in ways that allow personal dynamics to be ignored in understanding their structure or evolution.[17]

Two Forms of Structuration

Generalizations about the forms of complexity within regions of the social world would seem easily deduced from the theory of strong interaction, from Weber's theory of authority systems, and from numerous other theories. The typical sociological approach to understanding complex social organization, following Weber, emphasizes how hierarchical structuration appears in a region in conjunction with the spread or growth of culture in one form or another. Economists take the reverse perspective and emphasize how market structuration flourishes where hierarchical elements are weak or absent. These two styles of argument complement one another and speak to the same idealized phenomena—high-energy systems like markets, on the one hand, and low-energy systems like complex organizations, on the other.

HIERARCHICAL STRUCTURATION   Weber's examples of complex organization, as in his analysis of modern bureaucracy, are illustrations of hierarchical structuration. So, too, are examples of traditional hierarchy, such as systems of stratification based on status groups.

To stabilize and reproduce themselves, systems structured hierarchically depend on a cultural template, and Weberian analysis typically shows how such cultural terms for social differentiation emerge. Castes, for example, stabilize a society on the basis of religiously formulated beliefs, normatively constraining a society into a complex mosaic of horizontally and vertically differentiated regions. Such beliefs, like those prohibiting exogamous marriage, work to suppress tendencies toward the emergence of systems of interaction that might destabilize these arrangements. Other examples of hierarchical structuration based on status groups also arise in relation to normative codes, which likewise regionalize and restrict interaction, market exchange included (Nelson [1949] 1969).

MARKET STRUCTURATION   In classic microeconomic theory, markets are studied in relation to other "conditions" of exchange—specifically, conditions that introduce into relationships any considerations of a "nonmarket" nature. This market-nonmarket distinction is used by economists to isolate deviations from so-called perfect competition (see, e.g., Stigler 1950). Markets with small numbers of participants, high levels of uncertainty, weak information, and indivisibility of assets (including untransferable labor, information, skills, rights, etc.) are all subject to deviations from the behavior denoted by the concept of perfect competition. As these imperfect conditions appear, exchange takes on an increasingly bilateral quality—that is, it becomes dyadic and situational rather than a matter undertaken in relation to an impersonal market.

Consider just the nonmarketability factors associated specifically with changes in the generality of assets or resources. An administrative supply like paper, for example, is a nonspecific asset or resource—one a person or firm might get impersonally from any number of suppliers. Most firms use non-specific assets of this kind, but they also make use of other assets lacking this kind of generality (cf. Williamson 1975, 1981, whose discussion I follow here). Specificity in this sense is a quality assets acquire when they are specialized to particular relationships—for example, the semifinished goods a firm's machines are tooled specifically to complete. Other examples of "asset specificity" include any unique abilities of an exchange partner that affect a firm's costs, like a partner's specific "talents."

When discussing not firms but persons as "market actors" in a broader social exchange sense, many other specific nontransferable qualities of partners also come into view, such as an exchange partner's "responsiveness" or kinship. From a sociological perspective on such markets, in addition, an important matter always giving asset specificity to partners is particularism. It is particularism that prevents mothers from being indifferent as to which child they pick up at the daycare center.

In this market-and-hierarchies tradition of theorizing, economists and others have attempted to derive from imperfect competition an analysis of the conditions where nonmarket structuration should appear (e.g., Coase 1973; Williamson 1975; Dahl and Lindblom 1953; Lindblom 1977).

CULTURAL MODELS OF SOCIAL STRUCTURE   With the concepts of hierarchical and market structuration, we are able to speak of changes of structure, as when we use terms like loosening, opening, or slackening to describe loss of structure. These are useful distinctions because the processes by which structural gains or losses are produced—structuration and destructuration, respectively—powerfully affect the matter of sociocultural integration. Hierarchical structuration in particular is associated with increasing sociocultural integration and hence is connected with increasing the stabilizing force of cultural controls. Hierarchical destructuration, conversely, diminishes sociocultural integration and hence undermines cultural controls.

The reason hierarchical structuration is associated with normative culture is double-sided—stability is a condition of lasting expectations (normative or other), but lasting expectations in turn are governors of stability. Expectations are fundamental stabilizers in any social system, and they function effectively in this respect under two conditions—when they themselves are steady, and in proportion to their comprehensiveness in specifying relationships in a region. No cultural model is ever completely comprehensive, and all are in some sense limited by the information properties of the cultural channels in which they are stored and transmitted—oral devices such as stories, for example, being far less efficient (though perhaps no less comprehensive) than, say, written contracts or constitutions. When such a model appears, it tends to *become* normative—that is, to serve as a cultural template by which a system can subsequently replicate and stabilize itself.[18] As in the discussion of structuration in self, where we saw that only idealized selfobjects ultimately functioned to stabilize and consolidate self, we are here discussing an equivalent phenomenon at the level of larger systems.

Transferred to social systems, the model of structuration in self implies the same functional relationship between structuration culturally and socially we have been discussing above in other terms. On the one hand, that is, the spread of hierarchical structuration in a region tends to proceed lockstep with the appearance of ever more comprehensive (or at least articulated) cultural models; and, on the other, the correlation of structural and cultural growth yields—Kohut would say "consolidates"—sociocultural integration or system cohesion.

Sociocultural integration sometimes can be attributed to the appearance of a piecemeal process of structuration that serves macroscopically in the same functional way as an idealized selfobject in the interaction of infant and caregiver. A good example of this is provided by Stinchcombe, who describes elaborate "contracting" among parties involved in the development of oil resources in the North Sea. Contracting provides examples of "ways to construct social structures that work like hierarchies out of contracts between legally equal corporate bargaining agents in a market" (Stinchcombe 1984, 2). Contracting may not be hierarchy, but it counts functionally as such. In fact, contracting should also count as a cultural process, since it amounts to the legal specification of expectations presiding over a region.[19]

Religious officials, judges, elders, legislators, rulers, prophets, lawyers, teachers, bosses—all play some part in integrating, specifying, and elaborating models in functionally analogous ways, and all such figures serve in some sense either directly as "idealized selfobjects" or they create and interpret "cultural selfobjects." In general, the dynamics of authority systems connect the "responsiveness" of their incumbents to the idealizing needs of a constituency or audience, "generating" leadership in something like Parsons's (1967) sense. Leadership takes up where cultural direction itself leaves off, filling in the gap between dependency and autonomy in the way of a caregiver, or caregiver substitute. There is as much room for leadership in a social group as there is dependency—a matter that has a great deal to do with flaws in the supports for autonomy.

Such flaws constitute "deficits" in a social field and call forth leadership or its functional equivalents and substitutes—cultural direction, interpretation, divination, moralizing, deduction, guessing, law finding, and so forth. This sort of "function" covers the range from "telling a story" about self (or region) to promulgating elaborate legislation, professing knowledge, representing clients, or devising contracts. All introduce idealized structure into the "space" between the person and the caregiver, developmentally weakening attachments and supporting autonomy. This function necessitates some mixture of culture and structure—the patterned mixtures of culture and structure, for example, that Weber studied in the connections between different cultural foundations of legitimacy and the characteristic organizational properties of staffs, followers, or subordinates.

Only sometimes is this an intentional development extending into the elaboration of comprehensive cultural models of the sort that formalize expectations, as in detailed contracting. More frequently, the "cultural models" presiding over a region, or aggregation of regions, amount to various disconnected, fragmentary kinds of cultural direction, unevenly distributed among persons, the way, say, Geertz (1983) analyzes common sense as a "cultural system" or Schutz speaks of the "paramount reality" of everyday life. These expectations can extend from simple honorific terms of address like Sir or Lord, by which aspects of a person's status are designated, to complex models of social order. Feudal stratification, for example, produced such a "cultural model" for the world of the tenth century in parts of Europe—a feudal "conceptual scheme" (in Franklin Ford's [1963] phrase) that organized information about feudal society and allowed feudal actors to form expectations about others whose titles or social locations they recognized but about whom as persons they knew very little. Such prescriptive models, in other words, tended to absorb the personal into the social and cultural. When we find this close relationship between cultural model and social reality—where cultural model, operating normatively, produces a simplified but nonetheless "adequate" or "working" depiction of social reality—we have isolated another of the circumstances where macroscopic dynamics can override microscopic dynamics.

DISJUNCTION AND FIT   Where culture and social structure are closely integrated, as in feudalism or in stable organizational hierarchies, cultural models exhibit a high degree of "fit" to social life. Indeed, beyond being merely normative in a loose sense, such "fit" is sometimes legally instituted, as when sumptuary legislation has materially differentiated feudal ranks or separated castes by religiously instituted "styles of life." This, of course, does not guarantee that such cultural models will describe social reality. Just as frequently, such models fail to "fit" reality at all, and it is then that the disjunction of culture from social structure becomes important in its own right.

Disjunction is typically produced where there has been some disruption in the underlying distribution of resources in a region, where relationships among roles have accordingly been destabilized, and where persons have become mobile among positions. As resources are redistributed, persons begin to find themselves in circumstances where they can act apart from what others, under prevailing models, expect of them. Loss of structure in this sense, through disjunction of culture from social structure, is destructuration and produces effects that typically undermine the prescriptive and normative features of culture. When these effects are studied historically and comparatively, they provide strong evidence of how "failures" of culture as an environment for social action create conditions of sensitive dependence—conditions that stimulate processes of positive feedback and sometimes drive systems into far-from-equilibrium states. In addition, when culture fails in this sense by not describing reality—when it doesn't "fit" social reality—it stimulates the release of *disintegration anxiety*—the sense, as Durkheim's ([1902] 1933, [1897] 1951) arguments about anomie analogously formulated it, that the moral world has retreated from life, and that what most persons hold onto as "reality" is itself in danger of being lost (Hilbert 1986; Schwartz 1981).

A schematic diagram formulating this argument appears in figure 7.4, which also includes the functional equivalences argued above: disintegration anxiety in self (D) corresponds to anomie (A) at the level of sociocultural analysis. Notably, this claim preserves the assumption advanced in earlier chapters about constancy of process across changes of scale, specifically by suggesting how intrapsychic and microscopic phenomena studied in earlier chapters have functional equivalents on a macroscopic scale. This also draws together other arguments advanced in several earlier chapters—for instance, about cultural selfobjects. In this depiction of these matters, mirrored and idealized poles of self correspond in their respective dynamics to the workings macroscopically of markets and hierarchies. In addition, mirroring and market dynamics are functionally related, just as idealization and hierarchy are. Mirroring is the locus of energic dynamics in self, and markets of energic and resource dynamics in social systems.[20] Idealization is the locus of cultural stabilization in self, and hierarchy the locus in society. Where there is a prob-

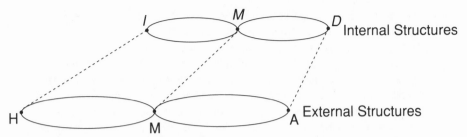

Fig. 7.4 Markets (M) and hierarchies (H) as external structures related to mirroring (*M*) and idealizing (*I*) dynamics in self

lem of cohesiveness or integration at either level, anxiety and anomie are its signals. Moreover, self is stabilized by the negative feedback inherent in the functional activity of idealized structures, just as markets are stabilized by the negative feedback inherent in hierarchy. M and *M* are positive feedback structures; H and *I* are negative feedback structures. By the logic of homeostatic processes investigated earlier, markets and hierarchies are thus related to one another functionally.

This argument makes a novel claim about markets, though a familiar one about hierarchies.[21] Both of these ideas, it must be remembered, are idealized concepts as employed here, and thus occasion a certain loss of reality even as we gain by their use simplicity in manipulating an argument. In particular, what I am calling a "market" is any system for matching or allocating "objects" (like products, substances, persons, etc.) over wants, appetites, demands, or preferences—labor markets, credit markets, commodity markets, friendship markets, dating markets, marriage markets, and so forth.[22] In figure 7.5, therefore, markets are systems within which consumers match wants to producers' "objects" and commodities. (Wants here are analogous

		Microscropic Processes Functions		Macroscopic Processes Functions	
		Mirroring	Idealizing	Markets	Hierarchies
Location	External	Mirroring Selfobject	Idealized Selfobject	Producers	Superordinate Positions
	Internal	Archaic Grandiose Self	Idealized Parental Imago	Consumers	Subordinate Positions
		Positive Feedback	Negative Feedback	Positive Feedback	Negative Feedback

Fig. 7.5 Structural analogues across microscopic-macroscopic change of scale

to merger demands— manifestations of deficits.) Similarly, hierarchies in figure 7.5 appear as systems structured by authority. Hierarchies organize superordinate positions (management, officials, priests, judges, parents, etc.), analogous to idealized selfobjects, in relation to subordinate positions (employees, constituents, laity, plaintiffs, children, etc.), analogous to idealized parental imagoes. Thus, for example, by the equivalences established in this argument, subordinate positions (macroscopic equivalents of the idealized poles of self) can operate without dependence on superordinate positions (macroscopic equivalents of idealized selfobjects) to the extent that they have been culturally structured (structured through transmuting internalizations).[23] Specification thus operates as the macroscopic equivalent of transmuting internalization.

If this analogy is correct, furthermore, the costs associated with markets will, under certain conditions, produce a "transfer" of function from markets to hierarchies, just as the infant, under certain "cost" conditions described in terms of frustration, will "transfer" omnipotence from the archaic grandiose self to an idealized selfobject. When it becomes obvious, say, that bazaar-type markets produce cost disadvantages to aspiring Third World entrepreneurs, incentives appear for organizing economic activity by means of firms (Geertz 1963)—that is, for seeking organizational alternatives to the multiplicity of ad hoc, high-risk bazaar transactions by which, in many traditional economies, goods and services are distributed. Whereas bazaar-type economies place competitive pressure on the transactions between buyers and sellers, firm-based economies create competitive pressure primarily between sellers.[24] This supports the appearance of impersonality in buyer-seller transactions and is hence another of the circumstances where macroscopic dynamics can damp microscopic dynamics.[25]

All empirical social systems are mixtures of hierarchical dynamics with those produced by markets and can be understood against the expectations pure concepts like these create. By this logic, for example, bilateral market exchanges, such as those in dating markets (Coleman 1961), can occasionally constitute positive feedback systems, subject to all the instability and wild fluctuation of two adolescent lovers. By contrast, coupling hierarchical dynamics in interaction systems generally strengthens their stability and integration.

Sensitive dependence in markets, even far-from-equilibrium instability, is not only familiar (think of the stock market as a casino), but something like it is assumed in theory—for example, in microeconomic theory as one of the conditions of perfect competition, and in rationality theory as a property (but, significantly, not the only property) of Economic Man.[26] Where we don't find sensitive dependence in markets, we get conditions economists don't like— stickiness, imperfections, and other sluggish behavior that are signals of too much negative feedback. Negative feedback enters into this process both in the form of controls on the sensitivity of the market and where decisions are taken to organize activity beyond the reach of market forces (as where markets create unacceptable costs). One such control on sensitive dependence in market behavior is *rationality,* which inhibits some choices (like indiscriminant and immediate matchings of wants to commodities) by interposing decision filters that give priority to some commodities over others (establishing preference orderings, etc.), insisting on delayed matchings to maximize search behavior and information, and introducing normative criteria of self-interest, efficiency, cost, taste, and other standards.

Transaction Cost Analysis: A Macroscopic Analogy Appropriated

Williamson's (1975, 1981) development of the normative economic argument about how "transaction costs" should dictate whether firms "internalize" functions (hierarchical governance) or leave them to markets has some parallels to this argument here. Markets operate to economize on transaction costs only under conditions where assets lack specificity, where uncertainty is low, and where transactions are frequent. Where assets are of a general nature and can be provided by a market, they will be provided most cheaply. But where they are highly specific to a firm, transaction costs can be reduced by moving the process of providing them out of the market.[27]

When asset specificity grows, "governance costs" associated with markets become large relative to those associated with firms. In theory, it is at this point when a decision should be taken to integrate the provision of the asset into the firm. Such a decision is regarded as rational by the criterion of minimizing transactions costs. Williamson (1981) illustrates this argument with a graph like the one in figure 7.6. (This tool becomes a useful simplifying device for our purposes as well, under assumptions I shall attempt to make clear.[28]) Production costs and governance costs, in Williamson's formulation, can each be considered in relation to asset specificity. Each of these cost differences is defined as the difference in dollar costs arising from market versus firm governance structures, that is, market procurement versus internal procurement. Thus, an argument implicit in figure 7.6 is that the governance costs of resolving disputes between autonomous market traders increase as the conditions associated with bilateral exchange appear. Holding uncertainty constant, an incentive appears in this region to move from markets to internal procurement. Firms, for example, can operate by fiat to resolve disputes arising over asset provision, avoiding expensive litigation, and are in better positions to make informed decisions. Thus, firms will enjoy transaction cost advantages in some cases—especially where conditions like asset specificity cause firms to lose whatever aggregation benefits might arise from a market. Allow *A* to represent "asset specificity" as we discussed it above, we can then

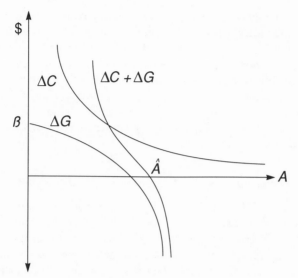

Fig. 7.6 Representative net governance and production cost differences (after Williamson 1981, 560)

examine both production cost differences and governance cost differences as functions of asset specificity. Following Williamson's argument, $\Delta C = f(A)$ is the "production cost difference between internal organization and the market," and $\Delta G = g(A)$ is "the corresponding governance cost difference" (1981, 560). Assuming for illustrative purposes that these two functions have the shapes and relative positioning shown in figure 7.6, then market procurement has the advantage where $\Delta C + \Delta G > 0$, internal procurement has the advantage where $\Delta C + \Delta G < 0$, and there is indifference between the two at the point where $A = \hat{A}$ (i.e., where $\Delta C + \Delta G = 0$).

TRANSACTION COST ANALYSIS IN SOCIAL INTERACTION   Applied to "social" exchanges, transaction cost logic would seem to account for such matters as introducing hierarchical governance structures like marriage contracts into love relationships—examples of bilateral exchange relationships marked by significant asset specificity. By contrast, the loss of asset specificity in marriage has a transaction cost rationale for divesting oneself of a spouse, or perhaps for recontracting the marriage relationship such that certain formerly endogenous assets are subsequently procured via market transactions—redrawing the firm's boundaries, in Williamson's sense. Moreover, by this same logic, because persons can have multiple friends, most friendships don't require contracting or institutionalization; persons can procure the benefits of friendship from several alternative sources, even though these alternate sources all supply assets with some specificity. In this perspective, particularism affects social exchange via the transaction costs associated with asset specificity. This has implications for bringing interaction theory more broadly into contact with transaction cost analysis and related traditions.

WANTS AND ATTACHMENTS   There are several theoretical problems to be kept in view here. One is how the larger analysis I have provided of strong and weak interaction relates to the transaction cost perspective. Another is whether microscopic interaction processes are affected by the specific macroscopic processes addressed in transaction cost theory. These questions are interrelated and ultimately involve answers that can be constructed within the same theoretical perspective. The connection is plain enough.

Behind particularism, as we have seen, are selfobject transferences—for example, the idealizing selfobject transferences in romance, or the mix of idealization and mirroring in charisma and personal power. Deficits in self-structuration, signalled by disintegration anxiety, motivate the transferences in strong attachments and interactions. Conceptually, these phenomena of deficit and attachment are related to what classic economic reasoning denotes by the concept of wants. Wants in the economic sense can be understood psychologically as merger demands on persons or as attachment behavior in which commodities serve functionally as selfobject substitutes. Wants can therefore be understood as giving rise to consumption behavior functionally like (but certainly not equivalent to) selfobject transference, as in the consumption of chemical substances.[29] A person's use of a chemical substance to control disintegration anxiety is the manifestation of a want—an appetite or craving arising from self. By this logic, the "utility" of an object to an actor is a measure in part of the strength of his or her dependence on it. Though, economically speaking, it is competition and not anxiety that creates utility or value in objects, one way to understand strength of attachment is as a function of scarcity or, as the psychological point of view emphasizes, dependency. In this view, disintegration anxiety creates wants we can observe in transferences and in cravings; these motivate attachments and consumption; and utility fluctuates with attachment or dependency. Since, in addition, attachment is also functionally motivated by the pressure to produce coherence or to optimize disintegration anxiety, markets can be viewed as dissipative structures that scavenge these anxieties by matching objects to wants, and firms can be seen as structures serving to regulate disintegration anxiety and to sustain the selection pressure behind structuration, in the functional sense reviewed in chapters 1 and 2.

THE PERSON AS A FIRM   To understand this analogy further we must deepen it to the level of the actor. Deepening the analogy is possible because similarities appear between the logical structure of the Winnicott-Kohut model of the person and the transaction cost model of the firm. Both depend on the spatial metaphor of internalization—of there being an inside and an outside to systems. One can thus partially rephrase either system in view of the other. Consider self psychology's model of development in view of transaction cost concepts: if the person is regarded as a firm, $\hat{A}$ in figure 7.6 becomes that point in interaction where frustration (cost) begins to take on an "optimal" character,[30] and consequently where the person-as-firm is motivated to internalize the provision of matters formerly left to external structures like markets (systems of external selfobjects like caregivers). Markets yield advantages to a person where internal structures (or their absence) create cost disadvantages, like being unable to raise or lower disintegration anxiety to an optimal level. Thus market dependence and internal provision of functions get mixed in a person's "efficient boundaries" (self-identity) in the same way self psychology leads us to recognize the mix of external dependency and internal structuration in an observed person's behavior. In the case of social actors, this reasoning has several corollaries implicit in our discussion all along—for example, that interaction itself is *always* a form of market behavior, however imperfect. Nonmarket behavior appears where the person has internalized functions formerly handled in a marketplace. By implication, autonomy is the property behavior acquires in proportion to a person's independence of interaction—a condition imaginable in theory but impossible in actuality. In fact, the constraints on autonomy arising from inherent limits on internalization contribute to various forms of social complexity.[31]

The Marketplace and Its Regulators

What *is* a social marketplace? Many persons, observing one another in competitive attachment processes, constitute an interaction system and form a social market. The simple example of two isolated persons engaged in interaction is a limiting and imperfect case of this market. Economic markets are special cases of interaction systems more generally. In this view, the M pole of self has its functional equivalent on a macroscopic scale in an interaction order marked by all the processes of competition, conflict, and attachment that scarcity induces among social actors. The I pole has its equivalents where we observe persons organized into collectivities that are more than simple aggregations—where, in fact, we observe structuration that *is* organization. External structuration in this sense subsumes everything from simple two-person systems of infants and caregivers to complex organization, and develops properties that depend on the boundary conditions of interaction we earlier derived from Weber.

Viewed this way, forms of complexity or structuration again come within reach theoretically. As before, they can be studied in relation to the supports for social order isolated in Weber's work—the mix of neutralization and information in culture that "carries" organization—and in relation to the conditions of perfect or imperfect competition studied by economists. In this way of thinking, for example, "rational organization" might then be defined as any pattern of structural complexity associated with maximizing the aggregation benefits arising from markets with the governance benefits arising from firms. The two benefits compete with one another, as Weber knew when he argued that bureaucracies hired professionals. Rationality mixes market and hierarchical forces, and concerts spheres of limited autonomy. In addition, regions of simple structuration that emphasize microscopic dynamics based on affect can be understood as systems in which more complex aggregations are unsupported by requisite boundary conditions. Such regions are those where internalization has failed to produce structures able to regulate disintegration anxiety, where there are not strong external cultural supports for autonomy, and where as a result strong attachments and strong interactions are common.

Interaction systems are always dissipative structures scavenging information from various processes. These include both those at the microscopic level where we focus on selfobject processes like identification, introjection, and differentiation, and at the market level, where we see complexity introduced into markets by combinations of actors in various organizational forms.

When Hierarchy Fails

Sociocultural Disjunctions

Even in the transaction cost perspective, hierarchy turns out to be another way of talking about culture—specifically, about sociocultural integration, the mix of leadership (caregiving) and information. Organization and hierarchy are hollow terms unless cultural instruments like contracts are binding—unless, that is, contracts produce forces that cause persons party to them to act in expected patterns. When sociocultural integration in this sense fails, hierarchy fails. Thus, studying the disjunction of culture from social structure is a way of isolating conditions where markets necessarily provide transaction cost advantages. Where culture fails, markets are all there are. And the strongest forces arising in such systems are the pressures they create toward defining the value of things—to retrieve in life some measure of worth.

Neo-Weberian and institutionalist traditions would support the arguments of sociologists and political scientists who have studied the markets-and-hierarchies literature and have concluded (as this theoretical analysis implies) that the real variable of interest for empirical studies is the mix of market and hierarchical systems (e.g., White 1981; Eccles and White 1988; also Stinchcombe 1984). Research on real-world settings thus must keep in view the way the forces underlying these two idealized structures can be understood to generate mixtures of centralization and decentralization, concentration and dispersion, authority systems and pricing systems. From a more general systems perspective, this amounts theoretically to understanding complex structures as mixtures of positive and negative feedback—mixtures of which interpenetrating markets and hierarchies are macroscopic instances.

OPTIMAL ANOMIE   Both markets and hierarchies of course occur in numerous forms to which Weberian analysis is sensitive. Viewing this newer literature from Weber's vantage means recognizing how the forces supporting macroscopic dynamics get mixed with the forces giving dominance to microscopic processes. In particular, this discussion helps again to frame the issue of how sociocultural integration is related to the work of interaction systems. To see this, the functional argument about macroscopic structures we have just advanced must be placed within the context of our discussion of structuration. This hybrid framework brings together Weberian and Durkheimian sociology and leads to certain predictions about the relative mix of market-like and hierarchy-like dynamics within regions. Immediately, for example, this functional theory shows us that *cultural failure,* as in the cases I called disjunction of culture from social structures, raises the level of anomie in a region.[32] This is signalled in a milieu by the appearance of unregulated behavior, a matter we now would be inclined to attribute to the cumulation of the effects of various kinds of positive feedback in markets. Fueled by disintegration anxiety, individual behavior in such circumstances tends again to come under the control of the selfobject transferences, and as such to be marked by sensitive dependence. In some cases, as we have seen, systems subject to such feedback can be driven into far-from-equilibrium conditions. Markets saturated by anomic forces, for example, begin to amplify disintegration within their immediate regions—a matter we can sometimes recognize in the specific forms of competitive and unregulated attachment behavior induced among individuals seeking to control their own anxieties. Macroscopic dominance gives way to microscopic dominance in these circumstances, as tremendous selection pressures build up among persons in such milieus for stabilizing attachments—that is, for attachments to other persons who can then function in their lives the way cultural selfobjects and macrostructures did in earlier periods. In the language of self psychology, pressures appear for finding new idealized selfobjects, and processes of competition build up in such markets for redefining the normative standards of social life.

This reasoning establishes a sociocultural framework for beginning to understand social change: disjunction creates conditions in which demand arises for new cultural models and where, indeed, markets are driven by powerful information hunger. When this occurs, microscopic dynamics again spread, amplified by anxieties. A repersonalization of social life is one of the more interesting products of disjunction.

The Renaissance provides evidence for many of the effects of destructuration and disjunction in this sense: the creation of circumstances where personal identity gradually surfaces from under the edifice of medieval stratification, where interest in persons as unique personalities appears for the first time in Western history since the end of the Roman era (except, of course, among persons at the very top of medieval institutions), and where extraordinary levels of gossip and interpersonal competition begin again to characterize social life. All of these matters are signals of the information deficit occasioned by disjunction. This is not the place to study the Renaissance in detail, but it reminds us that the surfacing of personal identity during this period is one of the central themes in scholarly treatments of the painting and sculpture of the time (e.g., Gombrich 1960; Wittkower and Wittkower 1963). Disjunction as evident elsewhere in Renaissance society also illustrates how macroscopic processes at the level of society lose integrative power more generally, as well as how this cultural circumstance is associated with an increase in the demand for new information of all kinds (Goldhamer 1978; Elias [1939] 1978–82, vol. 3).[33]

Determinant and Indeterminant Regions

A simple version of this argument is that structurally stable historical periods are associated with strong macroscopic dynamics, and unstable periods with strong microscopic dynamics. Straightforward though this claim may seem, it requires further illustration in the light of our theoretical expectations. The disappearance of the personal within structurally stable periods occurs in deceptive ways I have not yet made sufficiently explicit, and the reverse process of elevating market dynamics occurs with effects we shall be able to recognize from our earlier study of addictive behavior. The former can be illustrated, however, by considering examples of how cultural models supply a language for social relations that sometimes penetrates and encloses even close personal ties. The latter can be illustrated with an example of how failed models are associated with the dynamics of competitive social milieus built on reputation—with social markets.

The Great Chain of Being

JANE AUSTEN'S WORLD   Particularly instructive examples of how sociocultural integration submerges the personal are to be found in social novels describing courtship and marriage in the late eighteenth and early nineteenth centuries—the social landscapes described, say, by Jane Austen. As Asa Briggs (1959) has said of Austen, there are few novelists whose attention to the conventions of her time can tell us as much about the lives of her contemporaries. Viewed closely, of course, Jane Austen's characters straddle two worlds—one, the steady rural landscape of eighteenth-century gentry, and the other, the eddying, turbulent whorl of fashionable Society. In the behavior of her characters, we may thus observe the competing dynamics of these adjacent regions—one unsteadily ruled by macroscopic forces, the other by microscopic processes. By the end of the eighteenth century, a sort of watershed had been reached in the long death of feudal traditionalism. As Austen's characters moved from country to city, they moved from hierarchically settled regions such as those more typical of the past to a marketplace of personality such as that increasingly the hallmark of emerging modernity.

Recall the lines by which *Pride and Prejudice* opens: "It is a truth universally acknowledged that a single man in possession of a good fortune must be in want of a wife." Here is Jane Austen at her most ironic. So powerfully fitted to the lives of the English gentry in the late eighteenth century was the prevailing cultural template of their world that only brilliant personalities failed to be utterly absorbed into it. Or, at least, such was the power of the assumptions on which it ran. But by contrast to the gentle village life where Austen made her home, the urbane and aristocratic world of London society—of young Lord Byron, say, or of the milieu of the Prince Regent and the London dandies that began to appear at this time—showed powerful signals of decay and cultural disjunction. In the countryside we find a world over which prevailed an entrenched eighteenth-century conception of the good life, a conception tied deeply still to the land and to traditional notions of proper form. In the city, we find an exciting social whorl in which reality often seems to disappear behind appearances and where life flutters nervously across deceptive surfaces. The qualities celebrated by Addison were closer to those admired in Austen's villages than were the histrionic onstage appearances observable in Society. Indeed, Society itself had changed. Instead of the circle of sociability once constituted solely by the best families in England, it had become a milieu that formed itself at times altogether beyond the domestic arrangements of immediate kinship and locality. By the turn of the nineteenth century, it was a setting for exhibitionistic displays of entitlements to high status, and a shifting place of entrances and exits centering on individuals taken to be "important." Austen's characters dipped into such society but were more comfortable settled in the homes of their families and friends.

The city-country polarity explicit here dramatically brings into focus the uneven deterioration of traditional society, so much further along in great centers of commerce like London than in the small villages where Austen's novels by and large were set. Polishing the forms and practicing the amenities of a gentle sociability, as her characters did, elevated social life for them above the "vulgar economies" (as she once put it in a letter to her sister) found in classes less well positioned than her own. It also gave to the daily lives of the people she knew a security and regularity that enabled them to find comfort and cheer and invigoration in their mutual society. The forms they sought to map into their world smoothed and softened life, though sometimes, as her novels showed, at the expense of feelings. The exquisite success of some persons in fitting themselves into this society, in addition, made others seem unqualified and flawed. But this was one of the central and defining features of life in her circles—that there were standards generally accepted, forms sharply defined, values with definite content by which personal and social deficiencies were easily and quickly spotted. There was indeed a kind of social intelligence (of which she herself was an adept) by which the sensible and good person might with training educate and shape himself or herself to fit into such society.

Austen's social landscape was not a place of business or politics but of card parties and balls and visiting and letter writing, and of domesticity presided over by female voices. A man or a woman in the environs of one of her English villages was never the actor depicted (to borrow one of David Cecil's images) in one of those Watteau-like scenes of artifice from the Continent about which we read—Marie-Antoinette dressing up as Bo-peep in the vain effort to simulate rural relief from the ennui of her existence at Versailles—but the beefy reality of traditional English society and solid English convention. The life these gentry lived was, as Cecil says of the society of the eighteenth century, at once "polished and precise, disciplined and florid" ([1939] 1955, 17).

Here was a society, indeed, where a wife like Mrs. Bennet in *Pride and Prejudice* comfortably addresses her husband, "My dear Mr. Bennet." The distance we hear in these and other forms of greeting, like the formal stiff collars so much a symbol of the way forms shaped life more generally, are not evidence of emotional coldness and neutrality. They are evidence instead of how such a husband and wife affirmed in one another what they thought were important qualities—qualities worthy of their deference and honor. These qualities were derived from two processes—first, from realizing in their mutual relationship a form of association that echoed a valued concept of natural order and, second, from fitting one another into a larger society that itself was regarded as another manifestation of the same order. In particular, marriage in the eighteenth century was still regarded as a microcosm of a divine order evident in nature. Thus husbands and wives conventionally sought to reconfigure one another in view of these same deep principles of nature's arrangement. Intimacy and distance combine in conventional phrases that sound, to those unaccustomed to them, like oxymorons: "My dear Mr. Bennet" certifies Mr. Bennet not for how he so often acts in the novel, an ironic, distracted, selfish old grump, but for who he is, a beloved husband of the woman who so honors him. The institution of marriage mapped onto husband and wife status and dignity that it alone could impart—a settled, legitimate incumbency in a world still powerfully arranged by families and kinship.

This mapping of an external social template, driven by deep moral categories, even onto personalities intimately known to each other is a result of how the social structure of the age had settled traditional cultural formulations of worth and value into English life. It had done so throughout the eighteenth century (and for centuries before that) while benefiting from the stable and secure power of the landed classes. The formal then was still near at hand, the way in the twentieth century only the informal is. Arrangements of kinship and village life were the salient template into which the lives of Austen's characters were continuously being fitted—by personal efforts of conformity, as well as by the shaping sanctions of society itself. Lives were conventionalized in ways unheard of in more changing places. Collectively the titles and connections, the networks of kin and terms of honorific address in this world—its cultural models—worked together to constitute their society. It is not so much that the cultural terms for this arrangement of deference and rank actually did fit the lives of those who inhabited it, as that they were made to fit it. The possibility that they might not is a circumstance Austen's characters seek through various means to avoid. A woman like Mrs. Bennet is therefore enthusiastic about marrying one of her daughters to a gentleman who had just taken a nearby estate and who was reported to have "four or five thousand a year." It is an assumption as natural to her as that he would be in "need" of a wife. The story of course unfolds in ways that make it a commentary on how the pressures arising from position and the prejudices of such society may inhibit persons presented as belonging together from finding their way into one another's lives. All the formality and conventionalism of Austen's world may indeed be smoothing and supportive of amiability, but this it achieves at the expense of distancing persons socially. So unthinkable is it to evade the conventional channels of sociability and intercourse, so impossible socially to disappoint another's "proper" expectations and rights, that persons deeply attracted to one another are sometimes prevented from forming relationships. Macroscopic stability in Austen's world damps microscopic dynamics.

THE RHETORIC OF PERSONAL ADDRESS The English language, of course, collapses some of the distinctions between the formal and informal that other languages preserve. Let us sharpen the focus on these issues, and consider marriage itself. Where do the formal usages we have seen in the marriage of Mr. and Mrs. Bennet arise? This is a historical question without a clear answer, since the sources required to address such questions of personal usage do not extend further back than the sixteenth century, and even then are limited to the records of a literate minority of about 4 percent of the population. The first records of correspondence between husbands and wives—historical evidence surviving only from about the 1520s—indicates that prevailing beliefs about Natural Order—what Lovejoy (1936) called the Great Chain of Being—mapped onto marriage a rhetoric of public address derived from other sources. Marriage thus preserved a "natural" hierarchy, with husbands (among Puritans) sometimes even being addressed as "Father" and wives as "Child." By this logic, a wife counted merely as the oldest of the children in a household—hence as a child with disciplinary responsibility for those still younger than herself. In general, husbands were addressed with a public language that construed them as responsible adults, whereas women and children were addressed in language that construed them as natural dependents.

Because, moreover, the prefix *Mister* is ultimately a weakened form of *Master,* it derives from ancient usages like those describing other forms of hierarchical relations. The master-disciple arrangement of the guild system and the contract of personal service between a knight and his squire are medieval examples. Interestingly, this usage arrived in the English language from the Old French *mestier,* the modern word for which is *métier.* By this route, *Mister* serves as an honorific prefix, equivalent to that fitted in the Middle Ages to work (as in Mister Barber, Mister Craftsman, Sir Knight), which made its way into the division of labor in families—a concept of work and natural division, in both cases, related to the idea of duty in a calling.[34] Thus, an increasingly general honorific language had come to be applied both to marriage and to work, in both cases establishing an implicit equivalency between patterns of internal organization in families or workplaces and various beliefs about natural or divine order.[35] In part this rhetorical intrusion of natural hierarchy was necessary because of changes brought by the Reformation in the importance of marriage, elevating it above its former status as a second-class institution. This is reflected in the Tudor usage *Master* and *Mistress,* by which husband and wife were given honorific titles akin to those used to designate an office, an occupation, or a natural social division. Again, moreover, the usage preserved language implying natural dependency.

What these tracings show, of course, is that marriage as an institution, certainly in the form we observe in Austen's novels, displays some of its distant cultural history rather plainly: it continues to find itself organized by a language—hence, by a system of idealized cultural selfobjects—derived sometime in the past from stabilizing macroscopic processes. How persons conceived the natural ordering of gods and men, men and beasts, masters and apprentices were ways of thinking about the natural ordering of husbands, wives, and children; and each of these was connected to a scheme for conceiving the natural hierarchy of the world. If only imperfectly echoing an apprentice's relation to a master, a wife's role assumed some of its natural definition. In Austen's time, therefore, marriage continued to be an institution for the realization of a natural order among persons. The Great Chain of Being had been conventionalized into an ordering of the Mister and the Misses.

Even grossly deconstructed usages like these tell us something about the grammar of social institutions. This is because such rhetoric indicates that in the past other regions have served as important boundary conditions for an institution—in the case, boundary conditions for marriage. The rhetoric of religious calling and duty continued in marriage as a way of consecrating and instilling with sacred significance the otherwise personal connection of a husband and his wife. Though there are many ways to make functional sense of this historical pattern (such as the ineffectiveness of legal guarantees to contracts throughout considerable periods in Western history), a man and a woman were properly related to one another only when they recapitulated God's natural order. It is in this sense, then, that one can usefully speak of Mr. and Mrs. Bennet "realizing" in their relationship a microcosm of the larger natural order of the cosmos.

While the formal grammar and language of sacralized natural order saturated otherwise loving and personal bonds, its use in Austen's stories is no sociological marker of impersonality. What it signifies is culture and hierarchy—a macrosociological arrangement alive with voices echoing ancient conceptions of natural rank. Hierarchy in the eighteenth century still was carried by stabilizing images of a world organized naturally by forces that made the human sphere a microcosm of a divinized nature. Thus, the personal did not so much disappear as find itself absorbed into a larger and presumably stabilizing order of natural phenomena. Translate this into Prigoginism, and you see how conceptions of the world, controlled historically by religious institutions, had produced long-lasting dynamics that by and large continued to absorb and damp those arising from microscopic processes.

PERSONALISM AND STRUCTURAL STABILITY   To speak so sweepingly of a century in which profound scientific, technological, cultural, economic, and social changes were underway, of course, is to obscure many important facts. Austen's traditional eighteenth-century villages were often laboratories of drastic social change, and her characters moved excitedly and revealingly from the settled life of their provincial towns to the topsy-turvy, helter-skelter life of big cities. In the orbit of the social season, which took a family from the country to the city, we pass from a life ordered by the sanity and surety of earlier times to fragmented urban milieus full of competing forces. I have generalized about eighteenth-century English villages in ways false even to their own dynamism, but I have exaggerated to make a point. In the analysis of Weberian categories presented above, we saw how culture, acting as an environment for social action, sometimes "carries" complexity, but by complexity we specifically had in mind superior-subordinate relationships of the sort associated with neutralism, impersonality, and complex divisions of labor. In bureaucracies, social life is neutralized by general rules impersonally applied. But as Austen's society illustrates, the personal can also be absorbed by the social in conditions of hierarchical structuration. Stability in stratification in this sense means social life remains hierarchically ordered, and less subject to entropy. The old culture continues to be adequate to describe life as it is lived, even if only because persons fit themselves to it in acts of conformity. As such, it does not lose information faster than it can be replaced, and there is never so much change as to diminish its imposed fit to the world. Thus, there is less need to scavenge entropy in ways that sometimes build order out of disorder, as by the fast pulses of information spread through a milieu by gossip or fashion or electoral campaigns. Anxiety is confined in some optimal range by a balance of skill and challenge, and life generally feels good.

What such sociocultural circumstances further highlight, therefore, is· an important way culture sometimes carries organization and submerges (without eliminating) the personal. In formal organizations the personal is submerged because instituted cultural models diminish the amount of personal information organizational life is obliged to carry. But likewise, stable hierarchical culture within traditional social worlds can also carry organization apart from personal information. Where gridworks of titles and family connections supply enough information to support interaction apart from personal knowledge, such traditional settings depend on formality to maintain complexity. Formality is a kind of "equilibrium state" for such regions. Perturb such a region with a personal flux, and the region will "ignore" the perturbation. It will return to its former condition of formality. Nowhere does this mean such regions are devoid of personal information, but only that they run in view of preconstituted expectations above the level of the personal. In fact, stability in the larger social grid permits simplification of the models in terms of which persons themselves construct their own social worlds.

ELITE SOCIABILITY IN LONDON SOCIETY   Austen's characters were caught up not only in such traditional settings but also in a dramatically changing world—one where communication and travel had become faster and more common, where strangers were not infrequently encountered, where commerce kept up a constant background of market activity, where the middle classes controlled a greater share of wealth and power, and so forth. Thus there is a certain irony in her treatment of the rural social landscape—how its own terms obscure important forces in the lives of its inhabitants. In fact, Austen's world was being turned by the forces that had already made London a vortex. And the difficulties she wrote about in the lives of her characters reflected a slippage of social reality away from traditional culture. By the turn of the century, the sociocultural disjunction that had been underway since the Renaissance had produced unevadable strains. Feudalism persisted only as a hollow language, and beneath its terms real men and women struggled to locate a new language by which to construct their lives.

Destructuration had progressed furthest, perhaps, in the society of London's elite, unsettling the whole subject of worth. The assumptions by which aristocracy and hierarchy had traditionally been connected depended on finding in the nobility models of value. But as Ellen Moers has persuasively argued (1960), a central question of the social novel at this time had actually become, "What is a gentleman?" This question had been made all the more poignant because its answer could no longer reliably and consistently be derived from observations of aristocratic behavior. As often as not the aristocracy lived a hollow life, full of the sham nobility parodied by late eighteenth-century novelists like Richardson. As a class, their substantial entitlements to deference— money, land, culture, privilege—had also been weakened considerably, with the result that they were often impoverished, ill-mannered rustics who offered little by which the rising middle classes might define aristocratic behavior.

Seen in these terms, destructuration had led to the appearance by the end of the eighteenth century of a widening disjunction between culture and social life—between, that is, the moribund language of feudal titles and social organization, on the one hand, and the actual distribution of entitlements to deference, on the other. In such circumstances, culture failed as a source of negentropy. It certainly failed to supply information able to carry real social differences. Instead, what began to appear in its place were various forms of unstable structuration and complexity based on scavenging anxiety within the fragmenting social world of the elite in London society. In the terms of dissipative structure theory, London in places had become an indeterminant region, standing in sharp contrast to the more steady but still changing world of the countryside. In the vicinity of its exclusive clubs, salons, racetracks, and other establishments of the *haute ton* was a region specifically characterized by high levels of interpersonal competition, by extraordinary levels of gossip, by addictive patterns of sociability centered around gambling, racing, and fashion, and by the first modern culture of celebrity. Personality had again reemerged, this time as the focus of intense competitions over the fame that success in this capricious society could afford. Social life became an end in itself for many who became addicts of this world, a few of whom, like Byron or Brummell, also served as heroes of the age to many young, educated, urban, and aristocratic members of the elite. Where hierarchy had been the organizing principle of the social word Austen celebrated, the world Byron entered was increasingly structured by a market in which a powerful demand for new social models had combined with great rewards—the patronage of the Prince Regent, the adulation of the age—to induce many young men and women to enter its lists. London had always been a pulsing center for English life, but now it became a vortex that drew all England into its precincts.

What this contrast of countryside and city shows is that market dynamics intrude into hierarchically organized regions where disjunction is greatest. This occurs where cultural models can't supply negentropy, and hence where positive feedback can be amplified in ways that produce powerful nonequilibrium fluctuations. Austen's village world does not show us strong dynamics so much as hierarchical complexity—regions where personal matters were rarely driven into far-from-equilibrium conditions, and where complex social order was maintained by multiple sources of stability. By contrast to London society, for example, village social life was less "exclusive" and far less segregated by class, generation, and age. Heterogeneity of social settings meant that social contexts contained hierarchical damping mechanisms— parents with children, upper classes with lower, chaperons with courting youth, and so forth. Age and generational heterogeneity, always an important feature of traditional societies (Eisenstadt 1956), was one of the prevalent characteristics of such settings. By contrast, strong dynamics backed by positive feedback become increasingly obvious in certain regions within London Society, in part because the same negative feedback wasn't operating. Exclusivism, now again the marker of elite sociability, had become the tough membrane at the edge of an elite region, challenged by the advance of the middle classes into positions of great wealth and power in English society. Inside this increasingly defensive elite region the forces of identification became so powerful that a remarkable homogenizing of taste, manners, and style began again to transform the unsettled upper classes into a self-assured monolith of omnipotence and grandiosity. By its bearing and cultivation the English aristocracy attempted to maintain social significance in the nineteenth century—attempted, in effect, to answer the question, "What is a gentleman?" But it found the answers for itself by redefining concepts of noble life. In the transitional period from its settled rustic past to its London-centered, urban present, England's elite became a class with a renewed hold on forms by which to organize itself. But where the terms of hierarchy had failed, exclusivism provided a temporary substitute—a form of structuration based on repudiating others.[36]

THE DYNAMICS OF EXCLUSION Where the strains of disintegration are most deeply felt, its products become most visible. Aggression is foremost among them and signals the failure of a selfobject milieu. Kohut calls aggression a "disintegration product," meaning that it is one of the ways by which we might recognize the fragmentation of self—or, in this case, the fragmentation of a world. The exclusivism of London's elite world ran on this symptom. It was a world geared to the constant menace of the "cut"—vicious, bitchy, denigrating contests of wit, sarcasm, and mutual repudiation motivated by the dynamics of reputation. The private clubs, the exclusive dances and parties, the opera, the salons of the aristocracy, the parade each day into the best streets and shops of the best neighborhoods—all were organized by these dynamics. It was important to be seen, more important to be talked about, if one was to win the rewards this society offered—invitations and acceptance minimally, adulation and celebrity at its apex. More important, one had to win the attention and approbation of the persons whose opinions counted, and it was not always clear who these persons were.

Central to success in this matter, however, were skills at controlling sociability and interaction. Rewards in this elite milieu were such as to encourage competition. Visibility was organized like talk and could easily be monopolized at one's expense. Whoever held stage controlled a milieu. Thus talk became seductive, and was illuminated by all the effects that manners and artifice could bring to it. Clothing, comportment, speech—all became vehicles for attracting attention. By these stylistic triggers one demanded attention, identified with others of like standards, and implicitly repudiated others.

In psychological terms, of course, such aggressive repudiation served to support self-esteem. Typical dynamics were those of the false self, as we have already studied in detail. Compulsive conformity to an unreliable external milieu, driven by sensitive dependence, produced this symptom on a widespread basis—a defensive, other-centered self-identification. Aggression and social competition reigned in these precincts. The effect of disjunction in undermining hierarchical culture had been to trigger this market for idealization—for defining new models of worth. But its competitive dynamics saturated these milieus with repudiation. Indeed, reputations were won or lost depending on how well persons survived these contests of identification and attention management. Just beneath their surface, therefore, was rage—the same narcissistic rage we can see in an infant whose mother ignores it. Rage elicited by repudiation in turn supported more aggression, completing a loop back to the competitive dynamics that started it all. This worked as a simple positive feedback system, because those who won in these contests anticipated their own repudiation and were therefore defensively motivated toward yet further aggression and competition from others—certainly from those whom they had damaged.

Exclusivism enters this picture as one of the by-products of dissipative structuration, and arises from identification and differentiation. Structuration here corresponds only weakly to hierarchy, but it begins to resemble a primitive functional equivalent: namely, a milieu moved outside of the market. In a loose transaction cost sense, exclusivism is evidence of insiders having passed the point where they benefited from market "pricing," and who thereafter sought instead to stabilize their world by exclusionary judgments of worth. Moers (1960) had argued that exclusivism during the Regency was a "defensive" structure, aimed at excluding the middle classes from elite regions. While it was clearly that, it also was a way of diminishing disintegration anxiety by restricting competition, and in effect controlling the cultural discourse of idealization—defining whom to admit into society, and what to certify as the qualities of a gentleman. Those admitted inside elite precincts were persons who mysteriously passed a test of acceptance—who submitted to the implicit credentializing of this anxious stratum, and who fitted themselves into it. In effect, exclusivism tapped sensitive dependence to organize a selfobject milieu.

Indeterminant Regions and Change

The Limits of Social Integration

These complex historical examples of how failures of hierarchy spur market dynamics highlight equivalent processes on a smaller scale studied in previous chapters. Where hierarchical forces fail, microscopic processes predominate, setting into motion market dynamics in which persons observing one another compete in systems of interaction for attachment, regulation, and responsiveness. Drawn to the center of these markets are persons whose deficits make them prime candidates for addictive attachments—persons in need of responsiveness. Yet markets themselves get a push not alone from personal weaknesses but from systemic sociocultural conditions like disjunction—conditions producing the circumstances Durkheim described as anomie. As a systemic weakness in culturally supplied negative feedback, anomie drives idealization, and markets thrive where these processes spread competition for attention and responsiveness. The logic of hierarchy, by contrast, is to restrict markets—to stabilize and order preferences, and to create expectations out of some mix of leadership, caregiving, culture, and experience. Most empirical systems show a combination of these competing principles—conditions on the one hand that amplify sensitive dependence and market behavior, and conditions on the other that damp strong attachments and weaken interaction.

Stable complexity in social life, this argument implies, can arise in any number of ways. At one extreme are the high-energy dissipative arrangements emerging in markets—interaction systems with complex properties of structuration based on competition, attachment, repudiation, and conflict. At the other extreme are ordered, low-energy structures based on weak interactions—complex hierarchically organized systems founded on stable expectations. Studying the conditions of these various forms of stable complexity, this argument also suggests, helps to isolate how nonequilibrium fluctuations are associated with important social change. Though the detailed study of large-scale social change is beyond the scope of this book, this argument suggests such change cannot be fully understood without grasping how social systems are destabilized, driven into far-from-equilibrium conditions, and reorganized. The general logic of how this occurs is clear only up to a point.

1. Hierarchical failures (like sociocultural disjunction) result in destabilizing regions by leaving undamped the cumulative effects of positive feedback.

2. This drives systems into far-from-equilibrium conditions, elevating mi-

croscopic over macroscopic dynamics, creating incorrigible selection pressures in interaction systems toward strong attachments and interactions.

3. Where these strong attachments take on an optimal character, conditions are present favoring introjection and cultural development, each of which subsequently diminishes the force behind attachment and strong interaction. Conversely, where optimal responsiveness is not a property of attachment, high-energy marketlike structuration can nevertheless "organize" a system, especially when coupled to hierarchic regions providing havens from competition and repudiation. Put into this system of thought, Schumpeter's (1947) claims about capitalism's inherently revolutionary dynamics suggest how modern market economies thrive in part by optimizing nonequilibrium. More general, perhaps, is the suggestion that hierarchic structures appear to organize and drive market nonequilibrium in some conditions but not all; equally telling structural effects arise inside hierarchic regions from the far-from-equilibrium conditions producted by markets. The flow of effects from one region to the other appears to be best understood in view of the relative strength of macroscopic and microscopic forces.

Looseness and Order

The logic developed in this book amounts to a kind of nonequilibrium functionalism—a framework in which we end up speaking of how social order is possible only on the basis of inherent and inexorable tendencies toward disorder. I use the concept of nonequilibrium, as opposed to disequilibrium, for several reasons: first, to distinguish stable patterns of order in systems whose elements are themselves marked by instability and, second, to make explicit the temporal asymmetry and irreversibility involved in such systems. Though we shall discuss nonequilibrium properties in the next chapter, the immediate implication of this conception bears upon classic assumptions in social theory: in particular, it directs us to recognize real limits on social integration. Social systems by this logic are inherently loose, and they thrive only where their looseness is optimized. Where we observe strong links—passionate ties, repressive power and dependency, exclusivism, addictive dynamics—we are confronted paradoxically by evidence of social fragmentation—not evidence of strong social systems or strong organization, but of weak and fragmented social order.

This, of course, is something like what Mark Granovetter (1973) suggested in his classic argument about "the strength of weak ties." But where Granovetter's logic is driven by a Tocquevillian interest in networks as inherently important carriers of a social order sui generis, the perspective developed in this book takes the properties of networks as dependent variables; strong ties are the signals of deficits and unbreakable attachments, weak ties of boundary conditions in personal and social life able (within limits) to support autonomy and complexity.[37] Network properties are properties of structuration—a matter, as this chapter has emphasized, understandable only in view of how culture and organization support (or fail to support) one another. Network studies of friendship or consulting or the flow of information typically don't disclose the fixed grid of some crystallized social world but provide instead a snapshot of unstable dissipative arrangements of attachment and association. The same systems, viewed with more adequate measurement instruments geared realistically to the dynamism of the social world, would be seen to change endlessly, disorganized and reorganized by eddies and turbulences passing through them.

This kind of looseness naturally inherent in social life is perhaps the most important and most difficult of its textures to measure or explain. Looseness is connected to all the circumstances where social life feels good—to the "flow" produced by a balance of skills and challenge, to the optimal responsiveness of a partner to our needs, to the endless interest of talk and its subjects. Looseness is also a defining feature of weak interactions. The aim of this chapter was to discuss how weak interaction was even possible, especially in the face of what we recognize now as an incorrigible tendency toward particularism and strong attachment. The paradigm case of weak interaction for this argument is bureaucratic interaction, in Weber's sense—the kinds of interaction supported in organizations by cultural conditions enabling actors to know what is expected of them. The argument of this book is that weak interaction presumes persons capable (within limits) of autonomy, and that this capacity is supported not only by a personal history of optimal caregiving and psychological growth but also by stable and continuing cultural and social "boundary conditions" like those Weber identified in his studies of rationality and Durkheim isolated in his studies of sociocultural integration.

The strong forces present in face-to-face interaction get damped by the supports for autonomy social actors substitute for their caregivers. Ultimately, this amounts to damping the positive feedback incorrigibly present in face-to-face interaction, since caregiver substitutes function as damping mechanisms. But as we have seen, caregiver substitutes denote diverse matters like culture at work producing negentropy macroscopically as well as microscopically. Indeed, what this argues is that stability conditions of social interaction include circumstances where macroscopic processes override and control microscopic processes.[38] Wherever a person discovers regulation—in regions, as a person grows up, increasingly distant from parents—controls arise over attachment and interaction. Yet no region is really safe from microscopic dynamics and from positive feedback. All we need do is couple actors in conditions where damping is small relative to amplification, and positive feedback spreads. As it turns out, a significant fraction of the ordered complexity

in social life actually depends on precisely this spreading disequilibration—
or, more accurately, on maintaining the constraints operating on systems so
as to keep them in nonequilibrium conditions. Beyond face-to-face interaction, structuration appears when dissipative processes scavenge the anxieties
and positive feedback inherent in interaction systems and spread their effects
across changes of scale. Even in low-energy structures like hierarchies, only
processes favoring costs of organization over those of markets support hierarchy. In the final analysis, therefore, all social organization depends on instability and nonequilibrium.

8

Nonequilibrium Functionalism

Addictive Liabilities of Interaction

One aim of this book is to see how much of social life might be derived from a theory about elementary dynamics of social interaction. We have come a fair distance, but by no means have we reached the end of the trail cleared by the argument. How much farther we eventually get in this project ultimately depends on disentangling other subjects in view of a similar logic of feedback and control. We began in this book by studying "self" as an emergent of homeostatic structuration—homeostasis being one way, as part of physiological processes, positive and negative feedback get arranged—and haven't stopped until we discerned analogous embedded processes of feedback as the structuring principles in complex interaction systems like markets. But there are many subjects as yet barely touched by these terms and which seem amenable to future theoretical analysis. In this brief final chapter, I would like to consider from the point of view of metatheory the kind of analysis developed in the last seven chapters, thereby pointing the way to subjects where further development along these lines might occur.

Most of the argument about interaction in this book follows from regarding it as a process liable to being destabilized. Couple two responsive people in social interaction, and you get a potential explosion—emotional effects produced by positive feedback inherent in their selfobject transferences. This is an incorrigible tendency, one with roots probably best described as psychobiological—the predisposition every human being displays to recapitulate caregiving. It is also predisposed by the adaptively loose, open nature of the controls and structuration by which human systems otherwise are ordered. Systems of interaction scavenge the anxieties implicit in this ever-present social openness—from the degrees of freedom and indeterminacy social and personal life not only enjoy but exploit. Viewed functionally, systems of interaction transform these anxieties into the selection pressures behind object choices, attachments, interactions, and structuration of all kinds. As we have seen, this is a matter not of extinguishing anxiety but of optimizing it—keeping it at the level where experience is neither overwhelming in its novelty and challenge, nor boring and unstimulating.

The hard part of this argument is understanding how complex structuration emerges in large-scale interaction systems—how, say, a fashion process, superadded to interaction as a way to carry social differences, itself tends toward a dynamically steady state as a stable form of complexity: how it serves to formulate and stabilize social differences, based on scavenging anxieties at the level of its individual participants, and how it thereby adds information and complexity to the social world. Or how markets in one form or another arise on the basis of competitive attachment processes whose participants may be individuals but might just as well be firms or firmlike entities. The pure logic of these matters is that markets depend on positive feedback, organizations on negative feedback. Markets are high-energy forms of structuration based on dissipative processes, whereas most organizations aren't. Complex organizations in particular are low-energy systems based on boundary conditions like rational culture, able both to control or strictly specify interaction and to create conditions favorable to the autonomy and self-direction of their members. Without supports for autonomy, persons are prone to return to interaction to search for supportive external controls and regulation, and therein become liable to its addictive potential. This, of course, is not to argue that interaction is a bad thing, but only that it signals a want of responsiveness and the inherent qualities of incompleteness that make all of us human and necessarily bring us into relations of interdependence.

In some sense, these statements amount to truisms. Interaction freed of organization creates markets. But another way to put this kind of argument is to say that markets depend on interaction, organizations on interaction's control. Markets in fact flourish where systems of interaction create conditions of sensitive dependence and bring together large numbers of actors. Without interaction serving as the vehicle of positive feedback, there would be no market behavior. Organizations, by contrast, depend on creating circumstances where interaction can be minimized—circumstances where individuals can get along on their own, where their behavior is regulated, or where they are in strict relationships of dependency.[1] Since this kind of thinking argues that many forms of social complexity thus ultimately depend on underlying processes that scavenge anxiety, it implicitly argues that the processes behind social order are the same processes liable to produce disorder—potentiating mutual responsiveness, spreading disequilibrium, explosive feedback, and eventual disintegration. The seemingly paradoxical claims of this argument—for example, that order arises from disorder—give rise to a new kind of functionalism in sociological theory, a theory of far-from-equilibrium systems, nonequilibrium dynamics, and self-organization. Shorthand for this might be *nonequilibrium functionalism*—an expression that gives voice to how this kind of functionalism differs from the old kind.

Many of the best examples of the spread of nonequilibrium conditions and positive feedback in social systems have necessarily been left unstudied in this book. Studying them in the future constitutes an important avenue of further theoretical development for sociologists interested in this perspective.

Macrostructures and Microstructures

Methodological Individualism

One reason I find this way of thinking so potentially productive for sociology—and admittedly it remains decidedly vague in places—is that it enables descriptions of aggregates and social systems in view of forces reaching right down into brain chemistry. But rather than being merely reductionist, it suggests there are social processes like interaction, on which individuals are unevenly dependent, that carry the properties of social systems at the same time they are interdependent with how persons feel. This is a way of talking simultaneously about the properties of large-scale systems and the properties of their constituent elements—about macrosociology and microsociology—although it brings into view a problem of definition.[2]

Macrosociology typically is associated with analysis of the properties of social systems, particularly their stability and change. Microsociology typically is thought to concern the properties of individuals and small-scale social life, like face-to-face interaction. Yet where does the analysis of interaction cease to be microsociological? Or, better put, how does macrosociology establish itself apart from interaction? Clearly, the two fields of micro- and macrosociology enclose a continuous subject—even if one wants to postulate principles of action above the level of the person, and hence to take as units of analysis behavioral entities other than persons. This is of course possible and has long-standing precedents in social science. The argument advanced here allows one to talk about large-scale social systems, but it seeks to derive or synthesize the properties of these systems from the analysis of individual behavior. This is a version of methodological individualism, with roots in systems of behavior at once psychophysiological and interpersonal. Indeed, in this theory, the central interactive processes of social life seem intellectually and theoretically incoherent without themselves first being grounded in the psychophysiological functioning of those engaging in them—processes that allow sociologists to talk about feelings and to know them for what they are: biochemical changes, like those in neurotransmission, controlled from sources both inside and outside the individual. This is a strong metatheoretical position, not unlike that forcefully argued in other ways by Theodore Kemper (1978).

If we can characterize the behavior of individual social actors in terms of some principle of action and synthesize from their behavior the regularities of the systems of which they are members, we have a potentially powerful kind of theorizing. The principle of action we postulate in this theory involves the regulation of feelings: persons act so as to control their feelings. From this principle can be loosely "derived" all the accounts of attachment and inter-action offered in foregoing chapters, including those by which we end up describing complex interaction systems like markets.

Admittedly, we haven't gone very deep into these more complex systems, but at least we have reached them. Because of this shallowness, the current state of elaboration of this theory will justify a certain skepticism about whether this perspective by itself will ever reach so far as to synthesize from individual behavior, say, the regularities of complex market behavior or or-ganizational structure. It nevertheless comes close to producing theoretical descriptions that seem valuable—some indeed qualifying as "consequences" of the theory that, so far as I can tell, can't be derived from other theories. Moreover, the kind of functionalism on which it rests begins at the level of physiology, not at the level of the social system. This makes it unlike (or at least reduces its family resemblance to) the versions of structural-functionalism already familiar to sociologists and anthropologists. It offers no postulates at the level of the social system and is founded on an analysis of individual functioning that supports a more humane conception of personal life than is found in functionalism's more traditional forms. For example, it takes as axi-omatic the proposition that much of the "self-knowledge" individuals use to produce "cohesiveness" in themselves (or, put alternatively, to optimize their disintegration anxiety) arises as an emergent phenomenon, and that social interaction is its birthplace.

Nonequilibrium Systems

The concept of a "nonequilibrium system" stands in stark contrast to the kinds of systems traditionally postulated and studied in sociology. The usual assumption is that such systems behave like the thermodynamic systems stud-ied in classical physics. Perturb such a system, and it will exhibit behavior at first reflecting the perturbation but then returning the system to a point of equilibrium. The perturbation will have been erased, and the system will be-have as if it had no history—as if, therefore, time were reversible.

A nonequilibrium system lacks this ahistorical character, and it lacks this temporal symmetry. By contrast, it is a system whose every feature of order or disorder can be understood *only* in view of its history. In essence, nonequilibrium is a property of systems that themselves are maintained chronically out of equilibrium by constraints operating upon them—by psychological and social boundary conditions such as those we have studied, or by constraints such as those examined in studying the Bénard instability in chapter 4. States of organization *evolve* in such systems, and themselves exhibit a recognizable instability—whether as quasi-periodic temporal patterns, understandable patterns of flow, agitated bulk arrangements and rearrangements of molecules in systems of convection, escalating periods of conflict followed by intervals of quiescence, patterns of population growth and decline, merger followed by differentiation, elite circulation, or any of the many other examples of emergent organization appearing in such systems.

The hallmark of such nonequilibrium systems, then, is that they aren't marked by the amnesia of thermodynamic systems, but are exquisitely dependent—sensitively dependent, as we say—on initial conditions, and subsequently evolve in ways that reflect their own unique history. Moreover, the states of organization characteristic of them are emergent states that can't be understood solely on the basis of the behavior of the individual elements composing them. The behavior of the individual molecules in the Bénard instability is itself not easily predicted, but their bulk motion is. Similarly, the behavior of individual social actors in systems of interaction is not easily predicted, despite the ease with which certain aggregate patterns in their behavior are. Indeed, the aggregate patterns in interaction systems emerge only on the basis of instability at the level of the individuals. I may not have been able to predict who would buy certain articles of clothing in a nineteenth-century fashion system, but I would have been able to predict the way group boundaries were marked by the circulation of those fashions.

Though this kind of thinking remains ultimately a variant of methodological individualism—there are no aggregate patterns apart from individual behavior—it is clearly not a version based on a doctrine of reductionism in the ways reductionism is understood in traditional epistemology. While this theory keeps individual behavior strictly in view, and while it attempts to synthesize aggregate patterns from the behavior of individuals, the synthesis paradoxically is managed only by tracing out the implications of instability at the level of individual persons. Such instability at the level of individual persons becomes a fuel for stability at aggregate levels of organization.

Purposive Behavior

A fundamental assumption of this theory is that human behavior *is* largely purposive. "People act so as to . . ." This doesn't necessarily imply that people "know" what they are doing, the way purposiveness is conceived here. An organism motivated to interact with another by its aversion to anxiety is behaving purposively. The interaction aims to reduce (or optimize) its anxiety.

The assumption of purposiveness puts this kind of thinking in some familiar company—within reach, for example, of other frameworks like rational choice theory resting on the same assumption. How then does it compare to such frameworks? In its current versions, rational choice theory sometimes impresses feelings-oriented social scientists the way Ptolemaic astronomy must have impressed Copernicus: there are too many gyres and epicenters that the theory of rational choice requires at present to move the social world the way it can actually be seen to move with different telescopes. This seems particularly so when it comes to feelings and affect—matters that unquestionably require at least some degree of biological explanation. Describing the world isn't the only aim of good theory, as any normative theorist will remind us, but approximating the effects of brain chemistry on behavior with the use of rational models of constrained choice would seem to put the arrow on the wrong target altogether.

Some part of the aversion to rational choice I suspect is purely terminological—an unwillingness of twentieth-century sociologists, raised in the dark shadow cast by Freud, to admit that one person's "irrational" behavior might just be rational from another's point of view. Relativism aside, a symbolic interactionist doesn't like to be told his or her empathy is wanting. Another cause for aversion, however, may be precisely the difficulties such theory has dealing with behaviors like "addiction" that do not obey the law of diminishing marginal utility. From the point of view of economic theory, addicts behave in a seemingly anomalous way. Possessing large amounts of a good does not diminish their wants for more of the same good (Coleman 1990, 668–69; cf. Becker and Murphy 1988, for a rational choice examination of addictive behavior; also Stigler and Becker 1977). Needless to say, addiction is a problem we have paid considerable attention to here—indeed, it is an implicit paradigm for strong interaction itself. And for addiction I have suggested generalized conditions of abuse and disabuse—conditions, that is, of strengthening or weakening attachment and interaction.[3] Thus, we have sought to understand addictive behavior in a framework broad enough to embrace nonaddictive behavior as well—behavior, that is, like that conforming to a law of diminishing marginal utility. For example, in order for romantic partners to maintain their respective interest in one another, they eventually learn it is necessary to reduce their further mutual identification. This is a peculiar matter in which giving more of oneself to another person (in the specific sense of identifying with them) eventually obeys a law of diminishing marginal utility. Continuing mutual identification diminishes each partner's worth in the other's eyes and thus motivates their differentiation and introjection. This undermines addictive attachment and supports apartness—disabusing oneself of an "addiction" to a partner. Paradoxically, one can "have" the other only by separating from them. Overcoming addiction in a more general sense means developing psychological strengths allowing a person to stand apart from strong attachments. Psychological strengths in this sense support behavior in line with marginal utility theory's predictions.[4]

From the functionalist point of view developed in this book, moreover, the theoretical emphasis placed on nonequilibrium dynamics is also a matter that other purposive arguments like rational choice theory can appropriate without logical problems. The nonequilibrium states I have argued are associated in interaction with selection pressures toward structuration should be regarded as motivating conditions. Short-run disequilibrium conditions, and even long-term far-from-equilibrium conditions, result from entropic processes that release disintegration anxiety and motivate attachments and strong interactions. But anxiety itself—whether it is boredom or anxiety in the traditional sense—is what stands behind purposiveness in behavior.

Normal Addiction

An assumption of this book's arguments connecting addictive liabilities to attachment and interaction is that addiction is something like a ground form of the human condition. Without altogether eliminating distinctions between healthy and unhealthy dependence, this is a point of view that should blur sharp distinctions between pathological and nonpathological behavior. One way this becomes clear is in recognizing that addictive liabilities are a special case of the more general process of habituation—habituation of the brain, for example, to the presence of drugs in the blood. But understanding how the brain can become habituated to phenomena other than drugs—for instance, to perception and stimulation—enables the theorist to expand the perspective developed in this book to grasp both "normal" and pathological adaptations. Judging them one way or the other depends on normative criteria other than those central to the logic of this theory, however.

Decentering Analysis

The jump from two-person interaction to larger systems of interaction involved a sleight of hand. Suddenly we began talking of how such "systems" scavenge anxieties, when in fact such systems are conceptual entities. Clearly this won't do, certainly not for a theorist who regards purposiveness as a property of persons. In some cases, the regularities one can observe in interaction systems are purely the product of aggregating individual behavior. The convection of persons in a crowd toward and away from an emergent leader is such an aggregate regularity—an emergent based on a dissipative process at the level of individual actors. Some markets—dating markets in high schools, for example—are likewise emergents of large numbers of interacting persons. But trade and empire, and complex economic markets, involve regularities produced not alone by aggregation but by the introduction of collective actors—firms, governments, agencies, and so forth—and by boundary conditions like culture, specifically by norms. How to explain interaction systems in which actors are corporate entities—where large numbers of market participants, say, are the representatives of others, or where some participants are corporate entities and others are individual persons—has been rigorously studied in other theoretical traditions using different analytic tools, particularly those from economics and game theory. These traditions of study constitute potential avenues along which the theory developed here might be further extended. Still, the structural concepts connected with the theoretical perspective of this book help isolate how at least some of the properties of social systems themselves develop. Moreover, the analysis of the stability of these structures, as presented in this book, is unlike that produced in other theoretical perspectives, resting as this analysis does on concepts of underlying nonequilibrium conditions.

Strong Interaction and the Interaction Order

The Social System and the Interaction System

Because social interaction is an information-scavenging process by which human beings gear into a stabilizing interpersonal and cultural world, it is in some important senses a fundamental if not wholly irreducible matrix for understanding social life. The way we have studied it here, some of what we find in systems of interaction are processes serving subordinate systems, like the system composed of different forms of personal knowledge we call "self." Interaction is the process within which self emerges, and through which persons recapitulate significant caregiving relationships wherein their "strengths" as autonomous social actors emerged, are currently maintained, or are transformed. Some properties of interaction we can clearly synthesize from the uses persons make of one another—for example, in optimizing anxieties arising in these subordinate systems. Other properties of interaction appear as potential emergents, depending on the peculiar chemistry imparted to fields of interaction by the respective strengths and weaknesses of those present in them. The liability of such fields to strong forms of interaction, for example, depends on whether the respective weaknesses of interactants trigger mutual responsiveness, and whether such responsiveness in turn supports the distinctive positive feedback characteristic of strong interaction.

My emphasis in this book on studying interactions—interactions, as I originally characterized them, under the control of feelings—might seem to stand in some contrast to the recent attention sociologists (Rawls 1986; cf. Fuchs 1988) have given to Goffman's (1983) neo-Simmelian conception of an "interaction order" (e.g., Simmel 1950, 1971; cf. Levine 1980, 1981, 1989). But the concept of an interaction order sui generis, consisting of emergent phenomena different from phenomena on larger or smaller scales of analysis, is also something one might say is implied by the theory developed here. One difference is that the perspective developed here does not see these phenomena as *wholly* irreducible. The functional perspective developed in earlier chapters argues that interaction is one place individuals look for "objects" to control their feelings—my shorthand for talking about the complex ways persons apparently use one another (as well as mental representations of one another) to modulate effects arising through brain chemistry—for example, effects analogous to withdrawal symptoms, described loosely as anxiety. There is nothing unique about interaction viewed solely in this minimalist way—it is equifinal with many other forms of "object relations," as described in chapters 2 and 3, including addictive phenomena.

Viewed in other ways, however, there *is* something unique about interaction. Most important, it is the platform on which persons erect and maintain the "structures" of both the personal and social world. Without interaction, human life as we know it would be impossible. The architecture for it would never have been erected. Some of the structures supporting human personal and social life are interaction's own emergents—matters like self, memory, and relationships. Others confront it in what Alfred Schutz (1962; Schutz and Luckmann 1973) described as a "preconstituted" way—as facticities, the sedimented products of the interactions of predecessors (Berger and Luckmann 1966). Insofar as such matters are cultural, of course, they still depend on interpretation and on "realization" in the present. Yet other structuration is improvisational—contextual emergents, produced in concert with others in a vivid present. Some of these emergents may in turn have an adaptive effect on more or less stable generative structures, which are part of subordinate systems. Memories, for example, are reconstructed structures and are partly used by persons to control their feelings. Describing them as reconstructed means that through time memories are revised as a function of changes in emotional states, contexts, and other ambient phenomena (Barclay and Hodges 1990; Edwards and Middleton 1988; Neisser 1988a, 1988b; Nelson 1988; Barclay and Smith 1991). As they change, they themselves can produce further changes in a person's self-concept—in the conceptual structure by which a person maintains a more or less coherent identity.

What begins to sort itself out from these considerations (not that it hasn't been obvious all along) is the claim that social systems, as complex larger systems, are themselves fundamentally dependent on systems of interaction.

Interaction may be an order sui generis, but it is more plainly a system in some loose sense—a system related to other systems. It has properties of boundedness, coherence, and continuity, along with endogenous functional tasks, which give it distinctiveness as well as general properties of organization across persons. In its most important function, it is the sphere for "emergence"—the place social life depends on for the realization, instantiation, improvisation, specification, embodiment, and application of cultural controls. When we couple simple interaction systems into more complex systems, we begin to get something in theory that looks like a social system. Indeed, the social system itself then appears as an emergent of systems of interaction.

Social systems, of course, are generally conceived as more than aggregations of systems of interaction. They have stable properties as systems that survive apart from the subordinate systems of interaction that appear and disappear within them. These include matters like the various forms of complexity isolated in earlier chapters, as well as properties as systems that the work of Niklas Luhmann (e.g., 1982) has attempted to specify in general terms.[5] Some of these, like simple markets, are mere aggregations of interaction, but others are stable forms of organization, institutions, and other phenomena of a supraindividual character that survive apart from the persons whose actions constitute them. Nevertheless, a social system without interaction is a hollow fiction. Again, these statements amount to truisms, but they are truisms at times in danger of being eclipsed by analysis that slips into disembodied discussion of the easily reified theoretical categories found in macrosociology—categories, for example, like "society" or "social system."

Particularism Reclaimed

If this sort of theorizing accomplishes nothing else, it should at least contribute to sociological repatriation of the concept of particularism. So many of the assumptions of modern social theory lead away from the analysis of particularism that it has all but disappeared as a serious theoretical category in contemporary thinking. But what the theory of strong interaction brings to the forefront of attention is how important particularism is as a foundation for all of social life. All social actors depend for their psychological health and social well-being on the ability to recover from their interactions with one another the responsiveness and nurturance originating in caregiving. The search for responsiveness catches up everyone at one time or another. Finding it in the attentions of a friend, in the emotional resonance of a spouse, even in evanescent flirtations of strangers is an invitation to sociability and a marker of the trust on which social order of all kinds ultimately depends.

The odd property of this perspective is that a theory of love becomes a theory of economic life as well. Not a full theory in either case, but at least a perspective in which these former strangers can now share the same theoretical accommodations.

Sociology and the Nostalgia for Interaction

Sociologists have traditionally had a soft spot for the study of interaction. In the eyes of sociology's critics, this is in keeping with an implicit romanticism of the discipline. As against the claims of Enlightenment rationalism, sociologists have trained an eye on the "dark" side of human nature—on emotions, madness, prejudice, war, irrationality, and blind feeling. Toward the concept of a calculating, affectively straitjacketed *homo œconomicus* they have shown an allergic response. A fuller depiction of human nature, to many a sociologist, requires not just an acknowledgment of the emotional foundations of personal life but a recognition of how human nature gets its final sculpting within a social and cultural world. This has meant, among other things, keeping an eye not only on the macroscopic forces changing human history—revolution, democracy, egalitarianism, the spread of the market— but on the little things as well—the small-scale, face-to-face world of real men and women.

This orientation toward the microscopic has been one of the great strengths of modern sociology, particularly modern American sociology. Hand-in-hand with it has come the close and empathic study of personal reality and social worlds. Even the great macrosociologists at the turn of the century kept their eyes ultimately on the individual—Durkheim used individual explanation as a foil for his arguments about social facts, Weber as a foundation of his liberal humanism. How can you understand why men act as they do, admonished Max Weber, when you cannot understand their motives, their values, their points of view? Whether adopting Weber's *verstehende Soziologie* or not, sociologists have traditionally embraced work that has sought to describe and comprehend real life in a comparative and often a small-scale perspective— just as it presents itself to the understanding and empathic observer. Comprehending the city meant understanding its people—the ethnic enclaves, the community presses, the voluntary associations, the gangs, the skid rows, and the gold coasts everywhere. Intellectually, the historical source of this control over sociology's empirical agenda can be traced back to the University of Chicago in the era of Robert Park and W. I. Thomas and ultimately, therefore, to the writings of Georg Simmel—academic outsider, brilliant iconoclast, aphoristic *privatdocent* of the *fin de siècle*.

When Erving Goffman called for acknowledging an "interaction order" as a distinctive sphere of sociological analysis, the legacy of Simmel to modern sociology was heard one more time (1983). Here was something else distinctively sociological, a subject that constituted another focus for a separate discipline. Granted that sociology is defined by intellectual traditions and disciplines peculiarly its own, still some of the strongest claims sociology can make to its distinctiveness arise in relation to this most distinctive of its subjects—social interaction per se. This, as Simmel well knew, is the heart of the social.

I have argued in this tradition in this book, though not in terms Simmel would have approved. Interaction is where matters social originate, rooted even as they are in the biological relations of caregivers and infants. Especially because interaction is where substitutes for caregivers are discovered and where social regulation itself makes its way into the biological functioning of the organism—where, as some claim, the organism finds its ends—there is also a persistent nostalgia about it as a subject. Where there is interaction, there is passion, attachment, responsiveness, feeling, interest, love, play, power, and self. All of these primary emergents of face-to-face behavior must in the end serve to remind the observer of interaction of how epiphenomenal so many of the subjects of the social sciences really are. They are the creations of social interaction and constitute distinctive subject matters organized around topics like mind, self, and society—whether we call them self, personality, thought, or memory; whether power, influence, social control, or authority; whether groups, networks, organizations, institutions, markets, or social structure; whether norms, beliefs, culture, or information. Without interaction, these subjects evaporate. Whatever we may mean by many of them, they refer in the end to elusive entities it is the business of interaction to engender, maintain, service, and transform. The nostalgia for interaction is the nostalgia for a subject.

NOTES

Introduction

1. Even broadened to include attention to destabilizing matters like conflicting expectations, strain, alienative need-dispositions, and ambivalent motivation (1951, chap. 7), Parsons's formulation is still weighted by the classic emphasis on equilibration and order. Where positive feedback enters Parsons's system, it produces examples of deviance, matters phrased in a language—e.g., "cumulatively deepening vicious circle[s] of intensification of the alienative component" (1951, 271)—by which we recognize the analytic emphasis still placed by his system on explaining stability. Implicitly, of course, Parsons was aware that negative feedback, involved whenever actors sanctioned one another to conform to their respective expectations, was operating in the face of tendencies to deviate from conformity. Yet apart from discussing ways deviance sometimes "structures out" into crime or gangs or the sick role, he leaves inexplicit the part played by positive feedback in nondeviant or nonconformist interaction. More important, he fails to recognize how systems of interaction based on positive feedback drive certain institutions.

2. An important exception to this emphasis occurs in microeconomic theory, which assumes that rational markets are systems governed by conditions that maximize competiton and minimize forms of stability like monopolistic organization. That some markets are forms of order that arise from circumstances undermining organization, indeed augmenting instability at the level of their participants, is an idea we shall make use of in a later chapter. This conceptualization—markets as examples of aggregate forms of order arising from instability at the level of their participants—isn't relevant to the kinds of analysis usually undertaken in economic work but is consistent with assumptions economists make about "perfect" competition. More on this in chapter 7.

3. An obvious exception to this claim appears in the study of "collective behavior"

such as occurs in excited crowds (e.g., Turner and Killian 1957; Lang and Lang 1961; Smelser 1963b; Blumer [1939] 1946; etc.). Again, however, this is a conceptualization segregated from the study of everyday interaction—more work of the order assumption.

Other contemporary theories of interaction (or theories in which interaction is conceptualized) do not provide exceptions to the general claim I have made about the control of the dominant order assumption. Collins's (e.g., 1981, 1987) ideas about "interaction ritual chains," Luhmann's (1982, [1982] 1986) about interaction as a separate system level, Turner's (1988) synthesis of different traditions in a schematic model of interaction processes, Heise's (1977, 1979; Smith-Lovin 1987) affect control theory—all are controlled by the order assumption. Indeed, even Luhmann's appropriation of "self-organization" concepts is subordinated to the order assumption, and thus misses what is potentially revolutionary about these ideas for social theory.

Chapter 1

1. Kenneth Sayre, in his *Cybernetics and the Philosophy of Mind* (1976), makes a distinction between homeostatic and heterotelic feedback, the former being where a response is directed into a system to control the effect of some perturbation from the environment, and the latter being where a response is directed from the system back into the environment to control or affect the environment itself. In this sense, of course, human beings are both homeostatic and heterotelic.

2. A more general model of homeostatic processes, especially as they are described physiologically, is provided by D. J. Schneck 1987.

3. Viewed from the standpoint of our analysis of feedback, the question of where the signal originates is unimportant, but it must at least have been picked up by the infant and then returned to the infant by the parent's mirroring responses.

4. The clinical relevance of "omnipotence" originates with Freud's discussions of the "omnipotence of thought." Object relations theories such as Winnicott's appropriated the concept in conjunction with their postulate of magical thinking—the illusion the infant is believed to form that its own thoughts and wants and needs bring it relief. (See Pine 1985 for a useful discussion of this idea, particularly in relation to Mahlerian theory.) Kohut's idea of omnipotence depends on the infant's sense that the caregiver merges with it, not that it merges with the caregiver.

5. I do not want to argue that introjects are types, but that they are like types. They are specifically like types in being abstract and in requiring realization; they are specifically unlike types in being deep personal structures of self, rather than features of shared culture. It is reasonable, however, to argue that matters like memories (which in this scheme of thought are regarded as instantiations of introjects) might be conceptualized as forms of "personal culture." This reduces the difference between types and introjects.

6. To put the matter this way may annoy some clinicians, since it blunts the distinction between abnormal and normal object relationships in interaction. This implies that selfobject transference in clinical examples is evidence for similar (if less extreme)

phenomena in everyday social interaction. This argument is fundamental to understanding social interaction, which is saturated by just such functional "uses" of one another by interaction partners.

7. It is important to realize that pathological forms of disintegration anxiety can arise from values of T at both high and low extremes. This idea becomes more important in later chapters. Phrasing the matter this way would suggest that Kohut conflates the two extremes, or at least does not make theoretical use of this distinction. This would be inaccurate, since I am describing as anxiety subjective states he discusses in relation to concepts such as depression and the "empty self." In my way of conceptualizing these phenomena, depression (the more familiar clinical concept) is an affective manifestation of anxiety that arises in relation to absent responsiveness. The reader should be aware that this reasoning, though founded on Kohut's concepts, is based on my reading of his theory. In this reading, caregivers can fail to support mirrored strengths and self-esteem, for example, by being flat and underresponsive, or by being smothering and overresponsive. These two extremes produce values of T leading to pathological expressions of disintegration anxiety. The distinction becomes more important when we reach chapter 2 and consider various forms of strong attachment.

8. In this way of thinking, the selection pressure behind one of the merger demands is not proportional to the level of disintegration anxiety. Only low levels and high levels of disintegration anxiety, but not intermediate levels, yield merger demands. Moderate levels of disintegration anxiety are normal and are behind the continuing selection of existing structures of self to deal with temporary fluctuations in T.

9. "The self" is a secularized version of archaic religious and philosophical entities like the "soul." In sociology and social psychology where Meadian concepts have organized thought in this area, the tendency to reify this notion has proceeded without a critical perspective able to unearth the religious assumptions hidden in the idea. Mead was explicit about looking for a secular idea able to substitute for the "soul," which he got via Dewey from William James, and ultimately, therefore, from sources including the American romantics, many of whom were undisguised Platonists of one stripe or another. Recent critical work in this area has been immensely enlightening (e.g., Wiley 1986; Rochberg-Halton 1987; also Kuklick 1977).

Chapter 2

1. Actually, Kohut is inexplicably adamant about the approximate simultaneity of the appearance of the two poles of the self. Though this simultaneous emergence might have appeared to him as logically necessary or intuitively obvious, it is by no means obvious to the reader solely on the basis of the logic Kohut himself developed. In fact, however, his intuition is correct—as I shall show below. There can be no homeostatic self-equilibration without both poles of the self operating simultaneously.

2. It is useful to note that Kohut's developmental model modifies what he assimilated from Winnicott's (1965) influence on the psychoanalytic community. Kohut's revisionism manifests itself in the pattern $M \to M \to I \to I$. Were Kohut's concepts available to Winnicott, Winnicott might have argued that $M \to I \to I$. For Winnicott,

that is, the problem was to "release" idealized representations (illusions) and then to internalize representations of reality.

3. I am deliberately ignoring many of the conceptual issues around this subject raised by research in cognitive psychology. But one way of aligning this way of thinking with recent work in cognitive psychology is to suggest that the fragments of perception Kohut talks about being clustered around the mirroring and idealized poles of the self amount respectively, in their earliest status, to sensorimotor representations and early sorts of conceptual knowledge—the sorts of representations, on the one hand, that control perceptual recognition and motor activity and, on the other, that can be accessed independently of motor activity or perception (see Mandler 1988).

4. The loss of an introject's strength I will conceptualize in later chapters as a matter of decay, and therewith treat the subject more rigorously. Generally speaking, I mean by the "strength" of an introject its capacity to handle a function—that is, to do the work required to manage the person's feelings. This is roughly proportional to psychic structuration, in Kohut's model. One trouble with this notion is that it makes psychological strength a relative notion—that is, the self is strong relative to the problems of self-regulation it faces, and these are a function of the properties of the environments in which it has had transmuting experiences. More on this in chapter 3.

5. The logic of this process actually allows for the simultaneous selection of numerous equifinal structures, each contributing some increment to the function in question—say, soothing the anxiety or worry at issue. In the life of real actors, therefore, we would want to represent this process with more complex diagrams—allowing, for example, summing or otherwise aggregating the functional contributions of numerous selected structures.

6. The specific biochemistry at issue here is widely discussed in the pertinent literature. A good discussion is Milkman and Sunderwirth 1987. For the counterargument—for example, that endorphin levels have not consistently been shown to be related to running—see the summary in Peele 1988. Peele is particularly hostile to the neurological model of addiction proposed by Milkman and Sunderwirth, which is based on the argument followed here that "self-induced changes in neurotransmission" are involved in addictive experiences. He argues that this is social psychology masked as biochemistry, and that Milkman and Sunderwirth "cloak experiential events in neurological terminology without reference to any actual research that connects biological functioning to addictive behavior" (1988, 56). By contrast, one thing is fairly sure: the evidence based on asking people whether, say, they drink in order to feel better, or whether running diminishes their feelings of stress, speaks plainly enough about the fact that people attempt to regulate their feelings by certain of their practices. The question of evidence is whether neurotransmission levels are changed by addictive substances, and whether what people do by engaging in addictive behavior is to regulate their neurotransmission by attempting to control the way they feel. My argument is closer to the position of Milkman and Sunderwirth, though I am suggesting that there is a developmental precedent for addictive predispositions—namely, structural deficits in the self that arise from nonoptimal caregiving, and the initial infant position of "addictive" dependence on caregivers.

7. It turns out that the reason alcohol may be addicting is that it uses up the coenzyme NAD$^+$ necessary in the degradation of dopamine into 3,4-dihydroxyphenylacetate. This second-stage product backs up and becomes present in excess quantities. 3,4-dihydroxyphenylacetate begins then to react with unconverted dopamine to form another compound that is an example of the tetrahydroisoquinolines (THIQ)—a class of compounds that has effects believed to be like the effects of our own endorphins and of opiate narcotics (see the discussion in Milkman and Sunderwirth 1987, 73).

8. The burgeoning literature on cocaine is impossible to summarize, but a good introduction to the pharmacology is present in the articles in Redda, Walker, and Barnett 1989. Useful as well are Murray 1986, Arif 1987, Washton and Tatarsky 1984, and Grabowski 1984.

9. Just how much the concept of disintegration anxiety reduces to a withdrawal symptom I am unsure. But this possibility means that some of what we experience in the course of the disintegration of our attachments, of whatever kinds, from selfobjects or substances, may well be the psychological or psychophysiological expression of such withdrawal.

10. It is necessary to imagine consumer behavior more generally in relation to the addictive model of the self developed here. The effects of advertising on consumer demand, for example, are not unlike the effects of an addictive substance on disintegration anxiety. Consider how advertising a product affects consumer demand. This is a problem analogous to how addictive substances yield strong attachments.

The usual formulation is that advertising has cumulative lagged effects on the sales revenues of a firm (see the studies in Day and Parsons 1971). Firms are therefore motivated to continue advertising because each successive time period will expose further segments of the population to an advertising stimulus as well as reinforcing those segments previously exposed. Aside from the content of an advertisement—itself designed to arouse wants—sheer familiarity with a product through exposure to its advertising has effects a firm intends: it eventually makes a product seem familiar. Familiarity diminishes what attachment theorists call "stranger anxiety" and thus also diminishes disintegration anxiety. Psychological experiments have also long been able to demonstrate that familiarizing subjects with a stimulus—even when the stimulus is, say, nothing but a nonsense syllable—induces evaluations of the stimulus as "good" as opposed to the "bad" or unfamiliar stimulus. Repeated exposure to photographs of strangers, similarly, induces feelings of warmth toward the strangers on the part of experimental subjects.

It is important to note, however, that Michael Schudson (1986) takes exception to the claims made in research on the effects of advertising.

11. The concept of the "transitional object" also appears in Kohut's writing, despite Kohut's claim that he had never read Winnicott. When Kohut refers to the idealized selfobject as an "idealized (transitional) selfobject," as he does in *The Analysis of the Self*, he implies that this external structure is at first under the control of an internal representation or illusion—the equivalent, perhaps, of the archaic grandiose self. Clearly, the archaic grandiose self was such an illusion of omnipotence in the way he initially conceived of it. When one reads Kohut this way, it is clear his concep-

tual scheme is more closely aligned to Winnicott's than is generally recognized. (Similarities in their work are also noted by others, e.g, Greenberg and Mitchell 1983.) One should perhaps then reconceive the activity of the caregiver in Kohut's model also to include the job done by the "good-enough" mother in Winnicott's theory of development, namely, to encourage the surrender of illusions, replacing them with externally grounded attachments that might serve as a more realistic basis for introjection.

Chapter 3

1. This is not to argue that mirroring equals energetic regulation in Kohut's theory. It is to argue instead that what he discussed as mirroring is a process founded initially on energic dynamics. The clinical reader familiar with Kohut's writings will have to permit me some latitude here in developing uses for these ideas outside of the clinical setting. My argument is that, prior to the appearance of the infant's representational system, including what Kohut would have identified as a mirrored introject, infant-caregiver interaction is largely energic and homeostatic, with the caregiver serving as an external regulator of the infant's subjective states.

2. Though I shall not pursue the thought here, an "optimal" coupling might be defined with reference to the difference between the set point for a system and the actual reading of the system. "Perfect" adaptation of a mother to her infant, in Winnicott's sense, means that this difference is zero. Nonoptimal adaptation would mean that it exceeds some threshold that would have to be defined empirically. And "optimal" adaptation would mean that the system has some slack—that the furnace isn't caused to kick in, say, until the temperature drops by a fair amount. The adaptation then is "good-enough," but not perfect, and the infant thus experiences some discomfort before external devices begin to intervene in regulating it.

3. It is technically important to point out that identification does not necessarily or automatically imply introjection, which can happen only in conjunction with "optimal" disappointments and hence only when interaction has taken on a negative trajectory or, what is the same thing psychodynamically, when it exhibits movement apart, separation, or an associated moment of individuation—all phases of interaction connected, psychodynamically, with changing the values of I, specifically by increasing I. Hence the assumption of the constancy of the idealized introject during these positive phases of interaction is supported by the theoretical reasoning leading to the homeostatic model we began with.

4. Yet another angle on the matter of intimacy is provided by psychotherapy itself. The course of therapy might be described this way: therapists attempt to configure themselves in empathic relationships to their patients, establishing trusted and safe environments where relationships can become progressively deep. Maintaining continuing rapport with their patients, therapists must be able eventually to see patterns in their patients' observed and reported behavior. These patterns are typically hidden, "latent," or deep—beneath the level of patients' conscious awareness. They arise in a patient's past and reappear in the present. Typically, as well, they manifest themselves in the patient's relationship to the therapist, as part of what more classically is called "the transference." An important aim of therapy is to bring these matters,

formerly hidden from patients, toward the surface of their awareness. The talented and empathic therapist is able gradually to accomplish this function of therapy—bringing to the surface what is hidden, in the depths—through interpretation. Interpretation itself then further deepens rapport and enables the patient to see still deeper inside himself or herself.

Getting close to an interaction partner more generally also works like this process. Close relationships, certainly, are those where partners are encouraged by intimacy and trust to open up to one another, to interpret, and to bring depths to the surface. Closeness to an other means, in this sense, that each partner has admitted the other into the "foreground" of experience where feelings can be controlled. But it also means that close interaction partners have created a kind of transitional space that functions to contextualize inchoate personal depths. An implication of this argument turns out to be that intimacy is also driven by the flow that is achieved not solely by damping but by articulating anxiety. On the practical analysis of how psychotherapy actually works, see especially David Malan (1978).

5. Something similar often happens in reading. Part of the scholar's excitement in coming across a passage containing thoughts akin to his or her own is due to the sense of discovering an alter-ego. A relationship exists between persons who share common thoughts, or between whom a bridge might be built. Thus it never seems odd to write to strangers upon discovering such kinship, or to receive letters from them if they discovered it first.

6. Also *limen,* from the Latin for threshold, and meaning, in a psychological sense, the threshold of consciousness.

7. There are important differences between the dynamics of rituals of different types that should be treated separately. Some, like puberty rites, appear to work by generating positive feedback out of mutual idealizing transferences. Others, like the "rituals of rebellion" Gluckman (1963) studied among the Zulu, appear to generate solidarity by mobilizing social conflicts discharged in ceremonial catharsis. This is also true of the "festival," as modeled by Roger Callois (1959, 1961), which depends on "inversions of the moral order" to move interaction into liminality. Moral inversions make right into wrong, up into down, male into female, princes into paupers, and black into white, and function generally as disinhibiting processes—that is to say, displacements of the functioning of the idealized parental imago. Turning the social world inside out and upside down, as during Mardi Gras, supports excess and prodigality of all kinds and thus also functions dialectically, as in Turner's contrast. Excess, the code word for excitation and unregulated interaction based on positive feedback, is eventually stabilized in cultural selfobjects. Rituals of rebellion are more like elections in American politics—opportunities periodically to bring those on high down to earth and make them accountable by various humiliations. This operates retributively among the Zulu and is in a sense another way to tie the sacred (where the sacred has a concrete equivalent in the Zulu king) to the everyday life of the tribe—only this time the king is reminded not to become too high, too far away, or too arrogant.

8. It should perhaps be stressed that these functions (e^t, $cos\ t$) are descriptions of the behavior of $T(t)$ and $P(t)$ and are in no way prescriptive.

9. A singularity occurs with zeroes as the values for $Z(t)$. This is relatively trivial,

since in fact there is nothing unique about the representation of $F(t)$. I might just as well have taken the difference of the terms in the numerator and the denominator.

Chapter 4

1. Not without some dissensus in the ranks of physicists and mathematicians. See the work of the French mathematician René Thom, particularly his *Structural Stability and Morphogenesis* (1975), where a version of so-called catastrophe theory consistent with the older physics is developed. Thom's differences with Prigogine mainly have to do with his unwillingness to surrender deterministic conceptions, and his reinterpretation of stochastic ideas. He prefers, for example, to make determinism or instability a "local property of the process under consideration" (126). Prigogine regards catastrophe theory, where exact solutions happen to be available, as a description of a "very simple" and "exceptional" case of the more complex mathematical theory of bifurcations (1980, chap. 5).

2. Whether this will be an attractor is discovered by examining Lyapounov functions of the concentrations of the X_i, represented in figure 4.2 by the values of λ. If the value of $d\lambda/dt$ has a sign opposite that of λ, the equilibrium state will be an attractor.

3. Speaking of adverse gradients among "perceptual" phenomena introduces complexities not present in the Bénard instability, though it is a long-standing practice among social psychologists who study unbalanced dyads, cognitive dissonance, and related matters of disagreement. Such gradients might be (in all probability are) different for each interactant. This is necessarily the case in relationships involving mutual infatuation, where each partner idealizes the other. Thus, we have multiple adverse gradients, as many as there are interacting pairs. The Prigoginian analysis should be considered with this in mind. I ignore this complexity here in order to develop the basic point. (The analogy makes sense only if you accept the notion that interaction's equivalent of the adverse gradient arises in each actor, depending on how much each overestimates the strengths of their partners or themselves relative to their partners.)

4. The analysis in chapter 3, it will be recalled, suggests that this can occur when each partner interacts under the partial control of internal idealized strengths, as clustered around the archaic parental imago and its introjected derivatives. By contrast, when each idealizes the other, using the partner as an idealized selfobject in Kohut's sense, and hence engages in displacing introjected idealized controls with the external other, interaction has the potential of becoming a positive feedback system. Then mutual transferences are left undamped.

5. λ_1 and λ_2 refer to so-called Lyapounov functions of underlying variables whose concentrations we would be studying.

6. As Milkman and Sunderwirth summarize it, "The adrenal glands produce cortisol, a chemical that increases blood sugar and speeds up the body's metabolism. Other messages to the adrenal glands result in the release of the amphetamine-like stimulant epinephrine (adrenaline), which helps supply glucose to the muscles and the brain, and norepinephrine, which speeds up the heart rate and elevates blood pressure. The psychological byproducts of moderate chemical emergency are noticeable incre-

ments in one's feelings of physical prowess and personal competence, often associated with strong sensations of pleasure" (1987, 96–97).

7. This is an expression used by James S. Coleman in *The Mathematics of Collective Action* (1973) and subsequently by Laumann and Knoke in their study of policy-making at the national level, *The Organizational State* (1988). Both of these books have been a stimulus to the thinking I present in this section, though neither of them is concerned with individual-level processes of the sort I argue might be seen behind the cumulation of individual acts into macrostructures.

8. The several efforts of Roland Barthes to analyze fashion, as in his *Elements of Semiology* ([1964] 1967) and *The Fashion System* ([1967] 1983), establish a semiotic analysis that can be undergirded in self-psychological terms as well. In *Elements of Semiology* he offers the following analogy: (speech/language) = (dress/clothing). These relations hold true at the level of cultural analysis, since language and clothing are cultural systems. But when the numerators in the analogy are understood as "surface structures," they might also be seen as serving in some loose sense as instantiations of introjects. Culture provides vehicles in terms of which the deep structures of self find a way into behavior, shaping the person's acts of self-possession. Barthes's more penetrating semiotic analysis in *The Fashion System* has reference to fashion as a system of signs.

Chapter 5

1. Older, psychoanalytically derived ideas have influenced sociological analysis at various times. Freud's own remarks about the phenomenon appear in connection with the elaboration of his drive-structure model and involve an analysis of love as aim-inhibited (*zielgehemmte*) libido. Instead of serving in a consummatory mode, "objects" in such thinking undergo idealization, the cause of their worship and of the tenderness felt toward them. Willard Waller (1937, 1938) was later to discuss love as a "passion" that develops in response to the frustration of sexual aims, echoing the Freudian thought. Others like Parsons (Parsons and Bales 1955; Parsons 1964a; cf. Lasch's critique 1977) and Goode have used the language of psychoanalysis if not the exact logic, Goode, for example, when discussing love as a "strong emotional attachment, a cathexis" (1959, 41). The Freudian influence is otherwise thoroughgoing and ubiquitous.

2. Rational choice theory can accommodate phenomena like love by adding a better psychology to its models of preference, choice, and exchange. Sociology suffers from some of the same cognitive bias. In point of fact, models of preference, decision, and choice in sociology and social psychology have been evaluating matters of affect as if they were matters of cognition for some time. Balance theory, for example, is obviously more concerned with matters of liking and affect than with matters of cognition. In this respect, it is important for sociologists taken by the elegance of rational choice theory to realize the implications for theoretical analysis of psychological evidence about preferences. In Zajonc's forceful statement, "[F]or most decisions, it is extremely difficult to demonstrate that there has actually been *any* prior cognitive process whatsoever" (1980, 155). Understanding preferences and decisions requires first understanding affects and emotions. Choice is seldom the simple matter of evaluating

alternatives in the presence of uncertainty; choice involves likes and dislikes, and these are matters of affect—evaluative responses to objects based on simpler but more powerful affective coding of experience. Zajonc's observations, of course, have little to do with the status of rational choice theory as a normative perspective. (Jon Elster, working from a rational choice perspective, offers numerous provocative thoughts about love in various of his essays [e.g., 1984, 1985b] and also suggests in several places how passion might well be analyzed as a special case of "weakness of will" [e.g., 1985a, 1989]. "Weakness of will," from the perspective developed in this book, amounts to the circumstance described as an addictive predisposition—the absence of such inner "strengths" or self-structures as give rise to self-control and self-direction. Without these strengths, one is given to strong attachments, and so forth. In effect, what these predispositions produce, from a rational choice perspective, are such constraints on an actor's "opportunity set" as to effectively addict him or her to a given object.)

3. All but the most misanthropic of us display a readiness to discover attractive qualities in others we have just been introduced to. Our natural "responsiveness" often leads us to distort them apperceptively in view of our wishes, and we project into them qualities we would like to discover. So long as this idealizing transference is in place, it modifies the exchange rule operating in interaction. Above the qualities introduced initially into interaction by the requirements of good breeding, that is, there is a natural readiness among most people to idealize fresh acquaintances—a readiness that gives off signals of a desire to take them up should they seem at all ready to conform to our wishes. We are willing to pay more under such circumstances for their interaction than we would once our transference has been dispelled. This is a phenomenon related to the well-known effects first impressions have on us. Persons typically feel something about others they have never met, having a decided affective response about others prior to any so-called cold cognitions. This phenomenon speaks to what Zajonc calls *preferenda*—"a class of features [in others] that combine more readily with [our] affect and thereby allow us to make these evaluations, to experience attraction, repulsion, pleasure, conflict, and other forms of affect, and to allow us to have these affective reactions quite early after the onset of sensory input" (1980, 159). The features that combine readily with affect often include self-referenced items. Psychoanalysis would locate some of these in internal states of the individual that change as a function of interaction. Zajonc says, "If [*preferenda*] exist, they must be constituted of interactions between some gross object features and internal states of the individual—states that can be altered while the object remains unchanged, as, for example, when liking for a stimulus increases with repeated exposure" (1980, 159). Transferences make use of objects to control feelings, as we have seen.

4. It is useful to recognize that one source of the motivation to sustain bad relationships is an abstinence syndrome—the fear that giving up the bad partner may be painful and disorganizing in a degree not worth the costs emotionally. Generalizing from studies of addiction to studies of romance suggests yet other links, especially to underlying neurochemical processes affected in romance. This problem has been extensively developed elsewhere and is reviewed in Milkman and Sunderwirth 1987.

5. Strong "negative" attachments, like hate and prejudice, obviously serve integra-

tive functions for the self, particularly when they are shared by several persons. Such shared negative transferences, like the hatred directed toward an enemy during war, seems to reinforce strong positive attachments by a kind of balance rule. Hatred of others thus motivates strong attachments, or at least strengthens interaction, within a group of persons. Bettelheim and Janowitz (1964) discuss the "functions" of prejudice during adolescence in a similar vein—i.e., prejudices serve as ways to contain the identity diffusion characteristic of adolescence. (Erikson's [1968] concept of "identity diffusion" thus bears some resemblance to Kohut's notion of disintegration anxiety. Both signal fragmentation of self or lack of cohesiveness and produce behavior that can be interpreted as transferential and structure building.)

Chapter 6

1. The tendency to reify this concept of power is strongly entrenched in sociology and the other social sciences. Debates rage over what power is, forgetting that this concept is merely a seventeenth-century natural science borrowing from practical engineering, where the concept was useful for describing how much work a machine could do. And this, in turn, was merely the concept of how much energy was required to move an object a certain distance, and so forth. So how to define what power is, as a concept of something equivalent in the social world, is not a task that can be accomplished by pure theoretical debate but only by defining the concept in terms of observations. Power is a concept of something in the social world, not a thing in itself.

2. Weber's distaste for psychoanalysis per se had less to do with irreconcilable theoretical disagreements with Freud than with his repudiation of the more vulgar forms of "eroticism" evident in the lives of some of Freud's followers, like Otto Gross (Schwentker 1987).

3. Such attributions are not, however, automatic, and, Camic (1980, 18) cautions, "the extent to which such responses obtain is always a function of the social interaction between the extraordinarily needy and the figure they deem special. It must be determined empirically, not taken for granted."

4. "A desire to redeem his father and a sense of being chosen; a strong moral conscience and a love for 'activity on a large scale'; a long effort building up in oneself all the resources needed for the task to come; the capacity to make one's childhood crises representative of collective problems, to make one's personality the answer to an historical crisis, to fill a collective identity vacuum with one's own identity through one's acts or writings; the capacity to wait for the right moment, to engage one's whole personality when it comes, and to prefer settling for nothing rather than compromising one's integrity; a self-fulfilling (and early) sense of omnipotence and omniscience, combined with enormous energy and mental concentration; narcissism absorbed in charisma and lifted into deeds; a sense of being unique and unprecedented"—all are traits, derived from Erikson's analyses of Luther (1958) and Gandhi (1969), applied by Stanley and Inge Hoffmann (1968, 877) to Charles de Gaulle.

5. This ambivalence toward the holy, in Otto's sense, parallels the duality of sentiment toward the sacred, in Durkheim's analysis (1915).

6. Kohut (1985, 200) argued that "charisma" differed from "messianic" leadership

in the way Churchill differed from Gandhi. Churchill's "self" developed in such a way as to be largely identified with his "archaic grandiose self," whereas Gandhi's was largely identified with his idealized selfobject. This gave Churchill his unqualified self-assurance and empowered the British people through their identifications with him during World War II—Churchill serving as an idealized selfobject but confronting the enfeebled British public with the characteristic grandiosity and omnipotence that were so much a part of his personal appeal. Gandhi likewise served India as an idealized selfobject, though responding to the idealizing needs of his compatriots with a "self-righteousness" that reflected his personal development along lines emphasizing the consolidation of his own strengths around the pole of idealized strengths. This argument makes sense of the differences between Weber's contrasting concepts of exemplary and ethical charisma, though I do not believe Kohut was conversant with Weber's writings. (I discovered this essay of Kohut's only after having written the present chapter, and found that it converges with my own analysis.)

7. I deliberately omit consideration of what in all likelihood is the more common pattern—namely, the case where a leader fails to disappoint in the "incremental," "optimally frustrating," slow and piecemeal mode which, in the Winnicott-Kohut model, leads to successful "transmuting internalizations" of the sort that would support disciples' autonomy and growth. One must suppose that most failed claims, appearing in disappointing proofs—failed magic, lost battles, unsuccessful hunts, and so forth—lead to abrupt repudiations of leaders, and that follwers thereafter remain in the same needy condition, with equivalent needs for yet additional idealized objects.

8. The constituency becomes the salient source of negentropy for elected officials, so that the more closely electoral rules tie them to their constituents, the fewer degrees of freedom they have in their decision making. When this principle is discussed as a Burkean dilemma, it poses the potential incompatibility between internal and external information sources as sources of negentropy—a senator's conscience, say, versus the constituents' interests. The senatorial model presumes introjected self-reliant direction, whereas the "grass root" model in the House presumes external direction.

Chapter 7

1. Also, of course, this harkens back to Tönnies's thesis in *Gemeinschaft und Gesellschaft,* on the question of which Weber was not neutral. Though Weber clearly argued for the role played in change by social action centered on strong personal ties like those based on charisma, his ideal type of rational action still proscribed affect (see Shils's comments 1951; also Janowitz's introduction to Thomas 1966).

2. It should create no logical difficulties to imagine that social organization more generally might loosely be characterized in the same terms. This is not to suggest that there aren't limits to this logic.

3. Obviously there are certain ranges of these variables, left unspecified here, within which this relationship holds. Nevertheless, defining complexity in these rough terms is adequate to my purposes.

4. "Information richness" or "cybernetic richness" is a Parsonian notion. But this argument is not Parsons's; see, instead, Smith 1985; Smith and Ross 1984.

5. Or, perhaps better said, the degree to which culture supports autonomy depends on the information richness of culture itself. Leaders and persons in superordinate roles are specifiers. But outside of information-rich environments their specifying function does not establish the conditions of autonomy in the same degree.

6. There is a danger of thinking unrealistically about specification as a process that proceeds in relation to a single value or end, starting with its formulation at the top of a hierarchy and ending with job specs at the bottom. In reality, specification operates in some loose sense like this but also substantially involves all of the intermediate relations of authority and coordination of tasks in an organization. This means that it occurs with respect to various intermediate aims and projects, all of which are part of a division of labor.

7. This was one reason Weber spoke of bureaucracies employing "professionals." Organizations have to get their culture from someplace, and not all of it comes from the decision making of CEOs or boards of directors. One place is from hiring persons socialized into external cultural environments, who bring expertise and culture into an organization's decision making. Though this sets up the inevitable tension between bureaucratic and professional authority that naïve research has sometimes taken as evidence of an error in Weber's thinking about bureaucracy, professional culture is one of the inevitable sources of autonomy within the complex division of labor among bureaucratic offices. Likewise, it means that complexity can arise only from concerting the activities undertaken within such separate, autonomously functioning spheres of activity. Supporting this arrangement of spheres is the part played by codes and law.

8. I should note, too, that this formulation takes much of the mystery out of the much-studied relationship between increases in organizational "size" and so-called economies of scale. The way this has been handled in the research of Blau and his associates (e.g., Blau and Schoenherr 1971), size works its effects by principles out of view, as in the argument that size has effects because it produces economies of scale. Since economies of scale are equal to the administrative ratio changes, this is empiricism parading as theory. In the perspective suggested here, by contrast, size changes are correlated to changes in administrative ratios by the terms of the theory of specification. And in this theory, culture produces the interaction effect shown in figure 7.2.

9. See Weber's discussion in "The Protestant Sects and the Spirit of Capitalism" (1946, 302–22). Many other illustrations are available of how commitment to absolute ends in otherwise information-poor (unspecified) cultural environments works to neutralize attachments. It might be argued, for example, that an equivalent phenomenon is at work in ideological collectivities like the Bolshevik cells studied by Nahirny (1962). For an example of how ideological ties interfere with personal ties, see also Alberto Moravia's short story "Bitter Honeymoon" (1959). Martin King Whyte's *Small Groups and Political Rituals in China* (1974) presents another example—specifically, of how Chinese *hsiao-tsu* were coopted by the Communist Party and organized around political rituals based on criticism, hence mobilizing coercive small-group dynamics (as in the Protestant sects) that functioned (in Maoist theory) to break down the entrenched traditionalism of Chinese society. Undermining

traditionalism in this sense meant replacing particularism with universalism, a correlate of neutralization.

10. This is not to argue that other conditions later in life are not also able to support
universalistic values. Inkeles and his collaborators, for example, have shown that apart
from background factors, both experience and schooling encourage universalistic values (Inkeles 1983, 1974). A developmentalist with psychoanalytic training might look
at such findings as an indicator that one of the things schooling certifies is progress in
the "capacity to be alone"—progress, that is, in developing such psychological
strengths as support autonomy. Schools, after all, are also caregiver substitutes, whose
main function should be to socialize children to the point where (by some standard) it
is safe and socially responsible to release them on their own.

11. A good example of this is Edmund Leach's description, in *Political Systems of
Highland Burma* (1954), of what happened when a traditional hereditary chief turned
out to be feebleminded. (I am indebted to Arthur Stinchcombe for reminding me of
this example.)

12. Moreover, the cultural elaboration of traditional values in concrete, personalized ways shapes what we hope to discern in the particular incumbent of a traditional
role. A sacred kingship like that discovered among the Yoruba, for example, defined
a pattern of centralized particularism, where kings were perceived a priori as persons
uniquely possessed of certain sacred worth (see LeVine 1971 for a useful comparison
of Yoruba with Ibo and Hausa-Fulani cultures). The Yoruba practice illustrates one
form of the charisma of office, shaped by traditional culture. Complex traditional
societies, by this logic, depend on hierarchically focused transference to define and
redefine the content of traditional values, always "embodied" in "traditional" figures;
what is meant concretely by "traditional" in such cases depends on the culture in question and the particular incumbents of transferentially weighted roles. Less complex
(i.e., less hierarchical) traditional societies seem similarly to preserve their traditionality by means of practices by which the past, as it gets preserved and remembered in
stories, myths, bodies of traditional law, and so forth, is both transmitted and modified
by persons with traditional authority—elders, "schools" of teachers and religious
figures, storytellers, age groups, men's and women's groups, and so forth. Much simpler tribal societies, like the Ibo in eastern Nigeria, exhibited far less hierarchy, a
correlate of which was the absence of anything like the traditional "high culture" of
the Yoruba or of Islamicized tribes like the Hausa. Age groups, kinship groups, men's
and women's groups, and other matters in such societies (e.g., oracles that appeared
during the unsettled period of slaving in the eighteenth and nineteenth centuries) provided naturally occurring hierarchical systems in which the culture of such societies
was both preserved and transmitted (see also chap. 6).

13. Representing filtering interaction, a complex notion of variation, as a coefficient on interaction requires more detail than we need bother with here. But we can
skip over the difficulties of representing this in a precise form and adopt some conve-
nient simplifications. Define a new variable $\lambda = f(\eta, \theta)$, where λ (the same λ we discussed above) describes this structural-cultural environment, η is a measure of the environment's neutralization, and θ is a measure of the variable we have called cybernetic
level. (Let λ, η, and θ be continuous variables, and define η such that it takes on

larger values when neutralization increases and θ such that it takes on larger values when information richness increases. In this way, λ is defined as an increasing function of θ and of η.) With these definitions, we can represent the way λ filters transference as

$$F_{ij}(t) = \kappa\left(\frac{1}{\lambda}\right)\left[\frac{R_i(t)R_j(t)}{Z_i(t)Z_j(t)}\right].$$

In these terms, a macrosociological coefficient on the forces of attraction, $1/\lambda$, amounts to a set of conditions that either amplify or undermine the operation of role responsiveness, in Sandler's sense. When λ is a large number, as presumably it would be where the supports for rationality are present, there are powerful cultural filters that interpose themselves between the hypothetical actors in our interaction field, neutralizing them in each other's eyes and associating each with the other in a relational template specified organizationally and culturally. For all practical purposes, λ can be regarded as a constant when studying the behavior of $F(t)$, except where we are making comparisons over long periods of time or across contexts of interaction.

14. I am sidestepping the issue of where these so-called changes of scale occur, though it is apparently the case that for nonhuman populations a variable like population size operates empirically as the equivalent of what, in the study of physical systems, is called a bifurcation parameter. That is, as the n of a population changes, the population traverses these changes of scale, as might be observed in the appearance of new patterns of organization or complexity. The potential, with changes in n, for the emergence of new patterns of organization in human populations has been understood formally for quite some time, at least since Simmel's observations of the differences between dyads and triads, or perhaps Malthus's reflections on population. The change-of-scale argument associated with nonhuman populations has to do with matters like population density, carrying capacity of environments, and other supraindividual properties. It has been my argument, however, that at least some of the features of complexity in social organization isolated in comparative studies like Weber's are products not alone of changes in n but of interaction effects involving "environmental" variables like culture or information, stability, and so forth. Conceptualizing the operation of all of these matters simultaneously—size changes, divisions of labor, population density, and so forth—sounds like early Durkheim in *The Division of Labor in Society* a hundred years later. Cf. below, "When Hierarchy Fails."

15. Especially in this sense, Slater's (1963) conceptualization of strong two-person ties as instances of "dyadic withdrawal" assumes even greater relevance. Smith (1985) tries to put this idea into aggregate terms, studying the sensitivity in friendship rates to properties of corporate life like specification. In the framework of this book, the study of such rates of friendship choice becomes a way of showing how cultural variation in corporate life establishes fields of sensitive dependence and strong interaction.

16. Keep in mind that any system can be destabilized when positive feedback spreads beyond the interaction of two persons into larger aggregates. The stability conditions of larger systems, studied in this sense, is an important field of sociological analysis. One such stability condition, as sociologists have known for a long time, is the growth of multiple linkages connecting a system to other sources of stability—children to adults, groups to other groups, and so forth. Such linkages have the poten-

tial of damping positive feedback especially when they create cross-pressures—in particular, when stabilizing dynamics override positive feedback. On the concept of cross-pressures, see the work of Lazarsfeld and his associates (Lazarsfeld, Berelson, and Gaudet 1948; Lazarsfeld and Rosenberg 1955, etc.).

17. Again, this certainly does not mean there are no personal dynamics in such systems, but that when personal fluxes arise as part of larger systems they tend to produce small effects relative to those arising from macroscopic processes.

18. I do not mean to imply that all cultural models are prescriptive. Geertz (1973) makes the useful distinction between "models of" (descriptive) and "models for" (normative-prescriptive). Most models, like recipes, are a mix of description and prescription. Cf. Kroeber and Kluckhohn [1952] 1963, part 4.

19. The problem is more complex than this, since legal contracting is an example of how powerful macroscopic stability from one region can be used to damp and regulate potential disequilibrium arising in others. This was Max Weber's argument (albeit in different language) about why calculability in law was a condition for the rise of rational capitalism.

20. I am here conceiving of markets in the broadest possible sense. For example, power is a "market" emergent in this sense, and elections are a form of consumption behavior. Elections stabilize power in elected candidates; in such a scheme, candidates are idealized selfobjects who serve to stabilize the "omnipotence" of a system of voters. From a voter's viewpoint, power thus gets stabilized as authority by being "transferred" to electoral candidates. Parsons (1960, 1961, 1967) argued that, from a social systems viewpoint, the polity is a generative structure—it generates leadership. This is a similar conception to that advanced here, though I am working with a less "analytical" conception of "polity."

21. Though Stinchcombe (1984) comes close to this kind of statement, as in declaring his intention to "analyse . . . what kinds of social relations hierarchies consist of, and what functions they perform. This then provides an outline of . . . functions whose occurrence in contractual situations will lead to hierarchical elements in contracts" (2).

22. It is useful to remember that markets are not the only mechanisms of distribution and allocation. Kinship systems and government structures, for example, can also serve as allocative structures and assume important economic roles in nonmarket economies (see, e.g., Polyani, Arensberg, and Pearson 1957).

23. Cf. Kohut's language in describing how the accumulation of omnipotence through mirroring eventually produces a "transfer" of this property to an external idealized selfobject. See chapters 1 and 2.

24. A point made by Talcott Parsons and Neil Smelser (1956). Firms also rely on various internal pricing systems, such as those implicit in the competition between employees for promotion, and so forth.

25. Geertz's studies of bazaar economies in Indonesia (1963) and Morocco (Geertz, Geertz, and Rosen 1979) highlight this difference. In Geertz's words, firm-based economies enable "trade and industry to occur through a set of impersonally defined social institutions which organize a variety of specialized occupations with respect to some particular productive or distributive end" (1963, 28).

26. What saves Economic Man and Perfect Competition from being driven by positive feedback into disequilibrium is complete information. Thus, rather than far-from-equilibrium conditions, we get fast responsiveness, which is a form of anxious "rationality" and constitutes nonoptimal association in the extreme. Its analogue in the family is the sort of smothering caregiving Winnicott described as the style of the mother who is "unable to allow her child to be alone."

27. In Williamson's sense, specificity is an attribute a firm's assets acquire when, for example, the firm produces goods specialized to a particular transaction. "Asset specificity is both the most important dimension for describing transactions and the most neglected attribute in prior studies of organization. The issue is less whether there are large fixed investments . . . than whether such investments are specialized to a particular transaction. Items that are unspecialized among users pose few hazards, since buyers in these circumstances can easily turn to alternative sources and suppliers can sell output intended for one buyer to another without difficulty. Nonmarketability problems arise when the specific identity of the parties has important cost-bearing consequences" (1981, 555).

28. Williamson points out that "the main simplification is that ΔC (and possibly ΔG) is also a function of the amount produced." So the representation in figure 7.6 might be thought of "as a cross-section for a fixed level of output. Furthermore, the optimal level of A will depend on both demand effects and absolute cost effects" (Williamson 1981, 559). Even so, "only cost differences are shown in the figure."

29. Frank Knight's classic discussion of "wants" in this sense is especially useful. See Knight, [1921] 1965, chap. 3.

30. Optimal cost would be where $\Delta C + \Delta G = 0$, that is, where the specificity of assets has increased to the point where the person-as-firm economizes on transaction costs by internalizing their provision. The region around $\Delta C + \Delta G = 0$ would be called the "zone of proximal development" in Vygotsky's (1978) view of development.

31. It is worth noting, in addition, that Winnicott's developmental concept of how an infant allows its illusions to come under the control of reality—namely, by relinquishing them into a "potential space"—becomes equivalent here to allowing a formerly internalized function to be provided subsequently by a market mechanism. This happens, Winnicott says, when the infant begins to trust the environment—that is, to find it a reliable, responsive caregiver. Sociologically speaking, this is a psychological way to reconceive the market "rationalization" of social life Weber had in mind when he studied disenchantment.

32. This, from certain vantages, is a trivial consequence, since anomie *is* cultural failure. This new functional perspective, however, suggests that anomie is the macroscopic equivalent of disintegration anxiety and hence it is a variable it makes sense not to eradicate but to "optimize." Optimal levels of anomie, like optimal levels of anxiety, are behind the aggregate selection pressures supporting social structure and culture, and contribute to the subjective experience of flow in social life.

33. The onset of destructuration in Athenian history—evidence for which, in the unsettling of Athenian stratification, is discussed in Gouldner's neglected monograph *Enter Plato* (1966)—arguably provided the most significant cultural stimulus to the great age of Greek artistic and philosophic efflorescence. Destructuration also suggests

something similar to, though more general than, the kind of variation John Boswell, in *Christianity, Social Tolerance, and Homosexuality* (1980), suggests is behind those periods between the beginning of the Christian Era and the fourteenth century when homosexuals were not persecuted by reigning elites. Periods of cultural stagnation and of persecution are associated, among other things, with the "exhaustion of the urban elite" and the accompanying decline of urban cultural centers. Roman emperors, faced with declining birth rates among old elite families and with various other depleting conditions, replaced the old elite with wealthy provincials, a matter producing what Boswell calls a "ruralization" (his word) of the urban elite. This was a process that has its analogues in the history of the United States, particularly to the withdrawal of cultured, urban elites from the sphere of public life, and the abandonment of political institutions to provincials, especially the rural and working classes caught up in Jacksonian populism. Ruralization of elites is one of Boswell's ways of formulating the notion of stable, unchanging stratification dominated by conservative elites, leading to homophobia. Contemporary equivalents of this abound and can be discerned by observing geographic and socioeconomic variation in the appeals of authoritarianism, populism, nativism, xenophobia, ethnocentrism, homophobia, and related fears that are a function of illiteracy, downward social mobility, and disintegration anxiety.

34. Since these usages no doubt conceal even earlier roots, this chain of reasoning can be extended further. For example, *mestier* is related to the Latin roots *misterium* and *ministerium*. This would seem to be echoed in the concept of the calling, as it came to be applied to work—a root ultimately, therefore, connecting work to activity geared to guarding and preserving a mystery and, as the agent of such matters, to the glorification of God. In marriages, husbands were equivalent hierophants of God's natural order.

35. I say increasing generality because the *Oxford English Dictionary* notes that "phr[ases] like *all mister* (*men*), *what mister* (*man*) were subsequently misapprehended as = 'of all (what, etc.) class(es, kind(s'" (*Shorter Oxford English Dictionary*, 1959, 1263). *Sir* is a vulgarization of *Mister*, as in Sir Knight.

36. Redefining nobility may be understood as a process driven by pressures accumulating within the middle class to stabilize changes in its own self-conception, particularly conceptions of its own power and worthiness. In Kohutian theory, this would occur through transferring such equivalents of the infant's omnipotence to new idealized cultural selfobjects—in this case, through redefining aristocracy and nobility.

37. Democracy requires weak ties to diffuse information important in producing enlightened popular decision making, in Granovetter's perspective. But it is only the spread of information that "carries" weak ties in the first place, to invoke the argument developed here. My point is not that Granovetter is wrong—he isn't. It is that network structure might be regarded as a dependent variable, predicted by whether the boundary conditions were present to support weak ties.

38. To specify this matter in view of the damping of $F_{ij}(t)$, let us define a variable Ω as a measure of the degree of "fit" between a cultural model and the social world. The smaller the value of Ω, the better a model describes social life. (For example, Ω might be taken as a measure of how well contracting describes a system of transactions or, say, how well a ritual like the Javanese *slametan* described by Geertz

[1973] fits the reality of life in a Javanese village—not very well, according to Geertz.) Ω might then be written as a variable that interacts with the cultural coefficient on interaction λ, described above, allowing the coefficient to assume its full value only where the amount of "error" or disjunction measured in Ω approaches zero—writing it, say, as $1/\Omega$, and adding whatever other constraints are arithmetically necessary to keep this idea afloat (e.g., $\Omega \neq 0$).

We can then form an expression that becomes a theoretical tool for exploring the ways culture and social structure affect the appearance in interaction of the force of attraction, $F_{ij}(t)$:

$$F_{ij}(t) = \kappa \left(\frac{1}{\lambda}\right)^{\frac{1}{\Omega}} \left[\frac{R_i(t)R_j(t)}{Z_i(t)Z_j(t)}\right].$$

This expression condenses a logic with which we can organize a number of empirical observations and theoretical statements that currently stand separated from one another.

This variation arises from considering how closely culture and social structure are connected. Where the connection is near perfect, such that cultural models adequately describe relevant behavior of a system's incumbents, we can speak of a social equivalent of ordered, low-energy structuration as it appears in physical systems.

Chapter 8

1. Again, I am not arguing that organizations don't make use of interaction. They obviously do, especially where they create internal markets to stimulate competition and performance among employees. But where interaction is the vehicle, positive feedback is an inevitable liability—people falling in love, personalized power-dependency relations, unsettling selfobject transferences, and so forth. Interaction also scavenges anxieties inherent in organizational life, as where organizational cultures don't support autonomy, where superordinates subvert rules and behave tyrannically, and so forth.

2. Readers will discern here a metatheoretical perspective I learned listening to James Coleman. Coleman used to urge sociologists to attempt synthesizing properties of social systems from principles of action attributed to individuals—rather on the order of how one might synthesize Boyle's law from knowledge of the behavior of molecules in a system of gases, as in statistical thermodynamics. I was very impressed with this agenda. My way of thinking about these matters has become more biopsychological, though the perspective supplied by dissipative structure theory puts a new stochastic angle on these questions of synthesizing properties of systems from knowledge of the behavior of constituent elements. Coleman's work in the 1960s began to move away from the sorts of images supplied by social physics—the images still at work, say, in *The Adolescent Society* (1961) and *Introduction to Mathematical Sociology* (1964)—toward economics and rational choice theory, as in his magisterial *Foundations of Social Theory* (1990). A version of this metatheoretical perspective appears in *Foundations*, chapter 1.

3. Thus, the weak condition of an addictive process suggested in chapter 2—namely, $Pr\{a_{i+1} \mid q_1 \ldots q_n\} \geq Pr\{a_i\}$, where a_i is a "selection" on the ith cycle of

the process, and the qs are its effects—is a way of describing behavior that does not satisfy the law of diminishing marginal utility.

4. In point of observed fact, of course, much real addictive behavior is cyclic—that is, it is marked by binging and then by abstinence, followed later by another binge. The psychobiological reasons for this aren't clear in all cases. The neurochemical changes associated with ingesting a drug like cocaine, for example, are different from those associated with many other drugs of abuse. Cocaine is said to produce binging in part because the peak euphoric experiences associated with the drug's ingestion produce intense memories, and these then serve to tide over the person with a cocaine dependency between binges (see, e.g., Gawin and Ellinwood 1988). One hesitates to equate such flashbulb memories with psychological structure, but here is an example where a mental representation of a euphoric experience is said to substitute (for a time) for the experience itself. It is presumably when anxieties (i.e., withdrawal symptoms) begin to override the evoked representation of euphoria that binging recurs—though this is only a guess.

5. Luhmann theorizes in general terms about how social systems transcend the constraints at work in interaction systems, and how the two (along with organizational systems) form separate levels—in effect, offering an early version of the concept of an interaction order sui generis. In Luhmann's assumption that meaningfully interrelated actions among persons *constitute* a social system, however, he follows in the interpretive tradition of theorizing about social life whose origins in Weber and whose systems version in Parsons his own writing transmits and attempts to refine. Like Parsons's theory of interaction, Luhmann's gives greater weight to negative feedback in interaction, most explicitly by emphasizing how interaction is marked by an "overriding need for internal order" (1982, 72). Again, this is an example of how the dominant assumption of order has controlled an argument about interaction. Paradoxically, Luhmann's work discusses the right target even if it fails to hit it: he emphasizes ways social systems and interaction systems are self-organizing (right target) while failing to recognize the important part played in these processes not by stability and negative feedback but by instability and positive feedback. When he uses the concepts of self-organization, thus, he falsely assumes they describe only processes contributing to a system's coherence and integration.

REFERENCES

Abrams, M. H. 1971. *Natural Supernaturalism: Tradition and Revolution in Romantic Literature.* New York: Norton.

Abrams, M. H., E. Talbot Donaldson, Hallett Smith, Robert M. Adams, Samuel Holt Monk, Lawrence Lipking, George H. Ford, and David Daiches eds. 1979. *The Norton Anthology of English Literature.* Fourth edition. New York and London: Norton.

Ainsworth, M. D. S. 1973. "The Development of Infant-Mother Attachment." In *Review of Child Development Research,* vol. 3, edited by B. M. Caldwell and H. N. Ricciuti, 1–94. Chicago: University of Chicago Press.

Ake, C. 1966. "Charismatic Legitimation and Political Integration." *Comparative Studies in Society and History* 9:1–13.

Aldrich, Virgil. 1939. "Beauty as Feeling." *Kenyon Review* 1:300–307. Reprinted in *Reflections on Art: A Source Book of Writings by Artists, Critics, and Philosophers,* edited by Susanne K. Langer, 3–10. New York: Oxford University Press, 1961.

Alexander, Jeffrey. 1982–83. *Theoretical Logic in Sociology.* 3 vols. Berkeley: University of California Press.

Allen, John. 1977. *Assault with a Deadly Weapon: The Autobiography of a Street Criminal.* Edited by Diane Hall Kelly and Philip Heymann, with a foreword by Hylan Lewis. New York: McGraw-Hill.

Allport, Floyd H. 1924. *Social Psychology.* Boston: Houghton Mifflin.

Ambre, John J. 1989. "Cocaine Kinetics in Humans." In *Cocaine, Marijuana, Designer Drugs: Chemistry, Pharmacology, and Behavior,* edited by K. K. Redda, C. Walker, and G. Barnett, 53–70. Boca Raton, Florida: CRC Press.

Anselm. 1910. *Proslogium.* Translated by Sidney Norton Deane. London: Open Court Publishing Company.

Arendt, Hannah. 1965. *On Revolution.* New York: Viking Press.

Arif, A., ed. 1987. *Adverse Health Consequences of Cocaine Abuse.* Geneva: World Health Organization.

Aron, Arthur, and Elaine N. Aron. 1986. *Love and the Expansion of the Self.* New York: Hemisphere Publishing Company.

Arrow, Kenneth J. 1974. *The Limits of Organization.* New York: Norton.

Augustine. 1961. *Confessions.* Translated with an introduction by R. S. Pine-Coffin. New York: Viking Penguin.

Bales, Robert F. 1950. *Interaction Process Analysis.* Reading, Massachusetts: Addison-Wesley Publishing Company.

―――. 1953. "The Equilibrium Problem in Small Groups." In *Working Papers in the Theory of Action,* edited by Talcott Parsons, Robert F. Bales, and Edward A. Shils, chap. 4. Glencoe, Illinois: Free Press.

―――. 1970. *Personality and Interpersonal Behavior.* New York: Holt, Rinehart and Winston.

Barclay, C. R., and R. M. Hodges. 1988. "Content and Structure in Autobiographical Memory: An Essay on the Composing and Recomposing of One's Self." In *Acts du colloque européen: Construction et fonctionnement de l'identité,* 205–14. Aix: University of Provence.

―――. 1990. "La Composition de soi dans les souvenirs autobiographiques." *Psychologie Française* 1:59–65.

Barclay, C. R., and Thomas S. Smith. 1991. "Autobiographical Remembering: Creating Personal Culture." Paper presented at NATO Advanced Research Workshop: Theoretical Perspectives on Autobiographical Memory, July 9–12, 1991, Grange-over-Sands (Cumbria), England.

Barnes, Deborah M. 1988. "The Biological Tangle of Drug Addiction." *Science* (22 July): 415–17.

Barthes, Roland. [1964] 1967. *Elements of Semiology.* Translated by Annette Lavers and Colin Smith. Boston: Beacon Press.

―――. [1967] 1983. *The Fashion System.* Translated by Matthew Ward and Richard Howard. New York: Hill and Wang.

Bartlett, F. C. 1932. *Remembering: A Study in Experimental and Social Psychology.* New York: Cambridge University Press.

Bate, Walter Jackson. 1965. "The English Poet and the Burden of the Past." In *Aspects of the Eighteenth Century,* edited by Earl Wasserman, 245–64. Baltimore: Johns Hopkins University Press.

Bateson, Gregory. [1936] 1958. *Naven.* Second edition. Palo Alto: Stanford University Press.

Bateson, Gregory, Don D. Jackson, Jay Haley, and John Weakland. 1956. "Toward a Theory of Schizophrenia." *Behavioral Science* 1:251–64.

Baudelaire, Charles. [1863] 1965. *The Painter of Modern Life and Other Essays.* Translated and edited by Jonathan Mayne. London and New York: Phaidon.

Becker, Gary, and Kevin B. Murphy. 1988. "A Theory of Rational Addiction." *Journal of Political Economy* 96:675–700.

Bell, Daniel. 1976. *The Cultural Contradictions of Capitalism.* New York: Basic Books.

Bendix, Reinhard. 1960. *Max Weber: An Intellectual Portrait*. Garden City, New York: Doubleday and Company.

————. 1964. *Nation-Building and Citizenship*. New York: John Wiley and Sons.

Bendix, Reinhard, and Guenther Roth. 1971. *Scholarship and Partisanship: Essays on Max Weber*. Berkeley: University of California Press.

Bentley, Arthur E. [1908] 1953. *The Process of Government*. Chicago: University of Chicago Press.

Berger, Joseph, Morris Zelditch, Jr., and Bo Anderson, eds. 1966–72. *Sociological Theories in Progress*. 2 vols. Boston: Houghton Mifflin.

Berger, Peter. 1963. "Charisma, Religious Innovation, and the Israelite Prophecy." *American Sociological Review* 28:940–50.

————. 1967. *The Sacred Canopy: Elements of a Sociological Theory of Religion*. Garden City, New York: Doubleday and Company.

Berger, Peter, and Thomas Luckmann. 1966. *The Social Construction of Reality: A Treatise in the Sociology of Knowledge*. Garden City, New York: Doubleday and Company.

Besnard, Philippe, 1988. "The True Nature of Anomie." *Sociological Theory* 6: 91–95.

Bettelheim, Bruno. 1943. "Individual and Mass Behavior in Extreme Situations." *Journal of Abnormal and Social Psychology* 39:417–52.

————. 1962. *Symbolic Wounds*. Revised edition. New York: Collier.

Bettelheim, Bruno, and Morris Janowitz. 1964. *Social Change and Prejudice*. London: Collier-Macmillan.

Bhaduri, Amit, and Donald J. Harris. 1987. "The Complex Dynamics of a Simple Ricardian System." *Quarterly Journal of Economics* (November): 893–901.

Bion, W. R. 1959. *Experiences in Groups*. New York: Basic Books.

Blau, Peter M. 1964. *Exchange and Power in Social Life*. New York: John Wiley and Sons.

Blau, Peter M., and Robert K. Merton, eds. 1981. *Continuities in Structural Inquiry*. London and Beverly Hills: Sage Publications.

Blau, Peter M., and Richard Schoenherr. 1971. *The Structure of Organizations*. New York and London: Basic Books.

Blumer, Herbert. [1939] 1946. "Collective Behavior." In *New Outline of the Principles of Sociology*, edited by A. M. Lee, 165–220. New York: Barnes and Noble.

————. 1966. "Sociological Implications of the Thought of George Herbert Mead." *American Journal of Sociology* 71:535–44.

————. 1968. "Fashion." In *International Encyclopedia of the Social Sciences* 5: 341–45. New York: Macmillan.

————. 1969. *Symbolic Interactionism: Perspective and Method*. Englewood Cliffs, New Jersey: Prentice Hall.

————. 1970. "Fashion: From Class Differentiation to Collective Selection." *Sociological Quarterly* 10:3.

Bord, Richard J. 1975. "Toward a Social-Psychological Theory of Charismatic Social Influence Processes." *Social Forces* 53:485–97.

Boswell, John. 1980. *Christianity, Social Tolerance, and Homosexuality: Gay People in Western Europe from the Beginning of the Christian Era to the Fourteenth Century.* Chicago and London: University of Chicago Press.

Boulding, Kenneth. 1957. *The Image.* Ann Arbor: University of Michigan Press.

Bower, T. G. R. 1974. *Development in Infancy.* San Francisco: Freeman.

Bowlby, J. 1969. *Attachment and Loss.* Vol. 1, *Attachment.* New York: Basic Books.

Braiker, Harriet B., and Harold Kelley. 1979. "Conflict in the Development of Close Relationships." In *Social Exchange in Developing Relationships,* edited by Robert L. Burgess and Ted L. Huston, 135–68. New York: Academic Press.

Brain, Robert. 1976. *Friends and Lovers.* New York: Basic Books.

Brewer, W. F. 1986. "What Is Autobiographical Memory?" In *Autobiographical Memory,* edited by D. C. Rubin, 25–49. New York: Cambridge University Press.

Briggs, Asa. 1959. *The Age of Improvement.* London: Longman, Green.

Brown, Roger. 1989. "Pharmacology of Cocaine Abuse." In *Cocaine, Marijuana, Designer Drugs: Chemistry, Pharmacology, and Behavior,* edited by K. K. Redda, C. Walker, and G. Barnett, 39–53. Boca Raton, Florida: CRC Press.

Brubaker, Rogers. 1984. *The Limits of Rationality: An Essay on the Social and Moral Thought of Max Weber.* London: Allen and Unwin.

Burgess, Robert L., and Ted L. Huston, eds. 1979. *Social Exchange in Developing Relationships.* New York: Academic Press.

Byrne, D. 1971. *The Attraction Paradigm.* New York: Academic Press.

Calhoun, J. B. 1962. "Population Density and Social Pathology." *Scientific American* 206:139–46.

Callois, Roger. 1959. *Man and the Sacred.* Translated by M. Barash, Glencoe, Illinois: Free Press.

———. 1961. *Man, Play, and Games.* Translated by M. Barash. New York: Free Press of Glencoe.

Camic, Charles. 1980. "Charisma: Its Varieties, Preconditions, and Consequences." *Sociological Inquiry* 50:5–23.

Carlyle, Thomas. [1836] 1908. *Sartor Resartus.* New York: E. P. Dutton.

Cartwright, Dorwin, and Alvin Zander, eds. 1960. *Group Dynamics: Research and Theory.* Evanston, Illinois: Row, Peterson.

Cash, T. F., and V. F. Darlega. 1978. "The Matching Hypothesis: Physical Attractiveness among Same-Sex Friends." *Personality and Social Psychology Bulletin* 4:240–43.

Cavalli, Luciano. 1987. "Charisma and Twentieth-Century Politics." In *Max Weber, Rationality, and Modernity,* edited by Scott Lash and Sam Whimster, 317–33. London: Allen and Unwin.

Cecil, David. [1939] 1955. *Melbourne.* New York: Harmony Books.

———. 1980. *A Portrait of Jane Austen.* New York: Hill and Wang.

Chodorow, Nancy. 1978. *The Reproduction of Mothering: Psychoanalysis and the Sociology of Gender.* Berkeley: University of California Press.

Christian, J. J. 1960. "Factors in Mass Mortality in a Herd of Sika Deer (*Cervus nippon*)." *Chesapeake Science* 1, no. 2:79–95.

Clark, Margaret S., and Harry Reis. 1988. "Interpersonal Processes in Close Relationships." *Annual Review of Psychology* 39:609–72.

Cleary, J. P., and K. D. McIntire. 1989. "Behavioral Pharmacology of Drug Abuse." In *Cocaine, Marijuana, Designer Drugs: Chemistry, Pharmacology, and Behavior,* edited by K. K. Redda, C. Walker, and G. Barnett, 15–30. Boca Raton, Florida: CRC Press.

Coase, R. H. 1937. "The Nature of the Firm." *Economica* 4:386–405.

Coleman, James S. 1961. *The Adolescent Society.* New York: Free Press of Glencoe.

———. 1964. *Introduction to Mathematical Sociology.* New York: Free Press of Glencoe.

———. 1968. "The Mathematical Study of Change." In *Methodology in Social Research,* edited by Hubert M. Blalock, Jr., and Ann B. Blalock, 428–78. New York: McGraw-Hill.

———. 1973. *Mathematics and Collective Action.* Chicago: Aldine.

———. 1974. *Power and Society.* New York: Norton.

———. 1990. *Foundations of Social Theory.* Cambridge and London: Harvard University Press, Belknap Press.

Coleman, James S. and John James. 1961. "The Equilibrium Size Distribution of Freely-Forming Groups." *Sociometry* 24:36–45.

Collins, Randall. 1981. "The Microfoundations of Macrosociology." *American Journal of Sociology* 86:984–1014.

———. 1987. "Interaction Ritual Chains, Power, and Property." In *The Micro-Macro Link,* edited by Jeffrey Alexander, Bernard Giesen, Richard Münch, and Neil Smelser, 193–206. Berkeley and Los Angeles: University of California Press.

Commissaris, R. L. 1989. "Cocaine Pharmacology and Toxicology." In *Cocaine, Marijuana, Designer Drugs: Chemistry, Pharmacology, and Behavior,* edited by K. K. Redda, C. Walker, and G. Barnett, 71–83. Boca Raton, Florida: CRC Press.

Cook, Karen. 1975. "Expectations, Evaluations, and Equity." *American Sociological Review* 40:372–88.

Cook, Karen, and Richard M. Emerson. 1978. "Power, Equity, and Commitment in Exchange Networks." *American Sociological Review* 43:721–39.

Cook, Karen, Richard M. Emerson, M. R. Gillmore, and T. Yamagishi. 1983. "The Distribution of Power in Exchange Networks: Theory and Experimental Results." *American Journal of Sociology* 89:275–305.

Cooley, Charles Horton. [1902, 1922] 1956. *Social Organization and Human Nature and the Social Order.* With an introduction by Robert Cooley Angell. New York: Scribner's.

Coser, Lewis. 1956. *The Functions of Social Conflict.* Glencoe, Illinois: Free Press.

Csikszentmihalyi, M., and R. Larson. 1984. *Being Adolescent: Conflict and Growth in the Teenage Years.* New York: Basic Books.

Dahl, Robert, and Charles Lindblom. 1953. *Politics, Economics, and Welfare.* New York: Harper and Brothers.

Darwin, Charles. [1872] 1965. *The Expression of the Emotions in Man and the Animals.* Chicago: University of Chicago Press.

Day, Ralph, and Leonard Parsons, eds. 1971. *Marketing Models: Quantitative Applications.* Scranton: Intext Educational Publishers.

Day, Richard H. 1983. "The Emergence of Chaos from Classical Economic Growth." *Quarterly Journal of Economics* (May): 201–13.

DeCasper, A. J., and W. P. Fifer. 1980. "Of Human Bonding: Newborns Prefer Their Mother's Voices." *Science* 208:1174–76.

DeNora, Tia. 1986. "How Is Extra-musical Meaning Possible? Music as a Place and Space for 'Work.'" *Sociological Theory* 4:84–94.

Denzin, Norman K. 1987. *The Alcoholic Self.* Newbury Park, California: Sage Publications.

Derrida, Jacques. [1967] 1976. *Of Grammatology.* Baltimore: Johns Hopkins University Press.

————. [1967] 1978. *Writing and Difference.* Chicago: University of Chicago Press.

Dilthey, Wilhelm. 1962. *Pattern and Meaning in History: Thoughts on History and Society.* Edited by H. P. Rickman. New York: Harper and Row.

Dinnerstein, Dorothy. 1976. *The Mermaid and the Minotaur: Sexual Arrangements and Human Malaise.* New York: Harper and Row.

Dow, Thomas E. 1978. "An Analysis of Weber's Work on Charisma." *British Journal of Sociology* 29:83–93.

Driscoll, R., K. E. Davis, and M. E. Lipitz. 1972. "Parental Influence and Romantic Love: The Romeo and Juliet Effect." *Journal of Personality and Social Psychology* 24:1–10.

Duncan, Otis Dudley, William Richard Scott, Stanley Lieberson, Beverly Davis Duncan, and Hal Winsborough. 1959. *Metropolis and Region.* Baltimore: Johns Hopkins University Press.

Durkheim, Emile. [1897] 1951. *Suicide.* Translated by George Simpson. New York: Free Press.

————. [1902] 1933. *The Division of Labor in Society.* Second edition. Translated by George Simpson. New York: Macmillan.

————. 1915. *The Elementary Forms of the Religious Life.* Translated by J. Swain. New York: Free Press.

Duvignaud, Jean. 1965. "The Theater in Society: Society in the Theater." In *Sociologie du théâtre,* 7–25. Paris: Presses Universitaires de France. Translated by Tom Burns, in *Sociology of Literature and Drama,* edited by Elizabeth Burns and Tom Burns, 82–100. Baltimore: Penguin Books, 1973.

Eccles, Robert, and Harrison White. 1988. "Price and Authority in Inter–Profit Center Transactions." *American Journal of Sociology* 94, supplement: S17–S51.

Eckert, Roger. 1983. *Animal Physiology.* Second edition. San Francisco: Freeman.

Edwards, D., and D. Middleton. 1988. "Conversational Remembering and Family Relationships: How Children Learn to Remember." *Journal of Social and Personal Relationships* 5:404–16.

Eisenstadt, S. N. 1956. *From Generation to Generation: Age Groups and Social Structure.* Glencoe, Illinois: Free Press.

————. 1968. Introduction to *On Charisma and Institution Building: Selected Papers,* Max Weber, edited by S. N. Eisenstadt, ix–lvi. Chicago and London: University of Chicago Press.

————. 1981. "Some Observations of Structuralism in Sociology, with Special, and

Paradoxical, Reference to Max Weber." In *Continuities in Structural Inquiries*, edited by Peter M. Blau and Robert K. Merton, 165–78. London and Beverly Hills: Sage Publications.

Eiswirth, N. A., D. E. Smith, and D. P. Wesson. 1972. "Current Perspectives on Cocaine Use in America." *Journal of Psychedelic Drugs* 5:153–57.

Elias, Norbert. [1930] 1978–82. *The Civilizing Process*. 2 vols. Translated by Edmund Jephcott. New York: Pantheon Books.

Elster, John. 1984. *Ulysses and the Sirens*. Revised edition. Cambridge: Cambridge University Press.

———. 1985a. "Introduction." In *The Multiple Self*, edited by John Elster. Cambridge: Cambridge University Press.

———. 1985b. "Sadder but Wiser? Rationality and the Emotions." *Social Science Information* 24:375–406.

———. 1989. *The Cement of Society: A Study of Social Order*. Cambridge: Cambridge University Press.

Emerson, Richard M. 1962. "Power-Dependence Relations." *American Sociological Review* 27:31–40.

———. 1972a. "Exchange Theory, Part I: A Psychological Basis for Social Exchange." In *Sociological Theories in Progress*, edited by Joseph Berger, Morris Zelditch, Jr., and Bo Anderson, 2:38–57. Boston: Houghton Mifflin.

———. 1972b. "Exchange Theory, Part II: Exchange Relations and Network Structures." In *Sociological Theories in Progress*, edited by Joseph Berger, Morris Zelditch, Jr., and Bo Anderson, 2:58–87. Boston: Houghton Mifflin.

———. 1976. "Social Exchange Theory." In *Annual Review of Sociology*, edited by Alex Inkeles, James S. Coleman, and Neil Smelser, 2:335–62. Palo Alto: Annual Review.

Erikson, E. H. 1950. *Childhood and Society*. New York: Norton.

———. 1958. *Young Man Luther*. New York: Norton.

———. 1968. *Identity: Youth and Crisis*. New York: Norton.

———. 1969. *Ghandi's Truth: On the Origins of Militant Nonviolence*. New York: Norton.

Erikson, Kai T. 1966. *Wayward Puritans: A Study in the Sociology of Deviance*. New York: John Wiley and Sons.

Ezriel, H. 1950. "A Psycho-analytic Approach to Group Treatment." *British Journal of Medical Psychology* 23:59–74.

Fallers, Lloyd A. [1956] 1965. *Bantu Bureaucracy*. Chicago: University of Chicago Press.

———. 1966. *The King's Men*. Chicago: University of Chicago Press.

———. 1973. *Inequality: Social Stratification Reconsidered*. Chicago and London: University of Chicago Press.

Fararo, Thomas. 1972. "Dynamics of Status Equilibrium." In *Sociological Theories in Progress*, edited by Joseph Berger, Morris Zelditch, Jr., and Bo Anderson, 2:183–217. Boston: Houghton Mifflin.

———. 1973. *Mathematical Sociology*. New York: John Wiley and Sons, Wiley Interscience.

Fernandez, James W. 1974. "The Mission of Metaphor in Expressive Culture." *Current Anthropology* 15:119–45.

———. 1977. "The Performance of Ritual Metaphors." In *The Social Use of Metaphor: Essays on the Anthropology of Rhetoric*, edited by J. David Sapir and J. Christopher Crocker, 100–131. Philadelphia: University of Pennsylvania Press.

Festinger, L. 1957. *A Theory of Cognitive Dissonance*. Evanston, Illinois: Row, Peterson.

Feuer, Lewis, 1974. *Einstein and the Generations of Science*. New York: Basic Books.

Field, T. M., R. Woodson, R. Greenberg, and D. Cohen. 1982. "Discrimination and Imitation of Facial Expressions by Neonates." *Science* 218:179–81.

Foa, U. G., and E. B. Foa. 1974. *Societal Structures of the Mind*. Springfield, Illinois: Thomas.

Ford, Franklin L. 1963. "The Revolutionary and Napoleonic Era: How Much of a Watershed?" *American Historical Review* 69 (October): 18–29.

Forno, J. J., R. T. Young, and C. Levitt. 1981. "Cocaine Abuse: The Evolution from Coca Leaves to Freebase." *Journal of Drug Education* 11:311–15.

Fortes, M., and E. E. Evans-Pritchard, eds. 1940. *African Political Systems*. London: Oxford University Press.

Freeman, Mark. 1977. "Paul Ricoeur on Interpretation: The Model of the Text and the Idea of Development." *Human Development* 28:295–312.

———. 1984. "History, Narrative, and Life-Span Developmental Knowledge." *Human Development* 27:1–19.

Freud, Anna. 1936. *The Ego and the Mechanisms of Defense*. New York: International Universities Press.

Freud, Sigmund. [1900] 1953–74. *The Interpretation of Dreams*. Translated by James Strachey. In *The Standard Edition of the Complete Psychological Works of Sigmund Freud*, edited by James Strachey, vols. 4 and 5. London: Hogarth Press.

———. [1912] 1953–74. "Recommendations to Physicians Practicing Psychoanalysis." Translated by Joan Riviere. In *The Standard Edition of the Complete Psychological Works of Sigmund Freud*, edited by James Strachey, 12:109–20. London: Hogarth Press.

———. [1921] 1953–74. *Group Psychology and the Analysis of the Ego*. Translated by Joan Riviere. In *The Standard Edition of the Complete Psychological Works of Sigmund Freud*, edited by James Strachey, 18:65–143. London: Hogarth Press.

———. [1930] 1953–74. *Civilization and Its Discontents*. In *The Standard Edition of the Complete Psychological Works of Sigmund Freud*, edited by James Strachey, 21:59–145. London: Hogarth Press.

Friedman, E., S. Gershon, and J. Rotrosen. 1975. "Effects of Acute Cocaine Treatment on the Turnover of 5-Hydroxytryptamine in the Rat Brain." *British Journal of Pharmacology* 54:51–64.

Fuchs, Stephan. 1988. "The Constitution of Emergent Interaction Orders: A Comment on Rawls." *Sociological Theory* 6:122–24.

Garfinkel, Harold. 1956. "Conditions of Successful Degradation Ceremonies." *American Journal of Sociology* 61:420–24.

————. 1967. *Studies in Ethnomethodology*. Englewood Cliffs, New Jersey: Prentice Hall.

————. 1974. "The Origins of the Term "Ethnomethodology.'" In *Ethnomethodology*, edited by Roy Turner, 15–18. Baltimore: Penguin.

Garfinkel, Harold. and Harvey Sacks. 1970. "On Formal Structures of Practical Actions." In *Theoretical Sociology: Perspectives and Developments*, edited by John McKinney and Edward Tiryakian, 337–66. New York: Appleton-Century-Crofts.

Gawin, F. H., and E. H. Ellinwood. 1988. "Cocaine and Other Stimulants." *New England Journal of Medicine* 318:1173–82.

Gawin, F. H., and H. D. Kleber. 1985. *Cocaine Use in a Treatment Population*. National Institute of Drug Abuse Research Monograph Series 1985, 61:182–92.

————. 1986. "Abstinence Symptomatology and Psychiatric Diagnosis in Cocaine Abusers." *Archives of General Psychiatry* 43:107–13.

Geertz, Clifford. 1960. *The Religion of Java*. London: Free Press of Glencoe.

————. 1963. *Peddlers and Princes: Social Development and Economic Change in Two Indonesian Towns*. Chicago: University of Chicago Press.

————. 1965. *The Social History of an Indonesian Town*. Cambridge: MIT Press.

————. 1968. *Islam Observed: Religious Development in Morocco and Indonesia*. New Haven and London: Yale University Press.

————. 1973. *The Interpretation of Cultures*. New York: Basic Books.

————. 1977. "Centers, Kings, and Charisma." In *Culture and Its Creators: Essays in Honor of Edward Shils*, edited by J. Ben-David and T. Clark, 150–71. Chicago: University of Chicago Press.

————. 1983. *Local Knowledge*. New York: Basic Books.

————. 1984. "Anti Anti-relativism." *American Anthropologist* 86:263–78.

Geertz, Clifford, Hildred Geertz, and Lawrence Rosen. 1979. *Meaning and Order in Moroccan Society*. Cambridge: Cambridge University Press.

Gelanter, E., and M. Gerstenhaber. 1956. "On Thought: The Extrinsic Theory." *Psychological Review* 63:218–27.

Gibbs, J. C. 1979. "The Meaning of Ecologically Oriented Inquiry in Contemporary Psychology." *American Psychologist* 34:127–40.

Gibson, J. J. 1979. *The Ecological Approach to Visual Perception*. Boston: Houghton Mifflin.

Gilmour, Robin, and Steve Duck. 1986. *The Emerging Field of Personal Relationships*. Hillsdale, New Jersey: Erlbaum.

Gleick, James. 1987. *Chaos: Making a New Science*. New York: Viking Penguin.

Gluckman, Max. 1963. *Order and Rebellion in Tribal Africa*. New York: Free Press of Glencoe.

Goffman, Erving. 1959. *The Presentation of Self in Everyday Life*. Garden City, New York: Doubleday Anchor Books.

————. 1961. *Asylums: Essays on the Social Situation of Mental Patients and Other Inmates*. Garden City, New York: Doubleday Anchor Books.

————. 1963. *Stigma: Notes on the Management of Spoiled Identity*. Englewood Cliffs, New Jersey: Prentice Hall.

————. 1967. *Interaction Ritual*. Garden City, New York: Doubleday Anchor Books.

―――. 1969. *Strategic Interaction*. Philadelphia: University of Pennsylvania Press.

―――. 1971. *Relations in Public: Microstudies of the Public Order*. New York: Basic Books.

―――. 1974. *Frame Analysis: An Essay on the Organization of Experience*. New York and London: Harper and Row.

―――. 1981. *Forms of Talk*. Philadelphia: University of Pennsylvania Press.

―――. 1983. "Presidential Address: The Interaction Order." *American Sociological Review* 48:1–17.

Goldhamer, Herbert. 1978. *The Advisor*. New York: Elsevier.

Gombrich, E. H. 1960. *Art and Illusion: A Study in the Psychology of Pictorial Representation*. Bollingen Series 35, no. 5. Princeton, New Jersey: Princeton University Press.

―――. 1963. *Meditations on a Hobby Horse*. London and New York: Phaidon.

Goode, William J. 1959. "The Theoretical Importance of Love." *American Sociological Review* 24:38–47.

Goodman, Nelson. 1968. *Languages of Art: An Approach to a Theory of Symbols*. Indianapolis and New York: Bobbs-Merrill.

Goody, Jack. 1977. *The Domestication of the Savage Mind*. Cambridge: Cambridge University Press.

Gouldner, Alvin. 1966. *Enter Plato: Classical Greece and the Origins of Social Theory*. New York: Basic Books.

Grabowski, J., ed. 1984. *Cocaine: Pharmacology, Effects, and Treatment of Abuse*. Rockville, Maryland: National Institute on Drug Abuse.

Granovetter, Marc. 1973. "The Strength of Weak Ties." *American Journal of Sociology* 78:1360–80.

―――. 1985. "Economic Action and Social Structure: The Problem of Embeddedness." *American Journal of Sociology* 91:481–510.

Green, M. M. 1964. *Ibo Village Affairs*. New York: Praeger.

Greenberg, J., and S. Mitchell. 1983. *Object Relations in Psychoanalytic Theory*. Cambridge: Harvard University Press.

Greenfield, Liah. 1985. "Reflections on Two Charismas." *British Journal of Sociology* 36:117–32.

Greenson, R. 1966. "The Non-transference Relationship in the Psychoanalytic Situation." *International Journal of Psychoanalysis* 50:27–39.

―――. 1971. "The 'Real Relationship' between the Patient and the Psychoanalyst." In *The Unconscious Today,* edited by M. Kanzer, 213–32. New York: International Universities Press.

Greenspan, S. I. 1981. *Clinical Infant Reports*. No. 1, *Psychopathology and Adaptation in Infancy and in Early Childhood*. New York: International Universities Press.

Greenspan, S. I., and R. Lourie. 1981. "Developmental and Structuralist Approaches to the Classification of Adaptive and Personality Organizations: Infancy and Early Childhood." *American Journal of Psychiatry* 138:725–35.

Greenwald, Anthony G. 1980. "The Totalitarian Ego: Fabrication and Revision of Personal History." *American Psychologist* 35:603–18.

Halbwachs, M. 1925. *Les Cadres sociaux de la mémoire.* Travaux de l'Année Sociologique. Paris: Alcan.

———. [1950] 1980. *Collective Memory.* Translated by Mary Douglas. New York: Harper and Row.

Hazan, C., and P. Shaver. 1987. "Romantic Love Conceptualized as an Attachment Process." *Journal of Personality and Social Psychology* 52:511–24.

Heise, David R. 1977. "Social Action as the Control of Affect." *Behavioral Science* 22:163–77.

———. 1979. *Understanding Events: Affect and the Construction of Social Action.* Cambridge: Cambridge University Press.

Henderson, L. J. 1970. *L. J. Henderson on the Social System.* Edited with an introduction by Bernard Barber. Chicago and London: University of Chicago Press.

Hennis, Wilhelm. 1987. "Personality and Life Orders: Max Weber's Theme." In *Max Weber, Rationality, and Modernity,* edited by Scott Lash and Sam Whimster, 52–74. London: Allen and Unwin.

Heritage, John. 1984. *Garfinkel and Ethnomethodology.* Cambridge: Polity Press.

Hilbert, Richard A. 1986. "Anomie and the Moral Regulation of Reality." *Sociological Theory* 4:1–19.

Hochschild, Arlie Russell. 1983. *The Managed Heart: Commercialization of Human Feeling.* Berkeley and Los Angeles: University of California Press.

Hoffmann, Stanley, and Inge Hoffman. 1968. "The Will to Grandeur: De Gaulle as Political Artist." *Daedalus* 97:829–87.

Holmes, Richard. 1975. *Shelley: The Pursuit.* New York: E. P. Dutton.

Homans, George Caspar. 1961. *Social Behavior: Its Elementary Forms.* New York: Harcourt, Brace and World.

Huggins, W. H., and D. Entwistle. 1968. *Introductory Systems and Design.* Waltham, Massachusetts: Blaisdell Publishing Company.

Huizinga, J. 1950. *Homo Ludens: A Study of the Play Element in Culture.* Boston: Beacon Press.

Hummel, Ralph P. 1974. "Freud's Totem Theory as Complement to Weber's Theory of Charisma." *Psychological Reports* 36:683–86.

———. 1975. "Psychology of Charismatic Followers." *Psychological Reports* 37: 759–70.

Inkeles, Alex. 1974. *Becoming Modern.* Cambridge: Harvard University Press.

———. 1983. *Explaining Individual Modernity.* New York: Columbia University Press.

Jackson, Don D. 1957. "The Question of Family Homeostasis." *Psychiatric Quarterly Supplement* 31, part 1:79–90.

Jacobson, Edith. 1946. "The Effect of Disappointment on Ego and Super-ego Formation in Normal and Depressive Development." *Psychoanalytic Review* 33:129–47.

———. 1964. *The Self and the Object World.* New York: International Universities Press.

James, John. 1953. "The Distribution of Freely Forming Group Size." *American Sociological Review* 18:569–70.

Janowitz, Morris. 1960. *The Professional Soldier: A Social and Political Portrait.* New York: Free Press of Glencoe.

———. 1978. *The Last Half-Century: Societal Change and Politics in America.* Chicago and London: University of Chicago Press.

Jantsch, Otto. 1980. *The Self-organizing Universe.* Oxford: Pergamon Press.

Jasso, Guillermina. 1988. "Principles of Theoretical Analysis." *Sociological Theory* 6:1–20.

Johnson-Laird, P. N. 1987. "Reasoning, Imagining, and Creating." *Bulletin of the British Psychological Society* 40:121–29.

Jones, G. I. 1941. "Ibo Land Tenure." *Africa* 19:309–23.

Kalberg, Stephen. 1985. "The Role of Ideal Interests in Max Weber's Comparative Historical Sociology." In *A Marx-Weber Dialogue,* edited by Robert J. Antonio and Ronald Glassman, 46–67. Lawrence: University Press of Kansas.

———. 1987. "The Origin and Expansion of *Kulturpessimismus.*" *Sociological Theory* 5:150–64.

Katz, Jack. 1988. *Seductions of Crime: Moral and Sensual Attractions of Doing Evil.* New York: Basic Books.

Kelley, Harold H. 1979. *Personal Relationships: Their Structure and Process.* Hillsdale, New Jersey: Erlbaum.

Kelley, Harold H., E. Berscheid, A. Christenson, J. Harvey, T. Huston, G. Levinger, E. McClintock, L. Peplau, and D. Peterson. 1983. *Close Relationships.* New York: Freeman.

Kelley, Harold H., and John Thibaut. 1978. *Interpersonal Relations: A Theory of Interdependence.* New York: John Wiley and Sons.

Kemper, Theodore. 1978. *A Social Interactional Theory of Emotions.* New York: John Wiley.

Kemper, Theodore, and Randall Collins. 1990. "Dimensions of Microinteraction." *American Journal of Sociology* 96:32–69.

Kernberg, O. F. 1975. *Borderline Conditions and Pathological Narcissism.* New York: Jason Aronson.

Knight, Frank. [1921] 1965. *Risk, Uncertainty, and Profit.* New York: Harper and Row.

Kohut, H. 1971. *The Analysis of the Self.* New York: International Universities Press.

———. 1977. *The Restoration of the Self.* New York: International Universities Press.

———. 1984. *How Does Analysis Cure?* Edited by A. Goldberg and P. Stepansky. Chicago: University of Chicago Press.

———. 1985. *Self Psychology and the Humanities.* Edited with an introduction by Charles B. Strozier. New York: Norton.

Kroeber, Alfred L., and Clyde Kluckhohn. [1952] 1963. *Culture: A Critical Review of Concepts and Definitions.* New York: Random House.

Kubler, George. 1962. *The Shape of Time: Remarks on the History of Things.* New Haven and London: Yale University Press.

Kuhn, Thomas. 1970. *The Structure of Scientific Revolutions.* Chicago: University of Chicago Press.

Kuklick, Bruce. 1977. *The Rise of American Philosophy.* New Haven and London: Yale University Press.

Kumor, K. M., M. Shererm, and N. G. Cascella. 1989. "Cocaine Use in Man: Subjective Effects, Physiologic Responses, and Toxicity." In *Cocaine, Marijuana, Designer Drugs: Chemistry, Pharmacology, and Behavior,* edited by K. K. Redda, C. Walker, and G. Barnett, 83–97. Boca Raton, Florida: CRC Press.

Lakoff, G. 1987. *Women, Fire, and Dangerous Things: What Categories Reveal about the Mind.* Chicago: University of Chicago Press.

Lang, Kurt, and Gladys Lang. 1961. *Collective Dynamics.* New York: Crowell.

Langer, Susanne K. 1942. *Philosophy in a New Key.* New York: Mentor Books.

———. 1953. *Feeling and Form.* New York: Charles Scribner's Sons.

———. 1957. *Problems of Art: Ten Philosophical Lectures.* New York: Charles Scribner's Sons.

———, ed. 1961. *Reflections on Art: A Source Book of Writings by Artists, Critics, and Philosophers.* New York: Oxford University Press.

Lasch, Christopher. 1977. *Haven in a Heartless World: The Family Besieged.* New York: Basic Books.

Lasswell, Harold. 1930. *Psychopathology and Politics.* Chicago: University of Chicago Press.

———. 1948. *Power and Personality.* New York: Viking Press.

Laumann, Edward O. 1966. *Prestige and Association in an Urban Community.* Indianapolis: Bobbs-Merrill.

———. 1973. *Bonds of Pluralism: The Form and Substance of Urban Social Networks.* New York: Wiley.

Laumann, Edward O., and David Knoke. 1988. *The Organizational State.* Madison: University of Wisconsin Press.

Laumann, Edward O., and Franz U. Pappi. 1976. *Networks of Collective Action.* New York: Academic Press.

Lazarsfeld, Paul, Bernard Berelson, and Helen Gaudet. 1948. *The People's Choice.* New York: Columbia University Press.

Lazarsfeld, Paul, and Robert K. Merton. 1954. "Friendship as Social Process." In *Freedom and Control in Modern Society,* edited by Morroe Berger, Theodore Abel, and Charles Page, 18–66. Princeton, New Jersey: Van Nostrand.

Lazarsfeld, Paul, Ann K. Passanella, and Morris Rosenberg, eds. 1972. *Continuities in the Language of Social Research.* New York: Free Press.

Lazarsfeld, Paul, and Morris Rosenberg, eds. 1955. *The Language of Social Research.* New York: Free Press.

Lazarus, Richard. 1980. "Thoughts on the Relations between Emotion and Cognition." *American Psychologist* 37:1019–24.

Leach, E. R. 1954. *Political Systems of Highland Burma.* Cambridge: Harvard University Press.

———. 1970. *Claude Lévi-Strauss.* New York: Viking Press.

LeBon, Gustave. 1903. *The Crowd.* London: Unwin.

Leed, Eric J. 1979. *No Man's Land: Combat and Identity in World War I.* Cambridge: Cambridge University Press.

Levine, Donald N. 1980. *Simmel and Parsons: Two Approaches to the Study of Society.* New York: Arno Press.

———. 1981. "Sociology's Quest for the Classics: The Case of Simmel." In *The Future of the Sociological Classics,* edited by Buford Rhea, 60–80. London: Allen and Unwin.

———. 1985. *The Flight from Ambiguity.* Chicago: University of Chicago Press.

———. 1989. "Parsons' *Structure* (and Simmel) Revisited." *Sociological Theory* 7: 110–17.

LeVine, Robert. 1971. *Dreams and Deeds: Achievement Motivation in Nigeria.* Cambridge: Harvard University Press.

Levinger, George. 1979. "A Social Exchange View on the Dissolution of Pair Relationships." In *Social Exchange in Developing Relationships,* edited by Robert L. Burgess and Ted L. Huston, 169–93. New York: Academic Press.

Levinger, George, and L. R. Huesmann. 1976. "An 'Incremental Exchange' Perspective on the Pair Relationship." In *Social Exchange,* edited by K. J. Gergen, M. S. Greenberg, and R. H. Willis. New York: V. H. Winston.

Lévi-Strauss, Claude. [1949] 1967. *The Elementary Structures of Kinship.* Translated by James Harle Bell, John Richard von Sturmer, and Rodney Needham. Boston: Beacon Press.

———. 1963. *Structural Anthropology.* New York: Basic Books.

———. 1966. *The Savage Mind.* London: Weidenfeld and Nicholson.

Lindblom, Charles E. 1977. *Politics and Markets: The World's Political-Economic Systems.* New York: Basic Books.

Lovejoy, Arthur O. 1936. *The Great Chain of Being: A Study of the History of an Idea.* New York: Harper and Row.

Luhmann, Niklas. 1982. *The Differentiation of Society.* Translated by Stephen Holmes and Charles Larmore. New York: Columbia University Press.

———. [1982] 1986. *Love as Passion: The Codification of Intimacy.* Translated by Jeremy Gaines and Doris L. Jones. Cambridge: Harvard University Press.

McDougall, W. 1908. *Introduction to Social Psychology.* London: Methuen.

———. 1920. *The Group Mind.* Cambridge: Cambridge University Press.

McIntosh, D. 1969. "Weber and Freud: On the Nature and Sources of Authority." *American Sociological Review* 34:901–11.

Mahler, Margaret. 1968. *On Human Symbiosis and the Vicissitudes of Individuation.* Vol. 1, *Infantile Psychosis.* New York: International Universities Press.

Mahler, Margaret, F. Pine, and A. Bergman. 1975. *The Psychological Birth of the Human Infant.* New York: Basic Books.

Malan, David. 1978. *Individual Psychotherapy and the Science of Psychodynamics.* London: Butterworth and Company.

———. 1986. "Beyond Interpretation: Initial Evaluation and Technique in Short-Term Dynamic Psychotherapy: Parts I–II." *International Journal of Short-Term Psychotherapy* 1:59–82, 83–106.

Malinowski, Bronislaw. 1948. *Magic, Science, and Religion.* Boston: Beacon Press.

Mandelbaum, M., F. Gramlich, and A. R. Anderson, eds. 1957. *Philosophic Problems.* New York: Macmillan.

Mandler, Jean M. 1988. "How to Build a Baby: On the Development of an Accessible Representational System." *Cognitive Development* 3:113–36.

March, James G. 1962. "The Business Firm as a Political Coalition." *Journal of Politics* 24:662–78.

March, James G., and Herbert Simon. 1958. *Organizations.* New York: John Wiley and Sons.

Marcia, J. 1980. *Identity in Adolescence.* In *Handbook of Adolescent Psychology,* edited by J. Adelson, 159–87. New York: Wiley.

Markus, H. 1977. "Self-schemata and Processing of Information about the Self." *Journal of Personality and Social Psychology* 35:63–78.

Marshall, T. H. 1964. *Class, Citizenship, and Social Development.* Garden City, New York: Doubleday and Company.

Marske, Charles E. 1987. "Durkheim's 'Cult of the Individual' and the Moral Reconstitution of Society." *Sociological Theory* 5:1–14.

Mark, Karl. 1964. *Selected Writings in Sociology and Social Philosophy.* Edited by T. B. Bottomore and M. Rubel. New York: McGraw-Hill.

———. 1967. *Capital.* Vol. 1. New York: International Publishing Company.

Mauss, M. 1925. "Essai sur le don: Forme et raison de l'échange dans les sociétés archaïques." *Année sociologique,* n.s. 1:30–186.

Mayhew, Leon. 1968a. "Ascription in Modern Socieites." *Sociological Inquiry* 38:112–16.

———. 1968b. *Law and Equal Opportunity.* Cambridge: Harvard University Press.

Mead, George Herbert. 1934. *Mind, Self, and Society.* Edited by Charles W. Morris. Chicago: University of Chicago Press.

Meeker, B. F. 1971. "Decisions and Exchange." *American Sociological Review* 38:485–95.

Melges, F. T., and M. Swartz. 1989. "Oscillations of Attachment in Borderline Personality Disorder." *American Journal of Psychiatry* 146 (9): 1115–20.

Meltzoff, A. N. 1981. "Imitation, Intermodal Coordination, and Representation in Early Infancy." *Infancy and Epistemology,* edited by G. Butterworth. London: Harvester Press.

Meltzoff, A. N., and W. Borton, 1979. "Intermodal Matching by Human Neonates." *Nature* 282:403–4.

Merton, Robert K. 1957. *Social Theory and Social Structure.* Revised edition. Glencoe, Illinois: Free Press.

Milgram, Stanley, and Hans Toch. 1968. "Collective Behavior: Crowds and Social Movements." In *The Handbook of Social Psychology,* edited by Gardner Lindzey and Elliot Aronson, 507–610. Reading, Massachusetts: Addison-Wesley Publishing Company.

Milkman, H., and S. Sunderwirth. 1987. *Craving for Ecstasy.* Lexington, Massachusetts: Lexington Books.

Miller, Alice. 1981. *Prisoners of Childhood.* Translated by Ruth Ward. New York: Basic Books.

Miller, G., E. Galanter, and K. Pribram. 1960. *Plans and the Structure of Behavior.* New York: Holt.

Minuchin, Salvador. 1974. *Families and Family Therapy*. Cambridge: Harvard University Press.

Mitzman, Arthur. 1969. *The Iron Cage: An Historical Interpretation of Max Weber*. New York: Grosset and Dunlap.

Miyahara, Kojiro. 1983. "Charisma: From Weber to Contemporary Sociology." *Sociological Inquiry* 53:368–88.

Moers, Ellen. 1960. *The Dandy: Brummell to Beerbohm*. New York: Viking Press.

Moore, E. F., and C. E. Shannon. 1956. "Reliable Circuits Using Less Reliable Relays: Part I." *Journal of the Franklin Institute* 262:191–208.

Moore, M. K., and A. N. Meltzoff. 1978. "Object Permanence, Imitation, and Language Development." In *Communicative and Cognitive Abilities*, edited by F. D. Minifie and L. L. Lloyd. Baltimore: University Park Press.

Moraitis, George. 1985. "A Psychoanalyst's Journey into the Historian's World." In *Introspection in Biography*, edited by Samuel Baron and Carl Pletsch, 69–106. Hillsdale, New Jersey: Erlbaum.

Morrione, Thomas J. 1985. "Situated Interaction." In *Foundations of Interpretive Sociology: Original Essays in Symbolic Interaction*, Studies in Symbolic Interaction, supplement 1, edited by Norman Denzin, 161–91. JAI Press.

Münch, Richard. 1986. "The American Creed in Sociological Theory: Exchange, Negotiated Order, Accommodated Individualism, and Contingency." *Sociological Theory* 4:41–60.

Murray, John B. 1986. "An Overview of Cocaine Use and Abuse." *Psychological Reports* 59:243–64.

Murstein, B.I. 1972. *Theories of Attraction and Love*. New York: Springer.

Nahirny, Vladimir. 1962. "Some Observations on Ideological Groups." *American Journal of Sociology* 67:397–405.

Neisser, Ulric. 1987. "From Direct Perception to Conceptual Structure." In *Concepts and Conceptual Development: Ecological and Intellectual Factors in Categorization*, edited by Ulric Neisser, 11–24. Cambridge: Cambridge University Press.

———. 1988a. "Five Kinds of Self-Knowledge." *Philosophical Psychology* 1:35–59.

———. 1988b. "Time Present and Time Past." In *Practical Aspects of Memory: Current Research and Issues*, vol. 2, *Clinical and Educational Implications*, 545–60. New York: Wiley.

Nelson, Benjamin. [1949] 1969. *The Idea of Usury*. Second edition. Chicago and London: University of Chicago Press.

Nelson, K. 1986. *Event Knowledge: Structure and Function in Development*. Hillsdale, New Jersy: Erlbaum.

———. 1988. "The Ontogeny of Memory for Real Events." In *Remembering Reconsidered: Ecological and Traditional Approaches to the Study of Memory*, edited by Ulric Neisser and E. Winograd, 244–76. New York: Cambridge University Press.

Neusner, Jacob. 1972. *There We Sat Down: Talmudic Judaism in the Making*. Nashville and New York: Abingdon Press.

———. 1973. *Invitation to the Talmud*. New York: Harper and Row.

Newman, Ruth G. 1983. "Thoughts on Superstars of Charisma." *American Journal of Orthopsychiatry* 53 (April): 201–8.

Nicolis, Gregoire. 1988. "Physics of Far-from-Equilibrium Systems and Self-Organisation." In *The New Physics,* edited by P. C. W. Davies, 316–47. Cambridge: Cambridge University Press.

Nock, A. D. 1933. *Conversion: The Old and the New in Religion from Alexander the Great to Augustine of Hippo.* London: Oxford University Press.

Norton, David L., and Mary F. Kille, eds. 1971. *Philosophies of Love.* Totowa, New Jersey: Rowman and Allenheld.

Olds, James. 1958. "Self-stimulation of the Brain." *Science* 127:315.

Olds, James, and P. Milner. 1954. "Positive Reinforcement Produced by Electrical Stimulation of the Septal Area and Other Regions of the Rat Brain." *Journal of Comparative Physiological Psychology* 47:419.

Ornstein, A. 1981. "The Effects of the Holocaust on Life Cycle Experiences: The Creation and Recreation of Families." *Journal of Geriatric Psychiatry* 14:135–54.

Ortega y Gasset, José. 1957. *On Love: Aspects of a Single Theme.* Translated by Toby Talbot. New York: Meridian Books.

Ottenberg, Simon. 1959. "Ibo Receptivity to Change." In *Continuity and Change in African Culture,* edited by W. R. Bascom and M. J. Herskovits. Chicago: University of Chicago Press.

Otto, Rudolf. 1925. *The Idea of the Holy.* Translated by J. W. Harvey. London: Oxford University Press.

Park, Robert, and Ernest Burgess. [1921] 1969. *Introduction to the Science of Sociology.* Chicago: University of Chicago Press.

Parkes, A. S., and H. M. Bruce. 1961. "Olfactory Stimuli in Mammalian Reproduction." *Science* 134:1049–54.

Parsons, Talcott. 1951. *The Social System.* Glencoe, Illinois: Free Press.

———. 1954. *Essays in Sociological Theory.* Glencoe, Illinois: Free Press.

———. 1959. "An Approach to Psychological Theory in Terms of the Theory of Action." In *Psychology: A Study of a Science,* edited by Sigmund Koch, 3:612–712. New York: McGraw-Hill.

———. 1960. *Structure and Process in Modern Societies.* New York: Free Press of Glencoe.

———. 1961. "An Outline of the Social System." In *Theories of Society,* edited by Talcott Parsons, Edward A. Shils, Kaspar Naegele, and Jesse Pitts, 1:70–84. New York: Free Press of Glencoe.

———. 1964a. *Social Structure and Personality.* New York: Free Press of Glencoe.

———. 1964b. "Some Reflections on the Role of Force in Social Process." In *Internal War: Basic Problems and Approaches,* edited by Harry Eckstein, 33–70. New York: Free Press of Glencoe.

———. 1966. *Societies: Evolutionary and Comparative Perspectives.* Englewood Cliffs, New Jersey: Prentice Hall.

———. 1967. *Sociological Theory and Modern Society.* New York: Free Press.

———. 1982. "Action, Symbols, and Cybernetic Control." In *Structural Sociology,* edited by Ino Rossi, 50–65. New York: Columbia University Press.

Parsons, Talcott, and Robert F. Bales in collaboration with James Olds, Morris Zelditch, Jr., and Philip Slater. 1955. *Family, Socialization, and Interaction Process.* Glencoe, Illinois: Free Press.

Parsons, Talcott, Robert F. Bales, and Edward A. Shils, eds. 1953. *Working Papers in the Theory of Action.* Glencoe, Illinois: Free Press.

Parsons, Talcott, and Edward Shils, with the assistance of James Olds. 1951. "Values, Motives, and Systems of Orientation." In *Toward a General Theory of Action,* edited by Talcott Parsons and Edward Shils, 42–278. Cambridge: Harvard University Press.

Parsons, Talcott, and Neil Smelser. 1956. *Economy and Society: A Study in the Integration of Economic and Social Theory.* Glencoe, Illinois: Free Press.

Peckham, Morse. 1965. *Man's Rage for Chaos: Biology, Behavior, and the Arts.* New York: Schocken Books.

———. 1969. *Art and Pornography: An Experiment in Explanation.* New York: Harper and Row.

Peele, Stanton. 1988. *The Meaning of Addiction.* Lexington, Massachusetts: Lexington Books.

Peele, Stanton, with Archie Brodsky. 1975. *Love and Addiction.* New York: Signet Books.

Percy, Walker. 1958. "Symbol, Consciousness, and Intersubjectivity." *Journal of Philosophy* 55:631–41. Reprinted in *The Message in the Bottle,* Walker Percy, 265–76. New York: Farrar, Straus, Giroux.

———. 1975. *The Message in the Bottle.* New York: Farrar, Straus, Giroux.

Petersen, R. C. 1977. "Cocaine: An Overview." In *Cocaine: 1977,* edited by R. C. Petersen and R. C. Stillman, 5–14. Rockville, Maryland: National Institute on Drug Abuse.

Pine, Fred. 1985. *Developmental Theory and Clinical Process.* New Haven: Yale University Press.

Plato. 1892. *Phaedrus.* In *The Dialogues of Plato,* translated by B. Jowett, third edition, vol. 1. London: Oxford University Press.

———. 1892. *Symposium.* In *The Dialogues of Plato,* translated by B. Jowett, third edition, vol. 1. London: Oxford University Press.

Polyani, Karl, C. M. Arensberg, and H. W. Pearson, eds. 1957. *Trade and Market in the Early Empires.* Glencoe, Illinois: Free Press.

Prigogine, Ilya. 1978. "Time, Structure, Fluctuation." *Science* 201:777–85.

———. 1980. *From Being to Becoming: Time and Complexity in the Physical Sciences.* New York: Freeman.

Prigogine, Ilya, and Isabelle Stengers. 1984. *Order out of Chaos.* Foreword by Alvin Toffler. New York: Bantam Books.

Proust, Marcel. [1919] 1981. *Within a Budding Grove.* In *Remembrance of Things Past,* translated by C. K. Scott Moncrieff and Terence Kilmartin, 1:465–1020. New York: Random House.

Ramsöy, Odd. 1962. *Social Groups as System and Subsystem.* Oslo and Bergen: Norwegian Universities Press.

Rapaport, David. 1957. "The Theory of Ego Autonomy." In *The Collected Papers of David Rapaport,* edited by M. M. Gill. New York: Basic Books.

Rawls, Ann Warfield. 1986. "The Interaction Order Sui Generis: Goffman's Contribution to Social Theory." *Sociological Theory* 5:136–49.

———. 1989. "Simmel, Parsons, and the Interaction Order." *Sociological Theory* 7:124–29.

Redda, K. K., C. Walker, and G. Barnett, eds. 1989. *Cocaine, Marijuana, Designer Drugs: Chemistry, Pharmacology, and Behavior.* Boca Raton, Florida: CRC Press.

Ricoeur, P. 1970. *Freud and Philosophy: An Essay on Interpretation.* Translated by Denis Savage. New Haven: Yale University Press.

———. 1974. *The Conflict of Interpretations: Essays in Hermeneutics.* Edited by Don Ihde and translated by K. McLaughlin, R. Sweeney, W. Domingo, P. McCormick, and Charles Freilich. Evanston, Illinois: Northwestern University Press.

———. 1976. *Interpretation Theory: Discourse and the Surplus of Meaning.* Fort Worth: Texas Christian University Press.

Rochberg-Halton, Eugene. 1987. "Why Pragmatism Now?" *Sociological Theory* 5: 194–200.

Rodriguez, M. E. 1989. "Treatment of Cocaine Abuse: Medical and Psychiatric Consequences." In *Cocaine, Marijuana, Designer Drugs: Chemistry, Pharmacology, and Behavior,* edited by K. K. Redda, C. Walker, and G. Barnett, 97–113. Boca Raton, Florida: CRC Press.

Rorty, Richard. 1978–79. *Philosophy and the Mirror of Nature.* Princeton, New Jersey: Princeton University Press.

———. 1982. *Consequences of Pragmatism.* Minneapolis: University of Minnesota Press.

Ross, E. A. 1908. *Social Psychology.* New York: Macmillan.

Rossi, Ino. 1982. "Relational Structuralism as an Alternative to the Structural and Interpretive Paradigms of Empiricist Orientation." In *Structural Sociology,* edited by Ino Rossi, 3–21. New York: Columbia University Press.

Rostow, W. W. 1960. *The Stages of Economic Growth.* Cambridge: Cambridge University Press.

Roth, G. 1968. "Personal Rulership, Patrimonialism, and Empire Building in the New States." *World Politics* 20 (January): 194–206.

Rubin, Lillian. 1983. *Intimate Strangers: Men and Women Together.* New York: Harper and Row.

———. 1985. *Just Friends: The Role of Friendship in Our Lives.* New York: Harper and Row.

Ryle, Gilbert. 1949. *The Concept of Mind.* New York: Barnes and Noble.

Sander, L. W. 1962. "Issues in Early Mother-Child Interaction." *Journal of the American Academy of Child Psychiatry* 1: 141–66.

———. 1964. "Adaptive Relationships in Early Mother-Child Interaction." *Journal of the American Academy of Child Psychiatry* 3: 231–64.

Sandler, Joseph. 1981. "Unconscious Wishes and Human Relationships." *Contemporary Psychoanalysis* 17: 180–96.

Sandler, Joseph, and B. Rosenblatt. 1962. "The Concept of the Representational World." *Psychoanalytic Study of the Child* 17: 128–45.

Sandler, Joseph, and Anne-Marie Sandler. 1978. "On the Development of Object Relationships and Affects." *International Journal of Psychoanalysis* 59: 286–96.

Sapir, E. 1935. "Fashion." In *The Encyclopedia of Social Science* 6: 139–44. New York: Macmillan.

Sapir, J. David, and J. Christopher Crocker, eds. 1977. *The Social Use of Metaphor: Essays on the Anthropology of Rhetoric.* Philadelphia: University of Pennsylvania Press.

Sayre, Kenneth, 1976. *Cybernetics and the Philosophy of Mind.* Atlantic Highlands, New Jersey: Humanities Press.

Scheff, Thomas. 1977. "The Distancing of Emotion in Ritual." *Current Anthropology* 18:483–90.

———. 1986. "Microlinguistics and Social Structure: A Theory of Social Action." *Sociological Theory* 4:71–83.

———. 1988. "Shame and Conformity: The Deference-Emotion System." *American Sociological Review* 53:395–406.

———. 1990. *Microsociology.* Chicago: University of Chicago Press.

Schiffer, I. 1973. *Charisma.* Toronto: University of Toronto Press.

Schluchter, Wolfgang. 1979. *Max Weber's Vision of History.* Translated by Guenther Ross and Wolfgang Schluchter. Berkeley: University of California Press.

———. 1981. *The Rise of Western Rationalism.* Translated by Guenther Ross. Berkeley: University of California Press.

Schmalenbach, Hermann. [1915] 1961. "Die soziologische Kategorie des Bundes." In *Die Dioskuren,* vol. 1. Translated as "The Sociological Category of Communion," by Kaspar Naegele and Gregory Stone, in *Theories of Society,* edited by Talcott Parsons, Edward A. Shils, Kaspar Naegele, and Jesse Pitts, 1:331–47. New York: Free Press.

Schneck, D. J. 1987. "Feedback Control and the Concept of Homeostasis." *Mathematical Modelling* 9:889–900.

Schudson, Michael. 1986. *Advertising: The Uneasy Persuasion.* New York: Basic Books.

Schumpeter, Joseph. 1947. *Capitalism, Socialism, and Democracy.* New York: Harper and Brothers.

Schutz, Alfred. [1932] 1967. *The Phenomenology of the Social World.* Translated by George Walsh and Frederick Lehnert. Evanston, Illinois: Northwestern University Press.

———. [1951] 1971. "Making Music Together." In *Studies in Social Theory,* 159–73. The Hague: Martinus Nijhoff.

———. 1962. *Collected Papers.* Vol. 1, *The Problem of Social Reality.* Edited with an introduction by Maurice Natanson. The Hague: Martinus Nijhoff.

———. 1971. *Collected Papers.* Vol. 2, *Studies in Social Theory.* Edited with an introduction by Arvid Brodersen. The Hague: Martinus Nijhoff.

Schutz, Alfred, and Thomas Luckmann. 1973. *The Structures of the Life-World.* Translated by Richard M. Zaner and H. Tristram Englehardt, Jr. Evanston, Illinois: Northwestern University Press.

Schwartz, Barry. 1981. *Vertical Classification: A Study in Structuralism and the Sociology of Knowledge.* Chicago and London: University of Chicago Press.

Schwenkter, Wolfgang. 1987. "Passion as a Mode of Life: Max Weber, the Otto Gross Circle, and Eroticism." In *Max Weber and His Contemporaries,* edited by Wolfgang Mommsen and Jürgen Osterhammel. London: Allen and Unwin.

Shaver, P., and C. Hazan. 1987. "Being Lonely, Falling in Love: Perspectives from Attachment Theory." *Journal of Social Behavior and Personality* 2:105–24.

Shils, Edward A. 1951. "The Study of the Primary Group." In *The Policy Sciences: Recent Developments in Scope and Method,* edited by Daniel Lerner and Harold Lasswell, 44–69. Stanford, California: Stanford University Press.

———. 1957. "Primordial, Personal, Sacred, and Civil Ties." *British Journal of Sociology* 8:130–45. Reprinted in *Center and Periphery: Essays in Macrosociology,* 111–27. Chicago: University of Chicago Press, 1975.

———. 1958. "The Concentration and Dispersion of Charisma." *World Politics* 11: 1–19. Reprinted in *Center and Periphery: Essays in Macrosociology,* 405–21. Chicago: University of Chicago Press, 1975.

———. 1965. "Charisma, Order, and Status." *American Sociological Review* 30: 199–210. Reprinted in *Center and Periphery: Essays in Macrosociology,* 256–76. Chicago: University of Chicago Press, 1975.

———. 1972. *The Intellectuals and the Powers and Other Essays.* Chicago and London: University of Chicago Press.

———. 1975. *Center and Periphery: Essays in Macrosociology.* Chicago: University of Chicago Press.

———. 1980. *The Calling of Sociology and Other Essays on the Pursuit of Learning.* Chicago and London: University of Chicago Press.

———. 1981. *Tradition.* Chicago and London: University of Chicago Press.

Shils, Edward A., and Michael Young. 1956. "The Meaning of the Coronation." *Sociological Review* 1:63–82. Reprinted in *Center and Periphery: Essays in Macrosociology,* 135–52. Chicago: University of Chicago Press, 1975.

Short, James, and Fred Strodbeck. 1965. *Group Process and Gang Delinquency.* Chicago: University of Chicago Press.

Simmel, Georg. 1950. *The Sociology of Georg Simmel.* Translated by Kurt H. Wolff. Glencoe, Illinois: Free Press.

———. 1955. *Conflict and The Web of Group Affiliations.* Translated by Reinhard Bendix, with a foreword by Everett C. Hughes. Glencoe, Illinois: Free Press.

———. 1959a. *Essays on Sociology, Philosophy, and Aesthetics.* Edited by Kurt H. Wolff. New York: Harper Torchbooks.

———. 1959b. *Sociology of Religion.* Translated by Curt Rosenthal. New York: Wisdom Library.

———. 1968. *The Conflict in Modern Culture and Other Essays.* Translated with an introduction by K. Peter Etzkorn. New York: Teachers College Press.

———. 1971. *Georg Simmel: On Individuality and Social Forms.* Edited with an introduction by Donald N. Levine. Chicago and London: University of Chicago Press.

———. 1978. *The Philosophy of Money.* Translated by Tom Bottomore and David Frisby. London: Routledge and Kegan Paul.

Simon, Herbert. 1957a. *Administrative Behavior.* New York: Free Press and Macmillan.

———. 1957b. *Models of Man: Mathematical Essays on Rational Human Behavior in a Social Setting.* New York: John Wiley and sons.

———. 1983. *Models of Bounded Rationality.* 2 vols. Cambridge: MIT Press.

Slater, Philip. 1963. "On Social Regression." *American Sociological Review* 28: 339–63.

————. 1966. *Microcosm.* New York: John Wiley and Sons.

Smelser, Neil. 1959. *Social Change in the Industrial Revolution: An Application of Theory to the British Cotton Industry.* Chicago: University of Chicago Press.

————. 1963a. *The Sociology of Economic Life.* Englewood Cliffs, New Jersey: Prentice Hall.

————. 1963b. *Theory of Collective Behavior.* New York: Free Press.

Smith, Morton. 1973. *The Secret Gospel: The Discovery and Interpretation of the Secret Gospel according to Mark.* New York: Harper and Row.

————. 1978. *Jesus the Magician.* New York: Harper and Row.

Smith, Thomas S. 1968. "Conventionalization and Control." *American Journal of Sociology* 74:172–83.

————. 1968b. "Structural Crystallization, Status Inconsistency, and Political Partisanship." *American Sociological Review* 34:907–21.

————. 1974. "Aestheticism and Social Structure: Style and Social Network in the Dandy Life.' *American Sociological Review* 39:725–43.

————. 1976. "Inverse Distance Variations for the Flow of Crime in Urban Areas." *Social Forces* 54:802–15.

————. 1985. "Personal Ties and Institutionalized Action." In *The Challenge of Social Control: Essays in Honor of Morris Janowitz,* edited by Gerald Suttles and Mayer Zald, 23–51. Norwood, New Jersey: Ablex Publishing Company.

Smith, Thomas S., and Craig Barclay. 1990. "Interaction and Memory: Emotional Regulation through Joint Autobiographical Reconstruction." Presented at the 1990 Gregory Stone Symposium on the Sociology of Subjectivity, St. Petersburg, Florida.

Smith, Thomas S., and R. Danforth Ross. 1984. "Cultural Controls on the Demography of Hierarchy: Warfare and the Growth of the United States Army, 1960–1968." Manuscript.

Smith-Lovin, Lynn. 1987. "Affect Control Theory: An Assessment." In *Analysing Social Interaction,* edited by Lynn Smith-Lovin and David Heise, 171–92, special issue of *Journal of Mathematical Sociology* 13 (1–2).

Söderblom, Nathan. 1911. "Communion with Deity." In *Encyclopedia of Religion and Ethics,* edited by James Hastings et al., 736–40. New York: Charles Scribner's Sons.

Sohm, R. 1892. *Kirchenrecht.* Vols. 1–2. Leipzig: Duncker and Humboldt.

Sorokin, Pitirim. 1957. *Social and Cultural Dynamics.* Revised and abridged in one volume by the author. Boston: Porter Sargent.

Spelke, E. S. 1982. "The Development of Intermodal Perception." In *Handbook of Infant Perception,* edited by L. B. Cohen and P. Salapatek. New York: Academic Press.

Spelke, E. S., and A. Cortelyou. 1981. "Perceptual Aspects of Social Knowing: Looking and Listening in Infancy." In *Infant Social Cognition,* edited by M. E. Lamb and L. R. Sherrod. Hillsdale, New Jersey: Erlbaum.

Spence, D. P. 1982. *Narrative Truth and Historical Truth: Meaning and Interpretation in Psychoanalysis.* New York: Norton.

Spitz, R. A. 1959. *A Genetic Field Theory of Ego Formation.* New York: International Universities Press.

Steiner, George. 1975. *After Babel: Aspects of Language and Translation.* London: Oxford University Press.

Stendahl [Marie-Henri Beyle]. 1927. *On Love.* Translated by H. B. V. under the direction of C. K. Scott Moncrief. London: Boni and Liveright.

Stern, Daniel N. 1985. *The Interpersonal World of the Infant: A View from Psychoanalysis and Developmental Psychology.* New York: Basic Books.

Stern, Daniel N., and J. Gibbon. 1978. "Temporal Expectancies of Social Behavior in Mother-Infant Play." In *Origins of the Infant's Social Responsiveness,* edited by E. B. Thoman. Hillsdale, New Jersey: Erlbaum.

Stevens, Wallace. 1942. *The Necessary Angel: Essays on Reality and the Imagination.* New York: Vintage Books.

Stigler, George. 1950. "The Development of Utility Theory." *Journal of Political Economy* 58:307–27, 373–96. Reprinted in *Landmarks in Political Economy,* edited by Earl Hamilton, Albert Rees, and Harry Johnson, 380–452. Chicago: University of Chicago Press.

Stigler, George, and Gary Becker. 1977. "De Gustibus Non Est Disputandum." *American Economic Review* 67:76–90.

Stinchcombe, Arthur. 1965. "Social Structure and Organizations." In *Handbook of Organizations,* edited by James G. March, 142–93. Chicago: Rand-McNally.

———. 1968. *Constructing Social Theories.* New York: Harcourt, Brace, and World.

———. 1984. "Contracts as Hierarchical Documents." *Work Report no. 65.* Bergen, Norway: Institute of Industrial Economics.

———. 1986a. "Reason and Rationality." *Sociological Theory* 4 (2) (Fall): 151–66.

———. 1986b. *Stratification and Organization: Selected Papers.* Cambridge: Cambridge University Press.

Stouffer, Samuel. 1959. *Social Research to Test Ideas.* New York: Free Press.

Strauss, Anselm. 1959. *Mirrors and Masks: The Search For Identity.* Glencoe, Illinois: Free Press.

Sullivan, Harry Stack. 1953. *The Interpersonal Theory of Psychiatry.* New York: Norton.

———. 1964. *The Fusion of Psychiatry and Social Science.* New York: Norton.

Suttles, Gerald. 1968. *The Social Order of the Slum.* Chicago: University of Chicago Press.

Swanson, Guy E. 1965. "The Routinization of Love." In *The Quest for Self-Control,* edited by Samuel Z. Klausner, 160–212. New York: Free Press.

Tennov, Dorothy. 1979. *Love and Limerance.* New York: Stein and Day.

Thibaut, John W., and H. Kelley. 1959. *The Social Psychology of Groups.* New York: John Wiley and Sons.

Thom, René. 1975. *Structural Stability and Morphogenesis: An Outline of a General Theory of Models.* Translated by D. H. Fowler. Reading, Massachusetts: W. A. Benjamin.

Thomas, W. I. 1966. *On Social Organization and Social Personality.* Edited with an introduction by Morris Janowitz. Chicago: University of Chicago Press.

Tolpin, Marion. 1971. "On the Beginnings of a Cohesive Self." In *Psychoanalytic Study of the Child,* 26:316–52. New York and Chicago: Quadrangle Books.

Tönnies, Ferdinand. 1957. *Community and Society.* Translated by Charles Loomis. East Lansing: Michigan State University Press.

Trevarthan, Colin. 1980. "The Foundations of Intersubjectivity: Development of Interpersonal and Cooperative Understanding in Infants." In *The Social Foundation of Language and Thought,* edited by D. R. Olsen. New York: Norton.

———. 1983. "Emotions in Infancy: Regulators of Contact and Relationships with Persons." In *Approaches to Emotion,* edited by K. Scherer and P. Ekman, 129–57. Hillsdale, New Jersey: Erlbaum.

Trilling, Lionel. 1971. *Sincerity and Authenticity.* Cambridge: Harvard University Press.

Tucker, R. T. 1968. "The Theory of Charismatic Leadership." *Daedalus* 97: 731–56.

Tulving, E. 1972. "Episodic and Semantic Memory." In *Organization of Memory,* edited by E. Tulving and W. Donaldson, 381–403. New York: Academic Press.

Turner, Jonathan. 1988. *A Theory of Social Interaction.* Stanford, California: Stanford University Press.

Turner, Ralph. 1962. "Role-taking: Process versus Conformity." In *Human Behavior and Social Process,* edited by Arnold Rose, 20–40. Boston: Houghton Mifflin.

———. 1964. "Collective Behavior." In *Handbook of Modern Sociology,* edited by R. E. L. Faris, 382–425. Chicago: Rand-McNally.

Turner, Ralph, and Lewis Killian. 1957 *Collective Behavior.* Englewood Cliffs, New Jersey: Prentice Hall.

Turner, Victor, 1967. *The Forest of Symbols: Aspects of Ndembu Ritual.* Ithaca, New York: Cornell University Press.

———. 1969. *The Ritual Process.* Chicago: Aldine.

Vaillant, George. 1977. *Adaptation to Life.* Boston: Little, Brown.

Van Gennep, Arnold. [1908] 1960. *The Rites of Passage.* Translated by Monika Vizedom and Gabrielle Caffee. Chicago: University of Chicago Press.

Vygotsky, L. S. 1978. *Mind in Society: The Development of Higher Psychological Processes.* Cambridge: Harvard University Press.

Waller, Willard. 1937. "The Rating and Dating Complex." *American Sociological Review* 2:727–34.

———. 1938. *The Family.* New York: Dryden Press.

Walster, E., and G. W. Walster. 1963. "Effect of Expecting to Be Liked on Choice of Associates." *Journal of Personality and Social Psychology* 67:402–4.

Washton, A. M., and A. Tatarsky. 1984. "Adverse Effects of Cocaine Abuse." *National Institute of Drug Abuse Research Monograph* 49:247–54.

Watzlawick, Paul, Janet Bavelas, and Don Jackson. 1967. *Pragmatics of Human Communication: A Study of Interactional Patterns, Pathologies, and Paradoxes.* New York and London: Norton.

Watzlawick, Paul, John Weakland, and Richard Fisch. 1974. *Change: Principles of Problem Formation and Problem Resolution.* New York and London: Norton.

Weber, Max. [1904–5] 1958. *The Protestant Ethic and the Spirit of Capitalism.* Translated by Talcott Parsons with a foreword by R. H. Tawney. New York: Charles Scribner's Sons.

————. 1946. *From Max Weber: Essays in Sociology.* Translated, edited, and with an introduction by H. H. Gerth and C. Wright Mills. New York: Oxford University Press.

————. 1949. *The Methodology of the Social Sciences.* Translated by Edward A. Shils and Henry A. Finch. New York: Free Press of Glencoe.

————. 1968a. *Economy and Society.* Edited by G. Roth and C. Wittich. New York: Bedminister Press.

————. 1968b. *On Charisma and Institution Building: Selected Papers.* Edited by S. N. Eisenstadt, Chicago: University of Chicago Press.

Weinstein, F., and G. W. Platt. 1969. *The Wish to Be Free.* Berkeley: University of California Press.

————. 1973. *Psychoanalytic Sociology.* Baltimore: Johns Hopkins University Press.

Werner, Heinz. 1948. *The Comparative Psychology of Mental Development.* New York: International Universities Press.

White, Harrison. 1962. "Chance Models of Systems of Casual Groups." *Sociometry* 25:153–72.

————. 1981. "Where Do Markets Come From?" *American Journal of Sociology* 87: 517–47.

Whyte, Martin King. 1974. *Small Groups and Political Rituals in China.* Berkeley: University of California Press.

Wiley, Norbert. 1986. "Early American Sociology and the *Polish Peasant.*" *Sociological Theory* 4:20–40.

Williamson, Oliver E. 1975. *Markets and Hierarchies.* New York: Free Press.

————. 1981. "The Economics of Organization: The Transaction Cost Approach." *American Journal of Sociology* 87:548–77.

Willner, Ann Ruth, and Dorothy Willner. 1965. "The Rise and Role of Charismatic Leaders." *Annals of the American Acacemy of Political and Social Science* 358 (March): 77–88.

Wilson, Edmund. 1954. *Israel and the Dead Sea Scrolls.* New York: Farrar, Straus, Giroux.

Wilson, Thomas P. 1970. "Conceptions of Interaction and Forms of Sociological Explanation." *American Sociological Review* 35 (August): 697–719.

Winnicott, D. W. 1958. "The Capacity to Be Alone." Reprinted in *The Maturational Processes and the Facilitating Environment,* 29–36. New York: International Universities Press, 1965.

————. 1960. "The Theory of the Parent-Infant Relationship." Reprinted in *The Maturational Processes and the Facilitating Environment,* 37–55. New York: International Universities Press, 1965.

————. 1965. *The Maturational Processes and the Facilitating Environment.* New York: International Universities Press.

————. 1971. *Playing and Reality.* London: Tavistock Publications.

Wittkower, Rudolf, and Margot Wittkower. 1963. *Born under Saturn: The Character and Conduct of Artists: A Documented History from Antiquity to the French Revolution.* New York: Norton.

Wolf, E. 1980. "On the Developmental Line of Self-Object Relations." In *Advances in Self Psychology,* edited by A. Goldberg, 117–35. New York: International Universities Press.

Yanagita, T. 1973. "An Experimental Framework for Determination of Dependence Liability in Various Types of Drugs in Monkeys." *Bulletin of Narcotics* 25:57.

Zajonc, R. B. 1980. "Feeling and Thinking: Preferences Need No Inferences." *American Psychologist* 35:151–75.

Zajonc, R. B., and W. H. Smoke. 1959. "Redundancy in Task Assignment and Group Performance.' *Psychometrika* 24:361–69.

Zimmerman, D. H., and M. Pollner. 1970. "The Everyday World as a Phenomenon." In *Understanding Everyday Life,* edited by Jack Douglas. Chicago: Aldine.

AUTHOR INDEX

*(note numbers refer the reader to
the text pages on which notes are referenced)*

SUBJECT INDEX

Index